The Atlantic Slave Trade

The Atlantic Slave Trade

Effects on Economies,
Societies, and Peoples in Africa,
the Americas, and Europe

Edited by Joseph E. Inikori and
Stanley L. Engerman

Duke University Press 1992
Durham and London

Library of Congress Cataloging-in-Publication Data appear on the last
printed page of this book.

"The Numbers, Origins, and Destinations of Slaves in the Eighteenth-
Century Angolan Slave Trade," "Slavery and the Revolution in Cotton Textile
Production in England," and "Mortality Caused by Dehydration during the
Middle Passage" appeared originally in volume 13, number 4 of *Social Science
History*; "Private Tooth Decay as Public Economic Virtue: The Slave-Sugar
Triangle, Consumerism, and European Industrialization" and "British Industry
and the West Indies Plantations" in volume 14, number 1; "The Impact of the
Atlantic Slave Trade on the Societies of the Western Sudan" and "The Slave
Trade: The Formal Demography of a Global System" in volume 14, number 2;
and "The Slave(ry) Trade and the Development of Capitalism in the United
States: The Textile Industry in New England" and "The Ending of the Slave
Trade and the Evolution of European Scientific Racism" in volume 14,
number 3. All are reprinted by permission of the Social Science History
Association.

Contents

Preface

THE PAPERS included in this volume were presented at a conference entitled "The Atlantic Slave Trade: Who Gained and Who Lost?" held under the auspices of the Frederick Douglass Institute for African and African-American Studies of the University of Rochester in October 1988. The conference was held with the financial support of the Ford Foundation, through the Institute, and of the University of Rochester and its departments of economics and history. In addition to the presenters of the papers, some of whom also performed other roles, the attendees included: Stefano Fenoaltea; Philip D. Curtin, David Eltis, Stanley L. Engerman, and Henry A. Gemery (who served as discussants); and Tiffany R. Patterson and Robert L. Paquette (who chaired sessions). In preparing papers for publication in *Social Science History* as well as for this volume, we again benefited from the support of the Douglass Institute, particularly Charlette W. Henry, Anne S. Falvo, and Karen E. Fields, director, and of the department of economics. We also wish to thank Anne Keyl for her efforts in seeing the manuscript into book form.

The Atlantic Slave Trade

I
Introduction: Gainers and Losers in the Atlantic Slave Trade

JOSEPH E. INIKORI AND
STANLEY L. ENGERMAN

SINCE THE DEBATE in the late eighteenth and early nineteenth centuries between the proslavery interests in Europe and the Americas—the slave traders and slaveholders—and the abolitionist movements, conflicting arguments have been presented on a host of issues relating to slavery and the slave trade. These often center on questions of who were gainers and who were losers. The issues fall into three broad groups: (1) the social cost in Africa of forced migration; (2) Atlantic slavery and the rise of the Western world; and (3) Atlantic slavery, the world of the slaves, and their enduring legacies. Debate over these issues has become more and more frequent in the last two decades. Several conferences have been organized on some or all of these issues. Currently, the literature is growing so fast that a critical bibliographical essay is badly needed. While we are unable to do that here, we can at least highlight some of the main areas of contention and locate within them the papers in this volume.

THE SOCIAL COST IN AFRICA OF
FORCED MIGRATION

The literature on the costs and benefits of the Atlantic slave trade
for Africa generally distinguishes between private and social costs
and benefits (Inikori 1982: 51–52). It is generally agreed that
those who raided and took captives, and the African traders who
bought and sold the captives, all realized private gains. No quan-
tifiable evidence exists for detailed measurement of the private
gains and losses. But one can argue on the basis of human rationality that the raiders and traders would not have sustained the
captive business for centuries if there had been no private gains.
Given the low prices at which the captives were sold for export,
the questions have been raised of why it was not privately more
profitable for hegemonic African states to accept tribute from
potential captives rather than capturing and selling them; and why
it was not privately more profitable for African slaveholders to
employ the captives to produce goods and services for the domestic markets rather than selling the captives for export (Gemery and
Hogendorn 1974; Fenoaltea 1988). The question is answered in
the literature by pointing to the economic and political situation
that existed in tropical Africa in the fifteenth century, which was
reproduced and further worsened by the social cost of the Atlantic
trade (Inikori 1990b).

It is generally accepted that the export centers on the African
coast benefited economically and demographically from the trade.
Where they succeeded in insulating themselves from the sociopolitical upheavals provoked by the trade in their hinterlands,
these port towns (or city-states) realized short-term benefits that
have been equated with private gains (Inikori 1982: 51). Market
production of agricultural commodities to meet the limited needs
of the slave ships for foodstuffs was stimulated, their populations
expanded as the coastal traders retained some of the captives for
their business needs and for the production of their subsistence
products, and so on. These port towns or city-states typically grew
as enclave economies.

Some historians believe that these private and short-term micro-
regional gains were also social or macroregional benefits (Fage
1969; Northrup 1978; Miller 1988). This view has been criticized
for its failure to take into account the devastating consequences

of the trade for the much larger regions from which the captives were violently procured (van Dantzig 1975). Other researchers, employing structural analysis and discussing opportunity costs, describe far-reaching social costs of the trade for African societies. It has been argued, for example, that the Atlantic slave trade transferred to the New World part of Africa's relative advantage in the production of commodities for the evolving world market, and that this retarded the growth and development of commodity production for international trade in Africa. In turn, this helped to delay the development of market institutions and the general commercialization of economic activities in Africa (Inikori 1982, 1986; Inikori et al. 1986; Rodney 1969).

It has also been argued that the slave trade helped to structure African societies in ways that were inimical to capitalist development in Africa. The growth of chattel slavery in Africa has been linked specifically to the Atlantic slave trade (Klein and Lovejoy 1979; Meillassoux 1982), as has been the phenomenon of political fragmentation in nineteenth-century Africa. This phenomenon was characterized by the existence of systems of small-sized states, limited in geographical extent and population and dominated by military aristocracies. It is argued that politically the size and class structure of these state systems (which were a function of the Atlantic trade) were unfavorable to capitalist development (Inikori et al. 1986).

The controversy surrounding the structural analysis, as it relates to the societies of the Western Sudan, is discussed in this volume in the chapter by Martin Klein. Klein shows that the debate originated from the critical response of Senegalese and French historians to the arguments of Philip Curtin (1975). According to Klein, Curtin treated the slave trade in Senegambia as having developed much like any other type of trade. He did not address the issue of the structural impact of the slave trade on Senegalese societies. The Senegalese and French historians, in their efforts to demonstrate the historical origins of contemporary societal problems in Senegambia, reacted by detailing the structural impact of the Atlantic slave trade on Senegambian societies. The arguments, as summarized by Klein, show that the Atlantic trade transformed the class character of the state systems, causing them to become dominated by the warrior class. Widespread insecurity and exploitation by warrior aristocracies drove the masses to seek protection under Muslim leadership. This Islamic alternative, intended to contain the disruptive effects of the Atlantic trade, was soon caught up in the vicious circle of the forces it sought to control and ended up depending on slaving for survival. It is argued that the socioeconomic and political upheavals associated with the Atlantic slave trade also aggravated the effects of droughts on food supply and "eroded traditional mechanisms for dealing with natural disaster."

The chapter by Hogendorn and Lovejoy examines the efforts of the British colonial state to deal with the issue of slavery in northern Nigeria in the early twentieth century. Their subject is very much related to the issues Klein treats with respect to the Senegambia area. Hogendorn and Lovejoy do not specifically connect slavery in northern Nigeria with the Atlantic slave trade, but other scholars have done so. Meillassoux (1982) argues that slavery in the Sudanese region of West Africa developed originally in response to the socioeconomic and political conditions created by the trans-Saharan slave trade, but that the system was later sustained by the expansion of transatlantic slave exports. Humphrey Fisher (1988) argued that the growing enslavement of people in the Hausa states, used to supply the Atlantic trade from the 1780s, was a major factor in the jihad, aimed at suppressing slavery, that led to the creation of the Sokoto Caliphate in the early nineteenth century. This is much in line with developments in the Western Sudan discussed by Klein. To stress his point, Fisher called the leader of the Sokoto jihad in northern Nigeria "a Muslim William Wilberforce." But, like its counterparts in the Western Sudan, the Sokoto Caliphate soon became a major slaving machine, producing captives for export as well as for internal use. By the time it was taken over by the British in the early twentieth century, as Hogendorn and Lovejoy tell us, about 25% of the roughly 10 million people in all the emirates of the caliphate were slaves.

The contradiction in British colonial administration was that it consolidated and extended the influence, if not the real power, of the feudal class upon which it relied for the administration of its northern territories. And this was the very class that held the slaves. Abolition of slavery in northern Nigeria, therefore, became a delicate political issue for the British colonial state in

Nigeria. Lord Lugard's ingenious handling of this delicate matter is presented in minute detail by Hogendorn and Lovejoy.

Probably the aspect of the Atlantic slave trade that has received the most lively debate is its impact on African populations. The controversy begins with the numbers actually exported and ends with the interpretation of these numbers in terms of African historical demography. Disagreement about the numbers exported revolves around the estimate published over two decades ago by Philip Curtin (1969), based on the published data available at the time. Curtin's work served to raise questions about the then-available estimates based on earlier pamphleteers. Since 1969, detailed archival researches have been conducted on the volume of the traffic from particular ports, nations, and regions during particular time periods. Most of these researches have revised upward Curtin's original estimates, some by small, others by large margins. Nearly a decade ago, Paul Lovejoy (1982) provided a controversial synthesis of these researches, arriving at a global figure only slightly higher than Curtin's original estimate. However, further estimates since then, some still quite controversial, include those by Charles Becker (1986:668), who has raised the estimate of the French trade by over 50 percent to about 1.5 million in total. Ivana Elbl (1986: 487–88) presents an estimate for the Portuguese slave trade of the fifteenth and early sixteenth centuries (132,880 for 1450–1521) that suggests a doubling of Curtin's figures for the early period, raising the possibility of a further upward revision of his estimate. And David Richardson (1989:3) has raised Lovejoy's figures for the British trade in the eighteenth century by 342,700, although the magnitude of Richardson's adjustment is itself contested by Joseph Inikori (forthcoming). Inikori is now working on an estimate of the entire British trade from the seventeenth century to abolition. On the basis of these and other archival researches, many specialists believe that Curtin's original estimate has to be revised upward, but important disagreements on the magnitude of such revision remain; Lovejoy (1989:369) says that "the acceptable figures for the volume of the trade seem to inch upwards" (see also Eltis 1990). But how fast is the movement, and what final level can we expect? Making inferences based on the results of archival researches since 1976, Joseph Inikori (Inikori 1982; Inikori et al.

1986) has suggested a global figure of 15.4 million. This figure has been contested by some scholars, and while the process of revision continues, it seems probable that the ultimate figure is unlikely to be less than 12 million or more than 20 million captives exported from Africa in the transatlantic slave trade.

Interpreting the export figures in terms of African historical demography has posed as much of a problem as the computation of the export volume. For many years scholars were uncertain about the age and sex ratios of the exported population. That issue is now very much settled. The overall female ratio turned out to be higher than many had thought: over 35% (Geggus 1989; Eltis and Engerman forthcoming; Inikori 1990b). But the magnitude of the mortality between the time of capture and the final departure of slave ships from the African coast, as well as the numbers of deaths occurring during the process of capture, and the magnitude of further deaths caused by sociopolitical upheavals associated with the procurement of captives remain uncertain. The demographic consequences of the Moroccan invasion of 1591 in the Niger Bend of the Western Sudan have been used as one gauge of the effects of sociopolitical upheavals on populations of precapitalist agricultural societies (Inikori 1981). Ultimately the main source of disagreement on the subject is the differing conceptual frameworks employed by the scholars. Some have used models, such as the Malthusian population theory, claiming that the populations of tropical African societies had reached the limit permissible by available resources by 1400 (Miller 1982 and 1988). The demographic effects of the Atlantic slave trade have even been compared with the effects of emigration in the late nineteenth and early twentieth centuries from capitalist and semi-capitalist industrial countries (Eltis 1987: 67–68). These kinds of comparison were criticized by Joseph Inikori (1978:16–17) over a decade ago, who argued that each mode of production has a demographic law specific to it, and that it is therefore unwise to compare demographic behavior in precapitalist, preindustrial agricultural societies with that of capitalist and industrial societies. It is also contended that tropical African societies were land-surplus (open resource) between 1400 and 1850, under the existing agricultural technology (Gemery and Hogendorn 1974; Birmingham 1977: 549; Inikori 1981).

This demographic conundrum constitutes the focus of the chapters by Joseph Miller and Patrick Manning in this book. Miller examines the volume of the eighteenth-century Angolan slave exports, including the geographical origin of the slaves in west-central Africa and their distribution in Brazil. He concludes that the volume of the trade in west-central Africa in the eighteenth century was greater than was previously thought. A portion of the British and French trade from Angola had earlier been assigned to other African regions; hence, according to Miller, the larger measured volume of the Angolan trade does not affect the overall estimates of the volume of the slave trade.

The chapter by Patrick Manning, on the other hand, provides a detailed demographic model for analyzing the effects of the export slave trade from Africa on populations in Africa, the Middle East, and the Americas. The application of the model leads Manning to the conclusion that as a result of the export slave trade, Africa contributed about one-seventh of the current gene pool in the Americas and the Middle East, respectively. But the contribution in the Americas is more segregated than in the Middle East, where it is more broadly spread throughout the population. As for Africa, Manning's model shows that from 1700 to 1850, the population of sub-Saharan Africa as a whole stagnated or declined absolutely as a result of the slave trade. Since the populations of Europe, the Americas, and Asia expanded rapidly during this period, Africa's share of Atlantic basin population declined from about 30% in 1650 to roughly 10% in 1850.

From these four essays, it can be claimed that the social costs of the Atlantic slave trade for Africa completely dwarfed the private gains of a few members of the African elites. The structural impact left long-lasting adverse effects, politically and economically. It can be further argued that the demographic impact seriously delayed the commercialization of economic activities and thus retarded capitalist development in sub-Saharan Africa.

ATLANTIC SLAVERY AND THE EARLY RISE OF
THE WESTERN WORLD

The literature on the rise of the Western world has grown considerably since the early 1960s (Deane and Cole 1962; Davis 1973; North and Thomas 1973; Frank 1978 and 1979; Wallerstein 1974, 1980, and 1989; Rosenberg and Birdzell 1986; Jones 1981; Rostow 1975). Some writers focus exclusively on factors that explain the rise of the West. Others employ a broad perspective which locates the Western world within a world-historical process in which the same factors that explain the rise of the Western world also explain the stagnation and underdevelopment of other parts of the world. The extent to which the Atlantic slave trade and New World slavery enter the explanations of these scholars varies considerably. The reason for this wide variation is an intriguing historiographical question. Among other things, a major explanatory factor appears to be the theoretical framework which informs the issues raised, the data collected, and the analysis conducted.

It should be remembered that the neoclassical growth theories of the 1950s and 1960s were based on economic models in which international trade was downplayed, with the developing economies seen as lifting themselves by their own bootstraps. These bootstraps were fashioned from technology, agricultural productivity, and population change, with international trade generally not considered. Politics, the role of the state, the formation of class structure that determines the nature of state policy—these, too, were excluded. Since these growth theories were quite influential in the 1960s and 1970s, it is to be expected that they informed the agenda of many historical investigations and that the resulting historical investigations underrated the importance of international trade. K. E. Berrill (1960) criticized this tendency, which he thought the Keynesian revolution ought to have discouraged. Assigning a marginal role to international trade led automatically to the marginalization of the contribution of the Atlantic slave trade and New World slavery to the early rise of the Western world.

The portion of the literature specifically addressed to the role of the slave trade and New World slavery has tended to concentrate on profits from the trade and from the production by slaves in the Americas. And the debate on the subject centers on sections of Eric Williams's thesis (1944). Williams had argued that the slave traders in Europe and the Americas reaped enormous private profits from the slave trade, and that the slaveholders in the Americas also realized private profits from the commodities produced by slaves. This argument has attracted both critics and supporters (Hyde et al. 1953; Thomas and Bean 1974; Richardson 1975; Inikori 1981; Sheridan 1965; Fogel and Engerman 1974;

Ward 1978; Thomas 1968). Other scholars, who do not dispute the argument of Williams on the existence of profitability, have questioned the significance of the profits as a source of finance (Engerman 1972; Anstey 1975a and 1975b).

In recent times, scholars have argued for a broader view of the role of the slave trade and New World slavery in the early rise of the Western world (Inikori 1979 and 1981; Bailey 1986; see Solow and Engerman 1987). This argument is based on an evaluation of the historical forces that stimulated the growth and development of the fundamental institutions and socioeconomic structures of capitalism: market institutions; the division of labor; financial institutions; class formation, state power, and the direction of state policy; technology; and so forth. It is argued that the Atlantic slave trade and the employment of African slave labor in commodity production in the Americas offered, for the first time in the history of the world, immense opportunities for the development of a division of labor across diverse regions of the world, all linked together by the Atlantic Ocean. The market and consumption opportunities so created pulled subsistence producers in western Europe and North America irresistibly into production for market exchange. The growing Atlantic-wide division of labor and regional specialization within nations brought peasant crafts and the products that replaced them increasingly into the marketplace. Demographic behavior was altered as the expansion of manufacturing for export and for domestic markets offered growing nonagricultural employment (Inikori 1982), which further stimulated the growth of the domestic market. Colonial power, state policy, and internal socioeconomic structures influenced the direction in which the benefits flowed. The politics of profits and power reinforced the economic forces in hastening the pace of institutional change (Inikori 1990a). The winners in the politics of profits and power increasingly depended on the Atlantic system, as autarky increased generally in western Europe. This, the argument goes, was the environment that encouraged technological improvement and the growth of industrial capitalism, first in England and subsequently in other countries in western Europe and North America.

It is expected that these recent arguments will be subjected to criticism in the years to come. The criticisms that have appeared so far are based on a comparison of the magnitude of resources devoted to the Atlantic trade and those employed to meet internal needs (Eltis 1987; Eltis and Jennings 1988; O'Brien and Engerman 1991). It is argued that the volume of the Atlantic exchanges was too small for them to have played the leading role they have been assigned.

Four chapters in this volume deal with different aspects of the Western-world problematic. Through different routes all four arrive at the same conclusion concerning the connection between the slave trade and those who gained from it. The chapter by Joseph Inikori focuses on the development of the cotton textile industry in England, the key industry in the first Industrial Revolution. It is argued that cotton textile production in England was a typical import substitution industry. As such, it went through the usual vicissitudes of import substitution industries: early rapid expansion; then stagnation as output reaches the limit of preexisting domestic demand; and inefficient production methods due to limited competition behind tariff walls in a small domestic market. The English industry overcame its problems by moving into export markets in western Africa and the Americas, both of which were dependent on the slave trade and Atlantic slavery. The stimulating market opportunities and early exposure to competition with cheap, high-quality Indian textiles in western Africa induced the English producers to innovate in organization and technology, which enabled them to expand further into other export markets in Europe and Asia.

In their essay, Ralph Austen and Woodruff Smith discuss the role of slave-produced American sugar in the evolution of consumption patterns in the Western world. They argue that consumption is not merely a function of income, something that follows automatically as income grows. Patterns of consumption develop historically and create their own ideological support. Thus, imports not only meet existing needs but also help to create new needs. These needs provide markets and at the same time stimulate the supply of productive efforts. Austen and Smith then trace the contribution of sugar, particularly slave-produced American sugar, to the historical development of the consumption habits that were crucial for the early rise of the Western world.

Ronald Bailey's chapter examines the role of the Atlantic slave trade and New World slavery in the early development of industrial capitalism in the United States, with special reference to the cotton textile industry in New England. Bailey argues that the capital that financed cotton textile manufacturing in New England came initially from sources directly and indirectly related to maritime commerce and shipping. In turn, New England's maritime commerce and shipping were a function of the Atlantic-wide division of labor based on commodity production by African slaves. As New England exploited its initial comparative advantage based on its geographical location, the growth of regional specialization derived from the expansion of the slave-based cotton economy of the southern states offered a large and rapidly growing domestic market for New England's cotton textile industry. The growth of the domestic market was further sustained by the inflow of European immigrants, attracted by the booming U.S. economy, thanks to King Cotton.

In the final chapter on the Western-world problematic, William Darity, Jr., discusses arguments that seek to marginalize the contribution of the Atlantic slave trade and New World slavery to the rise of the Western world on the basis of income ratios. He argues that even by modern standards, the ratio of profits from the slave trade and from slave production in the Americas to the national income and to total investment in the then leading Western nation, England, was quite large from the point of view of economic development over time. Similarly, he argues, the share of imports and exports in the gross domestic product of the leading Western nations during the period in question was also large. Darity proceeds to examine the economic logic of mercantilist theories, which gave pride of place to the role of the Atlantic slave trade and New World slavery in Western development. He concludes that the British mercantilists thoroughly understood the economic forces of their time, and because Britain was the most thorough and single-minded "in pursuit of the grand mercantilist scheme of commercial conquest, naval power, colonialism, slavery, and metropolitan industrialization," she became "the world's industrial leader by the start of the nineteenth century."

Thus all four contributors to the Western-world problematic in this volume agree that the West reaped both private and social gains from the Atlantic slave trade and that these gains contributed significantly to the early rise of parts of the Western world. A similar set of views by an almost totally different group of scholars can be observed in the volume by Solow and Engerman

(1987). Can one interpret this as the emergence of a new trend in the historiography of the Atlantic slave trade? Or is it merely another temporary fluctuation? Only time can tell.

ATLANTIC SLAVERY, THE WORLD OF THE SLAVES, AND THEIR ENDURING LEGACIES

The experiences of the enslaved Africans—from the time of capture to the time in the Americas—and the enduring structures and ideologies to which these experiences gave rise across the globe have all been the focus of detailed historical research for many decades. The story of the untold sufferings of the enslaved, as they were marched to the coast, kept in barracoons under appalling conditions, packed into slave ships like cattle, and the horrors of the Atlantic crossing, euphemistically referred to as the middle passage, have all been vividly presented by historians. The magnitude of the deaths associated with these horrible conditions has been elaborately computed in recent publications (Klein 1978; Miller 1988). The regional distribution of slaves in the New World has also been the subject of careful historical investigation, as are the problems of slave resistance to oppression and exploitation, with the slaves fleeing to freedom or seizing it by force whenever possible. These enduring legacies have both positive and negative elements. The positive elements relate to the survival of Africans and their culture and to the contributions of African peoples to the cultural complexity of the Americas. The negative legacies have to do with ideological racism and the effects of the continued oppression of people of African origin in the Americas. When the full experiences and legacies are taken together, can we say that the enslaved people were losers, or were they gainers? There are conflicting views on the subject.

Much of the debate about the Atlantic slave trade and American slavery started with the controversy surrounding the politics of abolition and emancipation. The abolitionists charged that the Atlantic slave trade had caused, and was causing, considerable socioeconomic and political disruption in Africa and was inflicting great suffering on the slaves. In defense of their business, the slave traders claimed that the wars in Africa were not caused by European demand for captives. They argued that those wars occurred independently of European intervention and that the captives sold to the Europeans would have otherwise been slaughtered. They therefore contended that they were performing a rather humanitarian service in transporting the captives to the Americas.

Did the Western public find the case of the slave traders convincing? In the light of subsequent racist attitudes, it is hard to tell. Modern historians now know that the European demand for captives caused political upheaval and wars in Africa (Klein in this volume; Miller 1988). Nevertheless, arguments minimizing the cost of enslavement for the captives transported to the Americas can still be discerned in the recent literature. For example, it has been argued that the people exported from west-central Africa in the Atlantic slave trade would have died of starvation had they remained in the region (Miller 1988). Thus, any opportunity with some chance of survival might seem better than sure death, although there were captives who opted for sure death by jumping into the ocean instead of facing the suffering and humiliation of transportation and American slavery. It has also been argued that the African slaves in the Americas grew taller than the Africans left in Africa, and that this is evidence of better feeding and better nutrition for the slave population of the Americas (Eltis 1982). This may be interpreted as an unintended, and even undesired, gain for the enslaved. Against this, as an indication of the beliefs of the enslaved, is the evidence on slave resistance, revolt, and escape into remote and difficult territories (James 1963; Craton 1982; Geggus 1982; Genovese 1979; Hart 1980 and 1985).

As the enslaved struggled for survival in the American environment, they created distinct cultures, which included elements from their African origin (often adapted to their new environment) and new patterns of belief and behavior ingeniously brought into being to cope with their experiences. These cultural developments, which have contributed greatly to enrich contemporary societies in the Americas, have been extensively described in the literature (Bastide 1971; Fogel and Engerman 1974; Blassingame 1979; Simpson 1978; Genovese 1974; White 1985; Klein 1986; Fogel 1989; Mintz 1974; Gutman 1976). Diverse aspects of the story have been detailed, including that of the black family under and since slavery and the development of black religions, as well as white-black interactions in regard to racism and to access to power and resources—all of which contribute to the subject of gainers and losers.

Perhaps the most worrying legacy of African slavery in the New World is the persistent oppression of all people of African descent in the Americas. A recent quantitative study shows that up to about 1820, approximately five Africans were brought to the New World for each European migrant (Eltis 1983: 255; Engerman 1986: 318–22). But in the course of the nineteenth century all that changed, as the booming American economies attracted free migrants from Europe. This means that the African slaves did the back-breaking work, but as the fruits of this work began to mature others came in to reap the harvest, with the blacks continuing to be held back in bondage. Even after emancipation, legal and other forms of oppression still blocked black access to power and resources. Thus the process of capitalist accumulation passed them by, giving rise to a black population in the Americas generally characterized by poverty, extreme deprivation, lack of education, disease, and high rates of crime. Scientific racism interpreted these characteristics in genetic terms, which gave rise to heated debates in Western societies as to whether the conditions of the black population were the outcome of the hostile environment in the Americas or whether they were due to characteristics in the black gene pool. In the last decade of the twentieth century, the conditions of large black populations in the Americas remain extremely appalling. Members of the black population of Brazil, for example, had reason to say in 1988, one hundred years after emancipation, that they had nothing to celebrate except their poverty and oppression. (This observation was made during the conference on slavery held in Brazilian universities in 1988 and funded by the Brazilian government to mark one hundred years of the abolition of slavery in Brazil. Both of this volume's editors attended the conference.)

The five chapters in the third section contribute to different aspects of the debate relating to these issues. The chapter by Johannes Postma examines the regional distribution of the slaves transported to the Americas by the Dutch, in a contribution to the study of the historical demography of black populations in the New World. He points out that the present sizes of black populations in different regions of the Americas provide no indication of the magnitude or distribution of African slaves originally imported.

David Barry Gaspar's chapter is focused on the incidence and causes of slave resistance in Antigua in the 1720s. It is shown that in Antigua during the period, "running away was the most prevalent form of slave resistance." In spite of the severe punishment of those caught, the slaves continued to take the risk. Gaspar points out that flight occurred even when there was little possibility of any prolonged existence outside Antigua's plantation sector. Despite this, planters and slaveowners felt themselves forced to undertake "punitive and preventive action." Gaspar states, among other things, that the rate of new slave imports from Africa contributed to the nature and incidence of resistance in the island.

The chapter by Kenneth Kiple and Brian Higgins casts a fresh look at an old problem, mortality among the slaves during the Atlantic crossing. Historians have long been concerned with measuring the magnitude of deaths during the crossing and changes in these rates over time. When causes are discussed, one focus is on the extent to which so-called tight packing of slaves was the cause of death (Klein and Engerman 1976, Steckel and Jensen 1986). Kiple and Higgins have examined documented evidence relating to conditions on the slave ships during the crossing. They conclude that the conditions on the slave ships—extreme heat, poor diet, and limited medical intervention—gave rise to an extremely high rate of dehydration among the slaves, and that the symptoms reported by the surgeons confirm that dehydration was the major cause of death aboard slave ships. It is argued that the decline in mortality between the late eighteenth and nineteenth centuries, from about 25 percent to about 5 to 10 percent per voyage, was the result "not just of the construction of specialized ships intended for the trade, as has been suggested, but of the construction of specialized ships designed to carry more water than their predecessors and very likely to catch more water from rainfall as well."

The Kiple and Higgins essay provides a background for the one by Thomas Wilson and Clarence Grim, which deals with a subject that is currently intensively debated, the explanation of the greater prevalence of hypertension in blacks in the western hemisphere relative both to other populations in the Americas and to blacks in Africa. The experts are generally agreed that the incidence of hypertension and heart disease is far more common among the black populations in the Americas than among other populations in the world. What is disputed is how to account for it.

Wilson and Grim trace the historical origin of the problem

to the Atlantic slave trade. They argue that the conditions to which the slaves were subjected from the time of their capture, through the Atlantic crossing, to the markets in the Americas gave rise to a selection process in which the survivors were predominantly those with greater capacity to retain sodium in their system, while those with lower capacity perished. The selection mechanism was dehydration. Wilson and Grim hold that the black populations that grew out of the slave imports came to be dominated, through genetic inheritance, by people with extra capacity to retain salt in their system. And this, they conclude, is the main factor that explains the phenomenon in question.

This explanation is disputed by other medical scientists. The conflicting views of the contending scientists were summarized recently by Daniel Goleman (1990). According to Goleman, Elijah Saunders, a cardiologist at the University of Maryland Medical School and coauthor of a leading textbook on the subject, *Hypertension in Blacks*, holds that anger against racism is the principal cause of hypertension among blacks in the United States. Shirley Brown of the University of California Medical School in San Francisco agrees with Saunders. As Goleman reports, "Although there have been relatively few studies investigating the role of racism in hypertension, many physicians who treat blacks for hypertension say the link between black anger at racism and blood pressure problems is obvious in some cases."

This debate promises to be a long one, given the importance of the observed contemporary conditions. At this point in time, it is impossible to say which of the various conflicting explanations will be scientifically sustained in the end, but Wilson and Grim here present a widely cited argument for one interpretation of its causes. Whatever the outcome, however, the implication is that the enslaved individuals were clear losers.

The final chapter in this section deals with the historical development of scientific racism. Seymour Drescher points out that the process of abolition covered the same century during which scientific racism emerged in Europe. As the Atlantic slave trade was effectively brought to an end in the third quarter of the nineteenth century, scientific racism also reached its full development and became broadly diffused into the popular culture of the West at the same time. Both the abolitionists and defenders of slavery and the slave trade, especially planters such as Edward Long of

Jamaica, had earlier employed arguments that had racist implications. But as Drescher explains, it was only when the Atlantic slave trade was nearing its end that race became a central explanatory factor in accounting for variations among humans and thus that "biological and anthropological paradigms" were affected by both slavery and its abolition.

From the point of view of the papers in this volume, it is thus clear that western Europe and North America were gainers in the Atlantic slave trade. Tropical Africa was a loser. Not all gained in the former or lost in the latter, but these are the net patterns. On the whole, nevertheless, the greatest losers of all were, without question, the enslaved peoples of Africa and the Americas.

REFERENCES

Anstey, Roger (1975a) The Atlantic Slave Trade and British Abolition, 1760–1810. London: Macmillan.
———— (1975b) "The volume and profitability of the British slave trade, 1761–1807," in S. L. Engerman and E. D. Genovese (eds.) Race and Slavery in the Western Hemisphere: Quantitative Studies. Princeton: Princeton University Press: 3–36.
Bailey, Ronald W. (1986) "Africa, the slave trade, and the rise of industrial capitalism in Europe and the United States: A historiographic review." American History: A Bibliographic Review 2: 1–91.
Bastide, Roger (1971) African Civilizations in the New World. New York: Harper and Row.
Becker, Charles (1986) "Note sur les chiffres de la traite atlantique française au dix-huitième siècle." Cahiers d'études africaines 26:633–79.
Berrill, K. E. (1960) "International trade and the rate of economic growth." Economic History Review 12: 351–59.
Birmingham, David (1977) "Central Africa from Cameroun to the Zambezi," in Roland Oliver (ed.) The Cambridge History of Africa, vol. 3. Cambridge: Cambridge University Press: 519–66.
Blassingame, John W. (1979) The Slave Community: Plantation Life in the Antebellum South (revised and enlarged edition). New York: Oxford University Press.
Craton, Michael (1982) Testing the Chains: Resistance to Slavery in the British West Indies. Ithaca: Cornell University Press.
Curtin, Philip D. (1969) The Atlantic Slave Trade: A Census. Madison: University of Wisconsin Press.
———— (1975) Economic Change in Precolonial Africa: Senegambia in the Era of the Slave Trade. 2 vols., Madison: University of Wisconsin Press.
Davis, Ralph (1973) The Rise of the Atlantic Economies. London: Weidenfeld and Nicolson.

Deane, Phyllis and W. A. Cole (1962) British Economic Growth, 1688–1959: Trends and Structure. Cambridge: Cambridge University Press.

Elbl, Ivana (1986) "Portuguese trade with West Africa, 1440–1521." Ph.D. diss., University of Toronto.

Eltis, David (1982) "Nutritional trends in Africa and the Americas: Heights of Africans, 1819–1839." Journal of Interdisciplinary History 12:453–75.

——— (1983) "Free and coerced transatlantic migrations: Some comparisons." American Historical Review 88:251–80.

——— (1987) Economic Growth and the Ending of the Transatlantic Slave Trade. New York: Oxford University Press.

——— (1990) "The volume, age/sex ratios and African impact of the slave trade: Some refinements of Paul Lovejoy's review of the literature." Journal of African History 31:485–92.

Eltis, David and Stanley L. Engerman (forthcoming) "Fluctuations in sex and age ratios in the transatlantic slave trade, 1663–1864." Economic History Review 46.

Eltis, David and Lawrence C. Jennings (1988) "Trade between sub-Saharan Africa and the Atlantic world in the precolonial era." American Historical Review 93: 936–59.

Engerman, Stanley L. (1972) "The slave trade and British capital formation in the eighteenth century: A comment on the Williams thesis." Business History Review 46:430–43.

——— (1986) "Slavery and emancipation in comparative perspective: A new look at some recent debates." Journal of Economic History 46:317–39.

Fage, John D. (1969) "Slavery and the slave trade in the context of West African history." Journal of African History 10:393–404.

Fenoaltea, Stefano (1988) "Europe in the African mirror: The slave trade and the rise of feudalism." Paper presented at the University of Rochester conference on the Atlantic slave trade.

Fisher, Humphrey J. (1988) "A Muslim William Wilberforce? The Sokoto jihad as anti-slavery crusade: An enquiry into historical causes," in S. Daget (ed.) Actes du Colloque International sur la Traite des Noirs (Nantes, 1985), vol. 2. Paris and Nantes: Société Française d'Histoire d'Outre-Mer and Centre de Recherche sur l'Histoire du Monde Atlantique: 537–55.

Fogel, Robert William (1989) Without Consent or Contract: The Rise and Fall of American Slavery. New York: W. W. Norton.

Fogel, Robert William and Stanley L. Engerman (1974) Time on the Cross: The Economics of American Negro Slavery. 2 vols., Boston: Little, Brown.

Frank, André Gunder (1978) World Accumulation, 1492–1789. London: Macmillan.

——— (1979) Dependent Accumulation and Underdevelopment. New York: Monthly Review Press.

Geggus, David P. (1982) Slavery, War and Revolution: The British Occupation of Saint Domingue 1793–1798. Oxford: Clarendon Press.

——— (1989) "Sex ratio, age, and ethnicity in the Atlantic slave trade: Data from French shipping and plantation records." Journal of African History 30: 23–44.

Gemery, Henry A. and Jan S. Hogendorn (1974) "The Atlantic slave trade: A tentative economic model." Journal of African History 15:223–46.

Genovese, Eugene D. (1974) Roll, Jordan, Roll: The World the Slaves Made. New York: Pantheon.

———— (1979) From Rebellion to Revolution: Afro-American Slave Revolts in the Making of the Modern World. Baton Rouge: Louisiana State University Press.

Goleman, Daniel (1990) "Anger over racism is seen as a cause of blacks' high blood pressure." New York Times: 24 April: C3.

Gutman, Herbert G. (1976) The Black Family in Slavery and Freedom, 1750–1925. New York: Pantheon.

Hart, Richard (1980) Slaves Who Abolished Slavery. Vol. 1, Blacks in Bondage. Mona: Institute of Social and Economic Research, University of the West Indies.

———— (1985) Slaves Who Abolished Slavery. Vol. 2, Blacks in Rebellion. Mona: Institute of Social and Economic Research, University of the West Indies.

Hyde, C. K., B. B. Parkinson, and S. Marriner (1953) "The nature and profitability of the Liverpool slave trade." Economic History Review 5:368–77.

Inikori, Joseph E. (1978) "The origin of the diaspora: The slave trade from Africa. Tarikh 5:1–19.

———— (1979) "The slave trade and the Atlantic economies, 1451–1870," in The African Slave Trade from the Fifteenth to the Nineteenth Century: Reports and Papers of the Meeting of Experts Organized by UNESCO at Port-au-Prince, Haiti, 31 January to 4 February 1978. Paris: UNESCO: 56–85.

———— (1981) "Market structure and the profits of the British African trade in the late eighteenth century." Journal of Economic History 41:745–76.

———— (1982) "Introduction," in J. E. Inikori (ed.) Forced Migration: The Impact of the Export Slave Trade on African Societies. London and New York: Hutchinson University Library: 13–60.

———— (1986) "West Africa's seaborne trade, 1750–1850: Volume, structure and implications," in G. Liesegang, H. Pasch, and A. Jones (eds.) Figuring African Trade: Proceedings of the Symposium on the Quantification and Structure of the Import and Export and Long Distance Trade in Africa 1800–1913. Berlin: Dietrich Reimer Verlag: 49–88.

———— (1990a) "The credit needs of the African trade and the development of the credit economy in England." Explorations in Economic History 27:197–231.

———— (1990b) "Export versus domestic demand: The determinants of sex ratios in the transatlantic slave trade." Paper presented at the 1990 meeting of the Social Science History Association.

———— (forthcoming) "The volume of the British slave trade, 1650–1807."

Inikori, Joseph E., with the assistance of D. C. Ohadike and A. C. Unomah (1986) The Chaining of a Continent: Export Demand for Captives and the History of Africa South of the Sahara, 1450–1870. Paris: UNESCO.

James, C. L. R. (1963) The Black Jacobins. New York: Vintage.

Jones, E. L. (1981) The European Miracle: Environments, Economies, and Geopolitics in the History of Europe and Asia. Cambridge: Cambridge University Press.

Klein, Herbert S. (1978) The Middle Passage: Comparative Studies in the Atlantic Slave Trade. Princeton: Princeton University Press.

——— (1986) African Slavery in Latin America and the Caribbean. New York: Oxford University Press.

Klein, Herbert S. and Stanley L. Engerman (1976) "Facteurs de mortalité dans le trafic français d'esclaves au xviiie siècle." Annales: Economies, Sociétés, Civilisations 31:1213–24.

Klein, Martin and Paul E. Lovejoy (1979) "Slavery in West Africa," in Henry A. Gemery and Jan S. Hogendorn (eds.) The Uncommon Market: Essays in the Economic History of the Atlantic Slave Trade. New York: Academic Press: 181–212.

Lovejoy, Paul E. (1982) "The volume of the Atlantic slave trade: A synthesis." Journal of African History 23:473–502.

——— (1989) "The impact of the Atlantic slave trade on Africa: A review of the literature." Journal of African History 30:365–94.

Meillassoux, Claude (1982) "The role of slavery in the economic and social history of Sahelo-Sudanic Africa," in Joseph E. Inikori (ed.) Forced Migration: The Impact of the Export Slave Trade on African Societies. London and New York: Hutchinson University Library: 74–99.

Miller, Joseph C. (1982) "The significance of drought, disease, and famine in the agriculturally marginal zones of west-central Africa." Journal of African History 23:17–61.

——— (1988) Way of Death: Merchant Capitalism and the Angolan Slave Trade, 1730–1830. Madison: University of Wisconsin Press.

Mintz, Sidney W. (1974) Caribbean Transformations. Chicago: Aldine.

North, Douglass C. and Robert Paul Thomas (1973) The Rise of the Western World: A New Economic History. Cambridge: Cambridge University Press.

Northrup, David (1978) Trade without Rulers: Pre-colonial Economic Development in South-Eastern Nigeria. Oxford: Clarendon Press.

O'Brien, P. K. and S. L. Engerman (1991) "Exports and the growth of the British economy from the Glorious Revolution to the Peace of Amiens," in Barbara L. Solow (ed.) Slavery and the Rise of the Atlantic System. Cambridge: Cambridge University Press: 177–209.

Richardson, David (1975) "Profitability in the Bristol-Liverpool slave trade." Revue française d'histoire d'outre-mer 62:301–8.

——— (1989) "Slave exports from West and West-central Africa, 1700–1810: New estimates of volume and distribution." Journal of African History 30:1–22.

Rodney, Walter (1969) "Gold and Slaves on the Gold Coast." Transactions of the Historical Society of Ghana, vol. 10.

Rosenberg, Nathan and L. E. Birdzell, Jr. (1986) How the West Grew Rich: The Economic Transformation of the Industrial World. New York: Basic Books.

Rostow, W. W. (1975) How It All Began: Origins of the Modern Economy. New York: McGraw-Hill.

Saunders, Elijah (1985) Hypertension in Blacks: Epidemiology, Pathophysiology, and Treatment. Chicago: Year Book Medical Publishers.

Sheridan, Richard B. (1965) "The wealth of Jamaica in the eighteenth century." Economic History Review 18:236–57.

Simpson, George E. (1978) Black Religions in the New World. New York: Columbia University Press.

Solow, Barbara L. and Stanley L. Engerman, eds. (1987) British Capitalism and Caribbean Slavery: The Legacy of Eric Williams. Cambridge: Cambridge University Press.

Steckel, Richard H. and Richard A. Jensen (1986) "New evidence on causes of slave mortality in the Atlantic slave trade." Journal of Economic History 46:57–77.

Thomas, Robert Paul (1968) "The sugar colonies of the Old Empire: Profit or loss for Great Britain?" Economic History Review 21:30–45.

Thomas, Robert Paul and Richard N. Bean (1974) "The fishers of men: The profits of the slave trade." Journal of Economic History 34:885–914.

Van Dantzig, Albert (1975) "Effects of the Atlantic slave trade on some West African societies." Revue française d'histoire d'outre-mer 62:252–69.

Wallerstein, Immanuel (1974) The Modern World System. Vol. 1, Capitalist Agriculture and the Origins of the European World-Economy in the Sixteenth Century. New York: Academic Press.

———— (1980) The Modern World System. Vol. 2, Mercantilism and the Consolidation of the European World-Economy, 1600–1750. New York: Academic Press.

———— (1989) The Modern World System. Vol. 3, The Second Era of Great Expansion of the Capitalist World-Economy, 1730–1840s. New York: Academic Press.

Ward, J. R. (1978) "The profitability of sugar planting in the British West Indies, 1650–1834." Economic History Review 31:197–213.

White, Deborah G. (1985) Ar'n't I a Woman? Female Slaves in the Plantation South. New York: W. W. Norton.

Williams, Eric (1944) Capitalism and Slavery. Chapel Hill: University of North Carolina Press.

Part 1
The Social Cost in Africa
of Forced Migration

2

The Impact of the Atlantic
Slave Trade on the Societies of
the Western Sudan

MARTIN A. KLEIN

STUDIES OF the history of the Atlantic slave trade in Africa have focused on demography and within it on the number of slaves exported from Africa (Curtin 1969; Lovejoy 1982, 1983; Manning 1981). Seen from the perspective of African history, the question of the number exported is a window on larger fields of inquiry and an area open to research, but it is only a small part of the larger question of the impact of the trade on Africa. Working out a reasonable estimate of the number exported does not give us the number lost, for we can only estimate the number killed in wars and raids or the number who died while being moved toward slave markets. Even if the demographic question were the most important one, the most crucial aspect of it would not be the raw statistics of exports but the question of reproduction (Gregory and Cordell 1987). Reproduction involves a host of variables: nutrition, disease, agricultural productivity, security, political stability, and quality of life among others. Most of these are not amenable to precise answers.[1] Furthermore, the question of reproduction leads us to the larger questions of political, social, and economic relationships. This article examines the effects of the slave trade on the institutional structure of Senegambia and the western Sudan and the reproduction of the societies involved.

HISTORIOGRAPHY

The debate on the impact of the slave trade is the subject of what may be Philip Curtin's finest book, *Economic Change in Precolonial Africa* (1975). Thorough, rigorous, and imaginative, this book places slavery and the slave trade in the context of the larger economy. Curtin reminds us that a minority of Africans raided and traded for slaves, and that even they often had to do other things in order to feed and clothe themselves. However, it is Curtin's discussion of the slave trade that has drawn the loudest reaction, in particular his effort to differentiate between political and economic models of enslavement.

Like Curtin's *Atlantic Slave Trade*, *Economic Change* has drawn a heated response from Senegalese and French historians. The most thorough and persistent of Curtin's critics have been Boubacar Barry and Charles Becker. Barry argues that the slave trade contributed to the creation of a more arbitrary and centralized warrior state, that it magnified social conflict and increased violence, and that it led to a loss of population, a decline in productivity, and increased exposure to famine.[2] Becker (1977) has charged that Curtin minimized the effects of war, instability, and militarization of society (see also Becker and Martin 1975). These positions have been supported by several recent theses. Writing on the Soninke of Gajaga, Abdoulaye Bathily (1986, 1989: 237–52), a former research assistant of Curtin, has described an increase in violence, the militarization of the state, and diminished food production. Oumar Kane (1986) argues similarly on the Futa Toro. The Atlantic slave trade, he writes, contributed to a quest for arms.

> These arms were used less for defence against external aggression, though this was increasing, than for attacking and enserfing the innocent. . . . the social disequilibrium was accentuated because those charged with defending the people had become their principal oppressors. In addition, manual

labor depreciated; it was more and more debased in the popular mind because it tended to be reserved to slaves. [Ibid.: 360]

Similar lines of argument have been pursued by Mamadou Diouf and Jean Boulègue for the Wolof states.[3]

Many of Curtin's critics have seen in his work either an effort to minimize the importance of the slave trade or to apologize for it. In part, they have misread Curtin's agenda. Curtin was trying to be more scientifically rigorous, to place the slave trade within the context of both the South Atlantic system and the African trade networks and to see slaves as an item of trade much like any other. But Curtin has been insensitive to the agenda of Senegalese historians. Though no less anxious to be scientific, they want to understand Africa's backwardness and its continued exploitation. The debate often focuses on Curtin's conclusions; it does not always fully come to grips with some of his questions. In particular, Curtin asks two questions which force us to look at the nature of the societies we are examining. The first is why slave prices were so low. The second is whether slaves were captured for sale or were already enslaved. I would like to look at the second question first, largely because there is now a sizable body of literature that bears on it, and then to explore certain other effects of the slave trade.

ECONOMIC ENSLAVEMENT OR POLITICAL
ENSLAVEMENT?

This question is basic to our understanding of societies that enslave others. Is slaving the basis of their economy and political structure, or is it marginal to other activities? Is it one of many activities, perhaps merely an effort to get rid of prisoners, or is it the way the society meets some of its fundamental needs? Curtin (1975, 1: 156–68) answers this question by creating two models of enslavement, one political and one economic. Within the political model, slaves are made prisoner as a consequence of conflicts that always take place between states. Enslavement does not result from a conscious desire to enslave. Slaves are sold as an alternative to being killed or resettled. Within the economic model, slaving is a business. Slavers go raiding for no other reason than to enslave people. Curtin argues that if the economic model predominates, there will be relatively little fluctuation in slave supply. If the political model predominates, there will be sharp fluctuations, the production of slaves being most extensive during periods of warfare. Curtin's analysis balances between the two models, but it does show sharp fluctuations, particularly during major wars.

Since Curtin's book came out, there has been a significant body of research on slaving societies in the western Sudan, some of it in the form of well-documented theses. One of the major themes of this research is that these societies were restructured to become more efficient slaving operations during the late seventeenth or early eighteenth centuries, that is to say, during or just after the development of sugar plantations in the West Indies sharply increased the demand for slaves. This restructuring almost always involved the development of a corps of professional soldiers, usually of slave origins, and the emergence of a more centralized and predatory state. For some, the process began earlier. Both Barry (1972, 1988) and Boulègue (1986) are convinced that the process of change began in the sixteenth century, when the exchange of horses for slaves contributed to the breakup of the fragile Jolof empire and the emergence of smaller but more centralized states. Barry (1988: 79–82) also links the Portuguese trade to the rise of Kaabu in the Guinea coast area (but for an opposing view see Elbl 1986).

Toward the end of the seventeenth century, more profound changes paralleled the increase in demand from American plantations. In Wolof Kajoor, the Damel Lat Sukaabe (1695–1720) carried out a series of centralizing reforms, which included an increase in the number of slave warriors (Boulègue 1977, 1986, 2: 428–63). Bathily (1989: 307–52) describes an increase in violence and the militarization of political systems which followed the establishment of a French trading post in the upper Senegal River. S. M. Cissoko (1986) has described the emergence of the warlike kingdom of Khasso just northeast of Gajaga in the late seventeenth century. Emmanuel Terray (1974) describes Gyaman, founded about 1690. Kathryn Green (1984) describes the emergence of a warrior state in Kong about 1700 (see also Bernus 1960). The Wattara of Kong later created similar states in Bobo Dioulasso and Sikasso (Quimby 1972). The Bambara state of

Segu, founded about 1712, has been described by Bazin (1982: 362) as "an enormous machine to produce slaves" (see also Bazin 1975; Roberts 1980a, 1986). In each of these cases, slave raiding and trading were clearly crucial to the structure of the state.

The warrior states were closely linked to merchant cities. Often the major city was a juula community, while the ruling aristocracy lived in scattered villages, for example, in Kong (Bernus 1960), Bouna (Boutillier 1975), Bonduku (Handloff 1982; Terray 1974, 1975), and Bobo. In the Segu Bambara state, by contrast, there was a political capital, Segu, closely linked to a series of commercial cities, of which the most important were Nyamina and Sinsani (Roberts 1978, 1986: chap. 2). The merchants provided the horses and guns and marketed the slaves. Furthermore, though many juula towns claim distant origins, their traditions become concrete only from the late seventeenth or early eighteenth century (Roberts 1978). It seems clear that the eighteenth century was a period of increasing economic activity for many of the juula and a period during which many of the major trading families established their wealth and power. They not only traded the slaves but put many of them to work producing commodities (Klein and Lovejoy 1979; Meillassoux 1986: 237–303).

I argue not that the economic model predominated over the political model but that by its very nature the slave trade shaped the structure of the participating state. Curtin's distinction between an economic and a political model explains some of the fluctuations in the slave supply, but it does not explain how the long-distance slave trade shaped the state itself. The slave trade was the way the state reproduced itself. Bazin and Terray (1982: 24) explain: "The stock of slaves must be constantly renewed, either because the slaves are bit by bit integrated and thus less exploitable, or because slaves must continually be sold for the state to provision itself with firearms and horses." In his discussion of Bambara warfare, Bazin (1982: 360) is more explicit: "A social formation like the state of Segu . . . involves the permanent interplay of two distinct and complementary relations: first, by warfare, Segu extends its imperium over an increasing group of communities. . . . But second, by warfare, the state produces its own dependents, constantly increases the mass of them, and permanently reproduces their dependence."

When we look at Senegal again, we find a curious phenomenon. Having argued that the slave trade reshaped the structure of the Wolof states, Boulègue must confront the decline of slave exports from them after about 1730. He contrasts the large number of slaves taken and sold by the Moors from raids in northern Senegal and suggests that in spite of French efforts, the Wolof limited their slaving activities:

> The Wolof trade . . . was not a predation without limits. The taking of slaves, both on the external margins and in the interior of the kingdoms, was the object of regulation by the kings. . . . The companies never succeeded in shaping the slave trade in the Wolof states as they wished, and when in 1763, the French government thought it would motivate the kings to sell more slaves by removing price restraints, the kings took advantage of the rise in prices to reduce the number of slaves sold. [Boulègue 1986, 2: 605; see also Klein 1968: 28]

Becker and Martin (1975) insist that there was increased use of slaves within the Wolof states. James Searing (1988) has suggested that this was because of increased food production for the middle passage and for the towns of St. Louis and Goree, which fits in with Bathily's (1989: 278–82) suggestion that recurrent famines were a serious constraint on the Senegal River trade. Slave dealers would not buy slaves if they could not feed them.

WHY WERE SLAVE PRICES SO LOW?

If this answers the question why slaves were taken, it leaves us with the question of slave prices. When Curtin asks about slave prices, he is asking a question so simple its answer seems self-evident, but at the same time it is fundamental to any understanding of the larger question. Curtin (1975, 1: xxi) suggests that the Americas looked to Africa as the preferred source of labor because slaves could be procured so cheaply there. During the fifteenth century, a good horse could be exchanged for 14 or 15 slaves (ibid.: 222). While this price went down, during most of the eighteenth century the price of a slave on the coast fluctuated between £10 and £20 (ibid.: 159). "The real value of the goods received by the enslaver," Curtin (ibid.: 154) writes, "in Senegambia, at least, was very low—so low that no rational person with command over a slave's labor would give him up unless he showed genuine tendencies toward criminal activity or political 'trouble-making.' " Most slaves came from the interior. That meant that the profit was divided between the slavers and the slave traders. It also meant that they had to be moved, fed, and guarded. Profits were probably very slim. In an ordinary year, the price of a slave was about four times the cost of his subsistence for a year (ibid.: 169).[4] Thus, the cost of doing business threatened the potential profits. Furthermore, the mortality rate was high both for slaves being moved and for slaves being held in cool coastal areas (Bathily 1986: 276–78).

The slave trade was only a small part of the larger economy. During the early seventeenth century, the hide trade was more important than the slave trade, and by the end of the eighteenth century the value of the gum the French bought was probably greater than that of the slaves.[5] Furthermore, the desertside trade, millet and cloth for salt and livestock, was in most years more important than either (Curtin 1975, 1: 197). And certainly, most productive activity went into subsistence. Why then was slaving so crucial to political and social organization? One answer could be different notions of value. A gun is of more value in a society where guns are rare or absent than in one where they are numerous.[6] Most purchases were so valuable that people were willing to make sacrifices for them. But this answer clearly does not go far enough. It does not explain the price of a slave measured in terms of subsistence. Even viewed by African measures of value, the price of slaves was very low. The answer to our question must be seen in the way slaving shaped and strengthened the power of the state.

Slaving was not an easy business to get into. Kidnapping was a constant risk. Only those who commanded significant numbers of men could successfully slave. Thus slaving was done largely by armies or by raiding forces of professional warriors. At the same time, rulers needed men who stood outside kinship structures and by their very lack of status would be dependent. Young male slaves best fit this definition. Thus, only politically significant bodies could enslave, and that process strengthened the power of the state and its ruler. Two of the themes of Boulègue's thesis are the state-village conflict and the king-aristocracy conflict. In both cases, the creation of a force of dependent warriors gave the kings an advantage. Slaving also strengthened the state in other ways. First, slaves were exchanged for goods of value to the state. Weapons of war, metal goods, and luxurious textiles were all of value because they could be used to coerce or reward. The price of guns and horses was not as important as the power these scarce goods gave those who possessed them. The state also asserted itself through redistribution. Slaving enabled the state to redistribute prestigious goods that were available only from across the Atlantic or the Sahara and could be used to ensure the loyalty of warriors (Roberts 1986: 39).

If the state benefited, what was in it for the slave warrior? We know that slave warriors did not always act as expected. They could interfere with political processes and make or unmake rulers (ibid.: chap. 2; Diouf 1980). They generally did so not to undermine the system but to strengthen it and their position within it. And yet it is probable that they were poor. The low price of slaves meant that it was very difficult for slave warriors to feed and clothe themselves by their military activities. Wolof armies in the seventeenth century were estimated at 1,200 to 1,500 men, with forces up to 4,000 in the eighteenth century (Boulègue 1986, 2: 333–36).[7] This means that the number of warriors was many times the number of slaves marketed in any given year.[8] How did they live? Some accounts say they were supported by the lords they served (ibid.: 335). Others suggest they lived off pillage (Roberts 1986: 35). The most important kind of booty, however, was women. Slave warriors probably lived largely off the labor of their female slaves (M. Klein 1983), which freed them to pursue an adventurous life. They wore long hair and bright clothes and spent much time drinking. Their raids were not always successful. They often met resistance or retaliation. Sudanic walled villages were not easy to take (Bah 1985).

SLAVE USE

So far, my argument has dealt only with the slavers, but one-half of every slaving formation was the merchants who sold the slaves and provided the trade goods that rulers, aristocrats, and warriors wanted. "Newly captured war prisoners," Curtin (1975, 1: 155) writes, "had little or no value at the point of capture." For Meillassoux (1971: 55), "warfare and trade are complementary and opposed. The former feeds the second, uses it as an outlet, yet withdraws men from production. Hence two classes develop which are both solidary and antagonistic—a class of warrior aristocrats and a class of merchants." Solidly Muslim, the austere and puritanical merchants differed radically from the slave warriors in their values. They were, however, closely linked to the warrior states, for whom they marketed slaves and provided trade goods. The eighteenth-century expansion of their activities involved an extension of trade, capital from one kind of commerce being used for other kinds, and an increase in slave use. The networks noted by Curtin, which provided about 100,000 slaves a year on the coast, were capable of providing slaves for use within Africa. To do all this and to supply the Saharan trade, several times that number had to be enslaved in any given year. The endless files of slaves familiar to us from nineteenth-century explorer accounts were certainly also characterstic of the preceding century. These slaves did not necessarily move to the coast in one trip. Many were traded from place to place.[9] For each transaction there was always the choice of whether to keep the slave or sell him or her again.

There are several sources of evidence that many, probably most, slaves were kept within Africa. First, when the Atlantic trade ground to a halt in the nineteenth century, the drop in prices was not especially dramatic, though the number of slaves on the market was actually increasing. This clearly suggests that the capacity of Sudanic society to absorb and use slaves was quite high. Meillassoux (1971: 193) argues that in the nineteenth century a slave in the desertside town of Goumbou could earn the cost of his purchase in one to three years. An early-twentieth-century French administrator argued that a slave in the Senegal River region could earn for his master 40 to 50 francs a year and thus pay his purchase price in four to five years (Du Laurens 1904). We have no data about the profitability of slave labor in the eighteenth century, but its use was certainly increasing (Roberts 1986: 46–58).

There is another measure of the importance of slaves within Africa. Most slaves exported from West Africa were male, probably by a ratio of at least two to one, and probably higher in Senegambia (H. Klein 1983; Curtin 1975, 1: 175–77). Working from plantation data in Saint-Domingue, David Geggus (1989) found even higher ratios for peoples from the far interior; the longer the voyage to the coast, the higher the percentage of males. There is no doubt that women and children were a majority of those enslaved. They were easier to capture and to move. The predominance of men in the Atlantic trade clearly resulted from an African preference for women and children (Curtin 1975, 1: 175–77; H. Klein 1983: 36–37). Furthermore, a contrast between the ratio of women to men among those enslaved and among those exported suggests that a majority of those enslaved were kept within Africa, a majority that consisted largely of women and children (Klein 1987).

The importance of this is that western Sudanic societies were heavily dependent on slavery in a variety of ways. The long-distance slave trade did not create slavery within Africa; Bathily (1989: 180–84) argues that the slavery existed before the coming of Arab traders and that most slaves were exploited within the region. But the availability of slaves increased their use and transformed the mode of exploitation. Slavery was widespread in human society; it was almost universal in societies similar to those we find in precolonial West Africa. It is unlikely, however, that many medieval or early-modern societies were completely dependent on slave labor. By the late nineteenth century, many African societies were as much as two-thirds slave. Slaves were especially numerous in and around major political and commercial centers. Furthermore, there seems to have been some change in the way they were used. In earlier centuries, many communities were simply relocated from their original homes to areas where they could be forced to provide food for the court and army. This was clearly the case in the warrior state (Roberts 1986: 38–39; Bazin 1975: 135–82). Increasingly, however, slaves were used in mercantile centers to produce commodities for trade and were themselves commoditized (Meillassoux 1975a, 1986: 237–303; Roberts 1986: 46–50; Boutillier 1975). The availability of slaves probably increased production in many sectors of African society. Slaves were valued not because they worked more efficiently than nonslaves but because more labor could be extracted from them. Nehemia Levtzion (1986a, 1986b) and Lamine Sanneh (1979) have also argued that the exploitation of slave labor made possible the emergence of the rural-based Muslim clerics who provided much of the leadership for the jihads of the eighteenth and nineteenth centuries. Certainly, dependence on slave labor made study possible. It also made possible the creation of an alternative elite not dependent on commerce and with limited links to the rulers.

ISLAM AND THE SLAVE TRADE

Sometimes events have a logic that can be understood only as part of a dialectical process. Such a sequence is the process of Islamization in West Africa. A little over 18 years ago, Barry (1972) and Klein (1969, 1972) arrived independently at an interpretation of Senegal's past which stressed the role of Islam in resisting and providing an alternative to slave-trading political formations. The broad lines of this analysis have been accepted by most recent writers on Senegambian history (Diouf 1980; Bathily 1989; Boulègue 1986; cf. Curtin 1981). Islam is not hostile to either slavery or slave trading (Willis 1985a, 1985b; Levtzion 1985). Almost all slave traders in the western Sudan were Muslim. Muslim societies were also the most systematic in the exploitation of slave labor. Islam afforded the slave some protection, but not against heavy work (Brunschwig 1960; Hunwick 1988). More important, it explicitly prohibited the enslavement of Muslims. In Africa, the prohibition against enslavement of Muslims was often turned around and used to justify slaving by Muslims among pagan peoples (Willis 1985b; Farias 1985). Thus little in Islam itself would make it an anti–slave trade force.

The importance of Islam lay in its role as an alternative source of political power. When the first Portuguese explorers moved along the Senegambian coast, they identified Muslim clerics as Moors (Boulègue 1986, 2: 342–44, 1987: 93–99; Ca da Mosto 1937: 50; Fernandes 1951: 9). By the seventeenth century, Muslim leadership was black and rooted in local cultures. Many Muslim clerics were given land in reward for their services. Thus, there was a gradual buildup of communities that enforced Muslim law, strictly followed Muslim religious practices, and lived separately from the larger society (Boulègue 1986, 2: 365–80). The larger society was also influenced by Islam. Muslim clerics produced amulets, provided legal advice, and acquired a reputation for sanctity. Some participated in the political system. Many aristocrats and warriors were Muslim, though often not strict practitioners, at least not until late in life.

In the 1670s, a reform movement led by Nasir al Din seized

power in southern Mauritania (Boulègue 1986, 2: 381–408; B. Barry 1971, 1972: 101–31; Curtin 1971; Ritchie 1968; Hamet 1911; Norris 1969). It quickly spread south of the Senegal River, where local Muslims joined the movement and briefly overturned ruling dynasties of the Futa Toro, Waalo, Jolof, and Kajoor. Nasir al Din called on rulers to practice Islam, to limit themselves to four wives, to dismiss their courtiers, and to cease to pillage and enslave their subjects. Undertaken at a time when the slave trade had only begun to increase, antislavery cannot be considered the basis of the movement, but opposition to enslavement was a key demand.[10] The reform movement threatened both the French and various warrior elites, who united in suppressing it. Nasir al Din was killed in 1673, and within four years the traditional rulers were back in power. The demands made by Nasir al Din were, however, to be important to later reformers.

The ideological core of the subsequent jihads was the obligation of a Muslim ruler to enforce the shari'a, the Quranic law. In a number of cases, it was the inroads of the slave trade which called forth a new and more militant leadership. Thus, the Poular-speaking areas on both sides of the Senegal River suffered deeply in the eighteenth century from raids, first by Moroccan soldiers called Ormankobe and then by Mauritanians (Barry 1988: 154–64). Oumar Kane (1974, 1986: 510–43) sees the whole period from 1702 to 1776 as one of political crisis rooted in both internal conflict and foreign intervention, which eroded principles of legitimacy. The failure of the Denianke rulers to protect local peoples led many to turn to a Muslim reform movement under Suleiman Bal and Abdul Kader Kane, which effectively ended Mauritanian inroads and imposed a Muslim regime. Muslim policy in the Futa Toro was that no Futa Muslims could be enslaved or sold into the slave trade (Robinson 1975).

Barry argues that tensions between Muslims and the warrior elite led to Muslim revolts in Bundu (Senegal) in about 1690 and the Futa Jallon after 1725. Malik Sy, the founder of Bundu, had been a supporter of Nasir al Din. Barry (1988: 144) links the creation of a Muslim regime in Bundu to "a tendency for Muslim communities to try to consolidate themselves far from the coast to escape the oppression of warrior power" (see also Bathily 1989: 308–12; Curtin 1971). Barry (1988: 144–54) makes a similar argument for the Muslim coalition in the Futa Jalon.

There too, the new Muslim rulers prohibited the enslavement of Futanke Muslims (see also Robinson 1985: 63; Baldé 1975; Rodney 1968). During the nineteenth century, Islam provided an ideological basis for revolts, which rallied slaves and other oppressed groups against the rulers of the Futa (Barry 1978; I. Barry 1971; Botte 1988). The argument is even clearer for Masina, the fertile inner delta of the Niger. Masina was divided up among small pastoral polities, which were increasingly tied into the Bambara slave-producing machine and at the same time victimized by Tuareg slave raiders from the Sahara. Seku Amadu Lobbo rallied support from both slaves and Fulbe, received a flag from Usman dan Fodio, and threw off both the traditional Fulbe *ardos* and Bambara hegemony (Brown 1969).

Not every Muslim movement involved an anti–slave trade component. Most were open to recruits of slave origins, especially during the early years. Some jihad leaders, like Al Hajj Umar Tal, were careful not to offend the sensibilities of slave owners. As in the Futa Jallon and the Futa Toro, Umar prohibited enslavement of Muslims, but it was sometimes unclear who was a Muslim (Robinson 1985: 63). More important, even those jihads that started out with an anti–slave trade component were trapped in the conditions of their times. Thus, Masina, ruled by a small group of clerics, had to stabilize its population if it was to create a truly Muslim state. It did this by requiring all Fulbe to maintain a permanent residence. It also created a permanent army capable of striking north into the desert. Thus the herds could move north without the whole community moving with them. Sedentarization also meant increased reliance on slave labor. Masina under Seku Amadu and his successors was marked by a division between the pastoral Fulbe, who herded, ruled, and studied, and a mass of *rimaibe* agriculturalists, who produced the rice surpluses that made all other activity possible.

Jihad leaders elsewhere found themselves dependent on their ability to buy horses and firearms. Barry (1988: 151) argues that by the end of the eighteenth century "holy war . . . [has lost] its religious character and Islam serves as a pretext for a man-hunt against the infidels on the frontiers of the Futa Jallon. The predominance of slaves in exchange for European products explains the oppressive character of the new regimes toward non-Muslims, who, reduced massively into slavery, are sold on the coast or

simply gathered into slave villages." During the nineteenth century, the cost of maintaining an army increased rapidly as newer
and more sophisticated arms moved onto the market. Umar was
a striking case in point (Robinson 1985: 329–34; Roberts 1980a,
1986: chap. 3). He failed to create the new Muslim commonwealth he sought, in part because his Futanke were alien to the
areas they tried to rule. His sons and nephew were able to hold
on only by maintaining their superiority in weapons. They thus
had to keep open the strategic western corridor to Senegal; they
needed goods that could be exchanged for weapons; and they
needed booty, most notably slave women, with which to reward
their soldiers. There was no item of trade that could bring as quick
and sure a return as slaves. Thus, they had to slave to survive.

Other Muslims simply found slaving a way to bring in revenue.
Like other jihad leaders, Ma Ba Jaxoo in Senegambia rallied his
people against the slave-raiding warrior class. He was a deeply
devout Muslim cleric determined to create a state where Muslims
would be safe and the shari'a enforced (Klein 1968, 1977; Quinn
1972). After his death in 1867, many of his followers became slave
raiders. No raison d'état explains the slaving activity of Biram
Cissé in the upper Gambia and Fodé Kabba, the most successful
of a series of raiders who operated on the fringes of the densely
populated Diola communities on the South Bank in the 1880s.
Just as Muslims were the most effective raiders in this period, so
too were they the most systematic users of slave labor. This was
particularly true in coastal areas, where they produced commodities for sale to Europeans and in the desertside areas, where the
booming trade absorbed several hundred thousand slaves during
the last decades of the century.

The argument here, thus, is that under conditions of insecurity
engendered by the slave trade, significant groups of people sought
the protection of Muslim leadership (see also Barry 1978). This
leadership eventually acted not against the slave trade but against
its threat to their community. Furthermore, once in power, they
found themselves caught up in the same economic and military
pressures that shaped their predecessors. In this situation, Islamic
law justified and the struggle for power left few alternatives to a
continuation of slaving.[11]

ECONOMIC EFFECTS

There is a more complicated question. It is difficult for many studying the slave trade to imagine any kind of economic growth under the conditions of violence and insecurity that the trade promoted. Some have assumed that no good could come from such an evil. A closer examination of economic history often shows a more ambiguous picture. Certainly, in one area, the effect of the slave trade seems to have been negative. There was a decline in nonslave exports. The most important export from Senegambia during the late sixteenth and early seventeenth century was hides. These almost disappear from export data during the eighteenth century, only to reappear in the last years of the Atlantic trade, in the nineteenth century (Boulègue 1986, 2: 489–91; Curtin 1975, 1: 218–21). There was also a decline in exports of cotton cloth, but there are no data that clearly show that cloth production actually declined. Cotton cloth was used mostly for trade within Africa. There is also no clear evidence that the coastal trade did not continue to sell cotton textiles. Curtin (1975, 1: 211–14) suggests that a tripling of the cloth price in lower Senegal during the early eighteenth century made exports less profitable, but it also suggests strong demand within Africa (see also Boulègue 1986, 2: 491–92).

A more important question was food security. The eighteenth century was a period of endemic famine. During bad years, people often sold their children or themselves, and French slavers had difficulty feeding the slaves they bought. During the famine of 1757–58, the French commander turned about 500 slaves out of the fort to fend for themselves because he could no longer feed them (Curtin 1975, 1: 109–11, 168–73; Bathily 1989: 267–71; Barry 1972: 133). Charles Becker has argued that while these famines were caused by drought and locusts, the slave trade increased Senegambian vulnerability and eroded traditional mechanisms for dealing with natural disaster. Slave-raiding warriors pillaged and burned granaries; people moved to safer, though less productive, areas; and the young and strong were sold off (Becker and Martin 1975; Becker 1977, 1985, 1986). Bathily (1989: 278–83, 339–48) speaks of a general impoverishment of the upper Senegal River (see also Barry 1986: 161–68). Food supply was a constraint even on the French posts, which would not buy slaves if they could not feed them (Boulègue 1986, 2: 482–88). The sale of food to France's island bases and slave ships undoubtedly cut into reserves, thus exposing agriculturalists to the threat of hunger during periods of drought and warfare.

Other products fared better. Gum exports increased dramatically in the late eighteenth century and replaced slaves as the major export of northern Senegambia. In fact, the Moors were large purchasers of slaves. Desertside production seems to have increased. If cotton cloth production maintained itself or increased, as it seems to have done, we can suggest that production grew in those areas where slaves could be efficiently put to use in production. It is also clear that African merchants learned to cope with insecurity, as Curtin's (1975, 1: chaps. 2, 3, 7) description of trade diaspora indicates (see also Roberts 1980b). African merchants not only thrived during the eighteenth and nineteenth centuries but accumulated substantial amounts of capital. Regrettably, most of that capital accumulation took the form of slaves.

CONCLUSION

The slave trade produced islands of growth and prosperity, but these contrasted sharply with the misery of areas victimized by slave raiders and the harsh conditions of the slave village. Slaves could be efficiently exploited, and thus slave labor contributed to the growth of a slave-exploiting class and, in key areas, to an increase in production. There was a low ceiling to this growth. Much of the population was servile, at least a third of the total population (Klein 1987). Slaves were constrained in their enterprise, frustrated in their desire for a normal family life and limited in their incomes. Though some slaves rose above their origins, the masses were tightly circumscribed. The insecurity of life in the Sudan stimulated the development of walled villages and dissuaded ordinary people from venturing far from home. Merchants found ways to guarantee their security. Ordinary agriculturalists could only build walls.

The most important effect of the slave trade was the way it shaped the nature of the state. The slave trade was important not because of the global value of slaves compared to that of some other product but because it strengthened the state and shaped its nature. Dependence on slavery meant that the state had to constantly replenish the pool of slaves, both for trade and to staff itself with dependent servants. Ultimately, the great tragedy for those who lived in the area was that Sudanic political formations depended on slave labor and the slave trade. The inability of African states to move to other kinds of productive activity produced disaster in the late nineteenth century. The best measure of its effect is that during the earliest years of French rule, when slavery and the slave trade were still legal, slaves not only were a majority of the value traded but in many markets represented over 60–70% of what was being traded and probably most of the accumulated capital of the region.[12]

NOTES

1   Patrick Manning's efforts to use computer models to create hypotheses have been highly suggestive, though he makes some debatable guesses in order to construct his models (Manning 1981). Manning (1990) develops this approach further and links the question of demography to other questions. See also Thornton 1981, 1983.

2   Barry 1988 is an excellent synthesis of most recent research on Senegambia. It picks up many of the key themes of Barry 1972, which set the tone for much subsequent Senegalese historiography.

3   Boulègue's (1986) is the most thorough treatment of early-modern Wolof history. Its only serious flaw is his failure to address Curtin's analysis, even to cite Curtin's work. Boulègue's thesis is persuasive, however, because it is cautious and thorough. See also Diouf 1980, Boulègue 1977, and Colvin 1972.

4   Curtin goes on to explain that "the cost of holding slaves . . . must have been about half the purchase price per year, in an ordinary year." He then discusses the strategies of European and African traders. Europeans would often not buy slaves if they could not feed them and would sometimes release slaves they could not feed. Africans usually put slaves to work while they awaited shipment.

5   On hides, see Boulègue 1986, 2: 276–81, 489–91; Curtin 1975, 1: 218–21; on gum, see Boulègue 1986, 2: 494–95; Curtin 1975, 1: 215–18. Boulègue cites Golberry's (1802) estimate that for Senegambia as a whole, the gum trade was about two-thirds the value of the slave trade.

6   Curtin (1975, 1: 325) is critical of the guns-for-slaves stereotype, largely because the import of guns reached its maximum only in the 1730s, after the Senegambian slave trade had already hit its peak. Many other writers, however, have continued to place great stress on firearms. Boulègue (1986, 2: 506) presents a chronology similar to Curtin's but writes that "guns . . . were in the 18th century the principal article demanded by the kings in exchange for slaves." It is probable that horses were more important to

raiding because they made mobility possible, but with the introduction of guns there came an increment of power to those who procured them. Once again, Boulègue (ibid.: 438) writes of "the advantage provided by guns in the type of conflict which was most common among the Senegambian states. Progress was achieved with an increase in the number of guns and their use by cavalry, combining the advantages of the two major tools of war in the Africa of the time. Since all kingdoms got them, the equilibrium of Senegal was not broken."

7   In nineteenth-century Kajoor, there were 16 villages of slave warriors that belonged to the ruling *gueej* matrilineage (Monteil 1966: 85).

8   I am not in a position to make any estimate of the warrior population of Senegambia or bordering regions, but a modest projection from the Wolof data suggests the possibility of 100,000 or more in the western Sudan. Even if the number of slaves absorbed by African economies was several times the number exported, the number of warriors was much greater than the number of persons enslaved in any given year.

9   Binger (1892, 1: 30–31) talks of a young man taken prisoner in the nineteenth century, moved first to Jenne, a trip of 700 to 800 kilometers, then to Bandiagara, where he was sold to a chief from Kong, another trip of about 600 kilometers. Curtin (1975, 1: 193) tells the story of a man who was enslaved twice, sold at least five times, and in the process moved to Freetown, to a village near Labé in the Futa Jalon, down to the lower Gambia, and then up the river. Both cases involved slaves moving in the opposite direction from most of the traffic.

10 Kane (1986: 456–59) has criticized Barry's interpretation as too materialistic. He stresses the religious roots. He does not see the revolt primarily as a response to the Atlantic trade, though he recognizes that Nasir al Din's criticism of the rulers for pillaging and enslaving Muslims was a major issue. In other respects, his analysis of the slave trade and its impact on the Futa Toro is similar to Barry's.

11 For some reflections on why Gajaga is different from the rest of Senegambia, see Bathily 1989: 334–36. For a discussion of the response of the upper Senegal River to Umar and the jihad led by Mamadu Lamine Drame, see Bathily 1986. The second half of this thesis dealing with the nineteenth century should be published soon. See also Bathily 1972.

12 This is clearly indicated in commercial reports for the 1880s that are preserved in the Archives nationales du Mali and the Archives de la République du Sénégal.

REFERENCES

Archives de la République du Sénégal (1880s) Commercial reports, 1 D 79.
Archives nationales du Mali (1880s) Commercial reports, 1 E 18.
Bah, Thierno Mouctar (1985) Architecture militaire traditionelle et poliorcétique dans le Soudan occidental du dix-septième à la fin du dix-neuvième siècle. Yaoundé: Editions Clé.
Baldé, Mamadou Saliou (1975) "L'esclavage et la guerre sainte au Fuuta Jalon,"

in Claude Meillassoux (ed.) Esclavage en Afrique précoloniale. Paris: Maspero: 183–220.

Barry, Boubacar (1971) "La guerre des marabouts dans la région du fleuve Séné-gal de 1673 à 1677." Bulletin de l'Institut fondamentale d'Afrique noire 33: 564–89.

——— (1972) Le royaume du Waalo. Paris: Maspero.

——— (1978) "Crise politique et importance des révoltes populaires au Fuuta Jallon au dix-neuvième siècle." Afrika Zamani 8: 51–61.

——— (1988) La Sénégambie du dix-cinquième au dix-neuvième siècle: Traite négrière, Islam et conquête coloniale. Paris: Harmattan.

Barry, Ismail (1971) "Contribution à l'étude de l'histoire de la Guinée: Les Hubbu du Fitaba et les Almami du Fuuta." Mémoire du diplome de fin d'études, Institut Polytechnique Julius Nyerere.

Bathily, Abdoulaye (1972) "La conquête française du Haut-Fleuve Sénégal, 1818–1887." Bulletin de l'Institut fondamentale d'Afrique noire 34: 67–112.

——— (1986) "La traite atlantique des esclaves et ses effets économiques et sociaux en Afrique: Le cas du Galam, royaume de l'hinterland sénégambien au dix-huitième siècle." Journal of African History 27: 269–93.

——— (1989) Les portes de l'or: Le royaume de Galam (Sénégal) de l'ère musulmane au temps de négriers huitième–dix-huitième siècle). Paris: Harmattan.

Bazin, Jean (1975) "Guerre et servitude à Ségou," in Claude Meillassoux (ed.) Esclavage en Afrique précoloniale. Paris: Maspero: 135–82.

——— (1982) "Etat guerrier et guerres d'état," in Jean Bazin and Emmanuel Terray (eds.) Guerres de lignages et guerres d'états en Afrique. Paris: Archives contemporaines: 319–74.

———, and Emmanuel Terray (1982) "Avant-propos," in Jean Bazin and Emmanuel Terray (eds.) Guerres de lignages et guerres d'états en Afrique. Paris: Archives contemporaines: 9–32.

Becker, Charles (1977) "La Sénégambie à l'époque de la traite des esclaves." Revue française d'histoire d'outre-mer 64: 203–24.

——— (1985) "Notes sur les conditions écologiques en Sénégambie en dix-septième et dix-huitième siècles." African Economic History 14: 167–211.

——— (1986) "Conditions écologiques, crises de subsistance et histoire de la population à l'époque de la traite des esclaves en Sénégambie (dix-septième–dix-huitième siècle)." Canadian Journal of African Studies 20: 357–76.

———, and Victor Martin (1975) "Kayor et Baol: Royaumes sénégalais et traite des esclaves au dix-huitième siècle." Revue française d'histoire d'outre-mer 62: 270–300.

Bernus, Edmond (1960) "Kong et sa région." Etudes eburnéennes 8: 242–323.

Binger, Gustave (1892) Du Niger au Golfe de Guinée. 2 vols., Paris: Hachette.

Botte, Roger (1988) "Révolte, pouvoir, religion: Les Hubbu du Futa-Jalon (Guinée)." Journal of African History 29: 391–413.

Boulègue, Jean (1977) "Lat Soukaabe Faal ou l'opinatreté d'un roi contre les échanges inégaux au Sénégal," in Charles André Julien et al. (eds.) Les africains, vol. 9. Paris: Jeune Afrique: 169–93.

—— (1986) "La traite, l'état, l'islam. Les royaumes Wolofs du dix-cinquième au dix-huitième siècle." Doctoral thesis, University of Paris 1. 3 vols.

—— (1987) Le Grand Jolof. Paris: Karthala.

Boutillier, Jean-Louis (1975) "Les trois esclaves de Bouna," in Claude Meillassoux (ed.) Esclavage en Afrique précoloniale. Paris: Maspero: 253–80.

Brown, William (1969) "The caliphate of Hamdullahi, c. 1818–64." Ph.D. diss., University of Wisconsin.

Brunschwig, R. (1960) "Abd," in Encyclopedia of Islam, vol. 1. Leiden: Brill: 24–48.

Ca da Mosto, Alvise (1937) The Voyages of Cadamosto, trans. and ed. G. R. Crone. London: Hakluyt Society.

Cissoko, Sékéné Mody (1986) Contribution à l'histoire du Khasso dans le Haut-Sénégal des origines à 1854. Paris: Harmattan.

Colvin, Lucie (1972) "Kajor and its diplomatic relations with Saint Louis de Sénégal." Ph.D. diss., Columbia University.

Curtin, Philip (1969) The Atlantic Slave Trade: A Census. Madison: University of Wisconsin Press.

—— (1971) "Jihad in West Africa: Early phases and inter-relations in Mauritania and Senegal." Journal of African History 12: 11–24.

—— (1975) Economic Change in Precolonial Africa: Senegambia in the Era of the Slave Trade. 2 vols., Madison: University of Wisconsin Press.

—— (1981) "The abolition of the slave trade from Senegambia," in David Eltis and James Walvin (eds.) The Abolition of the Atlantic Slave Trade. Madison: University of Wisconsin Press: 83–98.

Diouf, Mamadou (1980) "Le Kajoor au dix-neuvième siècle et la conquête coloniale." Thèse du troisième cycle, University of Paris 1.

Du Laurens, R. (1904) Rapport sur la captivité (Podor). Archives de la République du Sénégal.

Elbl, Ivana (1986) "Portuguese trade with West Africa, 1440–1521." Ph.D. diss., University of Toronto.

Farias, Paulo Fernando de Moraes (1985) "Models of the world and categorical models: The 'enslavable barbarian' as a mobile classificatory label," in John Ralph Willis (ed.) Slaves and Slavery in Muslim Africa, vol. 1. London: Frank Cass: 27–46.

Fernandes, Valentim (1951) Description de la côte occidentale d'Afrique, de Ceuta au Sénégal. Bissau: Centro de Estudos de Guiné Port.

Geggus, David (1989) "Sex ratio, age, and ethnicity in the Atlantic slave trade: Data from French shipping and plantation records." Journal of African History 30: 23–44.

Golberry, Xavier (1802) Fragments d'un voyage en Afrique fait pendant les années 1785 et 1787 dans les contrées occidentales du continent. 2 vols., Paris: Treuttel et Wurtz.

Green, Kathryn (1984) "The foundation of Kong: A study in Dyula and Sonongui identity." Ph.D. diss., Indiana University.

Gregory, Joel, and Dennis Cordell (1987) "African historical demography: The search for a theoretical framework," in Joel Gregory and Dennis Cordell (eds.) African Population and Capitalism: Historical Perspectives. Boulder, CO: Westview: 14–35.

Hamet, I. (1911) Chroniques de la Mauritanie sénégalaise: Naçer Eddine. Paris: Leroux.

Handloff, Robert (1982) "The Dyula of Gyaman: A study of politics and trade in the nineteenth century." 2 vols. Ph.D. diss., Northwestern University.

Hunwick, John (1988) "Black slaves in the Mediterranean world: Introduction to a neglected aspect of the African diaspora." Workshop on the Long-Distance Trade in Slaves Across the Sahara and the Black Sea in the Nineteenth Century, Bellagio, December.

Inikori, Joseph, ed. (1982) Forced Migration. London: Hutchinson.

Kane, Oumar (1974) "Les maures du Futa Toro au dix-huitième siècle." Cahiers d'études africaines 14: 237–52.

——— (1986) "Le Fuuta-Tooro des Satigi aux Almaami (1512–1807)." Thèse d'état, University of Paris I.

Klein, Herbert (1983) "African women in the Atlantic slave trade," in Claire Robertson and Martin Klein (eds.) Women and Slavery in Africa. Madison: University of Wisconsin Press: 29–38.

Klein, Martin (1968) Islam and Imperialism in Senegal: Sine-Saloum, 1847–1914. Stanford: Stanford University Press.

——— (1969) "The Moslem revolution in nineteenth century Senegambia," in Daniel McCall, Jeffrey Butler, and Norman Bennett (eds.) Boston University Papers on Africa: History, vol. 4. New York: Praeger: 69–101.

——— (1972) "Social and economic factors in the Muslim revolution in Senegambia." Journal of African History 13: 419–41.

——— (1977) "Ma Ba ou la résistance forcée à la conquête française en Séné-gambie," in Charles-André Julien et al. (eds.) Les africains, vol. 8. Paris: Jeune Afrique.

——— (1983) "Women and slavery in the western Sudan," in Claire Robertson and Martin Klein (eds.) Women and Slavery in Africa. Madison: University of Wisconsin Press: 67–92.

——— (1987) "The demography of slavery in western Sudan in the late nineteenth century," in Joel Gregory and Dennis Cordell (eds.) African Population and Capitalism: Historical Perspectives. Boulder, CO: Westview: 50–62.

———, and Paul Lovejoy (1979) "Slavery in West Africa," in H. A. Gemery and J. S. Hogendorn (eds.) The Uncommon Market: Essays in the Economic History of the Atlantic Slave Trade. New York: Academic: 181–212.

Levtzion, Nehemia (1985) "Slavery and Islamization in Africa," in John Ralph Willis (ed.) Slaves and Slavery in Muslim Africa, vol. 1. London: Frank Cass: 182–98.

——— (1986a) "Rural and urban Islam in West Africa: An introductory essay." Asian and African Studies 20: 7–26.

——— (1986b) "Merchants versus scholars and clerics: Differential and com-plementary roles." Asian and African Studies 20: 27–44.

Lovejoy, Paul (1982) "The volume of the Atlantic slave trade: A synthesis." Journal of African History 23: 473–502.

——— (1983) Transformations in Slavery: A History of Slavery in Africa. Cambridge: Cambridge University Press.

Manning, Patrick (1981) "The enslavement of Africans: A demographic model." Canadian Journal of African Studies 15: 489–526.

——— (1990) Slavery and African Life. Cambridge: Cambridge University Press.

Meillassoux, Claude, ed. (1971) The Development of Indigenous Trade and Markets in West Africa. London: Oxford University Press.

——— (1975a) "Etat et conditions des esclaves à Gumbu (Mali) au dix-neuvième siècle," in Claude Meillassoux (ed.) Esclavage en Afrique précoloniale. Paris: Maspero: 221–52.

———, ed. (1975b) Esclavage en Afrique précoloniale. Paris: Maspero.

——— (1986) L'anthropologie de l'esclavage: Le ventere de fer et d'argent. Paris: Presses universitaires de la France.

Monteil, Vincent (1966) Esquisses sénégalaises. Dakar: Institut fondamentale d'Afrique noire.

Norris, H. T. (1969) "Znaga Islam during the seventeenth and eighteenth centuries." Bulletin of the School of Oriental and African Studies 20: 496–526.

Quimby, Lucy (1972) "Transformations of belief: Islam among the Dyula of Kongbougou from 1880 to 1970." Ph.D. diss., University of Wisconsin.

Quinn, Charlotte (1972) Mandingo Kingdoms of the Senegambia: Traditionalism, Islam, and European Expansion. Evanston, IL: Northwestern University Press.

Ritchie, Carson I. A. (1968) "Deux textes sur le Sénégal, 1673–1677." Bulletin de l'Institut français d'Afrique noire, ser. B, 30: 289–353.

Roberts, Richard (1978) "The Maraka and the economy of the Middle Niger Valley, 1712–1905." Ph.D. diss., University of Toronto.

——— (1980a) "Production and reproduction of warrior states: Segu Bambara and Segu Tokolor." International Journal of African Historical Studies 13: 389–419.

——— (1980b) "Long distance trade and production: Sinsani in the nineteenth century." Journal of African History 21: 169–88.

——— (1986) Warriors, Merchants, and Slaves: The State and the Economy in the Middle Niger Valley, 1700–1914. Stanford: Stanford University Press.

Robinson, David (1975) "Islamic revolution in Futa Toro." International Journal of African Historical Studies 8: 185–222.

——— (1985) The Holy War of Umar Tal. Oxford: Clarendon.

Rodney, W. (1968) "Jihad and social revolution in Futa Djalon in the eighteenth century." Journal of the Historical Society of Nigeria 4: 269–84.

Sanneh, Lamine (1979) The Jakhanke: The History of an Islamic Clerical People of the Senegambia. London: International African Institute.

Searing, James (1988) "Slavery in the Wolof states, 1700–1850." Paper presented at the annual meeting of the Canadian Association of African Studies, Kingston, Ontario, May.

Terray, Emmanuel (1974) "Long distance exchange and the formation of the state: The case of the Abron kingdom of Gyaman." Economy and Society 3: 315–45.

——— (1975) "La captivité dans le royaume abron de Gyaman," in Claude

Meillassoux (ed.) Esclavage en Afrique précoloniale. Paris: Maspero: 389–454.

Thornton, John (1981) "The demographic effect of the slave trade on western Africa," in Christopher Fyfe and David McMaster (eds.) African Historical Demography. Edinburgh: Centre for African Studies.

———— (1983) "Sexual demography: The impact of the slave trade on family structure," in Claire Robertson and Martin Klein (eds.) Women and Slavery in Africa. Madison: University of Wisconsin Press: 39–48.

Willis, John Ralph (1985a) "Introduction: The ideology of enslavement in Islam," in John Ralph Willis (ed.) Slaves and Slavery in Muslim Africa, vol. 1. London: Frank Cass: 1–15.

———— (1985b) "Jihad and the ideology of enslavement," in John Ralph Willis (ed.) Slaves and Slavery in Muslim Africa, vol. 1. London: Frank Cass: 16–26.

3
Keeping Slaves in Place:
The Secret Debate
on the Slavery Question in
Northern Nigeria,
1900–1904

JAN HOGENDORN AND

PAUL E. LOVEJOY

IT HAS BEEN widely recognized that British colonial policy toward slavery in Northern Nigeria was crafted by that territory's first high commissioner, Frederick Lugard. When Sir Frederick assumed the post in 1900, he implemented a number of ideas drawn from his experience in East Africa. By 1906, when he was transferred away from Northern Nigeria to become governor of Hong Kong, he could claim to have set in motion an irreversible transition in the slave economy and the condition of slaves in Northern Nigeria. In an earlier article (Hogendorn and Lovejoy 1989), we drew attention to the secret controversy between Lugard and his principal subordinates in the development and execution of these policies.[1] This chapter elaborates upon that controversy by identifying more fully the various ideological positions with which Lugard had to contend, and it establishes clearly that the secret debate was resolved in Lugard's favor by the summer of 1904.[2]

Why should it matter? As will be clear to specialists and should be more widely known, the Sokoto Caliphate which preceded the establishment of Northern Nigeria was the second largest slave society in modern history. Only the United States had more slaves in 1860 than the Caliphate had in 1900. Most of the Caliphate was conquered by the British, who thus had to decide what to do with the huge servile population that came under British jurisdiction between 1897 and 1903.[3] As we have shown elsewhere, the policy that was introduced abolished the legal status of slavery. This approach to slavery, which was an alternative to the compensated emancipation adopted in the British West Indies, did not end slavery but did remove the legal distinction between slave and free so that the courts could not be used to enforce the return of fugitive slaves and slaves could leave their masters without any formal emancipation. What the policy of legal-status abolition meant in practice is beyond the scope of this study. Our concern here is instead the controversy over its adoption, and most especially, the timing of the debate.

Other scholars have established that secrecy surrounded the slavery issue. Polly Hill (1977: 200) has pointed to a conspiracy of silence on the part of the authorities both in Northern Nigeria and at the Colonial Office, while Louise Lennihan (1982: 112) has claimed that Lugard's policy was shrouded in secrecy.[4] Both Hill and Lennihan focused on the important 1906 memorandum, which was handsomely printed by Waterlow & Sons in London, as the key document that Lugard atttempted to suppress.[5] Hill and Lennihan are certainly correct in noting that original copies of this memorandum are exceedingly rare, and it was not available to the public, Parliament, or the press. Yet Lugard's slavery policy as adumbrated in this article had been debated at length with the Colonial Office during the period 1900–1904, and the office had given its written approval to this policy. Lugard's secrecy was not aimed at the Colonial Office but at the British public and Parliament (Hogendorn and Lovejoy 1989). The Colonial Office knew full well what was going on and indeed was actively engaged in the controversy between Lugard and his subordinates. Even attempts to hide the situation from the public were largely abandoned by 1905. The rarity of the 1906 memorandum does not indicate Colonial Office ignorance of these matters.

POSITIONS IN THE CONTROVERSY

Lugard's views on slavery had been formed during his East African service from 1889 to 1892. In his book *The Rise of Our East*

African Empire (1893) and his influential article "Slavery under the British Flag" (1896), he advocated the abolition of the legal status of slavery followed by reforms enabling and persuading slaves to ransom themselves.[6] He thereby adhered to a policy that had been applied first in India in 1843 and was also adopted in Malaya in the same year, Ceylon and Hong Kong in 1844, the Gold Coast in 1874, and Zanzibar in 1897 (Hogendorn and Lovejoy 1989: 2). Legal-status abolition was also the cornerstone of the slavery policy of the Royal Niger Company, which enacted a decree similar to that of Zanzibar in 1897.

Lugard had already caught the attention of Joseph Chamberlain at the Colonial Office because of his activities in Uganda, and Lugard's famous march to Nikki in 1894 in the employ of the Royal Niger Company (RNC) that led to the confrontation with the French army added to his reputation. After an interlude in Bechuanaland in 1896, he received an Imperial government appointment to establish a military force (the West African Frontier Force, or WAFF) and serve as its commandant.[7] He was the obvious choice to serve as high commissioner of the new Protectorate of Northern Nigeria, which was established to govern the territory of the Royal Niger Company when that company lost its charter on 1 January 1900.

Even before he assumed office in Northern Nigeria, Lugard had to make decisions concerning slavery; indeed, he engaged in lengthy correspondence on the issue with Chamberlain during 1899. Clearly the Royal Niger Company's experiences with slavery had not been satisfactory. General misunderstanding and confusion existed among Royal Niger Company personnel. Many of the RNC's military officials, including James Willcocks (1904: 225–26), second in command of the new WAFF, and Seymour Vandeleur (1898: 191–92), another senior officer, believed that the emancipation of slaves must be instituted at once.[8] This opinion was widespread following the company's abolition of the legal status of slavery in 1897. The few missionaries under the protection of the RNC held a similar view. It appeared likely that this liberal, indeed humanitarian, view would resurface among the protectorate's officials, posing a threat to Lugard from the political left.

There was even greater pressure from the right. Two high officials of the RNC, who were to serve under Lugard from the first, were determined to hold the line against immediate freedom for slaves. They headed a group of colonial officials who were briefly known as the "Movement," a phrase coined by Reginald Popham Lobb, who had served as Lugard's personal secretary (Hogendorn and Lovejoy 1989: 10–20). William Wallace, the chief RNC administrator, took the post of deputy high commissioner under Lugard. Wallace clearly had not approved of the actions taken by RNC officials to encourage slaves to assert their freedom, and he was one of the first to announce openly the ultraconservative position that slavery should be continued. The other leader of the proslavery faction was Alder Burdon, commandant of the constabulary under the Royal Niger Company, who, like Wallace, became a senior official in the Lugard administration, first as Resident of Bida and later as Resident of Sokoto. Burdon was adamant in his belief that the RNC's decree abolishing the legal status of slavery must not be interpreted to mean that there was any intent to free slaves. The conservative stance of these two high officials eventually led to a major challenge to Lugard's policies concerning slavery.

There was yet another position, that of the Colonial Office itself, which wanted to rationalize slavery policies for all of British West Africa. Sierra Leone had entered history as a colony dedicated to emancipation (with, however, large numbers of slaves who remained legally in servitude until 1936). The Gold Coast slavery ordinance of 1874 set the stage for another response to "domestic slavery" in which Britain announced the abolition of the legal status of slavery and pledged a full-scale assault on the slave trade. Southern Nigeria followed yet another course. Opposition to the slave trade there evolved into a mechanism for allowing the continuation of slavery under the guise of "house rule" (Grace 1975; Ohadike 1988; McSheffrey 1983; Dumett and Johnson 1988: 78–82; Phillips 1989: 26–34). The Colonial Office certainly did not want to see an entirely different policy for Northern Nigeria, although in the end that is exactly what emerged.

THE SECRET DEBATE

The debate over slavery in Northern Nigeria highlights many issues concerning British attitudes towards this important issue, but it should be noted that the debate was largely held in secret, the reasons for which are even more revealing. Most officials believed that slavery had to continue. How to assure its continuation without drawing attention to the fact was a serious problem. In establishing the Protectorate of Northern Nigeria, the Colonial Office somehow had to mold its policies to allow for slavery, a fact that all of the protagonists in the debate realized. The debate was over how best to do so.

On 12 September 1899, Lugard submitted a draft proclamation that extended the Royal Niger Company's decree abolishing the legal status of slavery, sought to control slave raiding and dealing, and provided for the freedom of individuals born after a date to be specified later (PRO 1899). Legally, the RNC decree was revoked on 1 January 1900 because it was an "announcement" and not a "regulation." Only RNC regulations became law upon the assumption of the British Protectorate. The attorney general recommended a new proclamation, but Lugard rejected this suggestion because his own draft was under consideration. Instead, Lugard preferred "to bring into force the Niger Company Decree pro temp," which was enacted as Proclamation No. 11 of 1900 on 17 February 1900.[9] Lugard waited for action on his proposal.

Chamberlain finally responded to Lugard's draft on 25 May 1900, when he forwarded his own proposal for a proclamation, which was based on the Gold Coast Slavery Ordinance No. 1 of 1874 and was designed "with a view to uniformity of legislation in this important matter." Chamberlain's draft did not provide for the freedom of children born after a specified date (ultimately 31 March 1901). Chamberlain was more concerned with the termination of slave dealing, although it should be noted that he was in full accord with Lugard in upholding the abolition of the legal status of slavery (NNA, 1900a).

Lugard made some minor revisions to Chamberlain's draft, which he returned on 21 July 1900.[10] Far from being concerned with uniformity, Lugard observed that the West African colonies and protectorates were very different from each other. Northern Nigeria was "essentially a region of powerful Mohammedan States whose rulers for a long series of years past have exacted tribute from vassal states, paid annually in slaves. Thus a Slavery Decree in any other colony has a different meaning from what it has in Northern Nigeria." Lugard's own proposal had the intention of preventing slave raiding, ending the killing of people associated with raiding, and stopping tribute payments in slaves. He would even "confiscate slaves who have been recently caught and are on their way to Sokoto or elsewhere." If adopted, Lugard's draft would also have made the possession and transport of "raw slaves" illegal. The prohibition against "raw slaves" was not intended to interfere with a master traveling with his "domestic slaves," however. Lugard insisted on a date after which children would be born free. Even though this would have had little immediate effect, "twenty years hence no youth or girl would be legally held slave and after fifty years hence the race of slaves would be practically extinct." Otherwise Lugard's draft did not affect "domestic slavery" any more than Chamberlain's proposal did. The major difference related to the slave trade. Lugard did not think that it was time to move against the slave trade, which the adoption of the Gold Coast model would have entailed.

Lugard (NNA 1900c) reminded Chamberlain that *he* was the expert, noting that he had discussed his draft "clause by clause" with Sir George Goldie, who was responsible for the Royal Niger Company's decree, "and together we settled its terms. . . . I afterwards submitted it to Sir John Kirk—an intimate personal friend—who was the Plenipotentiary of Great Britain at the Brussels Slavery Conference, and is, I suppose, admitted to be the greatest living authority on the subject." Chamberlain would have known much of this, of course, and in the end he deferred. As if such name dropping was not sufficient, Lugard reinforced his position with the opinion of his attorney general, who agreed that the Gold Coast Ordinance did not go far enough. There had to be measures to obstruct slave raiding, even if it could not be enforced. Still Lugard "was not opposed" to enacting Chamberlain's draft.

Meanwhile, between the time Chamberlain sent his dispatch of 25 May and Lugard responded on 21 July, Proclamation No. 11 of 1900 was disallowed, which Lugard learned in a dispatch of 25 June 1900 (NNA 1900b). It was disallowed on technical grounds and also because Chamberlain thought that his own proclamation would be acceptable. Lugard responded to the disallowance on 25 September, pointing out that a proclamation was required since the Royal Niger Company Decree was not valid. Chamberlain sent a cable on 25 October 1900 agreeing to enact Lugard's draft proclamation and to withdraw his own, subject to certain amendments. The amended draft was forwarded to Lugard on 26 November 1900 and was enacted on 28 February 1901 as Proclamation No. 2 of 1901.[11] According to Lethem (1931):

> Prior to the enactment of the Proclamation which was in fact the first legal Proclamation in the Protectorate of Northern Nigeria, dealing with the question of Slavery, various memoranda had been circulated adumbrating the procedure to be observed in practice in connection with the disallowed Proclamation of 1900 and the Public Notification issued at the instructions of the Secretary of State. Copies of these earliest memoranda have not yet unfortunately been found. But in 1901 Lord Lugard, on his journey to England on leave, prepared a new set of three memoranda (Nos. 3, 4, 5) superseding the old ones. In these the meaning of the phrase "the abolition of the legal status of slavery" is fully defined, the reasons for non-abolition of domestic slavery are set forth and the procedure to be adopted by officers in administrating the new Proclamation outlined.

These three memoranda, dated 22 November 1901, were probably very similar to the earlier, secret instructions.

Lugard was firmly in control of the situation, or so it must have appeared. The new memoranda, which were the first of seven separate instructions issued between 22 November 1901 and 1 December 1902, elaborated on the Slavery Proclamation of 1901 to such an extent as to virtually nullify much of its apparent meaning. Lugard intended to obscure the slavery issue through legalisms and confusing (to some) instructions. As soon became apparent, Lugard had little tolerance for those who were bewildered and frustrated.

Memorandum No. 3, "Slavery," explained how "domestic slavery" was still in force, even though the legal status of slavery was no longer recognized. Memorandum No. 4, "Freed Slaves," outlined the policy that allowed slaves to purchase their own freedom or otherwise have their ransom paid by third parties. Memorandum No. 5, "Slavery: The System of Holding Persons in Pawn," distinguished between the pawning of persons, which was illegal, and the self-purchase or ransom of slaves, which constituted the basis of reformed slavery under British rule.[12] Special Memo No. 10 (Slavery) of 18 January 1902 defined fugitive slaves as vagrants who were to be denied rights to land and otherwise denied freedom of movement. This memo further explained the mechanism whereby slaves were to purchase their freedom. An addendum, dated 14 August 1902, warned against the wholesale desertion of slaves and in that event reaffirmed the policy that denied slaves access to land. Special Memo No. 32, "Disposal of Liberated Women," dated 1 December 1902, allowed that most matters pertaining to female slaves were to be considered a sub-category of matrimony, which enabled the transfer and redemption of female slaves under the guise of marriage and classified the estrangement of masters and female slaves as divorce, not escape from slavery. This memo also made it clear that most references to "slaves" were aimed at males. The establishment of the first freed slave home in early 1902 was intended to provide sanctuary for women and children who could not otherwise be disposed of through marriage or adoption and apprenticeship.[13]

It is our contention that these seven memoranda were virtually identical to the secret instructions, often verbal, that had been issued earlier, the first being to Acting Resident Cochrane in late January 1901. Burdon also received such instructions, and the testimony of Wallace and others suggests that these were widely known in Northern Nigeria (Hogendorn and Lovejoy 1989: 16–17). The pattern in Lugard's written communication is revealing. He issued lengthy and frequent directions, but there was extensive repetition from one set of instructions to the next. While Lugard elaborated upon and refined his policies, there is nonetheless re-markable consistency of wording and intent. We would predict that if the dispatches to Cochrane, Burdon, and others were to be located, they then would resemble the instructions of November 1901–December 1902. Secret though they may have been, it is highly probable that Lugard's ideas were already shaped when he became high commissioner in January 1900. He was com-mitted to an ideology based on the abolition of the legal status of slavery while in fact enforcing a gradual transition to a postslavery society.

His superiors at the Colonial Office and his subordinates in Northern Nigeria misunderstood the genius of Sir Frederick's strategy. The Colonial Office, preoccupied with a thousand and one problems of empire, was willing to defer on the issue, at least at first. Lugard's officers were less tolerant, since they had to deal with the reality of conquest and occupation. Hence the first serious opposition surfaced in Northern Nigeria. Wallace, while he was acting high commissioner during Lugard's second, lengthy leave of absence in 1901, wrote a series of letters to Chamberlain that dealt with issues of taxation, not slavery (NNA 1901a, b, c).[14] In a curious non sequitur, Wallace raised the issue of slavery in a manner that was bound to produce a strong reaction in the Colonial Office. "I am in complete touch and sympathy with the semi-civilized peoples of [the] Hausa States and I can assure you most positively that if a policy of wholesale liberation of domestic slaves is pursued it will mean the ruin of this Protectorate at no distant date" (NNA 1901b).

Chamberlain expressed his failure to understand the reference to the "wholesale liberation of domestic slaves." He reminded Wallace that the Proclamation of 1901 confirmed the abolition of the legal status of slavery and dealt with issues relating to slave dealing, "but it was not intended to interfere at this stage with domestic relations" (NNA 1901d). Wallace was told to explain himself.

Wallace responded to Chamberlain on 7 November. "I regret that in the first instance I did not make my allusion to 'the wholesale liberation of domestic slaves' more clear to you but I should like to explain that I did this advisedly as I hold strong views on this question which I considered it might be out of place for me to express at that time; now however that you call upon me for an explanation of my words, I have no hesitation in writing to you fully on the subject." Wallace charged that Proclamation No. 2 of 1901 "provides for a sweeping abolition of slavery, without distinction." In his opinion, this could not have been Lugard's intent, and he speculated that someone other than Lugard must have been the author of such a sweeping measure. Wallace was deliberately exposing the contradiction between what Lugard was proposing in Proclamation No. 2 and what he was instructing his officers to do.

Wallace referred back to the 1897 Niger Company Decree and its consequences—large-scale desertion from Ilorin and Jebba to Idah, also embracing Igala and Nupe canoe slaves ("the backbone of the river canoe traffic"). He estimated that 30,000 slaves had fled their masters in Bida Emirate alone by the end of 1899. "Before the first month [January 1900] of General Lugard's Administration had expired he had issued a Confidential Memo to

Residents on the subject [of mass desertions]. This, although full of very sound and practical advice, was so far as it referred to domestic and farm slavery rendered void by the emasculating sentence 'and it is even doubtful whether a British subject (including Residents) rendering up a fugitive slave to his master is not himself guilty of a criminal act.' " Prevailing opinion among officials, according to Wallace, held that there was "no such thing as slavery in any shape or form" as a result of the proclamation, and many WAFF personnel on the Wushishi campaign "proclaimed" that slavery was over. Emirate officials also believed this to be the intent of the proclamation, and consequently, to avoid the wholesale liberation of slaves as the British advanced, they gathered "their slaves from the farms before they could desert to the whiteman." Desertions were so extensive that the population of Wushishi, Bida, and Jebba had been "in a state of semi-starvation for months," according to reports from Molesworth, Eaglesome, and Burdon.

Wallace had avoided a similar crisis when he marched on Yola because he "clearly informed the Emir that we would on no account interfere with the domestic and farm or connubial slaves of himself and his people." Wallace had taken this action in the absence of Lugard, thereby "laying myself open to censure by His Majesty's Government." Now the emir of Zaria was requesting clarification of British policy on slavery; Wallace claimed written confirmation that the emir would acknowledge the British government if there was no interference with domestic slavery. Even stronger measures were adopted at Bida, where slaves were in open revolt. Burdon had acted to contain the fugitive crisis there by returning slaves to their masters. Wallace was in "total agreement" with "Burdon's good work" (NNA 1901f).[15]

According to Wallace, Burdon had "repeatedly broken clause 4 of the Slavery Proclamation and thereby rendered himself liable to six months' imprisonment with hard labour on different counts" (NNA 1901f).[16] Colonel Morland, who returned a female slave to her master "against her will," was also technically liable, and Wallace admitted that his action at Yola made him subject to criminal prosecution as well. He was not asking that charges be laid but that the proclamation be repealed and a new one introduced. In his opinion, "slaves in the Northern Nigeria Haussa States will be far happier and more prosperous in the future, if ruled by their present native law than by any new code which we could introduce." Wallace intended to "prepare a paper on the subject [of the real status of the domestic slave] . . . by the next mail" (NNA 1901f).

Burdon believed that Proclamation No. 2 of 1901 was full of contradictions: what could the abolition of the legal status of slavery possibly mean? If it meant that slavery was abolished, Burdon did not "understand why it was not made to say so in plain English." Slaves born after 31 March 1901 were free; slaves born before that date were not free, but what could that mean if there was no legal status? The effect was clear, nonetheless, and it was not in conformity with Islamic law, which held that concealing an escaped slave was a criminal offense similar to the English law concerning receipt of stolen property. Yet people could own slaves.

Burdon was of the opinion that Proclamation No. 2 of 1901 did not intend to free all slaves and that no slave was free unless he was duly and legally freed by a Protectorate Court. "The mere fact of flight from a master does not in itself constitute freedom." Nonetheless, if the proclamation were actually enforced, it would have resulted in "the most wholesale and sweeping abolition of slavery" (NNA 1901e). Consequently, Burdon was "governed by the confidential instructions issued by His Excellency Sir Frederick Lugard to Captain Cochrane when he was placed here [in Bida] as Acting Resident. His notes on that document are 'that the Slavery Proclamation is not to be too rapidly or drastically enforced.' " If slaves were allowed to flee, Burdon believed, starvation, death, and ruin would ensue for everyone, masters and slaves alike. Burdon had no choice: "I must restore or endeavour to restore, the original fugitives—then whether I succeed or not the remainder will not run away, knowing that they may be liable to capture or return." In this reading there was no middle ground; the rule had to apply to all fugitives or none.

Burdon had asked Lugard for advice in November 1900. He was told not to interfere in matters relating to slavery. Now even more confused as a result of his instruction, Burdon chose to act in accordance with what he thought Lugard wanted: the maintenance of slavery. To justify this decision, Burdon quoted Lugard himself on the necessity of returning fugitive slaves to their masters. He too inferred that "the Official who drafted the Slavery

Proclamation" could not have been Lugard, although there can be no doubt that indeed he was the author. That a draft may have been written by someone else could explain Wallace's and Burdon's willingness to absolve Lugard of blame, but this is of no consequence, since Lugard fully approved of the document and therefore was responsible for it.

Burdon "urgently" advised total "cancellation" of the proclamation. "Slavery must not be abolished—it must not even be tampered with—until we know something of the laws that govern [the Hausa emirates]." In Burdon's opinion, it would take "generations" to "teach the pagans who form the slave population the meaning of hired labour," and he argued that nothing must be done until that had been achieved. "NO—The system of slavery must be legalised. The native laws on it are wonderful in their mildness and liberal spirit and they must be learnt and endorsed by us." There must be penalties for "absconding" because with the abolition of slave trading recaptured fugitives could no longer be sold as a punishment (NNA 1901e).

Thus upon his return to Nigeria Lugard faced a serious crisis within his administration. His two most senior subordinates were in open opposition over the slavery issue, and there is enough information to suggest that they had support among other officials. More than slavery policy was at stake. His very hold on his own colonial service was in doubt. Lugard considered slavery "the most important question" of his early administration, and Wallace's "condemnation of my action and Policy" required the "use [of] some plain language" in defense. Lugard was condescending in his rebuttal, implying that Wallace was not capable of understanding "the meaning of the terms employed." Reference to Goldie and Kirk was further proof that the Movement had no legitimacy. Lugard turned the criticism around to blame everyone but himself for excesses and the failure to condemn them in the various military campaigns of 1900–1901. Wallace's judgment was repeatedly called into question. The complaints and charges of other officials were dismissed as distortions. Lugard made it clear that he wanted a full investigation and report on all such "domestic matters" within his administration (NNA 1901g).[17]

Wallace could not have avoided reading these instructions as an order to desist, although Lugard announced that he "would be glad to see the paper" that Wallace had proposed to write. The report never materialized. Finally, Lugard presented himself as a moderate who was an advocate of neither the "infinitely more drastic" measures of the Gold Coast Ordinance nor, by implication, the equally severe proposals of the Movement. He served notice that he would respond verbally to the "illogical deductions and mis-statements" that both Wallace and Burdon had made. The coup de grace was a reminder that British subjects were obliged to uphold British law (NNA 1901g).

Wallace was humble in his reply. He pretended that he did not have the "faintest idea" that Lugard had written Proclamation No. 2 of 1901. In reiterating his position, he requested that officials be instructed "not to interfere in slavery matters." There was little doubt in Wallace's mind that "the legal reading of it [the Proclamation] is that a slave need only be a slave with his consent." He reminded Lugard that the previous chief justice thought that the proclamation would have to be repealed and a clearer and unequivocal decree enacted. Wallace lamely insisted that he was only following orders in responding to Chamberlain's request for his opinions, although a reading of the correspondence would lead most people to believe that Wallace had deliberately provoked Chamberlain, forcing him to ask for Wallace's opinion. Wallace now claimed that his criticism was meant to "strengthen" Lugard's authority by allowing the high commissioner to "give clear and definite instructions on this most important matter." He believed that his dispatch had had a positive impact in securing Chamberlain's statement that "it is not the intention of the Government at present to interfere with Domestic Relations." Wallace noted that Chamberlain "avoided using the word slavery and I think rightly so" (NNA 1901h).

As this exchange makes clear, Lugard was often at his best when he was on the defensive. On 7 January 1902, he wrote to Chamberlain that he was now willing to consider Chamberlain's 1900 draft that was based on the Gold Coast Ordinance of 1874 because conditions had changed and Chamberlain's draft could "now be usefully enacted" (NNA 1902a). Earlier, Lugard had resisted attempts to declare slave trading illegal, but he was ready to do so now.

Lugard attempted to meet the criticisms of the Movement by containing the slave population and encouraging slaves to obtain their freedom through purchase. As Lt. Governor G. J. Lethem

(1931) accurately assessed the policy in Memorandum No. 10 of 18 January 1902, it "went so far as to encourage the payment of redemption by the slave to his former master in accordance with native custom and work was provided by Government in such cases in order that a slave who wished to free himself might save the necessary sum. The practice, too, of a man pledging his own labour for a limited time in redemption of a debt was countenanced by Memorandum No. 5, provided that the pawning was entirely spontaneous: but compulsory pawning of a debtor or the pawning of some person other than the debtor himself was illegal though the amount of time served in such compulsory labour was counted in liquidation of the debt." [18] The addendum of August 1902 was designed to prevent the immigration of large numbers of fugitive slaves by refusing to grant fugitives land on which to settle. Individual fugitives were not to be given government employment or permission to live in a government station. The intention was not to deny the right of a slave to desert, only to deter slaves from doing so (PRO 1902).

The issue of concubines and slave women was carefully separated from general considerations of slavery, a feature of slavery policy that has been noted elsewhere (Lovejoy 1988). As Lethem (1931) later noted with respect to "the freedom of a woman slave, the principle concerned was that of divorce and not slavery at all, since the applicants were usually actuated by 'a desire to leave one husband or man to whom they were concubines in order to live with another.' The right of the Native Court to deal with such cases was therefore recognised and compensation was admitted 'not as a debt due to the owner of a slave but on the principle on which damages were awarded in civilized divorce courts.' " [19] Memorandum No. 32 was specially directed against abuses associated with the so-called marrying of freed women "which was little better than actual legalized slave dealing." With the establishment of the first freed slave home early in 1902, women and children were to be sent to that institution "except in cases where women obtained satisfactory husbands or could be repatriated without delay" (Lethem 1931).

Slave raiding and slave caravans were dealt with in the harshest terms. The Addendum (Special Memo No. 2) of March 1903 was intended to prevent the enslavement of any person. Initially the trade in slaves between provinces (i.e., emirates) was banned; then all slave trading was prohibited.[20]

The disposal of freed slaves was the subject of Memo No. 4, November 1901, but further to dissuade his critics, Memo No. 32 of December 1902 gave more specific instructions: "The general principle was that all adults should be given an opportunity to return to their own countries and where this was not feasible men were allowed to go where they wished, women to select a husband they desired. The husbands and guardians of freed women or children slaves were subjected to continuous supervision and it was the Resident's duty to see that they fulfilled their obligations" (NNA 1902b).

On 7 January 1903, Lugard sent the draft of a new proclamation that combined his various instructions and finally incorporated Chamberlain's draft of 1900 on slave dealing (i.e., the Gold Coast Ordinance of 1874). The penalty for dealing in slaves was to be increased from six months' to seven years' imprisonment (PRO 1903a).[21]

The Colonial Office now entered the debate with its own proposal. As is clear, the office already had ideas different from Lugard's. Chamberlain wanted uniformity among colonies and protectorates, and serious consideration was given to the complaints of the Movement, although in the end the Colonial Office rejected its solutions. The office's reply to Lugard's submission, sent on 17 April 1903, asked for a response to Wallace's criticisms of 7 November 1901. Chamberlain wanted some assurance that Lugard's proposed proclamation did not "interfere with domestic relations" between slaves and masters; if so, it was time "to substitute for the institution of domestic slavery a legalised form of relationship between employer and labourer," specifically the Native House Rule Proclamation of Southern Nigeria. If that solution was not acceptable because of differences between Northern and Southern Nigeria, then Lugard was to offer his views on whether or not some other "legalised relationship for domestic slavery" should be enacted.[22]

Chamberlain's response gave Lugard's Nigerian critics a further opportunity to argue for legalized slavery. This time H. C. Gollan, the chief justice, led the attack. Gollan opposed the adoption of the Native House Rule Ordinance and any other substitute for domestic slavery. Instead he recommended that slavery be "fully recognized and regulated" through a "slight curtailment of the rights bestowed by the Slavery Proclamation, 1901." Gollan believed that legalization would put the colonial government "in a better position to overlook the upbringing of children born since the 31st March 1901 and prevent them from relapsing into the state of mind which, quite as much as the danger that would be created by a sudden destruction of the basis of native society, makes, in my opinion, the existence of a form of domestic slavery necessary, for the time being in this country, and which would, if not actively combatted, tend to give it continued existence" (NNA-I 1903a).

Gollan had not been in the vanguard of the Movement during the heated debate of late 1901, but it now became clear where his sympathies lay. He had become chief justice in November of that year in the midst of the fight, after serving as a Resident and as cantonment magistrate. In these various capacities he had dealt with the full range of slavery cases; as chief justice he only heard charges of enslavement, but as Resident he had handled cases between masters and slaves. On his own admission, he considered himself an expert on the issue of slavery: "During the whole of my service in this country, I have been keenly interested in this question and have taken every opportunity of gathering information on the subject."

Gollan's amending proclamation would have regulated the work of domestic slaves. It clearly articulated the obligations of slaves to their masters and the rights of slaves to work on their own behalf. Masters and slaves alike would have been subject to fines and/ or imprisonment for violating the terms and conditions regulating the work regime. Slaves would have been allowed to own property "of every kind and description," and there would have been clear provision for the "release of domestic slaves from customary obligations" through self-purchase, third-party redemption, and concubinage. Severe penalties would have been enforced if slaves attempted to desert their masters, and the courts would be able to force slaves to return, pay off their purchase price, or otherwise make arrangements to compensate their masters (NNA-I 1903b).

Lugard's marginal notes make it clear that he was not persuaded. Was there danger that slaves would escape as soon as they became aware that their masters had no legal recourse to secure their return, as Gollan claimed? Lugard minuted: "Vide my memos." Was there "an abundance of land available which any man can easily obtain leave to cultivate"? Lugard retorted: "The Government can make it not easy." And as for Gollan's proposal to legalize slavery, Lugard noted curtly: "I do not concur" (NNA-I 1903c).

Next Lugard turned on Chamberlain. His reply was stronger than the one he had made in 1901. He termed the proposal to adopt the Native House Rule Ordinance a "retrograde step" that tolerated "despotic control" in legal form, and he argued along these lines explicitly and at length. There was some remonstrance from the Colonial Office that the Southern Nigeria Ordinance did not legalize slavery de jure, but this was tantamount to an admission that for all practical purposes it did so.[23] Lugard suggested that the proper policy would be to "continue the existing anomaly and in practice to minimise as far as may be the attendant difficulties."[24]

Then he took the opportunity to review his policy in detail. Though that policy had been in effect at the latest from November 1901, Lugard now provided his most complete description for the Colonial Office. With his letter of 21 August 1903, he thus included a copy of his 1901 slavery memo to Residents, and he also enclosed the various supplements.[25]

His letter presented some additional aspects of the slavery policy that were not discussed in the memo. One of these aspects concerned the Islamic courts. Lugard asserted that these "native" courts had been allowed to retain an independent jurisdiction "especially . . . in order to deal with such matters as this of domestic slavery." He alluded to the substantial advantage of allowing slavery matters to be dealt with in that venue instead of in the protectorate courts, with their constricting British law. He noted how effectively fugitive slaves could be discouraged by a combination of land regulation and vagrancy law. In his subsequent article in *The Empire and the Century* he stated that Residents could ensure that village headmen would deny fugitive slaves land on which to settle, or, "if a vagrant in a city would allow the native courts to deal with the matter" (Lugard 1905: 853).

These points had a very practical significance. Without a community of interest between the British authorities and the slaveowning classes in preventing desertions, the slavery policy could not have been administered effectively. Only the local authorities could mobilize sufficiently large numbers of police (the emirs' *dogarai*) to deal with such "minor" matters of law enforcement on a wide scale.

Meanwhile the Colonial Office had delayed its considerations of Lugard's draft proclamation for a considerable period of time; on 1 February 1904, Lugard sent a letter reminding the Colonial Office that his draft had been submitted the previous year. He followed that on 7 June 1904 with yet another reminder; in this letter, Lugard proposed that at least some action be taken, perhaps adopting and updating those sections of the proposed revisions -that were virtually identical with the 1901 proclamation (NNA 1904a). At this point, Lugard also proposed that any canoes suspected of being involved in slave trading should be confiscated. This proposal appears to have been dropped shortly thereafter; there is no later mention of it. The letter included a copy of Lugard's earlier dispatch of 21 August 1903 and another copy of the draft slavery proclamation.

Alfred Lyttleton, who had replaced Chamberlain at the Colonial Office, sought the advice of P. H. Ezechiel, one of the Colonial Office secretaries. Ezechiel's summary, submitted on 6 August 1904, accurately described Lugard's policies on slavery and, moreover, recommended that the Colonial Office provide its full support. Lugard could not have outlined his policy any better: Ezechiel (PRO 1904) noted that slavery

> forms the basis of the whole labour system of the Protectorate. Ultimately it must be replaced. . . . But it cannot be so replaced at once without turning the country upside down and ruining both the masters and the slaves. . . . Therefore *domestic slavery must be maintained for the present* [italics in original]—not recognized by law but maintained in practice. . . . The practical difficulty is that when a slave runs away from his master, a British magistrate is forbidden both by local and by British law to order his return. Sir F. Lugard has instructed his officers . . . to evade the difficulty by a policy of temporary expedients, such as sending cases to be dealt with by native [i.e. Islamic] courts . . . , dealing with fugitive slaves as vagrants (to be sent back to their masters

as paupers were sent back to their parishes in England under the old Poor Law) and so on. Of course in deserving cases the magistrates are to set the slaves formally free.

Two weeks later, Lyttleton put his final seal of approval on Lugard's policies. On 19 August he wrote to Lugard: "I am willing . . . to accept your opinion that the substitution for domestic slavery of a system which would not be slavery and which could therefore be recognized by law, is not at present possible in Northern Nigeria; and I approve the enactment of the draft Proclamation enclosed in your despatch of the 7th June" (NNA 1904b).

Although he deferred to Lugard, Lyttleton tried again to explain the rationale for the Colonial Office proposal to adopt some version of the Native House Rule Ordinance. In Southern Nigeria, Lyttleton (NNA 1904b) pointed out, "domestic slavery has not been legalised *as such* [italics in original], but has been replaced by the house system, so that all former domestic slaves have been made members of a house. It is true that most of the practical features of domestic slavery have been retained; but this was precisely the object of the legislation, while slavery has been abolished not only in name, but also probably in the eye of the strict law, for it is at least very questionable whether a Court in this country would regard the house system as slavery." Lyttleton continued that there had never been any intention to legalize slavery in Northern Nigeria, thereby making it clear that the Colonial Office did not side with the Movement, "but that there should in substitution for it be a system which could be recognised by the law of the Protectorate without coming into conflict with British law. The legislation proposed by Mr. Gollan appears to be inadmissible, because by retaining the name of domestic slavery it would immediately challenge criticism in this country, and also because, so far as it purports to authorise a magistrate to make an order for the return of a slave to his master, it is probably ultra vires."

Lugard had won the day. Proclamation No. 27 of 1904 was enacted on 27 September of that year.

There were subsequent amendments and modifications of a minor nature, but the basic slavery policy was now firmly in place. On 12 June 1905, an amendment increased the penalty for slave trading to 14 years' imprisonment. Memoranda Nos. 3, 4, 5, 10,

12, and 32 of 1901 and 1902 were superseded by Memorandum No. 6 of March 1905; and in September 1906, Lugard published Memorandum No. 22 as an exposition of Islamic law and custom with regard to slaves.[26] Finally, Slavery Proclamation No. 17 of 1907, enacted 21 December 1907, combined the proclamations of 1904 and 1905 into a single proclamation.

In 1910, the Statute Laws Revision Proclamation incorporated the 1907 proclamation verbatim, with the exception of redundant sections referring to earlier measures. Chapter 11 of the schedule continued in force until the amalgamation of Northern and Southern Nigeria and its replacement by Ordinances No. 15 and No. 35 of 1916. Ordinance No. 15, later Chapter 21 of the Laws of Nigeria, was enacted on 16 May 1916. Ordinance No. 35, dated 16 August 1916, became Chapter 83 of the Laws of Nigeria. It was identical to earlier legislation, with the exception of superficial revisions (Lethem 1931).[27]

Those who opposed Lugard's policies made brief but ineffectual forays on behalf of the alternate strategies in 1906 and again in 1908, but there was really no serious threat to the official course after 1904.

AFTERSHOCKS

At the time of the Satiru uprising in February–March 1906, Burdon renewed his hard-line criticism of legal-status abolition (Lovejoy and Hogendorn 1990). He blamed the uprising on the fugitive slave crisis: "*The* [underlining in original] hardship caused by the [Slavery] Proclamation and not in any way remedied by the Memo [No. 6], is the impossibility of recovery of fugitive slaves."[28] Lugard (NNA 1906b) reminded him firmly that he was bound to the policy. "It is the law under which as a British subject, you were born, and I have no more power to alter it than to declare murder legal. I am sorry you are dissatisfied with it,—for my part, I should be very sorry to see it altered. Memo 6, if you read it carefully, does I think, give some practical methods of minimising consequential difficulties, and of preventing the desertion, which is better than the rendition of fugitives." Burdon remained silent after May 1906.

In January 1908, Chief Justice Ernest V. Parodi proposed to Governor Percy Girouard, Lugard's successor, what he considered a novel idea—the adoption of the Southern Nigeria House Rule Ordinance.[29] Parodi apparently was unaware of the earlier debate. Girouard, who appears to have been as ignorant on the matter as his chief justice, subsequently wrote a letter, dated 16 November 1908, to the Earl of Crewe at the Colonial Office suggesting either the adoption of the Southern Nigeria model or the granting of full emancipation to all slaves (NNA 1908b). The Colonial Office responded in disbelief, and the idea was quickly dropped (Hogendorn and Lovejoy 1989: 27–29).

SUMMARY

The four-way debate on the slavery issue thus reached a settlement, as far as British officials were concerned. The military officers favoring emancipation had lost out early on. The political officers of the Movement who had advocated retention of slavery in a legal capacity were bested as well. The Colonial Office officials who wanted to rationalize slavery policy and had therefore proposed that Northern Nigerian law be brought into line with those of the Gold Coast and Southern Nigeria acceded to Lugard's demur. Lugard's own chosen policy of legal subterfuge became the accepted method. Against an impressive array of opponents, Lugard had been able to impose his policy on the military, on his own political family, on the Colonial Office, and by so doing, on the slaves and masters of Northern Nigeria.

The Slavery Proclamation of 1904 was the outcome of the long debate. It remained a penal offense for British officials to participate in the return of fugitives; only then did the sale of slaves become illegal.[30] Nonetheless, there was a concerted effort to prevent slaves from escaping. Few wrote quite so openly about the countervention of official policy as did Major H. R. Beddoes in 1904, who stated that the return of fugitives was "continually being done by every official . . . with the connivance of the Government" (Beddoes 1904: 710; see also PRO 1905). By and large the Residents said little, either then or later. They quietly went about this particular task, though, as Margery Perham noted, some at least must have found their duty a painful one.[31]

At the start of 1906, Lugard could claim that he had successfully adhered to a narrow and even tortuous line between the antislavery principles espoused in Britain and the need to maintain political calm and economic stability in Northern Nigeria.[32] Through his compromise with the Movement he had made flight very difficult for the slaves, and so kept many of them at their labor. Yet at the same time he maintained the fiction that the legal status of slavery no longer existed, and the virtual silence in the scholarly literature might lead many to conclude that slavery had begun a gradual decline without any overwhelming economic or social catastrophe. Later it would be said that it is surprising that his policy did not engender greater overt opposition from the emirs (Perham 1960: 171). Lugard came to believe all this himself, or at least his public image required such an interpretation. His role as an antislavery expert in the League of Nations and his request for full documentation on the evolution of his policies in Northern Nigeria attest to this stance. Lethem willingly obliged the father of Indirect Rule in assembling the materials for his 1931 "Early History of Anti-Slavery Legislation," and Lugard maintained his image as an antislavery crusader.

What actually happened between 1900 and 1906 from the perspective of slaves and masters is another story, however. There was dramatic change during the Lugard years, including the massive flight of at least two hundred thousand slaves, a slave revolt in Nupe in 1901, and the Mahdist uprising at Satiru in 1906, which was supported by fugitive slaves.[33] Certainly the great majority of slaves did not participate in any of these movements, although most were somehow involved in the less dramatic but probably more important changes that were occurring then. In a very real sense slavery continued as a major institution for another two decades. The intense debate within the colonial circle is not only suggestive of the importance of the slavery issue but also provides an outline of the major transformations that were to occur under colonialism. In that sense, Lugard was successful. He set the agenda for the gradual demise of slavery.

NOTES

1   Also see Hogendorn and Lovejoy 1988. The subject of the ending of slavery will be examined by the authors in a forthcoming volume from Cambridge University Press.

2   Since the publication of Hogendorn and Lovejoy 1989, we have come across some important new information that fills in many gaps in the analysis of

British slavery policy. The most important new source is G. J. Lethem, lieutenant governor of Northern Nigeria (1931). This contains Lethem's long summary of the evolution of colonial policy on slavery and numerous documents and previously unavailable copies of memoranda and instructions. We wish to thank Ibrahim Jumare for his valuable assistance in searching for missing documents in our research on slavery.

3   We have estimated elsewhere that slaves constituted at least 25% of the population of the caliphate, whose thirty emirates probably had something on the order of ten million people in 1900.

4   Also see Hill 1976.

5   Memorandum No. 6, "Slavery Questions," in Lugard 1906.

6   See Lugard 1893, vol. 1, especially chapter 7; and Lugard 1896. These works were both widely read. Also see Hogendorn and Lovejoy 1989: 1–6.

7   For the details, see Perham 1956, parts 4, 5, and 6.

8   Also see Hogendorn and Lovejoy 1989: 6–8.

9   Minutes of Lugard, 15, 17 February 1900; Attorney General, 15, 16 February 1900; Lugard to Chamberlain, 6 April 1900, in Lethem 1931.

10   PRO 1900; also quoted in Lethem 1931.

11   For its text, see the *Northern Nigeria Gazette* 1901. Also see PRO 1904. This very useful document, dated 6 August 1904 and written as a summary of developments, is misfiled with Southern Nigeria in the PRO.

12   For an elaboration of this policy, see Hogendorn and Lovejoy 1988.

13   The various memoranda and addenda are summarized in Lethem 1931, to which are appended the complete instructions.

14   The letter of 2 August is also in PRO CO446/16, Despatch No. 368.

15   Also see CO446/17, Despatch No. 504. The serious unrest among the slave population in the area of Bida and Wushishi is examined in our forthcoming book with Cambridge University Press.

16   One clear example of Burdon's actions was reported to Wallace on 1 November 1901. In response to a request for details, Burdon reported that he had returned a slave girl to her master against her will; see NNA 1901e; also in Despatch No. 504, PRO CO446/17.

17   In Hogendorn and Lovejoy 1989 we stated that this correspondence had not survived, so far as we knew, but could be reconstructed from a letter sent by Lugard to the Colonial Office, 21 August 1903, in PRO CO446/36, No. 34322. The correspondence has now been found.

18   These memoranda are contained in Lethem 1931.

19   This is Lethem's (1931) interpretation.

20   For the evolution of British policy toward slave trading, see Ubah 1991.

21   Also see NNA 1903, enclosing the draft proclamation.

22   See PRO 1903b. The Southern Nigeria "House Rule" scheme had been proposed by Sir Ralph Moor and had resulted in a 1901 law that converted slaves into house members. The chief or head of a house was given legal authority over the members. The Colonial Office waxed enthusiastic over this scheme, which has been the subject of ridicule by Anene (1966: 305–8). Lugard himself presided over the repeal of this Southern Nigeria law when he was governor-general of united Nigeria in 1914. Repeal took effect on

1 January 1915. Lugard explained that "House rule was not thereby abolished, but the denial of the assistance of British courts in enforcing the will of the House, and of Government police in capturing fugitive members, struck a death blow to the system." In effect, Lugard thus abolished the legal status of slavery in Southern Nigeria as well. Among his numerous complaints concerning the system were that acceptance of the uncorroborated oath of the head of a house was sufficient to convict a vagrant; that arrest could be without warrant; and that the penalty, a year's imprisonment, was severe. See Cmd. 468 of 1919, "Report by Sir F. D. Lugard on the Amalgamation of Northern and Southern Nigeria, and Administration, 1912–1919," paragraph 23, p. 14; and Perham (1960: 458). A copy of the Southern Nigeria 1901 House Rule ordinance can be found in PRO 1908. Also see Talbot 1926: 693–707 (chapter 28, "Slavery").

23   One minute in No. 34322 of 1903 put it this way: "Our suggestion was not to legalise domestic slavery, but to substitute for it a relationship which, while having the same effect in practice as domestic slavery, would not bear the name of slavery & could be recognised by the law of the Prot[ectorate] without appearing to come into direct conflict with British law." Also see a letter from Chamberlain's successor, Alfred Lyttleton, to Lugard (NNA-I 1904). The letter defended the Southern Nigeria House Rule system but accepted that Lugard would have his way on the issue.

24   PRO 1904; also see the letter from Lugard to the Colonial Office, dated Abinger Common, 21 August 1903, in PRO 1903b.

25   To the best of our knowledge, two copies of the 1901 memo survive, one in Kaduna and one at the PRO.

26   The attorney general had to issue a ruling on paragraphs 24 and 25 of the Slavery Proclamation of 1904, which made all slave-dealing illegal, in November 1906, with regard to a case involving the division of an estate of slaves. The attorney general ruled that a slave could not be handed over to an emir in payment of court fees. The fact that the practice had occurred "shows how long the idea that slaves were realizable assets persisted in the minds of some administrative officers as well as in those of the natives themselves. . . . It should be noted, however, that the right of a Native Court to deal with cases in which slaves refused to work though they continued to live at their masters' expense was specifically upheld by paragraph 21 of this memorandum." See NNA 1906c.

27   An amendment in 1918 (Ordinance No. 20) permitted Native Courts to grant certificates of freedom in accordance with the principles of Muslim law, while Memoranda No. 6 of 1905 and No. 22 of 1906 were revised and published as Memorandum No. 6 of 1918.

28   Burdon continued: "The Slavery Memo while deprecating throughout desertion, distinctly forbids over and over again the *only* [emphasis in original] action that can prevent it, namely, rendition by Political Officers after enquiry. And my view is as it has always been, and as I have more than once submitted to Your Excellency, that the only way to minimise the upheaval caused by our interference with the foundation of all native social life and institutions, is to give to Political Officers, legally and above board, this power, the power to force a slave to return to and remain with his master

if satisfied that there is no just cause for the recognition of freedom." See NNA 1906a.

29   The chief justice was concerned with the fact that the proclamation contained "about two pages of printed matter . . . [on] the wholesale assertion of freedom [of slaves]" and 24 pages on "methods of dealing with cases of assertion of freedom," which in effect "explained away" a great deal of the proclamation. Parodi proposed the adoption of something similar to the Southern Nigerian Native House Rule Proclamation No. 26 of 1901. He claimed that Memorandum No. 22 was intended to achieve virtually the same result; the difference was that the Southern Nigerian solution authorized political officials to enforce compliance, while the Northern Nigerian solution afforded no legal protection to political officers. See NNA 1908a.

30   For the complete text, see "Slavery Proclamation No. 27 of 1904," *Northern Nigeria Gazette* 1904. Under the amended "Slavery Proclamation No. 12 of 1905," the penalty for nonnatives in violation of the slavery laws was a prison sentence of up to 14 years with or without hard labor, with fines also a possibility; see "Northern Nigeria Proclamations 1905–1913," PRO CO587/2.

31   For the Residents' presumed discomfort, see Perham (1960: 171–72).

32   This judgment follows Perham (1960: 171–72).

33   These issues will be examined in our forthcoming volume with Cambridge University Press, but see Hogendorn and Lovejoy 1988, Lovejoy and Hogendorn 1990, and Lovejoy 1986, 1988.

REFERENCES

Anene, J. C. (1966) Southern Nigeria in Transition 1885–1906. Cambridge: Cambridge University Press.

Beddoes, Major H. R. (1904) "The British Empire in West Africa." National and English Review 44: 701–17.

Dumett, Raymond, and Marion Johnson (1988) "Britain and the suppression of slavery in the Gold Coast Colony, Ashanti, and the northern territories," in Suzanne Miers and Richard Roberts (eds.) The End of Slavery in Africa. Madison: University of Wisconsin Press: 71–116.

Grace, John (1975) Domestic Slavery in West Africa, with Particular Reference to the Sierra Leone Protectorate, 1896–1927. New York: Barnes and Noble.

Hill, Polly (1976) "From slavery to freedom: The case of farm-slavery in Nigerian Hausaland." Comparative Studies in Society and History 18: 395–426.

——— (1977) Population, Prosperity and Poverty: Rural Kano 1900 and 1970. Cambridge: Cambridge University Press.

Hogendorn, Jan and Paul E. Lovejoy (1988) "The reform of slavery in early colonial Northern Nigeria," in Suzanne Miers and Richard Roberts (eds.) The End of Slavery in Africa. Madison: University of Wisconsin Press: 391–414.

——— (1989) "The development and execution of Frederick Lugard's policies toward slavery in Northern Nigeria." Slavery and Abolition 10: 1–43.

Lennihan, Louise (1982) "Rights in men and rights in land: Slavery, labor and small-holder agriculture in Northern Nigeria." Slavery and Abolition 3: 111–39.

Lethem, G. J. (1931) "Early history of anti-slavery legislation." SNP 17 15849, Nigerian National Archives, Kaduna.

Lovejoy, Paul E. (1986) "Fugitive slaves: Resistance to slavery in the Sokoto Caliphate," in G. Okihiro (ed.) In Resistance: Studies in African, Afro-American and Caribbean History. Amherst: University of Massachusetts Press: 71–95.

———— (1988) "Concubinage and the status of female slaves in early colonial Northern Nigeria." Journal of African History 29: 245–66.

Lovejoy, Paul E. and Jan S. Hogendorn (1990) "Revolutionary Mahdism and resistance to colonial rule in the Sokoto Caliphate, 1905–6." Journal of African History 31: 217–44.

Lugard, Frederick (1893) The Rise of Our East African Empire. 2 vols. Edinburgh: W. Blackwood and Sons.

———— (1896) "Slavery under the British flag." The Nineteenth Century 39: 335–55.

———— (1905) "West Africa," in Charles Sydney Goldman (ed.) The Empire and the Century. London: John Murray: 835–60.

———— (1906) Instructions to Political and Other Officers, on Subjects Chiefly Political and Administrative. London: Waterlow.

McSheffrey, G. M. (1983) "Slavery, indentured servitude, legitimate trade and the impact of abolition in the Gold Coast, 1874–1901." Journal of African History 24: 349–68.

Nigerian National Archives, Ibadan (NNA-I).

1903a. CSO 8/6/3 C. Gollan to Lugard, 24 June.

1903b. CSO 8/6/3 "Draft Amending Slavery Proclamation," 24 June.

1903c. CSO 8/6/3 Minutes on Gollan to Lugard, 24 June.

1904. CSO 1/28/4 Alfred Lyttleton to Lugard, 19 August.

Nigerian National Archives, Kaduna. SNP 17 15849 (NNA).

1900a. Chamberlain to Lugard, 25 May.

1900b. Chamberlain to Lugard, 25 June.

1900c. Lugard to C.O., 21 July.

1901a. Wallace to Chamberlain, 21 May.

1901b. Wallace to Chamberlain, 2 August.

1901c. Wallace to Chamberlain, 14 August.

1901d. Chamberlain to Wallace, 21 September.

1901e. Burdon to Wallace, 1 November.

1901f. Wallace to Chamberlain, 7 November.

1901g. Lugard to Wallace, 23 November.

1901h. Wallace to Lugard, 23 December.

1902a. Lugard to Chamberlain, 7 January.

1902b. Memo No. 32, December.

1903. Lugard to Chamberlain, 7 January.

1904a. Lugard to Lyttleton, 7 June.

1904b. Lyttleton to Lugard, 19 August.

1906a. Burdon to Lugard, 28 April.

1906b. Lugard to Burdon, 25 May.

1906c. W. W. Fraser, Circular No. 53, 29 November.

1908a. Parodi to Girouard, 9 January.

Nigerian National Archives, Kaduna. SNP 7 5711/1908 (NNA).

1908b. Girouard to Crewe, 16 November, in "Slavery Domestic, Proposed Legislation, Manumission."

Northern Nigeria Gazette (1901) 2: 28 February.

Northern Nigeria Gazette (1904) 5: 30 September.

Ohadike, Don (1988) "The decline of slavery among the Igbo people," in Suzanne Miers and Richard Roberts (eds.) The End of Slavery in Africa. Madison: University of Wisconsin Press: 437–61.

Perham, Margery (1956) Lugard: Part 1, The Years of Adventure, 1858–1898. London: Collins.

——— (1960) Lugard: Part 2, The Years of Authority, 1898–1945. London: Collins.

Phillips, Anne (1989) The Enigma of Colonialism: British Policy in West Africa. Bloomington: Indiana University Press.

Public Record Office, London.

1899. CO446/8: No. 24433, dated 12 September.

1900. CO446/10: Lugard to Colonial Office, 21 July 1900, Despatch No. 166.

1902. CO446/36: No. 34322, Addendum to Special Memo No. 10, 14 August (also contained in NNA).

1903a. CO446/30: "Draft Slavery Proclamation 1903," Despatch No. 4, 7 January.

1903b. CO446/36: No. 34322, "Domestic Slavery."

1904. CO520/95: P. H. Ezechiel, "Slavery in Northern Nigeria," dated 6 August.

1905. CO446/44: Despatch of 17 November.

1908. CO446/76: No. 46301 of 16 November.

Talbot, P. Amaury (1926) The Peoples of Southern Nigeria. Vol. 3, Ethnology. London: Humphrey Milford.

Ubah, C. N. (1991) "Suppression of the slave trade in the Nigerian emirates." Journal of African History 32: 447–70.

Vandeleur, C. F. S. (1898) Campaigning on the Upper Nile and Niger. London: Methuen.

Willcocks, Sir James (1904) From Kabul to Kumasi: Twenty-four Years of Soldiering and Sport. London: John Murray.

4

The Numbers, Origins, and Destinations of Slaves in the Eighteenth-Century Angolan Slave Trade

JOSEPH C. MILLER

THE "NUMBERS GAME" (Curtin, 1969: ch. 1; Darity, 1985) remains a favorite event in academic jousting over the Atlantic slave trade, not only because unexpectedly detailed quantitative records continue to turn up in archival repositories but also, more recently, because of the suppleness with which scholars have applied data discovered by the first generation of researchers[1] to new, and increasingly more sophisticated, historical problems.[2] Old, relatively formal, analytical categories—decades; large, internally diverse stretches of the African coast; colonial/national aggregates on the American side of the Atlantic—although comparable among themselves, now seem more revealing of the data than of the history of the trade and are very salutarily giving way to questions and issues arising more directly from the experience itself: the causes of slave mortality, the economic strategies of slavers, age and sex distinctions among the slaves, the meaning of slaving for specific regions in Africa, and the trade's contributions to events in Europe and the Americas.[3] Use of quantitative data now presupposes the discovery of historically relevant categories of analysis and at the same time informs the meaning of the categories employed.

Redeployment of the numbers reflecting the history of the southern Atlantic slave trade in the eighteenth century in this way distinguishes multiple groups of slavers who competed in it against one another.[4] These slavers may be sorted out along three distinct continua: (1) the west-central African suppliers feeding slaves to buyers at the coast, (2) Americans, particularly Brazilians, engaged—more prominently than in any other part of the Atlantic—in buying slaves from west-central Africa, and (3) the European national groups taking these slaves to American coasts from the River Plate to the Caribbean.[5] This three-way historical breakdown of the figures largely confirms the overall totals of slaves shipped, but the newer historical style of analysis allows us to derive inferences from the gains and defeats of the various participants in this highly contentious trade that fill gaps in the numerical data employed in the first generation of studies of Atlantic slaving. The refined quantitative estimates in turn support assessments of who won and who lost, when, and in what order during a series of sharply differentiated phases in slaving in the southern Atlantic.

STRUCTURES OF SLAVING IN THE
SOUTHERN ATLANTIC

The African supply points for slaves embarked south of Cape Lopes derived from the demography and commercial networks of the west-central portions of the continent. In very broad terms, the population of west-central Africa tended to be concentrated in a band of well-watered mixed woodland and riverine forest environments running east from the mouth of the Zaire River and in scattered fertile pockets to the south. Since more people lived in that subequatorial forest-savanna mosaic, open lands suitable for grain agriculture, richer soils, and large rivers filled with fish, these regions supplied more captives for the trade over the long run than the dry, sandy, and less densely inhabited higher elevations lying farther from the equator. The forest environments to the north did not become major sources of slaves before the nineteenth century, owing to their lower population densities, the greater ease of transportation along the numerous rivers there, the constant movements of people and foodstuffs in response to local subsistence crises, and the relatively low cost of delivering heavy commodities like ivory to the coast to sell in exchange for its residents' limited needs for imports from the Atlantic. To the south, people tended to cluster around isolated pockets of reliable rainfall or groundwater for agriculture, notably along the lower valley of the Kwanza River, in the middle valley of the Kwango, and on the central highland regions encircled by the great bends in the Kwanza and Kunene rivers. As time passed and the trade advanced farther south and east, denser populations of farmers living in the alluvial valleys of the upper Zambezi and the lower Kubango also fell prey to slavers, although the aridity of these areas on the margin of the Kalahari Desert made them decidedly less promising as sources of slaves than the populous wetter regions farther north.

Three distinct commercial networks drew slaves from these regions of denser population in the eighteenth century toward the Atlantic shores of west-central Africa.[6] The oldest had its main outlet at the Portuguese colonial seat at Luanda. Its trade routes approached the coast from the east along a narrow corridor along the lower Bengo and Kwanza rivers, but in the interior the trails feeding it fanned out toward the populous slopes of the central highlands south of the Kwanza and toward the numerous forest-savanna dwellers to the north. Directly to the east, Luanda traded through intermediaries in the fertile middle Kwango valley, principally the kingdom of Kasanje. The valley of the Kwango was itself a source of slaves, but most captives reaching Portuguese hands there came from remote eastern portions of the forest-savanna mosaic through slaving raids conducted by the armies of the powerful Lunda state, centered just to the south. Mbailundu and other kingdoms on the central highlands constituted the militaristic counterparts south of the Kwanza of these Lunda slave raiders (see Figure 1).

The same African suppliers who sent slaves toward Luanda also sold captives to both of the competing trading networks, one to the north that reached the Atlantic at the bays along the Loango Coast beyond the mouth of the Zaire River and a southern one concentrated at the small Portuguese town of Benguela. African merchants at the series of bays along the Loango Coast—Loango itself, Molembo, and Cabinda—sold slaves obtained from supply routes running directly to the east but seem to have acquired more of their captives from the same populous areas south of the Zaire

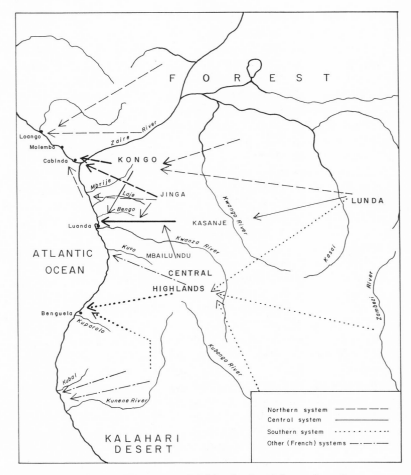

Figure I (sketch)   West-central Africa in the eighteenth century
(geography and schematic slaving networks)

as those that the traders serving Luanda regarded as their own
commercial hinterland. In the valley of the middle Kwango, Jinga,
the African state neighboring Kasanje to the north, tapped the
streams of slaves coming toward Luanda from the Lunda and diverted them off along a variety of routes to the north. The Kongo,
who lived in the regions between Luanda and Loango, sold slaves
north or south, depending on where they found greater advantage,

but they did most of their business to the north. Some western Kongo suppliers welcomed British or French buyers directly to the minor river mouths they controlled, but the Europeans tended not to load directly for the Atlantic crossing at these sites but rather to take the small numbers of captives available there down the coast in small launches and board them for the middle passage at Cabinda or Molembo. Far to the east, the Lunda themselves supplemented their trade toward Kasanje and Luanda with caravans headed toward the lower Zaire River and Cabinda through the eastern Kongo.

African traders north and south of the Zaire alike thus sold slaves originating in the same band of dense populations between about 6° and 8° S, but through distinct commercial networks. The intermediary states in the Kwango valley or the Kongo could send their captives southwest toward Luanda, directly west to the Loje or Mbrije rivers, or northwest across the Zaire to Cabinda. Slaves recorded in the shipping records as coming from the northern regions of "Loango" in fact fell into European hands as far south as the rivers adjacent to Luanda itself, though the English and French generally avoided exposing their ships, crews, merchandise, and slaves to the Portuguese military power—feeble though it was—concentrated at Luanda and seldom acknowledged their transgressions of Lisbon's claims to exclusive trading rights everywhere south of the Zaire.

The distinction in the south between Luanda and Benguela possessed a similar ambiguity in terms of the African commercial networks supplying the slaves embarked there. Slaves at Benguela arrived mostly from the western slopes of the highlands directly to its east, but the trade routes serving Benguela's proximate sources developed even minor sources of captives independent of Luanda's only in the far southeast, where they tapped the small pockets of population along the lower Kunene and other rivers flowing into the very dry margins of the Kalahari Desert. Eventually this southern network also reached the upper Zambezi, but as it gradually extended eastward it tended also to drain Lunda slaves away from Luanda along lines parallel to, but south of, those running to Kasanje. These northern edges of the Benguela trade also eroded the "back" side of the northern highland networks selling slaves toward the Kwanza River and thus, again, away from Luanda and the central portions of the Portuguese colony.

There in the south, however, Benguela encountered competition from the French similar to the incursions that Luanda experienced from non-Portuguese slavers to the north. Particularly during the expansive phase of French slaving everywhere in Africa after the Seven Years War (1756–63), roughly from 1763 to 1791, French ships seem to have called regularly at the mouths of the Kuporolo, Kubal, and Kunene rivers. In terms of the African supply networks, this French slaving in the far south drew slaves down the Kunene River away from Benguela traders, who approached the same sources, along the middle and lower Kunene and its tributaries, from their routes across the highlands to the north. At the peak of the French activity, the slaves sold in these southern locations supported elements of a fourth far-southern African commercial network, though the desert-edge population accessible through them was certainly too small to sustain it as an independent system in the long run. From time to time, the French and British also diverted slaves from the northern central highlands, particularly the Mbailundu kingdom, to the mouth of the Kuvo, not far up the coast from the Kwanza.

The different European slavers along the coast from Loango to the Kunene mouth appear only very vaguely in the quantitative records of the trade. The French presence has been particularly underestimated in first-generation volume-and-direction studies based on shipping records from France. However, the historical context reveals circumstances so convenient to savvy French merchants and captains—Portuguese military weakness, lengthy inland supply routes moving parallel to the coast to areas accessible more directly from remote rivers and beaches, and economic inefficiencies—that systematic smuggling in violation of Lisbon's claims to exclusive trading rights south of the Zaire mouth seems almost inevitable. French ships that called for slaves at the mouth of the Kunene seem to have continued down the coast to trade also at, or very near, Benguela itself, and then occasionally to have stopped again at the Kuvo and other small rivers south of Luanda, and, presumably only if necessary, to have finished up at the open ports of Loango.

The French course followed the winds and currents and the normal sailing route from south to north along the west-central African coast before turning west into the Atlantic toward the Americas (see Figure 2). Ships making for the coast south of

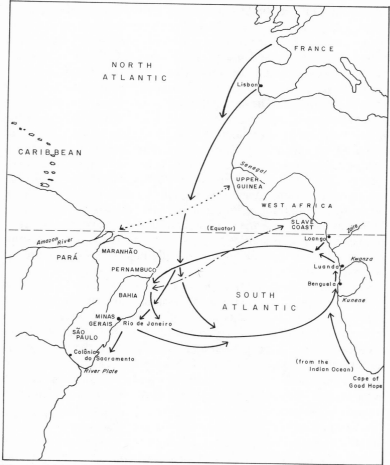

Figure 2 (sketch)   The southern Atlantic in the eighteenth century (Brazil, Africa, main sailing routes)

the Zaire necessarily sought landfall somewhere in the latitude of the Kunene mouth or beyond, whether coming from Europe around the southern Atlantic anticyclonic wind circulation from the west or returning around the Cape of Good Hope from the Indian Ocean and the east. The Kunene was so much farther from France through the western ocean voyage than other sources of slaves accessible to the French in Senegal, along the Slave Coast of Lower Guinea, or at Loango that few of the smugglers reported there would have followed this course out from Europe. The inbound route from India, on the other hand, passed right down those shores, and ships from the Indian Ocean arrived laden with the Asian cotton textiles that constituted the single most desired category of goods that Europeans sold in west-central Africa for slaves. The competitiveness of French slavers along Angolan coasts, the reported cheapness of their textiles, and the convenient geography suggest the plausibility, if not the probability, of such a strategy. The absence of references to this pattern from port records in France, notoriously vague about the destinations of French slavers in Africa, becomes readily explicable under the illicit circumstances. French captains, carefully reticent about their violations of Portuguese commercial rights recognized by the monarchy in Paris, and perhaps also contravening orders to deliver their Asian textiles to merchants in France before reshipment back to Africa, identified virtually none of these ventures in official records.[7]

Calculated French imprecision in this case closely matched the vagueness of the designation "Angola" that the English used for their voyages to coasts south of the equator, since they too encroached in their own ways on sources of slaves that the monarchies of Europe formally treated as exclusive to the Portuguese. The English, having woolens of their own to sell for slaves and thus in less need of Asian textiles to trade, usually approached west-central Africa directly from the north and thus concentrated their activities there on the Loango Coast. From that base, they bought the slaves gathered there by African traders and mounted small forays of their own to the Kongo ports south of the Zaire mouth. Occasionally, English ships turned up nearer Luanda, particularly early in the century, but their growing dominance in the north, Portuguese claims to monopoly in the south, and French superiority in smuggling there put the coasts beyond Kongo well outside the range of English slaving after the 1750s, in practice as well as in theory. Nonetheless, the term *Angola* served to cover a trade that, though based in the international ports north of the Zaire, effectively spread English goods throughout much of the trading hinterland claimed by the Portuguese.[8]

In economic terms, the trade considered Portuguese for diplomatic purposes, and treated as such in quantitative records organized by European monarchy, consisted of several distinct segments relevant to an explanation of its volume and direction. Broadly speaking, Portuguese-American traders based in Brazil competed at Luanda against a series of metropolitan interests and played an overwhelmingly dominant role at Benguela. In fact, the nominally Portuguese slave trade in the southern Atlantic was thoroughly Brazilian at its operational level. The ships that carried the slaves started their voyages to Angola, in the main part, in Brazil, and the captains and crews similarly tended to come from there. The Brazilians supplied the second most valuable component of the goods sold for slaves in west-central Africa, the harsh and fiery cane brandies known as *gerebita*. Only a few weeks distant across the southern Atlantic, they had better communication with the port towns of Angola than merchants in Lisbon, who were months away in another hemisphere and often in communication with their African agents only through intermediaries in Brazil. Thus, the Luanda and Benguela trades, though both nominally Portuguese, were so in reality mainly in the limited sense relevant to politics and official record keeping in Europe.

Lisbon, at such practical disadvantages, restricted its participation in slaving to the functional aspects of the trade and to the single port in which it enjoyed decisive advantages. In terms of geography, this strategy led metropolitan merchants to concentrate their trading at Luanda, where governors appointed by the king could sometimes, and with increasing frequency after about 1750, be held responsible for channeling business into the hands of resident factors representing the mercantile interests of the imperial capital. There, too, Lisbon merchants could expect judges appointed to the colony from Portugal to provide limited protection under the commercial laws of the realm. Benguela, in contrast, lay inaccessibly upwind to the south, was a notoriously unhealthy locale for immigrants from Portugal, offered none of the modest amenities of the colonial capital, and consequently remained almost entirely beyond Lisbon's control before the very end of the eighteenth century. Metropolitan merchants, accordingly, avoided trading there whenever possible, leaving Benguela's slaves to Brazilian buyers and, at certain periods, also to French in a favorable position to supply the Asian cottons that the Americans then supplemented with their cane brandies.

In terms of business organization, Lisbon merchants specialized in selling textiles—often English woolens and other northern European fabrics reexported through Portugal, but also cottons taken from India to Lisbon and then sent back out to Angola and, later in the century, domestic Portuguese fabrics—and in financing the trade. Lisbon's goods included mostly wares poor in quality and high in price relative to the Asian and northern European manufactures that its English and French rivals sold in west-central Africa. Its wines and brandies could not come close to the price or potency of the gerebitas of the Brazilians. It had only a rudimentary metalwares industry compared to the northern European sources available to other European slaving nations. Its roundabout reexports of Asian cottons and English woolens brought them to Angola at much greater cost than the French and English did. Even Portuguese smugglers, returning from India and dropping off goods according to a sensible strategy identical to the one inferred for the French, regularly thwarted Lisbon's attempts to penetrate markets in west-central Africa.

Lisbon countered both its poor colonial subjects from Brazil and its European competitors by making its uncompetitive merchandise available to novice Luanda traders and to African customers on lenient terms of credit. The Brazilians could seldom match the commercial wealth available to Lisbon, and the foreigners had no need to assume the high risks associated with a strategy of lending their goods to unreliable traders working areas of the interior far beyond the reach of Portuguese law. Accordingly, factors representing Portuguese merchants consigned their imported goods to Angolan slavers in touch with Kasanje or other trading points east of Luanda on terms requiring repayment in slaves months, in practice sometimes years, later.[9] Such trust arrangements seem to have been the principal strategy employed by a century-long succession of Lisbon interests active at Luanda to attract slaves away from the African commercial systems serving Loango and the trade networks focused on Benguela. Local Angolan exporters and Brazilian buyers paid in bills of exchange drawn on American commercial correspondents that allowed the merchants of the metropole thus to finance much of the Luanda trade in slaves by selling goods and buying commercial paper, usually without themselves owning significant portions of the human cargoes they sent across the southern Atlantic.[10] This economic organization of the trade left the operation of slaving itself to the Brazilians and further confined Lisbon to Luanda, since recovery of the highly risky debts owed by Africans and by colonial subjects depended vitally on the judicial, police, and sometimes outright military powers exercised there through colonial governors and judges.

The Brazilians came to Angola in at least three distinct groups, with sharply differing timing and strategies corresponding to strong regional variations in economic growth in Portugal's American colony and to the varying power of the metropole in the major port cities there. The sugar captaincies of the northeast, Bahia and Pernambuco, had dominated west-central African slaving in the seventeenth century but thereafter tended to decline in significance relative to Rio de Janeiro in the south. Because Brazil assumed an increasingly marginal role in world sugar production after about the 1650s, when the booming Caribbean islands of the English and French accounted for most of the demand from those nations that sent their slave ships to encroach on the African coasts south of the equator that the Portuguese claimed in the eighteenth century, slavers from the northeast found it more and more difficult to compete at Luanda.

Meanwhile, the gold of Minas Gerais, inland from Rio de Janeiro, led Brazil's economic growth in the first half of the eighteenth century, and the wealth of these mines propelled the southern city into the leading position among the Brazilians buying slaves in west-central Africa. Bahia redirected its own quest for African labor to the Slave Coast of Lower Guinea by developing a West African market for molasses-soaked third-grade tobacco, essentially a cheap by-product of the two major commodities that northeastern Brazil exported to Europe. Pernambuco receded in significance as a slaving port, having lost Angola to Lisbon and to Rio de Janeiro and lacking the means to match the Bahians in West Africa. Henceforth, at least with respect to slaving, Pernambuco became a passive market open to suppliers from Bahia and to Lisbon merchants seeking a Brazilian market devoid of strong America-based competitors. Rio slavers, on the other hand, became the major Brazilian carriers of slaves from Luanda and took advantage of Lisbon's weakness at Benguela to make the southern Angolan port virtually a trading preserve of their own. Benguela grew spectacularly as a source of slaves after about 1760, and it owed most of this growth to accelerating agricultural production in the southern Brazilian captaincies supplied with labor through Rio and to the dynamic combination of Rio traders, their gerebita cane brandies, and French smugglers and their Asian textiles concentrated there.

The peripheral Brazilian captaincies, tropical Pará and Maranhão in the north beyond Pernambuco and southern ports like Santos, an alternate entry route to São Paulo in the uplands behind Rio, or others functioning at least in part as clandestine access routes to Spain's colonies along the River Plate, seldom assumed significant positions in slaving in Angola. Pará and Maranhão took most of their modest needs for slaves from Cacheu and Bissau, conveniently close across the Atlantic in Upper Guinea. The smuggling business to the Spanish territories in the south played a larger role in Angolan slaving but fell to traders from Rio, so that most slaves leaving Angola for Spanish destinations appear in the records as captives bound ostensibly for south-central Brazil. There they continued on in coasting vessels to the Plate. Nonetheless, when imperial regulations permitted or when treaty arrangements between Portugal and Spain opened trade between their American colonies, ships declared directly for Santos, Montevideo, or the "Colônia do Sacramento," the main Portuguese smuggling port on the north bank of the Plate estuary. Otherwise, Bahia, Pernambuco, and Rio remained the sole legal Brazilian ports open to ships leaving Angola, and voyages declared to those three concealed the much wider variety of Brazilian captaincies actually receiving west-central African slaves reshipped through them.

Depending on the historical question at issue, the origins and destinations of the slaves from eighteenth-century west-central Africa are best understood in terms of distinctions only dimly visible in the official records of the trade. The slaves originated in several identifiable pools of dense population in Africa, but they arrived at the coast through three distinct African commercial networks capable of linking most of these populous regions to two or, in the case of the main band of population inland from Kongo, all three of the main regions of embarkation, Loango, Luanda, and Benguela. An incipient fourth network at times supplied slaves to the French along the lower Kunene as well. The foreign European buyers concealed their constant violations of Portuguese claims to commercial monopoly south of the Zaire mouth behind deliberately vague declarations of their intended destinations in Africa. Even from their declared bases at Loango, they intruded with their launches and through their African suppliers into areas virtually within sight of the principal Portuguese territories inland from Luanda. The Portuguese imperial shell, in turn, hid significant distinctions between metropolitan and colonial slavers and, among the colonials, the diverse histories of slaving at the major ports of Brazil. Even the ships headed to a single Brazilian captaincy must, finally, be understood as moving through no more than an intermediate stage in a complex redistribution to further destinations: Rio grew as a supplier to Minas Gerais but became a consumer of slaves in its own right, a route of access to São Paulo, and a smuggling station on the way to the estuary of the Plate. Slaves disembarked at Bahia continued south to Minas Gerais and north to Pernambuco and the Amazon.

THE DATA ON SPECIFIC BRAZILIAN DESTINATIONS

Systematic records of Angola's eighteenth-century exports of slaves begin in 1710 (Birmingham, 1966: 137), at a time when Lisbon, then preoccupied with the golden riches that had begun to flow from Minas Gerais just before 1700, turned its attention also to monitoring the Angolan sources of the African labor vital to mining there. Growing numbers of slaves leaving Angola presented the Crown with a further opportunity to increase its revenues, by letting tax-farming contracts on the duties imposed on slaves exported through Luanda to private interests in Lisbon. Presumably, seventeenth-century records of slave exports had remained in the hands of the earlier slave-duty contractors themselves or in those of the governors of the time, who may be presumed to have retained most papers from administrations that they ran very much as private enterprises.[11] Governors of the seventeenth century, often tied more closely to the Brazilian families from which they came than to the king who appointed them, took a particular interest in the colony's slaves. In either case, data on slaving before 1710 never reached ministers in Portugal, whose papers now constitute virtually the entire corpus of materials on Angolan slaving.

The opportunity to make money from selling slaves to the goldfields set Bahian merchants, hungry for markets beyond the relatively stagnant sugar economies of northeastern Brazil, against traders from Rio, who also meant to cash in on the mines' insatiable demand for African labor. Both groups of Brazilians petitioned Lisbon for favorable access to Minas markets during the second decade of the eighteenth century, and received quotas, but government reports distinguished the resulting shipments of slaves according to destinations in Brazil only after 1723. The annual series of government reports that followed, intended to assess contractor revenues from slave duties, runs—with gaps in 1716–17, 1729–30, and 1732–33—until 1772, the last year of the final contract, but they show the details of slaves' destinations in Brazil for only thirty-one of these fifty-one years (see Table 1).[12] Not infrequent minor differences in various reports of the data for given years arise from the variety of official purposes served by the parallel sets of records from which they come: some were current, and sometimes provisional, end-of-year reports; others were revised totals in summaries for the six-year period of each contract; still others were retrospective summaries compiled to examine specific issues. They also occasionally incorporated copyists' errors and, more often, reflected slightly differing technical definitions of the categories of slaves to be counted (e.g., Miller 1988b).[13]

The inconsistencies and incompleteness of the extant records of the trade thus reflect the politics of slaving at least as much as the vagaries of time. Under the government of the Marquis of Pombal, first minister to King D. José from 1755 to 1777, Lisbon attempted to strengthen its presence among the Brazilians and Angolans thriving at Luanda by setting up a chartered trading company, the Companhia Geral de Pernambuco e Paraíba (Pernambuco Company), with monopoly privileges in northeastern Brazil. It also intended to exclude the old-line Asian import interests behind the slave-duty contract in favor of other metropolitan merchants associated more closely with Pombal's efforts at domestic industrialization in Portugal. His government also replaced a number of the old tax farms with new, direct methods of collecting, and increasing, its revenues. These policies spelled doom for the slave-duty contractors in Angola, and they finally yielded, after years of resistance, in 1769, with the final contract terminating three years later.

The royal treasury thus became responsible for compiling the

Table 1 Slaves leaving Luanda, 1723–75, 1794, and 1802–26 (selected years), by destination in Brazil

Year	Rio de Janeiro	(%)	Pernambuco	(%)	Bahia	(%)	Other	(%)	Total
1723	3,403	(50.4)	519	(7.7)	2,830	(41.9)			6,752
1724	2,869	(47.0)	1,031	(16.9)	2,208	(36.1)			6,108
1725	3,080	(47.5)	703	(10.8)	2,701	(41.7)	242[a]	(3.6)	6,726
1726	3,559	(42.3)	318	(3.4)	4,156	(48.4)	497[a]	(4.8)	8,440
1727	3,591	(47.0)	842	(11.0)	3,200	(41.9)			7,633
1728	3,229	(37.8)	1,248	(14.6)	4,055	(47.5)			8,532
1731	3,111	(53.6)	318	(5.5)	2,379	(41.0)			5,808
1734	4,378	(50.2)	746	(8.6)	3,589	(41.2)			8,713
1738	4,735	(61.4)	617	(8.0)	2,361	(30.6)			7,713
1740	5,254	(64.6)	1,051	(12.9)	1,832	(22.5)			8,137
1741	6,143	(69.8)	980	(11.1)	1,675	(19.0)			8,798
1742	6,218	(64.1)	1,096	(11.3)	2,385	(24.6)			9,699
1744	5,123	(62.1)	1,515	(18.4)	1,618	(19.6)			8,256
1747	4,159	(48.9)	2,188	(25.7)					8,512
1748	5,834	(54.0)	2,661	(24.6)	1,917	(17.7)	384[b]	(3.6)	10,796
1749	2,839	(29.0)	1,455	(14.9)	3,502	(35.8)	1,981[b,c]	(20.3)	9,776
1758	4,870	(49.0)	3,235	(32.6)	821	(8.3)	1,012[d]	(10.2)	9,938
1762	3,808	(45.3)	1,666	(19.8)	1,347	(16.0)	1,594[d]	(18.9)	8,280[e]
1763	3,698	(48.4)	2,689	(35.2)	1,247	(16.3)			7,525
1764	3,491	(45.6)	1,834	(24.0)	519	(6.8)	1,720[f]	(22.5)	7,648[e]
1765	5,754	(52.0)	3,217	(29.1)	1,626	(14.7)	467[d]	(4.2)	11,065[e]
1766	3,617	(38.8)	2,380	(25.5)	3,333	(35.7)			9,330

Table 1—Continued

| | Port | | | | | | | | |
Year	Rio de Janeiro	(%)	Pernambuco	(%)	Bahia	(%)	Other	(%)	Total
1767	4,824	(53.5)	2,649	(29.4)	1,543	(17.1)			9,016
1769	3,432	(59.9)	758	(13.2)	1,543	(26.9)			5,733
1770	3,498	(46.4)	1,685	(22.3)	2,354	(31.2)			7,537
1771	3,462	(46.8)	1,704	(22.4)	2,341	(30.8)			7,606
1772	4,439	(59.0)	1,580	(21.0)	1,499	(19.9)			7,518
1774	4,000	(50.3)	2,082	(26.5)	1,853	(23.1)			7,935
1775	3,010	(38.6)	2,110	(27.1)	2,675	(34.3)			7,795
1794	7,502	(79.0)	—	—	1,607	(16.9)	384[c]	(4.0)	9,493
1802	5,160	(44.8)	3,622	(31.4)	1,881	(16.3)	855[f]	(7.4)	11,518[g]
1803	5,440	(39.2)	4,013	(29.2)	2,335	(17.0)	2,042[d,f]	(14.7)	13,830[g]
1804	4,556	(34.8)	3,325	(25.7)	2,063	(16.0)	3,071[d,f]	(23.5)	13,018[g]
1805	4,710	(34.4)	4,401	(32.1)	2,100	(15.3)	2,595[d,f]	(18.2)	13,711[g]
1809	7,323	(74.1)	2,492	(25.2)	72	(0.7)			9,887
1810	8,837	(75.3)	1,254	(10.7)	888	(7.6)	757[d,f]	(6.4)	11,736
1811	9,098	(77.9)	2,010	(17.2)	564	(4.8)			11,672
1812	6,891	(56.7)	2,489	(23.7)	401	(4.8)	700[d,f]	(6.7)	10,481
1813	6,126	(61.9)	3,265	(33.0)	169	(1.7)	334[f]	(3.4)	9,894
1815	7,370	(58.3)	3,911	(31.0)	1,028	(8.1)	325[f]	(2.6)	12,635
1816	6,115	(41.4)	5,499	(37.3)	1,700	(11.5)	1,446[d,f]	(9.8)	14,760
1817	5,425	(34.8)	5,932	(38.0)	1,213	(7.8)	3,025[d,f]	(19.4)	15,595
1818	4,645	(28.3)	7,702	(47.0)	1,329	(8.1)	2,703[d,f]	(16.5)	16,379

Year									Total
1819	4,873	(28.2)	6,863	(39.7)	1,566	(9.1)	3,997[d,f]	(23.1)	17,293
1820	8,215	(41.0)	7,816	(39.0)	1,034	(5.2)	2,987[d]	(14.9)	20,052
1822	9,415	(52.9)	3,203	(18.0)	637	(3.6)	3,120[d,f]	(27.5)	17,806
							1,430[c,h,i]	(8.0)	
1823		(41.4)		(17.7)		(2.3)		(17.5)[d,f]	
								(8.1)[c,h,i]	
1824		(62.2)		(23.4)		(10.1)		(4.3)[f]	
1825		(63.6)		(21.6)		(5.5)		(5.7)[h,j]	
1826		(60.0)		(21.6)		(5.5)		(4.5)[f]	
								(8.6)[c,k]	

Sources: E. g., Relação does navios que sahiram despachados desta cidade de Loanda para os portos do Brazil (1724), enclosed in letter from Francisco Pereira da Costa (*provedor da Fazenda Real*), 15 January 1725, Arquivo Histórico Ultramarino (Lisbon), Angola *caixa* (cx.) 16, and similar documents copied from the *livros de despachos* kept at Luanda in cxs. 17, 21–27ff. (old system). Cited in Miller, 1986.

[a] Unknown destination.
[b] Colônia do Sacramento.
[c] Santos.
[d] Maranhão.
[e] Includes small numbers of others.
[f] Pará.
[g] Original records list additional "children" without attributing them to individual ports.
[h] Rio Grande do Sul.
[i] Ceará.
[j] Montevideo.
[k] Santa Catarina.
Note: Not listed: intra-African destinations, three to São Tomé in 1803 and five in 1804; two to Cabinda in 1822.

data on Angola's slave exports on its own after 1772. It apparently never collected figures as detailed as those generated under the old regime, except for an encouraging, if belated and short-lived, start in 1774 and 1775. The data thus fell victim to Lisbon's unpreparedness to implement its initiatives in Angola at a time when much more urgent problems in Brazil demanded most of its attention. The apparent lack of competent metropolitan personnel at Luanda left record keeping there open to subversion by the local officials in the colonial government during the 1770s and early 1780s, decades in which Lisbon all but abandoned Angola to its residents, no champions of literacy of any sort and not eager to leave much evidence of the abandon with which they flaunted metropolitan regulation of their slaving. Those were the years in which the Angolans had smuggled actively with the English and French, then ubiquitous along Angolan coasts.

Lisbon attempted to regain control of record keeping at Luanda, and elsewhere throughout the empire, by creating a new customs administration that gradually took shape in Angola through the 1780s and 1790s (Miller, 1986). Fiscalization was a long, slow process to implement, and as a result annual aggregates appear to have been assembled for these last decades of the century only retrospectively, starting with figures for 1785, the year after the arrival of the governor, the Barão de Moçâmedes (in office 1784–90), who was sent out to impose the new customs regime on reluctant Angolans.[14]

A more detailed series drawn from current customs registries starts in 1802, the second full year after definitive establishment at Luanda of regular government inspection of imports and exports. It continues with impressive consistency through 1826, when Britain recognized Brazil's independence from Portugal. The only two years missing, 1806 and 1821, have ready explanations. In 1806, no governor was in residence at Luanda, and colonial smugglers, temporarily back in charge, kept no records of what must have been a bonanza of illicit imports and export duties unpaid. The confused years of 1821 and 1822 saw the Portuguese monarchy, removed to Rio de Janeiro since 1807–8, when France invaded Portugal during the Peninsular War, return from Brazil to Lisbon and Prince D. Pedro, who remained behind in Brazil, proclaim the colony's independence from Portugal. These dramatic political changes evidently disrupted the routine administrative business of reporting reasonably full and accurate economic statistics, including the numbers of slaves leaving the colony.

The end of this series in 1826 marks the beginning of a legal limbo, during which Angolan slaves crossed the southern Atlantic under very uncertain diplomatic status (Bethell, 1970; Eltis, 1987a). Britain was then intensifying pressures on Portugal to end its slave trade, and the treaties in effect at the time limited slaving to trade considered "domestic" and thus beyond the reach of international diplomacy, that is, among the colonial possessions within its empire. This condition remained innocuous enough while Angola and Brazil both were subjects of Portugal. However, Brazil's declaration of independence moved the major market for Angola's slaves outside that charmed imperial circle from the perspective of any nation that recognized the new country. Portuguese officials remained in charge in Angola after its abortive movements to follow Brazil in 1822–23. These Angolan officials asserted the colony's loyalty to Lisbon, which did not officially acknowledge Brazil's independence, partly by continuing to report its exports of slaves in detail, as if done legally through an intact imperial linkage with an American colony. But Britain formally acknowledged Brazil's independent standing, outside the empire, in 1826, and it must then have become clear to Lisbon that the less official documentation of the continuing flow of slaves across the southern Atlantic that their deputies in Angola created, the better. Official silence reigned thereafter until the end of the legal trade in 1830 and the termination of slaving in about 1850.[15] These data are summarized by decade in Table 2.

Detailed reporting of slave exports at Benguela began much later than at Luanda, and the southern port usually remained enveloped in the obscurity that the Brazilian-oriented interests in charge there carefully wrapped around the highly dubious trade they conducted.[16] Slaves boarding ships at Benguela were officially recorded at the contractor's factory in Luanda until the end of 1761, when the first separate registry book reached the southern port as part of the Pombaline fiscal reforms intended to capture duties unpaid by the Rio traders active there. Colonial military captains at Benguela operated almost independently of Luanda until 1779, when the town acquired a governor theoretically responsive to the Angolan governor-general, but no reliable records

Table 2 Slaves leaving Luanda, 1723–75, 1794, and 1802–26, by destination in Brazil (summarized by decades)

Decade	Rio de Janeiro	(%)	Pernambuco	(%)	Bahia	(%)	Other	(%)	Total
1720s	19,731	(44.6)	4,661	(10.5)	19,150	(43.3)	649	(1.5)	44,191 (6 years)
1730s	17,478	(57.5)	2,732	(9.0)	17,478	(33.5)			30,371 (4 years)
1740s	30,315	(54.3)	9,895	(17.1)	13,262	(23.8)	2,365	(4.2)	55,837 (6 years)
1750s	4,870	(49.0)	3,235	(32.6)	821	(8.3)	1,012	(10.1)	9,938 (1 year)
1760s	32,122	(48.6)	16,198	(24.5)	13,512	(20.4)	3,869[d,f]	(5.7)	66,134 (8 years)
1770s	15,011	(48.7)	7,476	(24.2)	8,368	(27.1)	97[a]		30,855 (4 years)
1780s	(no data)								

Port

1790s	7,502 (79.0)	—	1,607 (16.9)	384[c] (4.0)	9,493 (1 year)
1800s	36,026 (48.9)	19,107 (25.9)	9,339 (12.7)	9,220 (12.5)	73,700 (6 years)
1810s	58,758 (45.6)	49,233 (38.2)	9,004 (7.0)	15,518 (12.1)	128,761 (9 years)
1820s	(55.6)	(20.7)	(5.0)	(11.8)[d,f] (6.1)[c,h,i,j,k]	64,071 (5 years)
Total	209,441 (48.3)	82,906 (19.1)	109,302 (25.2)	31,630 (7.3)	433,279

Source: Table 1.

Note: See Table 1 for footnotes. Totals serve only for calculating intradecade percentages, as each is based on a different number of years (in parentheses) available from the period. The figures for slaves are not comparable vertically in the table, and only the percentages represent estimates of trends through time.

could be expected from Benguela at a time when the port crawled with French interlopers and when even the capital itself reported few economic statistics back to Lisbon (see Table 3).

Governor Moçâmedes nonetheless managed to obtain detailed data on slaves shipped from Benguela in 1784, the inaugural year of his new customs regime. No further record followed until 1791, when Benguela acquired political and administrative autonomy from Luanda and a governor of its own with rank equivalent to that of Luanda's. These appointees began to report directly to Lisbon. Even then, detailed reports from Benguela remained relatively spotty, and they exist now for only sixteen of the thirty-five years down to 1826, with an additional, anomalously naive set of figures for 1828, in the period of the trade's doubtful legality. For most of that period, Brazilian destinations are available only in terms of ships, with no surviving breakdown by slaves exported.

Slaves leaving Cabinda and other ports of the Loango Coast embarked without the benefit of Portuguese government inspection, as Lisbon never dared to establish an official presence north of the Zaire in the face of English and French dominance, particularly after the failure of an expedition Lisbon sent there in 1783 to occupy the trading beach while the northern Europeans remained distracted by their conflicts during the American War of Independence. In any case, few eighteenth-century Portuguese slavers possessed the merchandise or skills to compete successfully outside the shelter of Luanda bay, even when their rivals' slaving dropped off during wars in the North Atlantic.

Portuguese slavers moved north to the Loango Coast and into the estuary of the Zaire River in force after 1807, when the continental blockade eliminated French competition and the British ended their own subjects' direct participation in the trade. The Portuguese government, resident at the time in Rio de Janeiro, dared not establish an official presence on the Loango Coast for fear of arousing objections to a move that would have extended the permitted internal Portuguese slave trade to a highly productive part of the coast that London regarded as a free trade zone reserved for "legitimate" commerce. Records of the slaves taken in the 1810s and 1820s from ports north of Luanda, including the former British sites at the Mbrije and Loje river mouths, thus come only indirectly from data on arrivals in Brazil, nearly all of that from Rio de Janeiro.

Brazilian data on Angolan slaves reaching Rio come from one entry register covering the years from 1795 to 1811 [17] and from Klein's (1978: 73–94) compilation of Rio newspaper reports for 1825–1830.[18] In addition, starting in 1811, the British consuls stationed throughout Brazil began to report arrivals of slaves back to authorities in London, who were determined to suppress transatlantic slaving in the wake of Britain's abolition of its own trade.[19] These reports, along with scattered information from other Brazilian ports (Miller, 1975), extend a rough reconstruction of Angolan slave exports as they varied through the years among competing groups of Brazilians from Rio, Bahia, Pernambuco, and elsewhere down to virtually the end of the legal trade (Tables 1, 2, and 3).[20] The lacunae in the data distinguishing slaves exported by destination in Brazil may be partially filled by employing the numbers of Luanda ships making for each Brazilian port as a rough proxy. The results of this compilation, arranged as percentages of ships in each decade so as to show changing relative positions of each port in Brazil independent of the generally increasing absolute volume of shipping over the period, are shown as Figure 3.

Rio's dominance, established in the 1730s, is the most prominent feature of the figure, with Bahia's steady decline from the 1720s onward also apparent. Pernambuco tended to increase its role at Luanda, especially in the 1810s, with the exception of its improbably low percentage in the 1790s, based on a single, possibly anomalous year during a decade for which very few data bear on the distribution of the slaves Angola sent to Brazil. The declining proportions of slaves sent in the 1760s to Pernambuco, Pará, and Maranhão show how few slaves the Pernambuco Company and its sister, the Companhia Geral do Grão Pará e Maranhão (Maranhão Company), active mostly in that decade, were able to divert from their usual destinations to their monopoly preserves in northeastern Brazil. Pernambuco's increased share of Angolan slave exports after 1810 resulted from efforts by merchants remaining in Portugal during the monarchy's exile at Rio to restore a metropolitan presence at Luanda that had been severely threatened by traders based in Brazil and backed by enormous amounts of British capital pouring into the colony in the wake of a commercial treaty concluded in 1810. They achieved a modest success by shipping gunpowder and domestic cotton textiles through Pernambuco, the metropole's historical center of slav-

Table 3   Slaves leaving Benguela, 1784 and 1791–1828 (selected years), by destination in Brazil

				Port					
Year	Rio de Janeiro	(%)	Pernambuco	(%)	Bahia	(%)	Other	(%)	Total
1784	4,933	(64.8)	414	(5.4)	2,261	(29.7)	—	—	7,608
1791	4,450	(70.3)			1,450	(22.9)	429[c]	(6.8)	6,329
1792	5,988	(56.0)	1,309	(12.2)	1,613	(15.1)	1,788[l]	(16.7)	10,698
1793	7,573	(65.7)	1,897	(16.9)	1,701	(14.8)	350[l]	(3.0)	11,521
1794	7,493	(79.0)	—	—	1,604	(16.9)	384[c]	(4.1)	9,481
1796	6,714	(83.4)	1,171	(14.5)	—	—	164[l]	(2.0)	8,049
1797	5,679	(80.3)	385	(5.4)	—	—	1,005[l]	(14.2)	7,069
1798	4,512	(68.8)	—	—	912	(13.9)	1,130[l]	(17.2)	6,554
1801	5,693	(83.3)	—	—	821	(12.0)	320[l]	(4.7)	6,834
1802	6,639	(76.4)	—	—	1,021	(11.7)	1,027[d,l]	(11.8)	8,687

Year									Total
1806	4,288	(72.7)	—	—	467	(7.9)	1,147[f,l]	(19.5)	5,902
1808	4,050	(83.9)	—	—	—	—	778[d,l]	(16.2)	4,828
1809	5,129	(96.3)	—	—	—	—	196[l]	(3.7)	5,325
1811	4,514	(90.8)	—	—	341	(6.9)	115[l]	(2.3)	4,970
1812	4,345	(86.6)	—	—	—	—	670[l]	(13.4)	5,015
1813	4,404	(94.9)	—	—	—	—	236[l]	(5.1)	4,640
1815	3,576	(94.7)	—	—	—	—	200[l]	(5.3)	3,776
1819	2,936	(60.3)	939	(19.3)	—	—	992[d,f,l]	(20.4)	4,867
1828	4,692	(97.6)	—	—	—	—	116[l]	(2.4)	4,808
Total	97,608	(76.9)	6,115	(4.8)	12,191	(9.6)	7,920[l] (6.0) 3,127[c,d,f] (2.5)		126,961

Sources: Annual reports from Benguela, AHU (detailed listings in Miller, 1985).
Note: See Table 1 for all footnotes except l.
l Luanda.

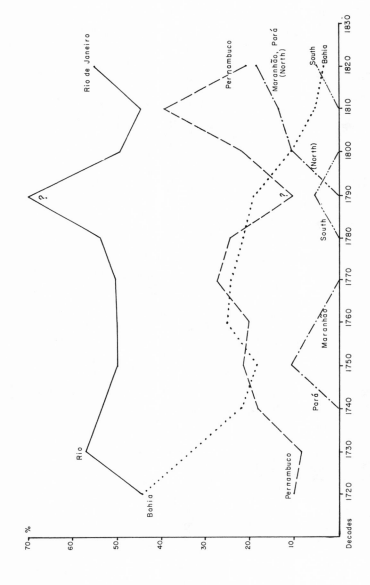

Figure 3   Percentages of ships leaving Luanda for Brazilian destinations

ing activity in Brazil, and avoiding the strong local commercial competition at Rio and Bahia. The presence of the Maranhão Company in the 1750s and 1760s is more evident, though at a very low level, as is the growing use that cotton growers in the Brazilian far north made of Luanda slaves beginning in the 1790s. Cotton animated Angola's early-nineteenth-century shipments of slaves to Pernambuco also. Luanda increased further in significance for northern and northeastern Brazil in the 1810s and 1820s as British pressure drove slavers from there south of the equator in search of labor. The occasional appearance of southern Brazilian ports—Santos, Santa Catarina, Rio Grande do Sul, and others— is a statistical artifact more than a reflection of changing flows of slaves, as southern Brazil (and the Spanish regions along the Plate estuary as well) normally received most of its slaves through Rio; ships began clearing directly for those ports from the 1790s owing to changes in the legal and diplomatic environments.

Although the accounts of the Pombaline-chartered commercial companies of the 1760s and 1770s provide additional details for slaves sent from Luanda (see Klein, 1987: 139–140), and rarely also from Benguela, to the captaincies in northeastern and northern captaincies of Brazil,[21] they are records of company purchases and sales only and do not include slaves the companies carried under the complex financial arrangements employed in the southern Atlantic, that is, for other owners. As such, they are most complete for the 1760s, the heyday of the companies and a time when they owned most of the slaves they transported. This period was covered well enough also by government documentation from Luanda. The company records become very problematic for the 1770s, unfortunately also an obscure decade in the government's statistics, owing to the Maranhão Company's virtually ceasing to buy slaves in Angola and to the Pernambuco Company's switching from owning the captives it carried to transporting slaves belonging to Angolan and other slaveowners. Its early aggressive strategy of making a massive investment in slaves had proved unsuccessful, and so it adopted a defensive posture aimed at maximizing returns from minimal further commitments of its own dwindling assets. Thus, the data reveal details about only the small, and decreasing, portion of slaves the company carried to Pernambuco on its own account and not the majority of its cargoes, owned by others.

ESTIMATES OF WEST-CENTRAL AFRICA'S
SLAVE EXPORTS, BY EUROPEAN NATION

These official Portuguese records provide relatively precise and complete indications of the numbers of slaves leaving west-central Africa only from the two Portuguese ports south of the Zaire, though much more clearly at Luanda than at Benguela. This affirmation of the essential accuracy—that is, within 5 percent or so—of the government data contradicts an assumption frequent in the secondary literature that they must be increased by a substantial factor, sometimes estimated as high as 50 percent to 100 percent, to account for smuggling to Brazil, through Luanda and Benguela but beyond the knowledge of the government authorities there, by Portuguese subjects. In fact, contraband in the Angolan trade consisted largely of the illicit merchandise (woolens, cottons) bought by Angolans from British and French interlopers along outlying parts of the coast and at Benguela itself. The slaves these colonial smugglers provided the foreigners in return did not go to Brazil but rather made their way to the Caribbean aboard the ships of other nations and to North America, where most, or nearly all, slaves leaving Angola without Portuguese government duties having been paid thus appear in independent data on slave arrivals in the islands of the West Indies, or in the shipping records of the British and French.[22] To add an allowance for these slaves to the Portuguese data also, above the official figures widely available in published form, would double-count most smuggling from west-central Africa.

Precisely because of the surreptitious character of much of this trade, British and French records of individual voyages specified the precise regions where they traded south of the equator too seldom for their activities along the Loango Coast to be distinguished from those in the Zaire estuary or as interlopers farther south near Luanda and Benguela.[23] One may, however, work from Portuguese expressions of concern about the competition they posed, tempered by knowledge of the general political and economic circumstances of the times as sketched here, to guess reasonably accurately at the volume and timing of their activity (Miller, 1988a: 226–234). These qualitative inferences, though loose and subject to further scholarly critique, in this case add precision to the vague quantitative data (which remain too crude to represent in tabular form). The Portuguese, French, and British bought slaves from the separate African supply networks and ports of embarkation south of Cape Lopes in the following approximate proportions (see also Figure 2).

At Benguela, the core of the most southerly of the three, Brazilian trade, mostly from Rio, grew from the demand in Minas Gerais after the 1710s and may have reached something on the order of two thousand slaves per year by 1730. The succeeding prosperity generally throughout southern Brazilian agriculture after the 1760s, supported by French smuggling, carried recorded slaving at Benguela to a peak of eight to nine thousand per year from about 1784 to 1795, a decade not coincidentally wracked also by the most severe west-central African drought known in the last four centuries (Miller, 1982). The disappearance of the French after about 1791 may have raised legal exports at the Portuguese town for the 1790s by diverting into official channels slaves formerly smuggled. Thereafter, the southern Brazilians tended to abandon Benguela. Intensified Portuguese administrative pressure there and, after 1810, the financial strength of metropolitan competitors in Rio who were backed by British capital decreased the attractiveness of what had always been something of a refuge for the smaller and peripheral traders in the Portuguese empire, and drove them off toward Mozambique and other outlying sources of slaves. Benguela's trade, accordingly, declined steadily until the late 1820s. Understandably, given the residual semi-licit flavor of slaving there, illegalization of the trade after 1830 brought a revival of its fortunes in the 1830s and 1840s.

French activity on the southern Angolan coasts around Benguela, mostly at the Kuvo, Kuporolo, Kubal, and Kunene river mouths, probably never amounted to more than a thousand slaves per year before 1756. After the Seven Years War, the French resumed trading in the vicinity in force and became major buyers through the 1780s, when they annually embarked three to five thousand slaves from Benguela and adjoining beaches alone. Presumably, French access to the Angolan town reduced their activity at the Kunene and other bays to the south. War in Europe eliminated the French after 1792, leaving the Brazilians, and eventually British-backed Portuguese from Rio, to take their places.

The English hardly traded at Benguela or beyond to the south. Nearer Luanda, at the small rivers upwind from the Kwanza, they showed up intermittently, particularly in the 1770s and 1780s. Together with occasional Frenchmen, they may have accounted for as many as one thousand slaves annually there by 1790–92.

The figures for Luanda, the heart of the second central African supply network, show the Portuguese-financed trade, in varying commercial combinations with Brazilian carriers, running at a relatively steady volume in the neighborhood of ten thousand slaves per year throughout most of the eighteenth century, though it tended to rise later in the period. Particularly with drought in Africa and prosperity in Brazil, it increased between the 1790s and 1809 to a range of thirteen to fifteen thousand annually, largely from the entry into the market of the thriving cotton growers of Pará and Maranhão. It then declined after 1810 as buyers moved off to the Loango Coast and the estuary of the Zaire after the end of British slaving opened those northern coasts to slavers from Brazil. It rose again, as high as twenty thousand slaves in the worst years, as a result of the efforts that metropolitan merchants, excluded at Rio, made between about 1816 and 1822 to develop Angolan markets through Pernambuco, and then declined until the end of the legal trade. The slaves that Angolans smuggled to eighteenth-century British and French buyers left not through the port at Luanda but rather through Benguela, the rivers to the south of the Kwanza, and the bays north of the city. After about 1815, Spaniards and North Americans replaced the northern Europeans, though in smaller numbers. The captives they bought therefore appear in the estimates of the non-Portuguese trade for those regions.

North of Luanda, from the Dande to the Zaire River, the British and French increased their slaving steadily through the eighteenth century to a peak in the 1780s that lasted until the withdrawal of the French after 1791. Non-Portuguese activity along that coast fell back into a shallow trough until 1809, when the Brazilians moved into the commercial niche left by the departed English. The Brazilians then abandoned Luanda to the Portuguese merchants based at Rio to seek slaves at Ambriz and other ports there. Pernambuco traders may, for example, have adapted the old French strategy of working down the coast from south to north in a pattern that included an initial stop at Benguela, perhaps a call at Luanda for provisions, though less often for slaves, and then further slaving in the Zaire estuary or at Cabinda. Luso-Brazilian trade north of the Dande increased through the 1820s, and the contacts that those engaged in this trade formed with African suppliers and Angolan smugglers at the time provided the base on which they built the region into a major source of slaves during the illegal trade after the mid-1830s. Merchants from Lisbon and the court-linked Portuguese slaving contingent in Rio enjoyed official favor at Luanda, and government administration had become efficacious enough by then that few of them had need to make more than occasional forays, none leading to long-term involvement, north of Luanda toward the Zaire.

The Loango Coast remained the primary central African slaving ground for the British and French throughout the eighteenth century. Their relative shares in this trade varied, with the Dutch accounting for significant purchases also in earlier decades. The total of this slaving, by Portuguese and other estimates, grew rapidly from a few thousand shortly after 1700 to ten thousand or more by the 1720s and 1730s, declined slightly in the 1740s and 1750s, and then rose to as many as fifteen thousand per year by the 1790s (Richardson, 1989). The British and French gradually drifted southward, away from the concentration of the Dutch in the 1600s at the Loango kingdom at the northern end of this stretch of coast, to ports like Cabinda, nearer the Zaire, that tapped the African commercial networks south of the river. This southerly movement thus constituted a move up the supply lines toward the band of dense population beyond the Zaire, and was part of a recurrent tendency among European buyers to beat their competition by intercepting African caravans proceeding diagonally toward the coast as near as possible to the sources of their slaves. For the same reason, by the 1820s and during the illegal trade, the Zaire estuary became a durable and reliable refuge from British cruisers as well as the point of earliest access to the major sources of slaves headed toward these northern coasts.

The Portuguese were utterly unable to meet the eighteenth-century British and French competition north of the Zaire, although factions not faring well at Luanda—for example, Lisbon merchants, all but excluded from the trade by Brazilians in the 1770s—sometimes made abortive attempts to intrude. After 1809, when British and French withdrawal finally made those coasts available to the Portuguese, tighter government control and favoritism at Luanda made it unnecessary for them to go there for slaves. The Brazilians began to trade in this area in the 1810s, when Rio-based merchants from the metropole assumed control at Luanda. Their strategy duplicated that of the Rio traders who in the eighteenth century had sought relief at Benguela from the power of the slave-duty contractors at the colonial capital. Cabinda in particular became a major attraction for them and remained so until the end of the legal trade.

Taking all these trading parties together, Portuguese and foreigners, perhaps ten or fifteen thousand slaves left the west-central African coast each year early in the eighteenth century, half of them or more from Luanda. From that time on, the trade dispersed outward to involve many sites, particularly as Loango and Benguela both developed independent slave catchment areas and began to draw slaves away from the indebted trading zone inland from the Portuguese colonial capital. Overall, in spite of the relatively stable volume of slaving at Luanda, exports increased steadily to a peak of around thirty-five thousand annually in the 1780s or 1790s. Volume leveled off in the 1790s and then dropped back substantially to a relatively stable range of thirty to thirty-five thousand until the end of the legal trade.

CONCLUSION

Figure 4 divides these changing totals according to the four major African supply systems contributing to them: Luanda; the coasts north of Luanda beyond the Zaire to Loango; Benguela; and the far southern latitudes beyond. It also presents a new revision of Curtin's pre-1810 estimates for the region (Richardson, 1989) and Eltis's (1986b: 168–169) data for the early nineteenth century for comparison.[24] The qualitative estimates for "Northern Coasts," "Luanda," and "Benguela" after 1810 merely subdivide Eltis's "Angola" and intuitively reallocate the trade north of Luanda to what Eltis would consider "Congo North," according to the geographical definitions employed for earlier decades in the figure.[25]

The larger totals, mostly between the 1740s and the 1790s, reached by summing the regional estimates drawn from the qualitative history of the trade result largely from the reticence in the first-generation quantitative data about French and British intrusions on Portuguese-claimed territory beyond the Zaire and in southern Angola. The qualitative evidence thus confirms the

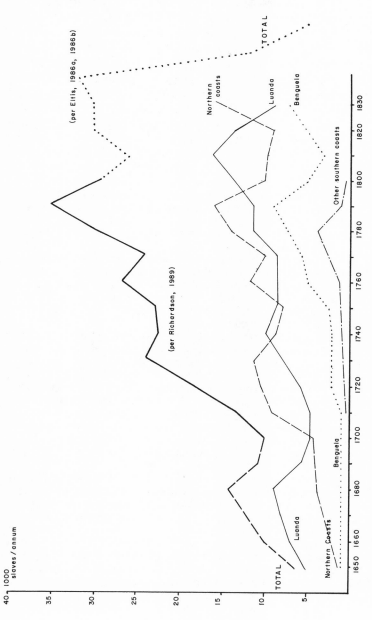

Figure 4   Estimated slave exports from west-central Africa (by decades, c. 1650–1860)

outline of recent statistical work (Richardson, 1989) in finding
the foreigners numerous and active there, identifies them as the
"smugglers" prevalent in Portuguese-claimed waters, and accounts for their presence as a logical strategy in terms of geography and the rivalries among the various Portuguese and Brazilian
participants in the trade. The higher regional totals, particularly
in the 1760s and 1770s, thus do not increase the volume of the
Atlantic trade as a whole but merely relocate in west-central
Africa a portion of French and British slaving formerly assumed
to have come from West African shores.

NOTES

1   Curtin's (1969) original survey represented only a preliminary summary of
published data available in the late 1960s. See Lovejoy, 1982, for a summary of the first generation of studies that focused on methodology and the
recovery of archival data not incorporated in Curtin; see Lovejoy, 1989, for
references to recent literature.

2   Eltis's monumental research on the nineteenth-century trade continued
through the watershed of the early 1980s and thus neatly encapsulates
the shift in emphasis from method and data to application and historical
problems; compare Eltis, 1979, to Eltis and Jennings, 1988, and note the
gradual displacement of the technical studies on data from Eltis's (1987a)
provocatively interpretive monograph.

3   Lovejoy's (1989) interim survey of new work, significantly, is phrased in
terms of a historical problem rather than in terms of evidence and method.
Healthy skepticism of the narrow emphasis on quantitative research as a
whole has correspondingly also made its appearance (Henige, 1986). Nonetheless, new data for the Atlantic still remain to be recovered and presented,
to judge from Becker, 1986, 1987. Ralph Austen's (1979a, 1979b, 1987,
1988a, 1988b) lengthening series of revisions of his estimates for the vastly
less well documented trans-Saharan, Red Sea, and Indian Ocean trades
record one cautious scholar's odyssey in a related area from hopeful tenta-
tiveness to confident acceptance of the limitations of the numbers relative
to the complexities of the problems.

4   Its Portuguese segment is well known in the abstract categories characteristic of the pioneering phase of the field thanks to the labors of Klein (1978),
preliminary studies cited there, and subsequent translations in Portuguese,
reworked most recently in Klein, 1987. Additional data arranged according
to more detailed categories are in Miller, 1975. Eltis (1986a, 1986b) has
also studied the activities of all European and American slavers active in the
nineteenth-century southern Atlantic trade within the context of his series
of papers on the trade as a whole. Also see Clarence-Smith, 1984, 1988.
New annual aggregates for the Portuguese trade at Angola are forthcoming,
as well, for the eighteenth century, though they appear only to nuance the
existing picture of overall volume and timing (see Curto, 1988).

5   The analysis presented here is documented and developed at length in Miller, 1988a.

6   This tripartite division based on African delivery systems contrasts with the two-part distinction, north and south of the mouth of the Zaire River, used in most studies of slaving in west-central Africa. The divide at the Zaire derives implicitly from the distinction in the origins of the data in anglophone or lusophone sources, not from the structure of the trade. One consequence of employing formal logic, rather than historical, in this case is that the method has lost track of much of the French trade on these coasts, for which geographically specified information in French sources has been slow to appear.

7   Though one searches Geggus, 1988, in vain for evidence of this pattern.

8   For new quantitative evidence along these lines, see Richardson, 1989.

9   The comparable British system of "advances" in the Indian context is sketched in Wallerstein, 1987: 226–227, 236–237. A recent stress on credit in Britain's nineteenth-century trade in West Africa is found in Mann, 1987.

10 Also found in the nineteenth-century "hypothecation system" in British India (Wallerstein, 1987: 248–249).

11 See the voluminous collection of personal papers from the term in Angola of the early-seventeenth-century governor Fernão de Sousa (in office 1625–30), recently edited and published by Heintze (1985, 1988). A similar private account book of a public servant from the 1680s–90s is known (Rau, 1956; further explication in Miller, 1984). No analytical study of the origins of the papers now in Lisbon's Arquivo Histórico Ultramarino (AHU) exists (though the current cataloging system is listed in Curto, 1988), but for the Luanda archives, which reflect the origins of the holdings of the AHU for Angola, see Miller, 1974, and Couto, 1979.

12 Curto (1988) gives variant overall totals from a number of different sources, including one for 1733, but without indicating its provenience.

13 These records are the documentation behind the statistical analysis in Klein, 1978: 51–72, 254–255, revised from an earlier version as Klein, 1972. Birmingham, 1966: 141, 154–155, has occasionally variant totals for most of the same years. See also the recent restatement of these data in Klein, 1987: 136, 139.

14 Curto (1988) has again found data of an unidentified sort for an additional year, 1783.

15 Knowledge thereafter depends on the apparently nearly complete record of imports compiled by British consuls stationed in Brazilian, and other American, ports to report illegal slaving back to London; see Eltis (all works listed).

16 Figures exist for 1730 and 1738, when officials grew concerned about Brazilian traders' failure to call at Luanda with slaves boarded at Benguela in order not to pay duties owed at the contractor's Luanda factory. The alarm over lost duties generated a continuous series starting in 1740. For a summary, see Curto, 1988: Table 3.

17 This register survives in the Biblioteca Nacional do Rio de Janeiro; see Klein, 1978: 51–72. It is studied independently in Miller, 1975.

18   The Eltis data (all references) are comprehensive for this period. For 1811–21, see Miller, 1976.

19   Recent work by Brazilian researchers (Tavares, 1988a, 1988b; Florentino, 1988) has apparently turned up few new figures.

20   This compilation of statistical reports from the Arquivo Histórico Ultramarino (Lisbon) supersedes the preliminary estimates attempted, mostly on the basis of inference and indirect data, in Miller, 1975, especially appendix 2.

21   For the data as most scholars have used them, see Carreira, 1967–69.

22   See the discussion of smuggling in the context of tight packing in Miller, 1988b.

23   Lovejoy (1982) acknowledges the inadequacies of the numerical evidence.

24   Curtin (1969) left Angola undistinguished in a general non–West African category of "Central and Southeastern Africa," but Lovejoy (1982) summarizes his understanding of the data for the eighteenth and nineteenth centuries under a heading of "West-Central Africa," presumably comparable to the definition of the coast used here (south of the equator from Cape Lopes to the Kunene River mouth), while acknowledging the impressionistic methods necessary to allocate relatively firm totals among specific African supply regions. Figure 4 represents my acceptance of Lovejoy's (ibid.: 493) invitation to "undertake more detailed work on each decade and coastal region," an opportunity seized also, from another perspective, by Richardson (1989).

25   The subtotals for the 1820s and 1830s incorporate Eltis's (esp. 1986a, 1986b) and Richardson's (1989) new work and represent a revision of the more preliminary estimates in a similar chart in Miller, 1988a: 233, Figure 7.1.

REFERENCES

Austen, R. A. (1979a) "The trans-Saharan slave trade: A tentative census," in H. A. Gemery and J. S. Hogendorn (eds.) The Uncommon Market: Essays in the Economic History of the Atlantic Slave Trade. New York: Academic Press: 23–76.
———(1979b) "The Islamic Red Sea slave trade: An effort at quantification," in Proceedings of the Fifth International Conference on Ethiopian Studies. Chicago: 443–467.
———(1987) "The Islamic slave trade out of Africa: An intermediate census report." Paper presented at the Congrès International de Démographie Historique, Paris.
———(1988a) "The nineteenth century Islamic slave trade from East Africa (Swahili and Red Sea coasts): A tentative census." Slavery and Abolition 9: 21–44.
———(1988b) "The Mediterranean Islamic slave trade out of Africa: Towards a census." Paper presented at the Workshop on the Long-Distance Trade in Slaves across the Sahara and the Black Sea in the Nineteenth Century, Rockefeller Foundation Bellagio Study and Conference Center, Villa Serbelloni, Italy.

Becker, C. (1986) "Note sur les chiffres de la traite atlantique française au dix-huitième siècle." Cahiers d'études africaines 26: 633–679.

——— (1987) "La place de la Sénégambie dans la traite atlantique française du dix-huitième siècle." Paper presented at the Congrès International de Démographie Historique, Paris.

Bethell, L. (1970) The Abolition of the Brazilian Slave Trade: Britain, Brazil, and the Slave Trade Question, 1807–1869. Cambridge: Cambridge University Press.

Birmingham, D. B. (1966) Trade and Conflict in Angola: The Mbundu and Their Neighbours under the Influence of the Portuguese 1483–1790. Oxford: Clarendon Press.

Carreira, A. (1967–69) "As companhias pombalinas de navegação, comércio, e tráfico de escravos entre a costa africana e o nordeste brasileiro." Boletim cultural da Guiné portuguesa 22: 5–88; 23: 301–454; 24: 59–188, 284–474.

Clarence-Smith, G. (1984) "The Portuguese contribution to the Cuban slave and coolie trades in the nineteenth century." Slavery and Abolition 5: 25–33.

——— (1988) "La traite portugaise et espagnole en Afrique au dix-neuvième siècle," in S. Daget (ed.) Actes du Colloque International sur la Traite des Noirs (Nantes, 1985), vol. 2. Paris and Nantes: Société Française d'Histoire d'Outre-mer and Centre de Recherche sur l'Histoire du Monde Atlantique: 425–434.

Couto, C. (1979) "Para a história arquivística em Angola—o primeiro inventário documental angolano (3.12.1754)." Studia 41–42: 227–271.

Curtin, P. D. (1969) The Atlantic Slave Trade: A Census. Madison: University of Wisconsin Press.

Curto, J. C. (1987) "The Angolan manuscript collection of the Arquivo Histórico Ultramarino, Lisbon: Toward a working guide." History in Africa 15: 163–189.

——— (1988) "Recounting the numbers: The legal Angolan slave trade, 1710–1830." Unpublished manuscript.

Darity, W., Jr. (1985) "The numbers game and the profitability of the British trade in slaves." Journal of Economic History 45: 693–703.

Eltis, D. (1979) "The export of slaves from Africa: 1820–43," in H. A. Gemery and J. S. Hogendorn (eds.) The Uncommon Market: Essays in the Economic History of the Atlantic Slave Trade. New York: Academic Press: 273–301.

——— (1986a) "Fluctuations in the age and sex ratios of slaves in the nineteenth-century transatlantic slave traffic." Slavery and Abolition 7: 257–272.

——— (1986b) "Slave departures from Africa, 1811–1867: An annual time series." African Economic History 15: 143–171.

——— (1987a) Economic Growth and the Ending of the Transatlantic Slave Trade. New York: Oxford University Press.

——— (1987b) "The nineteenth-century transatlantic slave trade: An annual time series of imports into the Americas broken down by region." Hispanic American Historical Review 67: 109–138.

———, and L. C. Jennings (1988) "Trade between sub-Saharan Africa and the Atlantic world in the pre-colonial era." American Historical Review 93: 936–959.

Florentino, M. G. (1988) "Notas sobre os negócios negreiros no porto do Rio de Janeiro 1790–1830." Unpublished manuscript.

Geggus, D. (1988) "The demographic composition of the French slave trade." Paper presented at the Escravidão—Congresso Internacional, São Paulo.

Heintze, B. (1985, 1988) Fontes para a história de Angola do século 17. 2 vols., Wiesbaden: Franz-Steiner-Verlag.

Henige, D. (1986) "Measuring the immeasurable: The Atlantic slave trade, West African population and the Pyrrhonian critic." Journal of African History 27: 295–313.

Klein, H. S. (1969) "The trade in slaves to Rio de Janeiro, 1795–1811." Journal of African History 10: 533–549.

——— (1972) "The Portuguese slave trade from Angola in the eighteenth century." Journal of Economic History 32: 894–918.

——— (1973) "O tráfico de escravos para o porto de Rio de Janeiro, 1825–1830." Anais de história 5: 85–101.

——— (1978) The Middle Passage: Comparative Studies in the Atlantic Slave Trade. Princeton: Princeton University Press.

——— (1987) "A demografia do tráfico atlântico de escravos para o Brasil." Estudos econômicos 17: 129–149.

———, and S. L. Engerman (1975) "Shipping patterns and mortality in the African slave trade to Rio de Janeiro, 1825–1830." Cahiers d'études africaines 15: 381–398.

Lovejoy, P. E. (1982) "The volume of the Atlantic slave trade: A synthesis." Journal of African History 23: 473–502.

——— (1989) "The impact of the slave trade on Africa in the eighteenth and nineteenth centuries." Journal of African History 30.

Mann, K. (1987) "Trade, credit, and the commodification of land in colonial Lagos." Paper presented at the conference "Reframing the Colonial Experience," University of Illinois at Urbana-Champaign.

Miller, J. C. (1974) "The archives of Luanda, Angola." International Journal of African Historical Studies 7: 551–590.

——— (1975) "Legal Portuguese slaving from Angola—Some preliminary indications of volume and direction, 1760–1830." Revue française d'histoire d'outre-mer 62: 135–176.

——— (1976) "Sources and knowledge of the slave trade in the southern Atlantic." Paper presented at a meeting of the Western Branch of the American Historical Association, La Jolla, California.

——— (1982) "The significance of drought, disease, and famine in the agriculturally marginal zones of west-central Africa." Journal of African History 23: 17–61.

——— (1984) "Capitalism and slaving: The financial and commercial organization of the Angolan slave trade, according to the accounts of António Coelho Guerreiro (1684–1692)." International Journal of African Historical Studies 17: 1–56.

——— (1986) "Imports at Luanda, Angola: 1785–1823," in G. Liesegang, H. Pasch, and A. Jones (eds.) Figuring African Trade: Proceedings of the Symposium on the Quantification and Structure of the Import and Export and Long Distance Trade of Africa in the Nineteenth Century (c. 1800–

1913) (St. Augustin 3–6 January 1983). Kölner Beiträge zur Afrikanistik, No. 11. Berlin: Dietrich-Reimer-Verlag: 165–246.

———(1988a) Way of Death: Merchant Capitalism and the Angolan Slave Trade, 1730–1830. Madison: University of Wisconsin Press.

———(1988b) "Overcrowded and undernourished: Techniques and consequences of tight-packing in the Portuguese southern Atlantic slave trade," in S. Daget (ed.) Actes du Colloque International sur la Traite des Noirs (Nantes, 1985), vol. 2. Paris and Nantes: Société Française d'Histoire d'Outre-mer and Centre de Recherche sur l'Histoire du Monde Atlantique: 395–424.

Rau, V. (1956) O "Livro de Razão" de António Coelho Guerreiro. Lisbon: DIAMANG.

Richardson, D. (1989) "Slave exports from West and West-Central Africa, 1700–1810: New estimates of volume and distribution." Journal of African History 30: 1–22.

Tavares, L. H. D. (1988a) Comércio proibido de escravos. São Paulo: Editora Ática.

———(1988b) "O capitalismo no comércio proibido de escravos." Revista do Instituto de Estudos Brasileiros 28: 37–52.

Wallerstein, I. (1987) "The incorporation of the Indian subcontinent into the capitalist world-economy," in S. Chandra (ed.) The Indian Ocean: Explorations in History, Commerce and Politics. New Delhi: Sage: 222–253.

5
The Slave Trade: The Formal Demography of a Global System

PATRICK MANNING

IF THE BEST-KNOWN aspects of African slavery remain the horrors of the middle passage and the travail of plantation life in the Americas, recent work has nonetheless provided some important reminders of the Old World ramifications of slavery (Miller 1988; Meillassoux 1986; Miers and Roberts 1988; Manning 1990a). Millions of slaves were sent from sub-Saharan Africa to serve in households and plantations in North Africa and the Middle East and suffered heavy casualties on their difficult journey. Millions more, captured in the same net as those sent abroad, were condemned to slavery on the African continent. The mortality of captives in Africa, therefore, included not only losses among those headed for export at the Atlantic coast but the additional losses among those destined for export to the Orient and among those captured and transported to serve African masters.

The purpose of this study is to address, at the global level and in analytical terms, the demography of this system of forced labor migration. What was the impact of the slave trade on Africa and on the Orient? How serious was the mortality and the demographic disruption brought by the slave trade to these Old World areas? How closely were New World slavery and African demography linked? What were the relative sizes of slave populations in the Occident, Africa, and the Orient? What was the rate at which African societies lost population to the slave trade? How distinctive were the structures of slave population in the Occident, in Africa, and in the Orient?

Figure 1 provides a framework for addressing these questions. It presents the slave trade as a single demographic system, linking the Occident, Africa, and the Orient through the migration of slaves. The hallmarks of this framework are found in both its regional and its analytical structure. It distinguishes the populations within Africa from those in the Occident and the Orient. It divides the population of each continental region into free, slave, and captive populations (where captives are those in the process of becoming slaves), and it accounts for the liberation of slaves.

The demography of slave trading, in turn, cannot be discussed in isolation from the economics of the slave trade. To phrase the linkage of demography and economics in simple terms, it was the New World demand for African slaves that created a demographic system, a world market for slave labor, spanning five continents in the years from 1700 to 1850.[1] The rising New World demand created a new, westward trade in slaves that competed with the older and smaller oriental trade, which continued to transport slaves across the Sahara and the Red Sea. The willingness of New World planters to pay relatively high prices for laborers brought an expanded supply response from those Africans willing to profit by selling slaves. Once the supply system had developed along the Western Coast of Africa, Africans developed a demand for slaves, especially female slaves, and the dimensions of the slave trade expanded further. The occidental slave trade then peaked at the end of the eighteenth century; in the early nineteenth century, prices for slaves declined as New World purchasers were driven out of the market, step by step, by abolitionist movements. But the lower slave prices only caused African and oriental purchasers of slaves to demand increased numbers, and the total volume of the slave trade changed little until after 1850.

As the nineteenth century proceeded, this global system of the slave trade broke down into a set of isolated, regional slave systems. Large-scale slave trading was suppressed in the Occident,

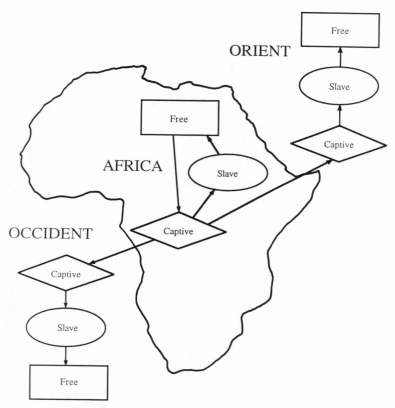

Figure 1   Populations in the slave trade

in the Orient, and finally in Africa. Nevertheless, in each of these areas slavery continued for generations after the end of the slave trade: slave owners reformed their plantations according to new and gentler regimes, within which it was sometimes possible for slaves to reproduce themselves biologically (Manning 1990b).

A cumulative total of over 10 million Africans reached the New World as slaves from 1500 to 1900; closer to 12 million were dispatched in ships from Africa, and over 1.5 million lost their lives in the middle passage. In the same period, some 6 million slaves were sent from sub-Saharan Africa to the Orient, and some 8 million people were enslaved and retained within the African continent. An estimated total of 4 million people lost their lives as a direct result of enslavement within Africa, while many others died young because of the hard conditions of slave life.[2]

The occidental slave trade reached an annual average of 70,000 slaves in the late eighteenth century; the combination of the occidental and oriental trades reached an annual average of over 100,000 slaves in the early nineteenth century, and the total number of people captured in Africa and either retained or transported abroad peaked at roughly 150,000 slaves per year in the early nineteenth century.

As a result of these exports of slaves, the population of the Western Coast of Africa—the region from Senegal to Angola from which most New World slaves were drawn—declined significantly from about 1730 to 1850. Further, since the slaves were removed at the rate of roughly two males for every female, the result was a relative shortage of males on the African continent: adult sex ratios fell to 80 men per 100 women in many areas, and to 50 men per 100 women in such hard-hit areas as Loango and Angola. In the East African region from Mozambique to Kenya, a serious population decline occurred later, from about 1820 to 1890, as slaves were taken both to Muslim areas in Arabia and the Persian Gulf and to European-ruled territories in the Indian Ocean and the New World. The sex ratio of slaves transported from East Africa was, on average, about even.

Mortality in the slave trade, though sometimes exaggerated by those seeking to underscore its immorality, was quite severe. Its severity becomes evident when all of its various elements are catalogued.[3] The best-known element of mortality is that of the middle passage. The summary figure of 15% is a good index of overall slave mortality for that voyage, though research has shown that it varied greatly with time, length of the voyage, and age of the slaves. On the New World side must be added the continued high mortality of slaves during the period of their seasoning as well as the normal mortality of slaves, which was higher than that for free persons in the New World.

Slave mortality in Africa had three dimensions, associated with the occidental, African, and oriental trades, respectively. Mortality among slaves headed for the Occident included the deaths of slaves during their capture, transport to the coast, and confinement on the coast in preparation for shipping. Here again, an overall average of 15% mortality is a useful guess, though it varied greatly with the age of slaves and the distance and duration of their journey to the coast. In the African slave trade, we may assume an equivalent 15% mortality among people enslaved and retained in Africa rather than exported. Similarly, for the oriental trade, mortality rates in transportation were comparable to those for the voyage to and across the Atlantic. The combination of the nearly 30% mortality in the occidental and oriental trades with the 15% mortality in the African trade thus yielded, for the global slave trade, a rate of mortality which probably exceeded 20% of all those enslaved, or some 5 million people over three centuries. Most of these people died in Africa.

The rise and fall of this modern, global system of black slavery entailed some remarkable transformations. In 1600 Africans at home and abroad were clearly a minority of the world's slaves; in 1800 they were the overwhelming majority of all slaves. In 1790 there were some 3 million New World black slaves, and they were perhaps the majority of all black slaves. By 1850 that total had risen to 5 million, but by then the population of slaves in Africa had risen to meet it, and went on to exceed it.

New World slaves usually married other slaves (though many male slaves were simply unable to marry for lack of women), and the resulting population was African in ancestry and slave in status. Slaves in the Orient, by contrast, were predominantly female, and they were frequently wedded to their oriental masters. Their children, as a result, were both African and Middle Eastern in ancestry, and often free in status. Today's New World population of 700 million includes roughly 100 million people of African ancestry. It may be true, remarkably, that the African contribution to the Middle Eastern gene pool is roughly of the same proportion as that in the New World—about one-seventh—but that this contribution is spread throughout the population of the Middle East, while it is segregated in the New World.

From 1700 to 1850, the population of sub-Saharan Africa as a whole stagnated or declined in size because of the mortality of captives, the drain of slaves, and continued high mortality resulting from social insecurity. This was precisely the period in which the populations of Europe, the Americas, and Asia began to grow rapidly. So while the African proportion of Atlantic basin population was perhaps 30% in 1650, it had declined to roughly 10% in 1850; adding in the African-descended populations of the

Occident and Orient would bring the African proportion up to 15% in 1850 (Manning 1990a).

THE MODEL AND ITS POPULATIONS

The remainder of this presentation focuses on the formal structure of the model underlying the interpretations summarized above. The model approximates a continuous process, like most such models, and is expressed in terms of five-year age groups (Keyfitz 1977). All the populations exist at each moment; they change in size and structure in response to their various rates of fertility, mortality, and migration. The populations are the variables in the analysis. The numerous rates of fertility, mortality, and migration are taken as parameters.[4] The analysis consists of determining which parameters are most important, both theoretically and historically, in setting patterns of population change. In the conclusion I offer a simplified history of the slavery of Africans in terms of changes in these key parameters.

In Africa and for Africans abroad, the broadest distinctions were among the free, slave, and captive populations. In Africa, the free populations were usually the largest, though in a significant number of instances—for example, the Western Sudan in the late nineteenth century—slaves outnumbered the free (Klein 1987). The free populations included those liberated either by manumission or by escape.

The captives, while always the smallest of the three groups, had sufficiently distinctive characteristics that they must be identified and analyzed as populations distinct from the slaves they became. Captives were people recently placed in captivity; they were in transit to their destinations or undergoing training and seasoning (socialization) prior to becoming productive slaves. In demographic terms, the mobility of captives and the extremely poor conditions in which they lived meant that their rates of fertility and mortality were far more unfavorable than those of settled slaves.

The same three broad categories, free, slave, and captive, apply to populations of African descent abroad. Here *abroad* means, primarily, the slave plantation colonies of the Americas, but it also refers to the significant numbers of slaves who were settled in North Africa and the Middle East, in the Sahara Desert, in the islands of the Indian Ocean, and in Europe. In each of these areas the captives were those newly arrived from sub-Saharan Africa, fresh off the boat or the caravan, or undergoing the process of seasoning. The slaves dominated the populations of African descent in these slave-importing regions. In addition, however, there were significant numbers of free persons of African descent.

Flows of Migration and Change in Status

The demographic logic of the analysis takes the form of a multiregional, multistage process (Rogers 1985): multiregional because it addresses several geographical and social regions (i.e., African, occidental, and oriental regions; free, captive, and slave populations within each region), multistage because several populations undergo decrement both by death and by out-migration (through enslavement or liberation), and also because people may enter one of several populations either by birth or by in-migration.

Further, the path of migration from one region to another affects the outcome of migration, as migrants experience distinct patterns of fertility and mortality along the way—for instance, the heavy mortality of slaves during the middle passage across the Atlantic. In one sense, this amounts simply to adding more stages to the process described above. In another sense, however, it may be useful to think of the model as assuming *eventful* migration. The migration is assumed to be slow and eventful, rather than rapid, so that the path of the migrants and the events they undergo must be included explicitly in the analysis. This approach contrasts with that of many migration models, in which only destination and not the path of migrants is included; in effect, such models assume migration to be instantaneous (ibid.).

Within Africa, people are assumed to have migrated as a result either of enslavement or of its opposite, liberation. When a man freed his slave wife, the woman's status changed but she was not displaced physically. To utilize the standard analytical simplification, however, we may consider her change from the status of slave to that of a free person as a migration from one population to another. In the New World and other slaveholding areas abroad, migration similarly took place through absorption of the imported captives into the slave population, and through the liberation of slaves by manumission or escape. The liberation of

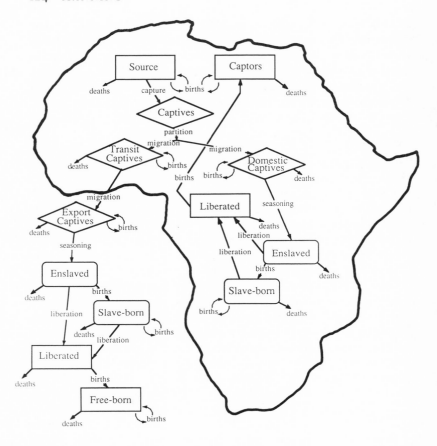

Figure 2   Reproduction and migration in the African and occidental slave trades

slaves, in this version of the model, is assumed to be uneventful and instantaneous, in contrast to the slow and painful migration of captives.

Figure 2 focuses, for heuristic purposes, on the slave trade from Africa to the New World. It shows, in more detail than Figure 1, the various populations and their births, deaths, and migrations. The divisions I have made are as follows: Free persons in Africa are divided into Source and Captor populations, plus the Liberated; free blacks abroad are divided into the Liberated and the

Free-born. Slaves in Africa are divided into the Enslaved (or first-generation slaves) and the Slave-born (subsequent generations of slaves); slaves abroad are divided in the same way. Captives in Africa are divided among the Domestic captives (who are to become slaves in Africa) and the Transit captives (who are to be sent abroad). Once outside sub-Saharan Africa, the surviving Transit captives become Export captives and ultimately become Enslaved abroad.[5]

Under similar principles, this model could allow for finer distinctions, such as the division of the African population into subpopulations corresponding, for instance, to the western coast, the savanna, and the eastern coast, and could allow for slave raiding of greater or lesser complexity among them. Similarly, the model could distinguish regions in the Occident or the Orient.

Discussion of the model for the case of the slave trade to the New World is sufficient, however, to display its basic properties. Thus, although various populations of slaves abroad—for instance, in Jamaica and in Arabia—differed greatly in composition and reproduction, they may each be described in terms of a single set of variables and parameters; it was the differing values of the variables and parameters which made these two populations so different. Let us turn, therefore, to cataloguing the modifications brought to the populations shown in Figure 2 through the slave trade.

Identification of Key Parameters

The most basic parameters in the analysis are the age-specific rates of birth and death for each population. These rates are assumed to be distinct for the free, slave, and captive populations. Further, among free persons, rates of birth and death are assumed to be different in Africa and abroad, and for Source, Captor, and Liberated populations within Africa. Within slave populations, rates are distinct for the Enslaved and the Slave-born. Among Captives, rates are distinct for Domestic, Transit, and Export, and further distinctions could be made within those groups. The remaining parameters consist of age-specific rates of migration: of *capture* from the Source population,[6] of *partition* among captives to be held in Africa and exported, and of *liberation* of slaves (both the Enslaved and the Slave-born).[7]

The simplest assumption for the parameters is that they remained constant (really, as constant matrices) for any given analysis. Over time, however, it is clear that all the parameters varied. In fact, the life-course and migration parameters might also be treated as functions. Thus the rate of escape was a function of the availability of open land within reach of the slaves; the rate at which captives were exported was a function of the relative prices of slaves in markets in Africa and abroad.

In the discussion below, the parameters are labeled as follows (all are age- and sex-specific):

W: annual rate of capture of persons in the Source population
$X = 1 - W$: annual proportion of Source population avoiding capture
Y: proportion of captives selected for export
Z: annual rate of liberation of slaves
$P = 1 - Q$: five-year rate of survival
F: annual rate of female births to women

The main relationships involving the parameters may be summarized schematically as follows:

Source $\times W$ = Captives
Source $\times X$ = Source population remaining after capture
Captives $\times Y$ = Transit captives
Captives $\times (1 - Y)$ = Domestic captives
Slaves $\times Z$ = Liberated
Population $\times P$ = Surviving population
Female population $\times F$ = Female births

The Base Population: Projection of
Nonmigrating Populations

We turn now to the specifics of population projections, first for a closed population and then for migration. Let us consider a free African population which is neither losing population through enslavement nor gaining population through the flight of slaves. A projection of the size and composition of this population over time then follows the standard projection for a closed population. As indicated above, this projection is based on an analysis of five-year age groups from 0–4 to 80+, five-year periods, and a single-sex model of reproduction.

Mortality in each age group above birth is calculated as the age-specific survivorship rate multiplied by the previous population. For the Captors:

$$_5^C N_x^t = {}_5^C N_{x-5}^{t-5} \times \frac{{}_5^C L_x}{{}_5^C L_{x-5}} = {}_5^C N_{x-5}^{t-5} \times {}_5^C P_{x-5}$$

For survivors to age 80+, the survival rate is taken as $T80/T75$.[8] The population in each age group, as estimated for the middle of each five-year period, for Captors, is then

$$\frac{{}_5^C N_x^{t-5} + {}_5^C N_{x-5}^{t-5} \times {}_5^C P_{x-5}}{2} = \frac{{}_5^C N_x^{t-5} + {}_5^C N_x^t}{2}$$

Female births in each population are calculated as the age-specific annual fertility rate multiplied by the midperiod population, then by five years of exposure, and summed over all childbearing years.[9]

$$^C B^{f,t} = \sum_{x=\alpha}^{\beta} \left[\frac{({}_5^C N_x^{f,t-5} + {}_5^C N_{x-5}^{f,t-5} \times {}_5^C P_{x-5})}{2} \times {}_5^C F_x^f \times 5 \right]$$

Survivorship among those born in the current period is calculated as the number of female births multiplied by the female birth survival rate. Male births in each population are calculated as a constant proportion of female births (usually 1.03); survivorship of male babies is determined by the male birth survival rate.

The crude birthrate is then the sum of all male and female births in each five-year period divided by the midpoint population of all age groups totaled. The crude death rate is the sum of all deaths divided by the midpoint population. The crude rate of natural increase is the sum of the birth and death rates.

Population Projection with Migration: Selected Cases

Migration, of course, increases the complexity of population projection, but a few examples are sufficient to illustrate all of the principles involved in the projection of free and slave populations undergoing enslavement and liberation. These examples are presented in this section. Meanwhile, the smaller captive populations, which logically intervene between those of free and slave, involve still more complexity in projection: they are considered in the following section.

In Africa, the Source population remaining after the loss of Captives in each period is as follows:

$$\,_5^S N_x^t = \frac{(\,_5^S N_x^{t-5} + \,_5^S N_{x-5}^{t-5} \times \,_5^S P_{x-5})}{2} \times X_x \times 5,$$

where X_x (or $1 - W_x$) is the annual age-specific rate of retention by the Source population. This is the midperiod Source population multiplied by the annual rate of retention, over five years of exposure.

The Captor population, in turn, gains liberated slaves in each period, where the liberated slaves come from the Domestic slave population (both Enslaved and Slave-born), and Z_x is the annual age-specific rate of liberation.[10]

$$\,_5^C N_x^t = \,_5^C N_{x-5}^{t-5} \times \,_5^C P_{x-5} + \,_5^C M_x^t,$$

where

$$\,_5^C M_x^t = \left[\frac{\,_5^{D1} N_x^{t-5} + \,_5^{D1} N_x^t}{2} + \frac{\,_5^{D2} N_x^{t-5} + \,_5^{D2} N_x^t}{2} \right] \times \,_5^D Z_x \times 5$$

The Domestic enslaved population gains in-migrants from surviving Captives and loses out-migrants to liberation:

$$\,_5^{D1} N_x^t = \,_5^{D1} N_{x-5}^{t-5} \times \,_5^{D1} P_{x-5} + \,_5^{DC} N_x^t - \frac{(\,_5^{D1} N_x^{t-5} + \,_5^{D1} N_x^t)}{2} \times \,_5^D Z_x \times 5$$

For the domestic Slave-born population, there is no in-migration (except at birth, as shown below), but there is out-migration because of liberation:

$$\,_5^{D2} N_x^t = \,_5^{D2} N_{x-5}^{t-5} \times \,_5^{D2} P_{x-5} - \frac{(\,_5^{D2} N_x^{t-5} + \,_5^{D2} N_{x-5}^{t-5})}{2} \times \,_5^D Z_x$$

Births into this population include births to the Slave-born but also all births to the Enslaved. That is, all children born to Enslaved women are treated as members of the Slave-born populations: they face rates of mortality at birth appropriate to the Enslaved populations, though all deaths (as all survivors) in this group of

infants are accounted for with those of the Slave-born populations. For the Slave-born population, female births to Slave-born
women are

$$
D2B^{f,t} = \sum_{x=\alpha}^{\beta} \left[\frac{(D2\atop 5 N_x^{f,t-5} + D2\atop 5 N_{x-5}^{f,t-5} \times D2\atop 5 P_{x-5})}{2} \times {}^{D2}_5 F_x^f \times 5 \right]
$$

Female births to Enslaved women are

$$
D1B^{f,t} = \sum_{x=\alpha}^{\beta} \left[\frac{(D1\atop 5 N_x^{f,t-5} + D1\atop 5 N_{x-5}^{f,t-5} \times D1\atop 5 P_{x-5})}{2} \times {}^{D1}_5 F_x^f \times 5 \right]
$$

Survivors age 0–4 in the Slave-born population are

$$
{}^{D2}_5 N_0^{f,t} = {}^{D2}B^{f,t} \times {}^{D2}_5 P_{\text{birth}} + {}^{D1}B^{f,t} \times {}^{D1}_5 P_{\text{birth}}
$$

Projections for Captives

The projection of captive populations involves the further com-
plication that, during any five-year period, captives experience
several different rates of fertility and mortality as they move from
freedom to captivity to enslavement.

It is assumed that Captives in Africa, be they the Domestic
captives retained in Africa or the Transit captives on their way
to the coast, suffer one year of exposure to the high mortality
rates (and perhaps low fertility rates) of captives in Africa. It is
assumed that those who survive to become captives abroad suffer
one year of exposure to the high mortality rates (and low fertility
rates) of captives crossing the Atlantic, the Sahara, the Red Sea,
or the Indian Ocean.

Capture is assumed to take place, on average, in the middle
of each five-year period. As a result, in the five-year period of
their capture, most captives are exposed to the fertility and mortality rates of the free Source population for the time before their
capture, that is, one-half of the period, or 2.5 years. Similarly,
those who survive to become slaves within the five-year period
are exposed, at the conclusion of their migration, to the fertility
and mortality rates of the Enslaved population within Africa, or,
alternatively, those of the Enslaved population abroad. The analysis requires, therefore, a decision as to how much exposure each

group of captives experienced to the several different rates it faced during the period of capture.

Figure 3 displays a schematic summary of the assumed exposure of migrating Domestic captives to various rates of fertility and mortality. Each of five persons is assumed to be captured, successively, in the middle of the first, second, third, fourth, and fifth years of a given period; on average, capture thus occurs at midperiod. Each captive then experiences one year of exposure to Domestic captive rates of fertility and mortality and during the remainder of the period is exposed to Enslaved African rates. The figure includes 25 person-years of experience: the exposures to each set of rates are totalled and divided by 5 to give the portions of a five-year period for each set of rates. Under these conditions, the averages are 2.5 years of exposure to Source rates, 0.9 years of exposure to Domestic captive rates, and 1.6 years of exposure to Enslaved African rates.

One problem remains: A slave captured in the middle of the fifth year experiences one-half year of exposure to Domestic captive rates in this period, and another one-half year of the same exposure in the next period. To account for this systematically, it would be necessary in each period to account for the equivalent exposure for captives left over from the previous period. This would require a complex system of accounting for a very small population. As a simple and close approximation, therefore, it is assumed that the extra half year of exposure to captive rates takes place in this period rather than in the next, and that a half year of exposure to Enslaved African rates is displaced in exchange from this period to the next. As a result, the average estimated exposure of the five captives is 2.5 years at Source rates, 1.0 years at Domestic captive rates, and 1.5 years at Enslaved African rates.

Figure 4 displays the equivalent exposure for Transit captives and Captives abroad. As before, capture is assumed to take place at midperiod. Captives then undergo one year's exposure to Transit captive rates, one more year's exposure to Captive abroad rates, and the remainder of the period to Enslaved abroad rates.

Average exposures for the captives in a five-year period are 2.5 years' exposure to Source rates, 0.9 years' exposure to Transit captive rates, 0.7 years' exposure to Captive abroad rates, and 0.9 years' exposure to Enslaved abroad rates. Even more complex than before, however, would be the accounting necessary

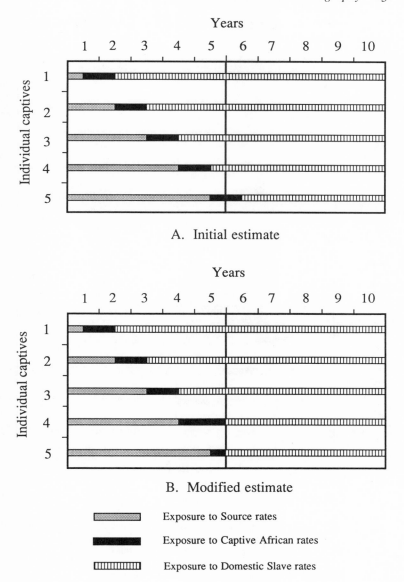

Figure 3   Exposure of new Domestic captives

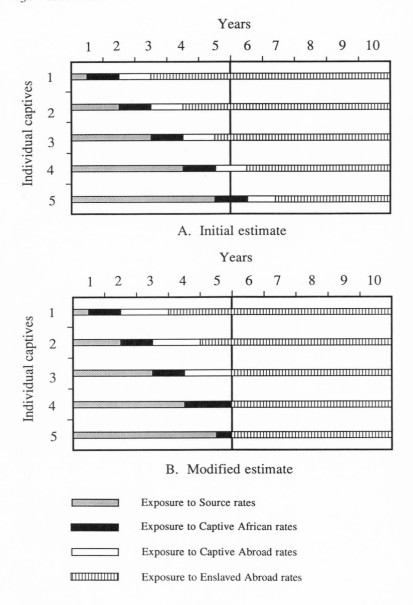

A. Initial estimate

B. Modified estimate

Exposure to Source rates

Exposure to Captive African rates

Exposure to Captive Abroad rates

Exposure to Enslaved Abroad rates

Figure 4   Exposure of new Export captives

to keep track of the 0.5 years' Transit captive exposure and the 1.5 years' Captive abroad exposure in the following period. By the same logic as above, therefore, Enslaved abroad exposure in this period is exchanged for captive exposure in the next period, and the results remain a close approximation of the more accurate but more complex formulation. In sum, the allocation of the 5.0 years' exposure of these captives is 2.5 years at Source rates, 1.0 years at Transit captive rates, 1.0 years at Captive abroad rates, and 0.5 years at Enslaved abroad rates. (These varying periods of exposure must be kept in mind when one calculates, as we do below, the number of person-years lived in each period for calculations of crude rates of birth, death, and growth.)

These rates of exposure may now be used in calculating the fertility and mortality of migrating captives. For Domestic captives, the number of captives for each age and sex is the midperiod Source population multiplied by the annual enslavement rate (X) and by the complement of the partition rate $(1 - Y)$, which gives the number of captives intended for slavery in Africa:

$$
{}^{DC}_{5}N^t_x = \frac{\left({}^{S}_{5}N^{t-5}_x + {}^{S}_{5}N^{t-5}_{x-5} \times {}^{S}_{5}P_{x-5}\right)}{2} \times {}_5X_x \times 5 \times (1 - {}_5Y_x)
$$

Survivorship for Domestic captives is the product of three rates of survival over a period of 5.0 years: those of the Source population (2.5 years), of Domestic captives (1.0 year), and of Enslaved Africans (1.5 years):

$$
{}^{DC}_{5}N^t_x = {}^{DC}_{5}N^{t-5}_{x-5} \times {}^{S}_{2.5}P_{x-5} \times {}^{DC}_{1}P_{x-5} \times {}^{D1}_{1.5}P_{x-5}
$$

Fertility among Domestic captives is the sum of three rates of fertility, multiplied by the midperiod female population for each childbearing age group:

$$
{}^{DC}B^{f,t} = \sum_{x=\alpha}^{\beta} \left[\frac{\left({}^{DC}_{5}N^{f,t-5}_x + {}^{DC}_{5}N^{f,t}_x\right)}{2} \times (2.5 \times {}^{S}_{5}F^f_x \right.
$$

$$
\left. + 1.0 \times {}^{DC}_{5}F^f_x + 1.5 \times {}^{D1}_{5}F^f_x) \right]
$$

Survivors among the newborn female Domestic captives are calculated as female births multiplied by the product of the three birth survival rates, at the relevant exposure. Male births, as elsewhere, are 1.03 times female births, and survivorship is determined by male birth survival rates.

Surviving Domestic captives enter the Enslaved population in Africa as in-migrants. That is,

$$^{D1}_{5}N^t_x = {}^{D1}_{5}N^{t-5}_{x-5} \times {}^{D1}_{5}P_{x-5} + {}^{D1}_{5}M^t_x,$$

where

$$^{D1}_{5}M^t_x = {}^{DC}_{5}N^t_x.$$

The captives sent abroad first enter the Transit population, then the Export captive population, and the survivors join the Enslaved population abroad. The initial Transit population in each period is the complement of the initial Domestic captive population:

$$^{CE}_{5}N^t_x = \frac{({}^{S}_{5}N^{t-5}_x + {}^{S}_{5}N^{t-5}_{x-5} \times {}^{S}_{5}P_{x-5})}{2} \times {}_5X_x \times 5 \times {}_5Y_x$$

Survivorship for the Transit population is calculated as the product of two survival rates over the 3.5 years of each five-year period which the average exported captive spends in Africa:

$$^{CE}_{5}N^t_x = {}^{CE}_{5}N^{t-5}_{x-5} \times {}^{S}_{2.5}P_{x-5} \times {}^{DC}_{1}P_{x-5}$$

Fertility among Transit captives is the sum of two rates of fertility:

$$^{CE}B^{f,t} = \sum_{x=\alpha}^{\beta} \left[\frac{({}^{CE}_{5}N^{f,t-5}_x + {}^{CE}_{5}N^t_x)}{2} \times (2.5 \times {}^{S}_{5}F^f_x \right.$$

$$\left. + 1.0 \times {}^{DC}_{5}F^f_x) \right]$$

Survivors among the Transit captives leave sub-Saharan Africa as Export captives.

For Export captives, finally, mortality is calculated over the 1.5 years of each five-year period which the average export captive spends abroad.[11]

$$^{CE}_{5}N^t_x = {}^{CE}_{5}N^{t-1.5}_x \times {}^{CE}_{1}P_x \times {}^{E1}_{0.5}P_x$$

Fertility among Export captives is:

$$
{}^{CE}B^{f,t} = \sum_{x=\alpha}^{\beta} \left[\frac{({}^{CE}_{x}N^{f,t-1.5}_{x} + {}^{CE}_{5}N^{f,t}_{x})}{2} \right.
$$

$$
\left. \times (1.0 \times {}^{CE}_{5}F^{f}_{x} + 0.5 \times {}^{E1}_{5}F^{f}_{x}) \right]
$$

Survivors among the Export captives enter the Enslaved population abroad as in-migrants at the end of the current period. That is,

$$
{}^{E1}_{5}N^{t}_{x} = {}^{E1}_{5}N^{t-5}_{x-5} \times {}^{E1}_{5}P_{x-5} + {}^{E1}_{5}M^{t}_{x},
$$

where

$$
{}^{E1}_{5}M^{t}_{x} = {}^{CE}_{5}N^{t}_{x}.
$$

Of the many elaborations which could be made to this model, let us mention those which seem most relevant to issues which have been discussed in the slave trade literature. Captives headed for service in Africa could be divided into those marching and those undergoing seasoning. Transit captives could be divided into those marching and those living in barracoons. Captives abroad could be divided into those on ships and those undergoing seasoning.

Population Projections for the Liberated

Where Captives are defined here as people captured within the current five-year period, the Liberated population includes any person liberated during this *or a previous* five-year period. As noted above, it is assumed that the migration from slavery to freedom is instantaneous and uneventful, while the migration from freedom to slavery is fraught with peril. The Liberated population in Africa, for instance, is calculated as the forward projection of the previous Liberated population plus the number of liberated in-migrants from both the Enslaved and the slave-born populations.[12]

Calculating Crude Demographic Rates

For each population, we may use the information from the above population projections to calculate crude rates of birth, death, migration, growth, and decline. The crude rate of migration for any population, for instance, depends on the age-specific rates of birth, death, and migration and on the age and sex composition of that population. (The age-specific rates of birth, death, and migration are taken as data, or sometimes by assumption, in the model.) All of these crude rates can be calculated in straightforward fashion from the population projections outlined above.

Thus, the crude birthrate in Africa during any period is calculated as the total of births among Free, Slaves, and Captives divided by the midperiod population total for Free, Slaves, and Captives (excepting Captives who have been sent abroad). The crude birthrate among Africans abroad is calculated as the total of births among Free, Slaves, and Captives abroad divided by the midperiod population total for Free, Slaves, and Captives abroad. Death rates are calculated similarly.[13]

Some additional useful variables may be calculated for study of the slave trade and expressed in terms of crude rates. One of these is *excess deaths:* deaths occurring because of the slave trade over and above those which would have occurred in the African Source population.

Four distinct rates of African population loss provide a useful composite picture of the demographic toll of the slave trade. The *crude rate of out-migration* from Africa is calculated as the midperiod Transit population divided by the midperiod total for Free, Slave, Domestic captive, and Transit populations. The *crude growth rate* of African population is calculated as the number of births less the number of deaths among the Free, Slaves, and Captives in Africa, less the number of out-migrants (Captives abroad), divided by the midperiod total for the Free, Slave, Domestic captive, and Transit populations. The *crude rate of decrement* in African population leaves out the births; it is calculated as the number of deaths among Free, Slaves, and Captives in Africa plus the number of out-migrants (Captives abroad), divided by the midperiod total for Free, Slave, Domestic captive, and Transit populations. The *crude rate of enslavement decrement* in African population is calculated as the number of excess deaths among Captives in Africa plus the number of out-migrants, divided by the midperiod African population total.

In addition, the model allows for the aggregation of migrants into *cumulative totals.* The best-known example of a cumulative total is Curtin's estimate of 9.6 million slaves landed in the New World between 1500 and 1850. This type of figure, while often quoted in migration studies, has an analytical weakness in that, because it has no dimension of time, it cannot be compared to a population at risk. Nonetheless, a substantial body of historical research and debate is built on cumulative totals of African slave migrants (Curtin 1969; Thomas 1968). The model allows for the estimation of cumulative totals not only for captives arriving in the New World but for the number of captives, enslaved, liberated, and even excess deaths, and for the Orient and within Africa.

Practical implementation of the formal model requires that one link it to historical data on slave populations. While data are very scarce for many of the variables specified in the model, the process of migration links the variables sufficiently closely that limited historical data may provide important insights into broad patterns of slave demography. Information on the age and sex composition of slaves making the middle passage (Export captives, in the terminology used here) yields powerful inferences about the age and sex composition of the population remaining in Africa. Estimated growth rates of New World slave and free black populations, respectively, suggest limits for the estimation of equivalent rates in Africa.

On the other hand, for certain crucial variables the absence of sound historical data greatly weakens the analytical and predictive power of the model. We face a serious shortage of data on overall rates of capture and on the age and sex breakdown of captives; on the rates of partition among domestic and export slaves; and on the rates of mortality for captives within Africa. Similarly, we need more information on rates of fertility and liberation (Manning 1988).

CONCLUSION: A "PARAMETRIC" HISTORY OF THE
AFRICAN SLAVE TRADE

I conclude with a simple application of the model, describing the rise and fall of black slavery in terms of changes in the five types of parameters included in the model: rates of capture, partition, liberation, fertility, and mortality.

Rates of capture in Africa increased from the sixteenth to the early nineteenth centuries, not only for Africa as a whole but for most regions on the continent. For East Africa and the northern savanna, rates of capture roughly doubled in the early nineteenth century. Rates of partition, initially biased heavily toward export, moved gradually toward retention of more slaves in Africa; in the early nineteenth century, as New World demand declined, partition rates moved sharply toward retention. Rates of liberation were generally higher in Africa and the Orient than in the Occident and were probably higher in the Orient than in Africa. Rates of liberation rose sharply in the New World in the mid-nineteenth century and rose somewhat later in the Orient. Rates of liberation in Africa may actually have declined in the mid-nineteenth century as slavery expanded rapidly, but they rose at the turn of the twentieth century.

The fertility of slave-born persons was higher than that of the Enslaved in the New World; perhaps the same was true in Africa. It is not likely that fertility rates changed significantly for a given type of population during the slave trade. Mortality rates probably fluctuated with changing local conditions; the expansion of the slave trade or of slave labor in a given area tended to raise mortality levels in the short run, but the maturation and systematization of the slave trade or slavery allowed mortality rates to decline. Mortality rates declined generally in the Occident and the Orient during the nineteenth century, but not in Africa. Captive survival rates improved with the passage of time (most clearly for the middle passage), though exposure to them increased as the voyages of slaves became longer. For instance, many nineteenth-century slaves going to Brazil came to the Angolan port of Luanda from distant Lunda or Kazembe or took the long ocean route from Mozambique.

By about 1850, the slave export rates collapsed to zero: the New World was cut off from the import of African slave labor, and slavery was replaced by new labor systems. The same came to be true for North Africa, the Middle East, and the Indian Ocean by about 1900. In sub-Saharan Africa, slavery continued to expand until the European conquests of the late nineteenth century. From the 1890s to the 1930s, African slavery survived in a regulated state. Rates of capture declined almost to zero and rates of liberation increased. That is, African slavery continued well into the twentieth century, with no more slave imports but with local "slave dealing"; it was comparable in many ways to slavery after 1807 in the U.S. and the British West Indies.

NOTES

1   The period of the large-scale Atlantic slave trade was from 1650 to 1850. In a more detailed interpretation (Manning 1990a), I argue that, within this period, the years 1700–1850 were the time of a world market in slave labor and the years 1730–1850 were the time of general decline in the population of West and West-Central Africa.

2   These and succeeding quantitative estimates of the impact of the slave trade are based on a simulation analysis. For details on the simulation, see Manning and Griffiths 1988 and Manning 1988. For the estimates themselves, see Manning 1990a. The demographic model on which the simulation is based is the subject of the present article; see also Manning 1981.

3   For instance, Buxton (1839) assumed that fully 50% of those captured died before embarkation at the Atlantic coast. At the same time, he neglected the capture and mortality of the large number of slaves retained in Africa.

4   The variables and the parameters are each matrices, with dimensions of age and sex: in this case, 2 sexes by 17 age groups (0–4 to 80+).

5   For each population in Figure 2, one may catalog the sources of in-migration and the directions of out-migration. For instance, the Enslaved abroad receive in-migrants from the Export captives and send out-migrants to the Liberated and (via birth) to the Slave-born. The Slave-born, in turn, receive in-migrants as births from the Enslaved abroad and send out-migrants to the Liberated.

6   Two possible modifications may be noted here. People already in slavery could be captured and carried off to a new slavery. More broadly, instead of dividing the African population into discrete Source and Captor populations, with only the Source at risk of capture, one could assume that any free African was at risk of capture, or that Source and Captor populations raided each other.

7   The single schedule of rates of liberation could reasonably be broken down into separate schedules for manumission and escape. The manumission schedule would include high rates for the young and old and for females; the escape schedule would include high rates for adults and for males.

8   N is population by age group (subscript 5 indicates five-year age groups, and x indicates ages x to $x + 5$; superscript C is the index for Captors, and t indicates time t). L indicates the number of life-table persons living in each five-year age group; P indicates the probability of survival, in this case from age $x - 5$ to age x. T indicates the total number of life-table person-years lived in the indicated age group.

9   B is the total number of births, where superscripts f and t refer to female births and to the period ending at time t, respectively. Alpha and beta are

women's minimal and maximal ages of childbirth. F is the annual fertility rate, where subscript 5 refers to five-year age groups and x refers to women's age at childbirth; C is the index for the Captor group.

10   This assumes, in effect, that all liberated slaves are manumitted. If it were assumed that some were escapees, one could rewrite the model to include a rate of escape, with the escapees migrating to the Source population.

11   Note the change of indices from previous calculations: the full exposure to mortality comes, on average, within the last half of the period.

12   Here it is assumed that the rate of liberation, Z_x, is the same for both Enslaved and Slave-born populations. This assumption could, of course, be relaxed.

13   For Captive populations, crude rates could be calculated in two ways. The first would include only the births or deaths during the period of capture, transit, and seasoning (one or two years in a five-year period), as a proportion of person-years lived during the one or two years in question. The second would include the births or deaths during a five-year period including capture, as a proportion of person-years lived during the five years. Death rates calculated in the first way would be higher than those calculated in the second way.

REFERENCES

Buxton, T. F. (1839) The African Slave Trade. London: John Murray.

Curtin, P. D. (1969) The Atlantic Slave Trade: A Census. Madison: University of Wisconsin Press.

Keyfitz, N. (1977) Introduction to the Mathematics of Population, with Revisions. Reading, MA: Addison-Wesley.

Klein, M. (1987) "The demography of slavery in western Soudan: The late nineteenth century," in D. D. Cordell and J. W. Gregory (eds.) African Population and Capitalism: Historical Perspectives. Boulder, CO: Westview: 50–61.

Manning, P. (1981) "The enslavement of Africans: A demographic model." Canadian Journal of African Studies 15: 499–526.

——— (1988) "The impact of slave trade exports on the population of the western coast of Africa, 1700–1850," in S. Daget (ed.), De la traite à l'esclavage. Nantes: Société française d'histoire d'outre-mer: 111–34.

——— (1990a) Slavery and African Life. Cambridge: Cambridge University Press.

——— (1990b) "Slavery and the slave trade in colonial Africa." Journal of African History 31: 135–40.

———, and W. S. Griffiths (1988) "Divining the unprovable: Simulating the demography of African slavery." Journal of Interdisciplinary History 19: 177–201.

Meillassoux, C. (1986) Anthropologie de l'esclavage: Le ventre de fer et d'argent. Paris: Presses universitaires de France.

Miers, S., and R. Roberts, eds. (1988) The End of Slavery in Africa. Madison: University of Wisconsin Press.

Miller, J. C. (1988) Way of Death: Merchant Capitalism and the Angolan Slave Trade, 1730–1830. Madison: University of Wisconsin Press.

Rogers, A. (1985) Regional Population Projection Models. Beverly Hills, CA: Sage.

Thomas, B. (1968) Migration and Economic Growth, 2d ed. Cambridge: Cambridge University Press.

Part II
Atlantic Slavery and
the Early Rise
of the Western World

6

Slavery and
the Revolution in
Cotton Textile Production
in England

JOSEPH E. INIKORI

FROM THE point of view of the preindustrial world, the development of the English cotton textile industry in the eighteenth century was truly revolutionary. The industry was established early in the century as a peasant craft (section 2; note 2), and by 1850 it had been almost completely transformed in terms of the organization and technology of production. Of the total work force of 374,000 employed in the industry in 1850, only 43,000 (approximately 11.5 percent of the total) were employed outside the factory system of organization. In terms of technology, the industry was virtually mechanized by this time: there were 20,977,000 spindles and 250,000 power looms in the industry in 1850. What is more, steam had become the dominant form of power used in the industry—71,000 horsepower supplied by steam as opposed to 11,000 supplied by water (Mitchell, 1962: 185, 187). Value added in the industry by this time exceeded by about 50 percent that in the woolen textile industry, the dominant industry in England for over four centuries. This rate of development was something that had never been experienced in any industry in the preindustrial world. Indeed, the Industrial Revolution in England, in the strict sense of the phrase, is little more than a revolution in eighteenth-century cotton textile production.

This extraordinary development of the cotton textile industry has been explained variously by modern writers. Like the general debate about the Industrial Revolution itself, the explanations fall within three areas of emphasis: whether the industry was revolutionized by the autonomous development of technology or by the pressure of demand; if the latter, whether the growth of internal or the growth of external demand offers the main explanation.[1] All of these explanations, however, suffer from one fundamental weakness: they are not posited within the framework of development economics, in spite of the important insights offered by recent advances in development studies.

One area of development studies with clear insights that are relevant to a study of the Industrial Revolution in England, but more to the revolution in cotton textile production, is the analysis of *import substitution industrialization* (usually referred to as ISI). ISI as an analytical concept has been well developed since the 1960s and applied to the study of industrial development in the Third World, especially Latin America (Hirschman, 1958, 1968; Chenery, 1960; Ahmad, 1978; Morawetz, 1974; Felix, 1968; Krueger, 1975; Baer and Maneschi, 1971; Bruton, 1970). Students of eighteenth-century industrialization in England are apparently unaware of the relevance of these studies to their subject. Their neglect of the insights offered by these studies has led them to pose the wrong questions in several instances, which has encouraged controversy to thrive. The analysis in this article is informed by the theoretical framework of import substitution industrialization.

The argument elaborated here is that the cotton textile industry developed in England in the eighteenth century as an import substitution industry, an industry whose products replaced those previously imported from India. As such, the industry expanded rapidly in the first few years on the basis of preexisting domestic demand. As the expansion reached the limits of the protected preexisting domestic market, stagnation set in. The crisis of stagnation was resolved through the exploitation of export opportunities in the transatlantic slave trade from Africa and in the slave-based economy of the Atlantic system. These early export opportunities were crucial to the subsequent transformation of the industry for a number of reasons. First, the larger market offered by export demand helped to enlarge the total number of firms in the industry at an early stage, which contributed to the development of its competitiveness. Second, the operation of the export producers outside the protected domestic market exposed them to stiff competition with cheap and high-quality Indian cotton goods in West Africa, and this induced them to adopt innovations that reduced costs and raised quality. These developments in the first three-quarters of the eighteenth century enabled the industry to successfully invade major European markets and those of the Americas from the late eighteenth century onward. The rapid expansion of exports which followed, together with the multiplier effects on the domestic market for cottons and other manufactures, provided the favorable environment for the rapid transformation of the industry's technology and organization between the late eighteenth and mid-nineteenth centuries.

A brief exposition of the theory and application of the concept of import substitution industrialization is offered in section 1. Section 2 examines the creation of a domestic market for cotton textiles in England through the import of East India cotton goods in the seventeenth century, and the subsequent development of a native cotton industry under import control measures adopted by the British government. The discussion and analysis in section 3 center on the development of the export sector of the industry on the basis of the slave trade and the slave economy of the Atlantic system. Section 4 summarizes the evidence and analyses in the preceding sections in order to demonstrate the overall implications.

1. IMPORT SUBSTITUTION INDUSTRIALIZATION

The term *import substitution industrialization* refers to a process of industrial development propelled by the substitution of domestically produced manufactures for previously imported ones. Early modern writers who employed the term in their analyses of the development process include Albert O. Hirschman (1958) and Hollis B. Chenery (1960). It has been suggested that Chenery was the first to apply the term as an analytical and measurable concept (Ahmad, 1978: 11). Chenery's problem was to identify the factors that could cause the industrial sectors to grow more rapidly than the rest of the economy during the development process and to measure their relative contributions. These factors he identified as "(1) the substitution of domestic production for imports; (2) growth in final use of industrial products; (3) growth in intermediate demand stemming from (1) and (2)" (Chenery, 1960: 639).

The second factor needs some elaboration. Growth in the final use of industrial products may come from one, or a combination, of three sources: a change in the composition of domestic final demand due to increases in per capita income; a change in the composition of domestic final demand arising from a social redistribution of income; the growth of external demand for manufactures. Increases in per capita income bias demand in favor of manufactured goods. The main explanation for this is Engels' law, that as the incomes of consumers increase beyond a certain level, the proportion spent on food declines. On the other hand, a redistribution of income in favor of the lower classes shifts demand to mass consumer goods, while a redistribution in favor of the upper classes concentrates demand on luxury products.

The third factor, the growth of intermediate demand stemming from the first and second factors, depends very much on the size of the domestic market because of the special properties of intermediate and capital goods, as will be shown below. However, a small country with an initially narrow domestic market can expand production for export in import substitution consumer goods industries. This will sufficiently increase the domestic market for intermediate and capital goods to allow the country to produce them efficiently domestically, in lieu of importing all or most of them.

The foregoing analysis maps out theoretically the factors to look for and measure in explaining disproportionate growth in any industrial sector.

Further development of the ISI concept and application of it to the study of historical cases in the more recent past reveal the essential characteristics of this pattern of industrial growth. One important characteristic is that there are two identifiable stages of import substitution industrialization. The first stage usually entails the domestic production of previously imported consumer goods, while the second stage involves the domestic replacement of previously imported intermediate goods, machinery, and consumer durables. During the first and easy phase, the sectors experiencing import substitution grow more rapidly than the rest of the economy. Once domestic production of import substitutes has been sufficiently expanded to absorb the preexisting demand, however, the growth rate of output declines to the rate of increase in domestic consumption. At this point, maintaining high industrial growth rates requires moving into either production for export or second-stage import substitution, or both (Balassa, 1981: 7).

Another important characteristic of import substitution industrialization is the state's provision of protection for the import substitution industries through the use of import duties, quotas, or prohibition. Depending on whether protection takes the form of moderate or high import duties or outright prohibition, import substitution industrialization tends to produce sellers' markets, especially in small countries with relatively narrow domestic markets. This limits competition and gives rise to high production costs, which in turn limit the growth of sales and therefore output.

What is more, moving from first- to second-stage import substitution industrialization entails considerable difficulties arising from the peculiar characteristics of intermediate and capital goods. These products tend to be highly capital-intensive and are subject to significant economies of scale. For efficient production, there has to be a sufficiently large market as costs rise quickly at lower levels of output (ibid.: 7).

In empirical studies of import substitution industrialization, one observes that third world countries undergoing this pattern of development fall into three categories: those that embarked on aggressive promotion of export production of manufactures after the completion of first-stage import substitution industrialization (Korea, Singapore, and Taiwan); those that moved into second-stage import substitution industrialization after completing the first stage, but later adopted export promotion policies in the face of difficulties (Brazil, Argentina, Colombia, and Mexico); and those that limited production virtually to the domestic market (India, Chile, and Uruguay). The performance of these three groups of countries may indicate the elements that are crucial to successful industrial development through import substitution.

Bela Balassa's (ibid.: 17) study of these groups of countries shows that the rate of capacity utilization was highest in the first group of countries and increased considerably in the second group after the countries adopted export promotion policies, while it remained low in the third group. Balassa's summary of his findings is best presented in his own words:

> Manufacturing employment increased by 10 to 12 per cent a year in Korea and Taiwan, leading to reductions in unemployment rates. *Pari passu* with the decline in unemployment, real wages increased rapidly as the demand for labor on the part of the manufacturing sector grew faster than the rate at which labor was released by the primary sector. After the 1966 policy reforms, real wages increased also in Brazil. By contrast, real wages declined in India, Chile, and Uruguay.
>
> Furthermore, income increments were achieved at a considerably lower cost in terms of investment in countries that consistently followed [an] outward-oriented strategy [export promotion]. . . .
>
> The operation of these factors gave rise to a positive correlation between exports and economic growth. The three Far Eastern countries had the highest GNP growth rates throughout the period [1960–73], and the four Latin American countries that undertook policy reforms [adoption of export promotion] considerably improved their growth performance after the reforms were instituted, while India, Chile, and Uruguay remained at the bottom of the growth league. [Ibid.: 18]

These findings agree with those of other studies (Morawetz, 1974; Felix, 1968; Krueger, 1975; Baer and Maneschi, 1971; Bruton, 1970). Thus, the theoretical literature demonstrates the contribution of import substitution to early industrial growth while indicating the problems that logically arise after the first stage of import substitution. The conclusions in the theoretical literature are confirmed by empirical studies, which show conclusively that opportunity for export production by import substitution industries offers the most effective solution to the problems which inevitably arise after the first stage of import substitution industrialization. These findings give important insights into the role of exports in an industrialization process propelled by import substitution in a predominantly market economy.

2. RISE OF THE BRITISH COTTON
TEXTILE INDUSTRY

It is quite difficult to give a precise date for the establishment of a cotton textile industry in England. However, the evidence suggests, and writers generally agree, that while cotton manufacture of a sort existed in England in the seventeenth century, the development of the industry was an eighteenth-century phenomenon. As P. J. Thomas (1926: 121) wrote,

> It is now really difficult for us to realize that 200 years ago hardly any genuine cotton cloth was made in England. It is true that "cottons" were spoken of even in the sixteenth century; and in the seventeenth we have definite records mentioning the manufacture of cloth from cotton wool imported from the Levant, but these were not genuine cotton cloth but the hybrid fustians made of linen warp and cotton weft. English artisans did not know in those days how to make cotton strong enough to serve for warp.[2]

The growth of the industry in England in the eighteenth century is a typical example of industrialization working its way through import substitution in the sense of Albert Hirschman's (1958: 123) postulate that "import fulfils the very important function of demand formation and demand reconnaissance for the country's entrepreneurs." In this particular instance, the role of imports was played by Indian cotton goods. The usual role of the state in the control of imports was also very crucial.

The English East India Company began test imports of East India cotton goods into England in 1613. Before then, the company had been involved in the sale of these goods in Indonesia in exchange for pepper and other spices which were later taken to England. At first only a few thousand pieces were imported. The company's sales in 1613 amounted to 5,000 pieces. They increased to 12,500 pieces in 1614. The company seems to have met with early success in the trial sales, as the imports increased considerably in the 1620s. One hundred thousand pieces were imported in 1620, 123,000 pieces in 1621, and 221,500 pieces in 1625. The imports declined in the 1630s but began to rise again towards the end of the decade (Chaudhuri, 1965: 191–193).

Table 1   East India textiles ordered by the English East India
Company, 1661–94

Year	Pieces
1661	253,000
1662	96,000
1663	292,000
1664	55,000
1669	298,000
1670	290,000
1671	376,000
1672	306,000
1673	555,500
1674–75	609,500
1675–76	711,500
1676–77	647,000
1677–78	643,000
1678–79	919,500
1679–80	715,000
1680–81	1,227,000
1681	1,370,000
1682	3,445,000
1683	2,522,000
1684–85	802,000
1686–87	501,000
1687–88	832,000
1688	1,671,000
1693	1,181,000
1694	1,400,000

Source: Krishna, 1924: ch. 6, appx. A, p. 301.
Note: The combined orders for 1696 and 1697 amounted to 2,571,000 pieces
(ibid.: 141).

From the middle decades of the seventeenth century, the East
India cotton goods built up considerable popularity among English consumers of all classes due to their cheapness, the high
quality of the texture, and the sheer beauty and fastness of their
colors (Table 1). Contemporary writers wrote about high-class
English ladies appearing "all the morning in muslin night-rails,"
visiting and receiving visitors in that dress. Even the queen and the
court ladies regularly wore Indian muslins and calicoes (Thomas,
1926: 29).

The Indian goods created in England new demand for cotton goods among the poorer classes, who previously could not afford the expensive woolen and silk goods produced in England. However, an important part of the demand for East India cotton goods by English consumers in the seventeenth and eighteenth centuries was the shift in demand from English woolen and silk goods.

As some of the East India textiles imported into England were later reexported to the British colonies, West Africa, and continental Europe, the quantities annually imported do not accurately represent the size of the English domestic market for cotton goods in the late seventeenth century. Evidence presented to the House of Commons in 1703 shows that during the years 1699–1702, East India goods of all kinds reexported from England, using the sales prices in London, amounted to £2,538,933. Of this, £1,053,725 was for calicoes and £536,210 for silk goods, or a total of £1,589,935 for all East India textiles reexported (Krishna, 1924: 138). Thus, for these four years, East India cotton goods reexported amounted to £263,431 per annum. For all East India textiles, the annual average for the same years was £397,484. It is safe to assume that the Indian cotton goods retained for the domestic market in the late seventeenth century could not have been less than the reexports. In fact, contemporary observers generally claimed that about one-half of all East India goods imported into England at this time were reexported (ibid.: 136–137).

Combining the foregoing evidence with the figures produced by Ralph Davis (1969a), we can form a reliable impression of the size of the domestic market for cotton textiles in England by the end of the seventeenth century. Davis's (ibid.: 96–97) figures show that East India calicoes imported into England for the years 1699–1701, as recorded in the import ledgers of the British Customs, amounted on average to £367,000 a year and the reexports to £340,000. The clear indication here is that the reexports were valued on the basis of sale prices in London. Since the sales value in London would have been at least double the purchase value in India as recorded in the import ledgers, the actual value of the imports for the years 1699–1701, at current prices in London, comes to £734,000. Deducting the reexports gives £394,000 for the yearly domestic consumption of East India cotton goods in England in those years.

As already noted, the imports of East India textiles for the domestic market and for reexports had adverse effects on the demand for woolen and silk goods produced in England. This provoked noisy agitation by the woolen and silk manufacturers in the late seventeenth century. With their political clout, the latter secured a protective act early in the eighteenth century. The law stipulated that from 29 September 1701, all silk goods and painted, dyed, printed, or stained calicoes imported into England from China or the East Indies could not be worn in England or Wales. The law allowed the prohibited goods to be imported and warehoused for reexportation; it also allowed white calicoes from India to be imported and printed in England for the domestic market and for export. Muslins were not affected by the law and were therefore free to be imported and sold for domestic consumption in England (Thomas, 1926: 114–115).

The prohibition of printed East India calicoes stimulated the growth of calico printing in England in the first two decades of the eighteenth century. Calico printing is said to have started in England in 1676 with methods copied from India; the goods were sold as East India products. But it was not until after the prohibition act that the cotton-printing industry expanded and developed to provide the foundation for the cotton textile industry in England. This expansion was so great that a contemporary observer wrote in 1706 that "greater quantities of calicoes had been printed and worn in England annually since the importing of it was prohibited than ever was brought from India" (ibid.: 125). The growth of the industry is reflected in the following import figures for white calicoes: 1717, 676,082 pieces; 1718, 1,220,324 pieces; 1719, 2,088,451 pieces (ibid.: 125, 162).[3]

Once again, the silk and woolen manufacturers called upon Parliament for more protection. Bowing to their pressure, Parliament first imposed import duties on the white calicoes and excise duties on the calicoes printed in England from the imported plain ones, on which import duties had already been paid. The printers calculated that all the duties put together amounted to 82 percent ad valorem (ibid.: 125–126). Not satisfied with the effects of these duties, Parliament then enacted a law, effective from 25 December 1722, prohibiting the consumption in England of printed, painted, stained, and dyed calicoes (ibid.: 160). Muslins, neckcloths, fustians, and calicoes dyed all blue were excepted. Printed East India calicoes could still be imported for reexport, and plain calicoes were allowed to be imported and printed for export. But the home market was closed for these goods.

While this extreme protectionism was intended to favor the woolen and silk industries, it was the cotton textile industry that reaped the benefits. The prohibition stimulated the domestic production of cotton goods for the printing industry, which had relied on imported white calicoes in the first decades of the eighteenth century (Wadsworth and Mann, 1931: 144). This is somewhat reflected in the sudden expansion of retained raw cotton imports between 1715 and 1724 (Deane and Cole, 1962: 51, Table 15). From this point we can begin to observe the development of cotton textile production in England as an import substitution industry, with all the expected characteristics.

There are no reliable figures of total output for the industry in the first half of the eighteenth century. What is available is the indirect evidence of retained raw cotton imports. The decennial averages for the period 1711–60, in pounds, are as follows: 1711–20, 1.48 million; 1721–30, 1.51 million; 1731–40, 1.72 million; 1741–50, 2.14 million; 1751–60, 2.76 million (computed from Mitchell, 1962: 177). The retained raw cotton import figures indicate that after the rapid expansion of the first two years following the promulgation of the new law (retained imports were over 2 million pounds in 1722 and 1723), there was stagnation for the rest of the decade. Hence, the average for the 1720s exceeded that for the preceding decade by only 2.0 percent. It is not quite clear whether this means that production was expanded to the limit of the preexisting domestic demand within a few years following the prohibition act. Other evidence seems to point in that direction. The existing estimates of total output in the industry indicate that the home market for cotton textiles in England grew very little, if at all, in the first half of the eighteenth century. According to the estimate by Postlethwayte, the gross value of output in the industry in 1766 was £600,000, of which £379,241 represented domestic consumption and £220,759 export (Hobson, 1926 [1894]: 44). If we recall the size of the domestic market for cotton textiles before the prohibitions of the early eighteenth century, we see that little or no growth took place in the first half of the century. Of course, it is true that some classes of Indian cotton goods, such as muslins, were still allowed into the domestic market. And some smuggling of the prohibited ones may have occurred (Thomas, 1926: 162). Hence, domestic sales of English cotton textiles would not represent the size of the entire domestic market for cotton goods during the period. Even so, the evidence suggests strongly that the growth of domestic demand for English cotton textiles after the completion of first-stage import substitution in the industry was decidedly slow.[4]

This seems to be borne out by the timing of the export drive by the cotton textile manufacturers. As has been suggested, "the international market is highly competitive and considerable effort is required to be successful. Few sensible entrepreneurs would choose to operate in that market if their alternative was a comfortable, sheltered domestic market" (Krueger, 1975: 114). The manufacturers must have been forced to look for markets abroad in the third and fourth decades of the eighteenth century as the expansion of output reached the limit of the preexisting demand. This is suggested by the evidence of the manufacturers presented to a House of Commons committee in 1751. Samuel Touchet of Manchester, owner of one of the largest firms in the industry at this time, stated that production of cottons mixed with linen had begun in England about "forty years ago" (that is, about 1711), and none of the products had been exported "till about twenty-five years since" (about 1736; House of Commons Reports 2, 1738–65: 290–293). Other export producers who testified gave similar dates for their entry into export production. For example, James Johnson of Spitalfields, a very large export producer at the time, said he had been in the business for "16 or 18 years" (that is, since 1735 or 1733; ibid.: 294–295). Another export producer, Thomas Tipping, who held that export was "the most advantageous" trade, stated that he had been in it for "15 or 16 years" (that is, since 1736 or 1735; ibid.: 293–294).[5]

It took some time for the English cottons to establish a reputation in the export markets. This is why the progress of the industry remained unimpressive throughout the first half of the eighteenth century. During this period, it has been observed, the industry "was a minor trade, little more than a subsidiary occupation for a few thousand agriculturalists" (Deane and Cole, 1962: 183). Through persistent effort by the manufacturers, however, overseas demand began to grow from the middle of the eighteenth century.

3. THE EXPORT MARKET

The export market that developed in these difficult decades of the cotton textile industry in England was dependent almost entirely on the slave economy of the Atlantic system. This is borne out by both quantitative and qualitative evidence.

Statistical evidence shows that the export centered on a mixture of cotton and linen checks. From appendix 1 below, it can be seen that this branch of the industry provided a preponderant share of total English cotton textile exports from 1750 to 1774, varying between 48 percent and 86 percent during the period. In fact, between 1751 and 1774, the lowest share of cotton and linen checks in total cotton exports was 56 percent in 1773. Except for that year and 1765, 1766, and 1774 (60 percent, 59 percent, and 59 percent, respectively), it remained above 60 percent; in the years 1753–58 it was above 80 percent. It is therefore clear that the export sector of the English cotton textile industry began with the check branch. The rapid expansion of the export sector in the last quarter of the century can be traced to the experience gathered in this branch.

The check manufacturers produced mainly for export, although a small quantity of their products was sold in the home market. Throughout the third quarter of the eighteenth century, cotton checks were the most important branch of the English cotton textile industry. The largest of the mercantile and manufacturing houses at this time were in the check branch. These men employed a large number of the weavers of Ashton, Oldham, and Royton. In 1758, one of them claimed to have five hundred weavers in his employ (Wadsworth and Mann, 1931: 173, 211, 243).

The important point to note is that the manufacture of cotton checks for export was almost entirely a function of the British slave trade from Africa and the employment of African slaves on plantations and in mines in the New World. The cotton check branch specialized in the production of goods in imitation of Indian piece goods for the market of West Africa. These goods also became very important as clothing material for the African slaves in the New World. For example, in 1739 the total export of English cotton checks amounted to £5,279. Of this, export to West Africa was £4,339, or 82.2 percent, and the rest went to the New World slave plantations. The figures in Table 2 illustrate the pattern up to the American War of Independence, specifi-

Table 2   Distribution of English cotton check exports in selected years

Year	Total export of cotton checks	West Africa		New World plantations	
1750	£ 9,743	£ 7,839	80.5%	£ 1,904	19.5%
1759	80,605	39,090	48.5	40,850	50.7
1769	142,302	97,972	68.8	40,597	28.5

Source: Wadsworth and Mann, 1931: 146, Table 2.

cally, that as the population of African slaves on the plantations in the eighteenth century increased, the export of English cotton checks to the New World colonies also increased. However, West Africa remained the main market for the cotton checks, except during a few war years. This is borne out by the more detailed information in appendix 1, which shows that between 1750 and 1802 the export of English cotton checks to West Africa was less than 50 percent of the total only in sixteen years, and that for most of these sixteen years the African share was above 40 percent. For the rest of this period of fifty-three years, the African share varied between 50 percent and 94 percent and often was 70 percent or more. When this variety of English cotton goods lost its popularity in West Africa, its exports gradually became insignificant.

The evidence thus makes it clear that the check branch of the English cotton textile industry owed its growth and development in the eighteenth century to the slave trade from Africa and New World slavery. Since it was demonstrated above that the export sector of the cotton industry was founded upon the export of cotton checks, the inference can be drawn that the development of the export sector was a function of the slave trade. It was when the check makers found their markets in West Africa and on the New World plantations interrupted by the American War of Independence that they turned their eyes to Europe.

Many check makers had manufactured some other varieties of cotton goods as a sideline to the production of checks for the slave trade when the check branch was the most important branch of the industry. When the check makers moved to Europe, it was natural that some of these varieties should be tried in the European markets. The discovery that "Manchester cottons and velverets" were popular among European consumers must have been the outcome of trial-and-error searching for a product suitable for a new market in the face of problems in the old markets. This variety was developed from the fustian branch (ibid.: 174–175), which was closely related to the check branch. Thus there was a relatively easy transfer from checks to the new leading branch.

The Manchester firm of William and Samuel Rawlinson, for example, which for a long time was a considerable producer of checks for the slave trade, had at the same time produced fustians as a sideline. When Samuel Rawlinson decided to give up the check branch, he concentrated on articles in the fustian branch. In his letter of 26 November 1789 to James Rogers, a Bristol slave trader, after reporting that he had given up the "check business," Rawlinson added, "P/S The cotton branch, say all kinds of fustians, muslinetts, dimitty, jeans, jeanett, cords, velitts [velverets?], etc., etc., is carried on as usual by W. & S. R. [William and Samuel Rawlinson] who will be glad to receive your favours in that line" (PRO, 1789). His brother, William, continued with the check business, and in April 1790 he complained to James Rogers of being short of capital, "for to be open I find myself at present so very poor on acct. of the large sums I have paid my brother since his relinquishing the African concern that it has caused such a diminution of capital that to up an old phrase, I am enabled to have half the number of eggs in the same basket as formerly" (PRO, 1790b).

Even Samuel Taylor, one of the largest producers of cotton checks for the slave trade in the last quarter of the eighteenth century, who boasted of specializing in the few products he could best manufacture, still combined checks with articles in the fustian branch. He wrote in April 1785 to inform James Rogers that

> the order you send us for 100 ps. of printed linen & calicoes with bordering is not an article that we manufacture and print, & it is not the practice of our house (Haberdasherlike) to clap on a profit upon everything we can lay our fingers on; we are anxious to both give satisfaction to our customers & get something by them too. Therefore we supply only our own manufacture & what we are masters of—those are the various articles in the CK [check] & stripes way for Africa, the West Indies & America. [PRO, 1785]

But he added, "Likewise the various articles in the Fustian Branch for any part" (ibid.).

It was the production of articles in the fustian branch as a sideline to checks that made the shift to Europe by check makers easy and successful. The evidence suggests very strongly that check manufacturers led the way in the development of cotton exports to Europe from 1775 onwards. It is particularly important that by the time the check makers turned to Europe, they had acquired much competitiveness from their long-drawn battle with East India piece goods in West Africa. In fact, it can be argued that the success of the English cotton textile industry in expanding the sale of its products in European markets in the last quarter of the eighteenth century resulted from the beneficial effects of protracted competition with Indian cottons in West Africa. This subject is very important for our analysis. It is therefore necessary to pursue it at some length.

As an import substitution industry, cotton textile production grew in England in the early eighteenth century in a protected domestic market. Although the import restriction and prohibition laws were not specifically designed for the cotton industry, naturally the domestic market for cotton goods created in England by the East India cottons was inherited by the English cotton industry. Under these circumstances, the industry had little or no opportunity for competition in the domestic market. Only those manufacturers who were compelled by the limited size of the home market to produce for export faced stiff competition with the Indian cottons that had been kept away from the English market by law. This competition occurred mainly in West Africa.

From the early years of English trade to West Africa, when the Royal African Company had a monopoly of it under a royal charter, East India cotton goods formed a large proportion of the exports. As the limited size of the domestic market forced some of the English cotton producers to move into the markets of West Africa, they came face to face with the Indian cottons. Here there was no question of the British government providing any protection, as all the European nations were entirely free to trade in West Africa and carry there whatever commodities they thought would sell. Under these conditions, English producers of cotton textiles in imitation of Indian piece goods for the West African markets had to stretch their ingenuity to be equal to the fight, which to some seemed futile; pamphleteers in England had begun to complain in the late seventeenth century of the impossibility of the English competing with Indian labor at a half penny a day (Davis,

1969a: 82). The English producers employed a simple method of advertisement. They requested officials of English companies resident on the African coast to promote among the inhabitants of the coastal states a comparison of English imitations with the Indian originals, noting the reaction of the African consumers.

To illustrate, in February 1750 the Committee of the English Company of Merchants Trading to Africa bought from Thomas Norris and Company of Chorley some cotton bafts of eighteen yards per piece at eighteen shillings each. In the letter accompanying the goods, Thomas Norris stated that he

> should be extremely glad to have them [his own bafts] compared with Indian bafts at the same price & if the committee of Company of Merchants trading to Africa would make further tryal by sending a few pieces in different ships to different parts of the Coast, that would be the readyest way to find out which goods have the preference, at the same time giving orders to their factors to take notice how such goods was [*sic*] approved of by the Negroes. [PRO, 1750]

In 1751, this firm claimed that the prices of its goods were already lower than those of their Indian equivalents. In a letter of 7 May 1751, the firm pointed out that though the goods sent to the English Company of Merchants were "charged higher than the price you there limit to us I make not the least doubt but they will be very agreeable if compared with India bafts that are 2 to 3s per piece higher & I should be greatly obliged to you to promote their being compared if [when] they are opened" (PRO, 1751a). Norris seems to have become so confident of the quality of the firm's products that he could ask the company to

> write upon them Chorley Superfine Cotton Bafts which I forgot than after they were packed. I here inclose you two partons [patterns] & Beg You'll shew them to some of the knowing ones. We are making a large quantity of them for the Liverpool merchants and are rather too Backwards with our orders or would have sent a piece of each sort by way of sample. [Ibid.]

English imitations of East India cotton goods seem to have established some reputation on the African coast by the 1750s. Thomas Melvil, governor of the English Company of Merchants, who was resident on the Gold Coast (Ghana), wrote to the company's committee in London in July 1751 that "to Windward Manchester checks and Grass green long Ells are greatly in demand," and reported that Manchester goods were as popular as Indian goods on the coast (PRO, 1751b). In 1753, he specifically asked for "large quantities of checks cross barred & Manchester" in "our supply" (PRO, 1753).[6] Then, in August 1754, Melvil reported, "If the Ashantee paths open, the goods wanted will be guns, Gunpowder, Pewter basons [basins], Brass pans, Knives, Iron, Cowries, Silks, The Bejutapauts will go out. Of these Touchet's are preferred to India" (PRO, 1754).[7]

These reports give the impression that English cotton manufacturers had ousted Indian cottons from West Africa by the 1750s. This was by no means the case. Subsequent decades saw further intense competition. What made the competition particularly difficult for the English producers was that English merchants trading to West Africa were confronted in the slave trade with merchants from other European nations. Since the slave trade from Africa was completely open to all nations, and the African traders bought freely from whoever sold goods of the best quality and at the lowest price, what determined one's success in the trade was the ability to sell goods in demand and at the lowest possible prices. English merchants, though they wished, from national attachment, to export homemade goods, were compelled by the conditions of the West African markets to export other goods that would not place them at a disadvantage with their European rivals. This fact is spelled out clearly in a memorial addressed to His Majesty's Treasury by the Merchants of Liverpool Trading to Africa in March 1765.

> The trade to Africa being free and open to all the Nations of Europe, it becomes necessary for your Memorialists, not only to carry such goods as are in demand, but also to be able to purchase them as cheap as other Nations, otherwise they can't long support the Rivalship, & this so valuable a branch of Commerce must inevitably languish and decay. That the East Indian Company for many years past, have not had a sufficient quantity of sundry sorts of Goods proper for the African Trade, denominated Prohibited Piece Goods etc. which has obliged your memorialists to send several ships to Holland for the same, the consequence of which is, a great

sum of money is laid out there, in buying other goods for assortments, as also, in the equipments of the ships, which wou'd otherwise have centred amongst the Manufacturers & others of this Kingdom. That the manufactures of this Kingdom exported to Africa are woollens, arms & other iron-ware, hats, gunpowder, brass and copper wares commonly called battery, Pewter, lead etc. as also checks & other goods made at Manchester in imitation of East India Goods, when the latter are at high prices, or not to be got, but some they cannot imitate & their imitation of many kinds is but indifferent. That the trade on the coast of Africa differs from the trade in civiliz'd Nations, & is carried on chiefly by Barter, the certain consequence of which is, if a ship there wants a commanding article brought by one of another Nation, the first must wait till the latter is dispatched, which is often fatal to the lives of the seamen & Negroes, & renders the success of the voyage very precarious. That your memoralists bound both by ties of inclination & interest, do always give the preference to the manufactures of their own country, & several branches of them, they can with pleasure say, have the preeminence, & it is with great reluctance they are forced to purchase any part of their cargoes elsewhere, but in so precarious a Trade as this, they must either have proper assortments of goods, or not adventure to those parts. [PRO, 1765]

These Liverpool merchants requested permission to go to the different markets in Europe and bring the required goods directly to their own port, "on payment of half the old subsidy, & to be kept in warehouses, under the locks of His Majesty's officers, for exportation to Africa only" (ibid.).

It was this peculiar character of the slave trade from Africa which imposed extra strains on the English check manufacturers in their struggle to take over the West African market from Oriental textiles. The evidence shows that they made an impressive effort, one aspect of which was their ready adoption of the available technology. Of all the English cotton manufacturers, they led the way in applying the textile inventions which transformed the cotton industry. The first of the series of inventions which revolutionized cotton textile production in England was Paul's spinning machine, patented on 24 June 1738. The first manufacturers who encouraged Paul with their patronage were check manufacturers supplying the markets in West Africa.

> Of the three men engaged in the cotton trade who took up the machine two—Johnson and Touchet—were intimately connected with the manufacture of checks for Africa, and their interest in cheap yarn of a quality comparable with that from India was evidently great enough to encourage them to take considerable risks in the hope of obtaining it. [Wadsworth and Mann, 1931: 447][8]

James Johnson purchased 150 spindles and Samuel Touchet 300 (ibid.: 427, 444–445). The spinning machine had to wait for later improvements before it became fully productive. However, the evidence shows clearly the dynamic attitude of the check producers supplying the African markets to available technology.

The Liverpool merchants, in their memorial, were unfair in some ways to the English cotton manufacturers. It may be assumed that by 1765 English imitations of Indian cottons still had some way to go to achieve perfection. But no doubt considerable progress had been made before the American War of Independence disrupted English cotton exports to West Africa. When the war was over, some producers who had switched their products to Europe may have failed to resume production for the slave trade, some may have combined both, but others did resume full-scale production of African goods. It is not correct to say that Manchester manufacturers failed in their competition with Indian cottons on the African coast in the eighteenth century (ibid.: 164).[9]

Appendix 2 shows the official figures of East India and English cottons exported from England to West Africa from 1751 to 1807. (The figures for East India cottons from 1751 to 1780 are in pieces only, so a direct comparison may not be easy to draw for these years.) English cottons seem to have made great progress; from £14,573 in 1751, they had reached £125,343 by 1767. Further progress was hampered by the political upheavals in the American colonies, which affected the slave trade. Indian goods were higher in value than English cottons in the early 1780s, but from 1783 to 1794 the competition was fairly even. From 1794 to 1801 Indian cottons again were significantly higher in value than English cottons; from 1802 to 1807 English cottons were back in full force.

The achievements of the English cottons were quite impressive, given that Indian cottons had completely dominated the West African market at the beginning of the eighteenth century. What is more important, however, is that the ceiling on English cotton exports to West Africa in the late eighteenth century seems to have been fixed not by the greater popularity of Indian cottons on the coast, but by the inability of the producers to expand production adequately to meet growing African demand. A combination of the quantitative and qualitative evidence for the years 1790 to 1792 points strongly to this conclusion.

On the basis of the statistics in appendix 2, it is clear that English cottons lost ground to East India cottons from 1786 to 1792, except for the sudden swell of English cottons in 1792. Export of East India cottons rose significantly in 1790, 1791, and 1792. When we turn to the qualitative evidence, however, we discover that, at least in 1790, 1791, and 1792, English cotton manufacturers producing African goods had more orders than they could fill. For example, in January 1790 Captain William Woodville wrote to James Rogers of Bristol, a slave trader:

> I arrived this morning in Manchester & applied to the different gentlemen here who deal in African goods & found everything bought up by the Liverpool people except a very small quantity & Mr. Rawlinson who had but few goods by him except the Romals you ordered some time since, advised me to look amongst the different manufacturers—but very kindly took that trouble upon himself & by using very great exertions he has procured a sufficient quantity for us. [PRO, 1790a]

A bill for one thousand pounds had to be drawn on Rogers for immediate payment for these goods, as Mr. Rawlinson was obliged to pay cash for them; "otherwise it had been impossible to procure a single piece" (ibid.).

The letter of Joseph Caton, a Liverpool merchant who undertook to prepare for the slave trade one of Rogers's vessels, is even more revealing. In December 1790 he wrote:

> Sir I received your letter at Mr. Robinsons and Heywoods and had at last engaged your two small cargoes but the Tradesmen at this time is rather full of orders as they say which I believe to be the case, and the short time allowed

to have them ready makes it more difficult to get what you want, particularly windward Coast goods as they cannot get weavers to work that article. . . . I must beg leave to tell you the cunning and art of these Old Tradesmen. In the first place, they are all combined together and you cannot do one thing with any of them but all the rest knows it before you get to the second House. . . . the Old Tradesmen is [*sic*] grown so arrogant that they compell one to do as they please. They keepd [kept] me running from one house to another for two days desiring I would try to get what I could at other houses. . . . I would advise you to divide your future orders equally amongst these people then you are sure of being served, for when you employ one man in general and goods much wanted as is often the case then your friend cannot supply you in your time, then you go to another, then he immediately says how do you expect me to supply you if you could get them at another House. [PRO, 1790c]

The letter of a manufacturing firm may serve to show some of the factors responsible for the supply problems. In May 1791 Robinson and Heywood wrote to James Rogers, "We have in hand engagements for more goods than we can manufacture in the next six weeks which must be sent as they come from the looms; and our workpeople are so much our masters at present that we cannot this spring add to our manufacture" (PRO, 1791). Finally, we may cite a letter from 1792, also from a manufacturer of African goods. William Green, writing to James Rogers and Company in November 1792, acknowledged receipt of their letter of "the 19th current" but complained that "Mr. Parke is not yet returned from Lpool and I don't know what engagements he may make during his absence, but from what I am acquainted with I am confident it will not be in his power to supply your order of the 1st inst. [instant] under five or six months" (PRO, 1792).

It is sufficiently evident from the foregoing that the ceiling for English cotton exports to West Africa in the late eighteenth century was not fixed by a limited demand for them on the African coast. On the contrary, the demand from exporters to West Africa was pressing exceedingly hard on limited production capacity. As some of the above letters show, the supply of labor seems to have been one of the crucial bottlenecks for cotton manufacturers producing African goods in the late eighteenth century. In regard to popularity, Manchester manufacturers can be said to have achieved remarkable success in their competition with Indian cottons in West Africa. In fact, they were so successful that even before Manchester cottons had really established their supremacy in Europe, manufacturers producing African goods had begun to supply them to continental merchants trading to Africa.

The success achieved by English producers in the manufacture of cotton textiles for the slave trade was the first development in the cotton industry to catch the eye of continental merchants; it served to popularize the industry's products with continental consumers. Samuel Taylor told a Privy Council committee in 1788 that

> about twelve months after the Peace, various French African Merchants from Bourdeaux, Nantes, but particularly from Havre, came over here, and examined the species of goods destined for Africa in several warehouses, but particularly in my own, and expressed their surprise at the quality and Price of these goods, the expedition with which they can be furnished, and the credit at which they were sold, and they told me that if I or any other capital manufacturer would establish a House of the same extent, and upon the same plan at Rouen, they should be ready to give me, or such manufacturer every encouragement from Government. [PRO, 1788b]

In answer to a question, Taylor told the committee that before the Anglo-French Commercial Treaty of 1786, "all Manchester goods destined for the African trade were . . . by a special Edict, allowed to be imported into France free of Duty, and warehoused for that purpose" (ibid.).[10] If France, of all countries, depended on Manchester cottons for her slave trade, it can be safely said that no slave trader on the continent could do without Manchester cottons in the late eighteenth century.

As we have seen, the protracted competition of Manchester cottons with East India piece goods in West Africa and the level of achievement attained there were important elements in the growth of Manchester exports to Europe in the last quarter of the eighteenth century. The link is further demonstrated by the share of West Africa and the New World plantations in the total export of

English cottons in the eighteenth century. For example, in 1722–24, exports to West Africa and the plantations accounted for 83 percent of the official value of all English cotton exports; in 1752–54, for 94 percent; and in 1772–74, for 80 percent (Davis, 1969b: 120). Additional details of exports to West Africa are shown in appendix 1. Column 6 shows the share of English cottons exported to West Africa as a percentage of total English cotton exports from 1750 to 1807. It can be seen that the West African markets predominated from 1750 to 1775. During this period of twenty-six years, the share was 40 percent or above in eleven years. For most of the other years, it was above 30 percent; at its lowest, it was 29 percent in 1757 and 1762.

The disturbances in the American colonies and the war that followed caused the share of cotton exports to West Africa to fall off from 1774 onwards and reach a new low in 1780; from 1774 to 1781 the check makers switched to Europe. Arthur Young had been told in 1769 that the interruption caused by the political upheavals in the American colonies was deeply felt by every workman in the check branch (cited in Wadsworth and Mann, 1931: 164), and by the time war actually broke out and trade to West Africa and the New World plantations came to a virtual halt, the effects of the dislocation on the check makers must have been very serious indeed. Their turning to Europe can be seen in the sudden expansion of exports of Manchester cottons to Europe after 1775. The records show no exports up to 1770. In 1775, the exports were worth £74,683; in 1776, £86,384; in 1777, £110,185; in 1778, £117,447; in 1779, £207,626; and in 1780, £159,565 (ibid.: 169, Table 8). That the product found to be popular in Europe was within the fustian branch of the industry is quite significant, if we recall the link between the fustian branch and the check branch. These manufacturers could now apply the lessons they learned from their operation in the West African markets to Europe, where they were also confronted with East India cottons (ibid.: 141).[11]

4. SUMMARY AND CONCLUSIONS

We can now pull together the implications of the foregoing discussion for the revolution in cotton textile production in England. It has been established in the article that the cotton textile industry in England grew as an import substitution industry in the late seventeenth and the eighteenth centuries. In section 1, the characteristics of import substitution industrialization were logically and empirically demonstrated. Again, a central tendency of industrial growth propelled by import substitution is rapid expansion during the first few years of first-stage import substitution, followed by protracted stagnation as production expands to the limit of preexisting domestic demand. The evidence marshalled above shows that the cotton textile industry in England displayed this tendency in the first half of the eighteenth century. It was also logically and empirically established in section 1 that the most effective way to sustain rapid industrial growth after the completion of the first and easy phase of import substitution is through the expansion of export production in the import substitution industries. Again, this was exactly what the cotton manufacturers did from the 1730s.

The implication of the evidence and analysis presented here, therefore, is that it was the rapid expansion of the export sector from the middle decades of the eighteenth century that solved the problem of stagnation for the English cotton textile industry in the eighteenth century. As this expansion of export production provided growing employment and income for the lower classes, it contributed to the growth of population and the domestic market for mass consumer goods in England.[12] It is important to note that the other industrial sectors, such as the linen industry and metal manufacturing, were also expanding at the same time through import substitution, and that they followed the pattern of the cotton industry in developing a rapidly growing export sector after the first stage of import substitution.[13] All these contributed to the growth of the domestic market. The cotton industry, because the character of its products makes it a mass industry par excellence, was a major beneficiary of this expansion of the domestic market.

Even so, the export market continued to grow more rapidly. Table 3 shows the relative shares of exports and domestic consumption in the value of the total output of cotton textiles from 1760 to 1817. Apart from the years of the American War of Independence, when exports were disrupted, the table shows clearly both the magnitude and the higher rate of growth of the export sector.[14] It was the rapid growth of the market for cotton textiles, stimulated largely by the growth of exports, that created the con-

Table 3   Share of exports and domestic consumption in gross value of English cotton textiles

Year	Gross value cotton textiles (£ million)	Export at current prices (£ million, %)		Domestic consumption (£ million, %)	
1760	0.6	0.2	33.3	0.4	66.7
1772–74	0.8	0.3	37.5	0.5	62.5
1781–83	3.0	0.6	20.0	2.4	80.0
1784–86	5.4	1.1	20.4	4.3	79.6
1787–89	7.0	1.5	21.4	5.5	78.6
1795–97	10.0	3.5	35.0	6.5	65.0
1798–1800	11.1	6.8	61.3	4.3	38.7
1801–3	15.0	9.3	62.0	5.7	38.0
1805–7	18.9	12.5	66.1	6.4	33.9
1811–13	28.3	17.4	61.5	10.9	38.5
1815–17	30.0	17.4	58.0	12.6	42.0

Source: Deane and Cole, 1962: 185, Table 42.
Note: There is a discrepancy between the gross value of cottons and the sum of value added and value of retained raw cotton imports in Deane and Cole's original table. The gross value of cotton textiles in the above table is the sum of retained cotton imports and value added as shown in Deane and Cole's original table. To eliminate some errors detected in the exports as shown by Deane and Cole, we have used their method of converting the official values to current values with the customs figures presented in appendix 1. Only the figures for the years 1801–17 are taken directly from Deane and Cole's original table.

ditions for the technological innovations in the industry in the late eighteenth century.

The production of textile machines in England in the eighteenth century may be likened to movement into second-stage import substitution industrialization in present-day third world countries. It should be noted that third world countries undergoing import substitution industrialization have the difficult problem of overcoming the temptation to import intermediate goods and machinery because they are available in the world market. England, on the other hand, had the problem of inventing them, because they did not yet exist. In either case, however, the market requirement is essentially the same. Eighteenth-century England was certainly a small country. At the point in the first half of the century when production was expanded to the limit of the preexisting demand, the size of the domestic market for cotton textiles in England was far too small to have stimulated the production of cotton machines and their adoption by cotton manufacturers. The evidence also shows that the rate of growth of domestic consumption of cotton textiles, after the completion of first-stage import substitution, was decidedly low. Such slow growth could not have provided the market conditions for the production of cotton textile machinery. The rapid growth of cotton exports from the middle decades of the eighteenth century created pressures which stimulated the inventions. These pressures can be seen from the sample letters of traders and manufacturers cited in section 3, which show the pressure of exporters' demand. What is more, a large enough market was provided to make the production of cotton textile machines economical and their employment in cotton production profitable.

We have demonstrated that the export sector grew out of the production of cotton textiles for the slave trade in Africa and for the clothing of the African slaves on the New World plantations. This point cannot be overstressed; the evidence for it is overwhelming. To summarize, we can do no better than let the manufacturers who knew the industry well speak. Samuel Taylor, who was commissioned by the Manchester cotton manufacturers to present their case to the Privy Council committee on the slave trade in 1788, stated:

The value of goods annually supplied from Manchester and the Neighbourhood for Africa, is about £200,000, from which, if I deduct the small value which is taken for the purchase of wood, Ivory, etc. which cannot amount to £20,000, there remains upwards of £180,000, for the purchase of Negroes only. This value of manufactures employs immediately about 18,000 of His Majesty's subjects, men, women and children. . . . This manufacture employs a capital of at least £300,000 including that part of the capital which belongs to the Dealers in the materials who sell them to the manufacturer. The coarse kinds of goods serve for a School or means of improvement to Workmen to enable them in time to work finer goods. Besides the manufactures which are directly furnished by the manufacturers of Manchester for the African trade, they equally furnish for the West India Trade, which is intimately connected with the former, upwards of £300,000 a year worth of manufactures, in the making of which a still greater number of hands are employed. [PRO, 1788a][15]

Even in the last decade of the century, when the European and American markets had become far more important, the Manchester cotton manufacturers were still sufficiently disturbed by the attempt in the House of Commons to abolish the export of slaves by British traders to non-British colonies to issue the following petition:

> During the extreme distress which for several months past has prevailed, and now prevails, among the manufacturing poor of this country, occasioned by the stagnation of Trade, and the depression of commercial credit, it has been [a] matter of great satisfaction to the petitioners, that they have been able, by the stock of goods which they have been encouraged to provide for the African trade, to give employment to very great numbers of the said poor. [House of Commons Journals 49, 1794]

The prolonged competition with Indian cottons in West Africa was particularly important in building efficiency and competitiveness into the industry at an early stage. We have shown the dynamic attitude towards the available technology of the producers who supplied the African market, a fact connected with the competition offered by the Indian cottons in West Africa. The technologically innovative activities of these producers must have had a significant demonstration effect on the other producers in the industry. The application of the analytical framework of import substitution industrialization to the available evidence thus makes it clear that the revolution in cotton textile production in England owed a great deal to the slave trade from Africa and African slavery in the New World.[16]

Appendix 1   Percentage shares in English cotton goods exported from England, 1750–1807

	From England to all parts		From England to West Africa		Percentage shares		
	1	2	3	4	5	6	7
	All cottons exported	Cotton and linen checked	All cottons exported	Cotton and linen checked	2 as %	3 as %	4 as %
Year	(£)	(£)	(£)	(£)	of 1	of 1	of 2
1750	20,155	9,743	7,839	7,839	48	39	80
1751	43,548	29,585	14,573	13,969	68	33	47
1752	73,045	57,871	35,752	35,747	79	49	62
1753	115,355	96,181	67,328	67,328	83	58	70
1754	85,049	73,192	49,740	49,740	86	58	68
1755	65,491	54,347	28,503	28,503	83	44	52
1756	100,888	84,993	35,486	35,486	84	35	42
1757	124,129	101,319	35,918	35,918	82	29	35
1758	116,284	94,515	47,565	47,565	81	41	50
1759	112,863	80,605	39,125	30,090	71	35	49
1760	167,022	125,174	52,264	52,264	75	31	42
1761	151,218	108,066	59,672	55,570	71	39	51
1762	183,003	127,203	52,413	51,832	70	29	41
1763	399,203	302,683	119,402	118,242	76	30	39
1764	200,190	140,107	100,438	99,067	70	50	71
1765	248,852	148,599	119,925	102,640	60	48	69
1766	223,503	132,376	85,784	85,020	59	38	64
1767	272,822	182,019	125,343	112,387	67	46	62
1768	213,265	133,181	64,568	63,480	62	30	48
1769	211,604	142,302	98,674	97,972	67	47	69
1770	198,824	122,761	72,702	70,833	62	37	58
1771	310,802	210,332	118,486	116,250	68	38	55
1772	245,247	161,050	123,711	121,714	66	50	76
1773	180,655	101,884	72,190	69,799	56	40	69
1774	258,049	152,932	95,544	92,961	59	37	60
1775	252,427	83,146	76,132	71,850	33	30	86
1776	289,434	103,853	91,480	90,000	36	32	87
1777	245,550	44,286	31,368	30,135	18	13	68
1778	191,157	18,429	14,148	14,117	10	7	76
1779	303,357	23,496	8,402	7,825	8	3	33
1780	306,156	17,754	4,995	4,716	6	2	27
1781	296,385	18,101	17,304	12,324	6	6	68
1782	405,005	50,498	48,777	45,031	12	12	89

Appendix 1—Continued

	From England to all parts		From England to West Africa		Percentage shares		
	1	2	3	4	5	6	7
	All cottons exported	Cotton and linen checked	All cottons exported	Cotton and linen checked	2 as %	3 as %	4 as %
Year	(£)	(£)	(£)	(£)	of 1	of 1	of 2
1783	746,291	165,597	162,724	151,648	22	22	91
1784	847,603	155,394	141,735	124,722	18	17	80
1785	826,368	130,081	147,892	118,630	16	18	91
1786	872,415	263,189	279,864	247,481	30	32	94
1787	1,025,067	109,024	111,666	92,027	11	11	84
1788	1,149,753	173,068	175,137	150,659	15	15	87
1789	1,089,229	117,236	121,501	97,865	11	11	83
1790	1,456,268	244,446	200,977	174,656	17	14	71
1791	1,636,838	180,197	188,535	148,682	11	12	83
1792	1,921,930	328,945	437,370	287,310	17	23	87
1793	1,653,260	100,716	128,867	66,531	6	8	66
1794	2,279,901	231,429	206,511	152,176	10	9	66
1795	2,308,539	127,143	69,231	46,475	6	3	37
1796	3,061,495	232,766	134,786	93,334	8	4	40
1797	2,464,376	229,972	133,980	105,574	9	5	46
1798	3,621,516	207,624	204,645	130,783	6	6	63
1799	5,859,289	90,295	317,381	46,507	2	5	52
1800	5,851,449	30,032	166,259	7,530	1	3	25
1801	6,941,281	116,317	187,163	44,998	2	3	49
1802	7,666,757	70,065	336,306	33,728	1	4	48
1803	7,143,361	8,034	288,246	—	0	4	0
1804	8,791,554	18,113	352,304	253	0	4	1
1805	9,652,816	11,731	282,834	—	0	3	0
1806	10,482,250	23,462	418,982	250	0	4	1
1807	10,287,301	3,168	270,274	—	0	3	0

Sources: Columns 1 and 2: Schumpeter, 1960: 29–34, Tables 10 and 11. England and Wales, 1750–91; Great Britain, 1792–1807. Columns 3 and 4, 1750–80: Customs 3/50-80; 1781–1807: Customs 17/7-29.

Note: Percentages are rounded to the nearest whole number.

Appendix 2   Official value of East India and English cotton goods exported from England to West Africa, 1750–1807

| Year | East India cottons | | English cottons |
	Pieces	Value (£)	Value (£)
1750	—	—	7,839
1751	54,958	—	14,573
1752	42,683	—	35,752
1753	20,580	—	67,328
1754	33,385	—	49,740
1755	30,831	—	28,503
1756	31,090	—	35,486
1757	17,390	—	35,918
1758	24,328	—	47,565
1759	72,032	—	39,125
1760	71,440	—	52,264
1761	52,606	—	59,672
1762	40,100	—	52,413
1763	63,037	—	119,402
1764	74,917	—	100,438
1765	50,974	—	119,925
1766	52,635	—	85,784
1767	74,908	—	125,343
1768	97,368	—	64,568
1769	110,181	—	98,674
1770	113,637	—	72,702
1771	138,145	—	118,486
1772	149,896	—	123,711
1773	127,455	—	72,190
1774	147,297	—	95,544
1775	147,513	—	76,132
1776	71,876	—	91,480
1777	36,794	—	31,368
1778	28,224	—	14,148
1779	45,226	—	8,402
1780	63,071	—	4,995
1781	80,419	72,622	17,304
1782	76,319	71,244	48,777
1783	154,675	153,212	162,724
1784	122,846	122,545	141,735
1785	128,265	116,390	147,898
1786	183,453	175,778	279,864
1787	176,697	186,258	111,666

Appendix 2—Continued

	East India cottons		English cottons
Year	Pieces	Value (£)	Value (£)
1788	186,780	165,744	175,137
1789	136,573	171,454	121,501
1790	185,032	222,051	200,977
1791	191,406	241,674	188,535
1792	413,652	348,809	437,370
1793	71,717	93,133	128,867
1794	170,664	213,275	206,511
1795	133,059	159,024	69,231
1796	168,984	214,560	134,786
1797	236,376	289,332	133,980
1798	372,187	437,852	204,645
1799	394,595	464,952	317,381
1800	366,491	402,729	166,259
1801	354,689	408,769	187,163
1802	258,334	306,561	336,306
1803	200,951	235,491	288,246
1804	342,313	389,479	352,304
1805	279,580	322,666	282,834
1806	312,786	364,315	418,982
1807	152,462	175,119	270,274

Sources: Columns 1 and 2, 1751–80: Wadsworth and Mann, 1931: 160; 1781–1807: Customs 17/7-29. Column 3, 1750–80: Customs 3/50-80; 1781–1807: Customs 17/7-29.

NOTES

1 Much of the explanation is implicitly stated in works whose main concern is the Industrial Revolution rather than the cotton textile industry per se. Some of the main works arguing the case of autonomous scientific, technical, and technological development include Musson, 1972: introd., and Mokyr, 1977; for an opposing view see Inikori, 1987: 775–76n.5; see also Hall, 1974. For a work relating specifically to the British textile industries, see Coleman, 1973. As Coleman (ibid.: 12–13) puts it, "If applied science, which was undoubtedly important at some stages and in some sectors of the industrial revolution, contributed hardly anything to the onset of that mechanisation, towards which so little progress had been made earlier, then the implication is surely that economic pressures must have become remarkably urgent; or at least that contemporaries came rapidly to see them

as so pressing that relief could no longer be obtained in the traditional way but had to be sought via a new way."

2   For the early history of the cotton textile industry in England, see also Wadsworth and Mann, 1931. Thomas Ellison's view is also the same as that of P. J. Thomas, quoted in the text. Ellison (1968 [1886]: 3) wrote that "the first recorded import of cotton into England took place in 1298. It was used for the manufacture of candle-wicks. . . . Mention is made of 'Manchester cottons' as early as 1352 and at various dates down to 1641; but these were really not cotton goods, but fabrics composed of wool and cotton or linen and cotton."

3   The growth of cotton printing in the first two decades of the eighteenth century means that raw cotton imports do not give an accurate indication of the quantity of cotton goods available for domestic consumption and for export. Nor do they give a proper picture of the infant cotton industry at this time. Thus, while cotton printing was expanding, retained imports of raw cotton stagnated between 1695 and 1714 (see Deane and Cole, 1962: 51, Table 15).

4   Application of the import substitution framework makes it easy to see the error in the thesis by A. H. John (1969) that the fall in food prices in the first half of the eighteenth century released workers' incomes for the consumption of manufactured goods, and that this led to the growth of the domestic market, which in turn stimulated industrial growth during the period. The contribution of the domestic market to industrial growth in England in the first decades of the eighteenth century was through import substitution and not through the growth of final domestic demand for manufactures. The evidence shows that very little happened in the latter area. (Import substitution industrialization in early-eighteenth-century England included a number of other industries apart from the cotton textile industry.)

5   As will be shown later, the West African market was the first important export market for the English cotton manufacturers. There is clear, though indirect, evidence that the English cotton manufacturers were not yet much interested in that market in the first two decades of the eighteenth century. This is suggested by the total absence of petitions from cotton manufacturers during the great struggles between the Royal African Company and the private traders over the African trade in the late seventeenth and early eighteenth centuries. A large number of petitions came from woolen manufacturers, some supporting the company and others supporting the case of the private traders. But there were none from cotton manufacturers (see House of Commons Journals 16). This indirectly confirms that in the first two decades or so of the eighteenth century, the cotton manufacturers concentrated their efforts on the protected domestic market. Some limited quantity of fustians had been exported since the late seventeenth century. But they did not command much external demand. The export market developed around cotton checks, the type produced by Samuel Touchet from about the second decade of the eighteenth century.

6   The salaries of the company's officials resident on the coast of West Africa were paid in goods supplied from England. These goods were sold by the

officials to the African consumers on the coast. As the popularity of the goods among the African consumers determined the governors' purchasing power, they took pains to ensure that only goods in popular demand were sent down from England.

7 Samuel Touchet was a wealthy Manchester cotton manufacturer who produced considerable quantities of cotton checks for the slave trade. The "Bejutapauts" were a variety of East India cotton goods. Their English imitations went by the same name.

8 Mann states earlier that "the first manufacturer to be associated with him [Paul] was James Johnson the younger, of Spitalfields, who had begun to make goods for the African trade in 1735 and had carried on business on a large scale. It will be remembered that by 1740 imitations of Indian cottons for Africa had had a considerable success. Good and cheap yarn was essential for them, and London was dependent on imported yarn, of which there must have been a shortage in 1738–40" (Wadsworth and Mann, 1931: 425).

9 This view may be due to the fact that Wadsworth and Mann (1931) end their study with 1780. Furthermore, they are wrong to say that by 1780 checks had ceased to be an important branch of the cotton industry (ibid.: 166). The share of checks in total cotton exports fell during the war but rose again afterwards, reaching 30 percent by 1786. Though it then continued to decline, it remained significant until after 1793, when it fell off rapidly (see appx. 1, col. 5).

10 During one of the seminars at the Institute of Historical Research, University of London, F. Crouzet, an eminent French economic historian and a participant, confirmed Taylor's evidence concerning the edict on Manchester African goods imported into France.

11 According to Wadsworth and Mann (1931), the use of Indian cottons was not prohibited in Germany, Holland, or Switzerland. Indian cotton goods thus dominated these countries' domestic markets.

12 For a demonstration of the relationship between the growth of manufactured goods export, population growth, and the expansion of the domestic market for mass consumer goods in England in the eighteenth century, see Inikori, 1987.

13 The details of this point are being worked out in a manuscript in progress.

14 The extraordinary expansion of domestic consumption during the war years was associated with increased government spending that greatly expanded employment and income for the middle and lower classes.

15 On 8 March Samuel Taylor further informed the committee that he had "been concerned in this Trade [the manufacture of cotton textiles] for 27 years; about three fourths of my trade is in goods for Africa, and the rest for the West Indies; I have raised and supported by it a family of ten children" (PRO, 1788b).

16 It should be noted that we have not treated the contribution of slavery to the relatively low cost of the industry's raw material, cotton. Since demand for the industry's product was highly price-elastic, the price of the industry's raw materials is clearly important in determining the level of

sales and output. Initially, the raw cotton came from the slave plantations of the Caribbean, but between 1790 and 1860, the slave plantations of the southern U.S. cheaply provided the bulk of it. Thus the contribution of slavery to the growth of the industry did not end when England abolished the slave trade in 1807. Indeed, the expansion of British exports to Latin America in the first half of the nineteenth century was very much connected to the slave economy of Latin America. A comprehensive assessment of the contribution of slavery to the revolution in cotton textile production in England will have to include these important considerations.

REFERENCES

Ahmad, Jaleel (1978) Import Substitution, Trade and Development. Greenwich, CT: JAI.

Baer, Werner, and Andrea Maneschi (1971) "Import substitution, stagnation and structural change: An interpretation of the Brazilian case." Journal of Developing Areas 5: 177–192.

Balassa, Bela (1981) The Process of Industrial Development and Alternative Development Strategies. Princeton: Princeton University, Department of Economics, International Finance Section.

Bruton, Henry J. (1970) "The import substitution strategy of economic development: A survey." Pakistan Development Review 10: 123–146.

Chaudhuri, K. N. (1965) The English East India Company: The Study of an Early Joint-Stock Company 1600–1640. London: Frank Cass.

Chenery, Hollis B. (1960) "Patterns of industrial growth." American Economic Review 50: 624–654.

Coleman, D. C. (1973) "Textile growth," in N. B. Harte and K. G. Ponting (eds.) Textile History and Economic History: Essays in Honour of Miss Julia de Lacy Mann. Manchester: Manchester University Press: 1–21.

Davis, Ralph (1969a) "English foreign trade, 1660–1700," in W. E. Minchinton (ed.) The Growth of English Overseas Trade in the Seventeenth and Eighteenth Centuries. London: Methuen: 78–98.

———(1969b) "English foreign trade, 1700–1774," in W. E. Minchinton (ed.) The Growth of English Overseas Trade in the Seventeenth and Eighteenth Centuries. London: Methuen: 99–120.

Deane, Phyllis, and W. A. Cole (1962) British Economic Growth, 1688–1959: Trends and Structure. Cambridge: Cambridge University Press.

Ellison, Thomas (1968 [1886]) The Cotton Trade of Great Britain. London: Frank Cass.

Felix, David (1968) "The dilemma of import substitution—Argentina," in Gustav F. Papanek (ed.) Development Policy—Theory and Practice. Cambridge: Harvard University Press: 55–91.

Hall, A. Rupert (1974) "What did the Industrial Revolution in Britain owe to science?" in Neil McKendrick (ed.) Historical Perspectives: Studies in English Thought and Society in Honour of J. H. Plumb. London: Europa Publications: 129–151.

Hirschman, Albert O. (1958) The Strategy of Economic Development. New Haven: Yale University Press.

————— (1968) "The political economy of import-substituting industrialization in Latin America." Quarterly Journal of Economics 82: 1–32.

Hobson, J. A. (1926 [1894]) The Evolution of Modern Capitalism: A Study of Machine Production. London: Walter Scott.

House of Commons Journals 16 (1708–11).

House of Commons Journals 49 (1794) Petition of the manufacturers of the Town of Manchester to the House of Commons: 304.

House of Commons Reports 2 (1738–65).

Inikori, Joseph E. (1987) "Slavery and the development of industrial capitalism in England." Journal of Interdisciplinary History 17: 771–793.

John, A. H. (1969) "Aspects of English economic growth in the first half of the eighteenth century," in W. E. Minchinton (ed.) The Growth of English Overseas Trade in the Seventeenth and Eighteenth Centuries. London: Methuen: 165–183.

Krishna, Bal (1924) Commercial Relations between India and England (1601 to 1757). London: G. Routledge.

Krueger, Anne O. (1975) The Benefits and Costs of Import Substitution in India: A Microeconomic Study. Minneapolis: University of Minnesota Press.

Mitchell, B. R. (1962) Abstract of British Historical Statistics. Cambridge: Cambridge University Press.

Mokyr, Joel (1977) "Demand vs. supply in the industrial revolution." Journal of Economic History 37: 981–1008.

Morawetz, David (1974) "Employment implications of industrialization in developing countries: A survey." Economic Journal 84: 491–542.

Musson, A. E. [ed.] (1972) Science, Technology and Economic Growth in the Eighteenth Century. London: Methuen.

Public Record Office (PRO), United Kingdom. Customs 3 and 17, Ledgers of Imports and Exports of Great Britain.

————— (1750) Thomas Norris and Co. to Committee of the English Company of Merchants Trading to Africa, 25 February. T. 70/1516.

————— (1751a) Thomas Norris to William Hollier (secretary to the African Company), Chorley, 7 May. T. 70/1516.

————— (1751b) Thomas Melvil to Committee, Cape Coast Castle, 23 July. T. 70/1520.

————— (1753) Thomas Melvil to Committee, Cape Coast Castle, 24 April. T. 70/1520.

————— (1754) Thomas Melvil to Committee, 10 August. T. 70/1523.

————— (1765) Memorial of the Merchants of Liverpool Trading to Africa to the Commissioners of His Majesty's Treasury, 16 March. T. 1/447/LA17.

————— (1785) Samuel Taylor to James Rogers and Co., Manchester, 29 April. C. 107/8.

————— (1788a) Evidence Taken before the Committee of Privy Council Appointed by an Order in Council, 11 February 1788, to Consider the State of the African Trade; Evidence of Samuel Taylor, 6 March. BT. 6/12.

————— (1788b) Evidence Taken before the Committee of Privy Council Appointed by an Order in Council, 11 February 1788, to Consider the State of the African Trade; Evidence of Samuel Taylor, 8 March: 309–317. BT. 6/9.

———— (1789) Samuel Rawlinson to James Rogers and Co., Manchester, 26 November. C. 107/9.

———— (1790a) Captain William Woodville to James Rogers, Manchester, 29 January. C. 107/13.

———— (1790b) William Rawlinson to James Rogers and Co., Manchester, 2 April. C. 107/9.

———— (1790c) Joseph Caton to James Rogers, Liverpool, 2 December. C. 107/13.

———— (1791) Robinson and Heywood to James Rogers and Co., Manchester, 13 May. C. 107/8.

———— (1792) William Green to James Rogers and Co., Manchester, 23 November. C. 107/10.

Schumpeter, E. B. (1960) English Overseas Trade Statistics 1697–1808. Oxford: Oxford University Press.

Thomas, P. J. (1926) Mercantilism and the East India Trade: An Early Phase of the Protection v. Free Trade Controversy. London: P. S. King.

Wadsworth, A. P., and J. de L. Mann (1931) The Cotton Trade and Industrial Lancashire. Manchester: Manchester University Press.

7
Private Tooth Decay
as Public Economic Virtue:
The Slave-Sugar Triangle,
Consumerism, and
European Industrialization

RALPH A. AUSTEN AND

WOODRUFF D. SMITH

> The only group of clear gainers from the British trans-Atlantic slave trade, and even those gains were small, were the European consumers of sugar and tobacco and other plantation crops. They were given the chance to purchase dental decay and lung cancer at somewhat lower prices than would have been the case without the slave trade. [Thomas and Bean 1974: 914]

ALTHOUGH the quotation above represents a radical departure from earlier economic assessments of the Atlantic slave trade, it shares with them an almost universal assumption: that the real significance of the Atlantic sugar triangle lay in its contribution to the productive capacity of Europe. Thus, concluding that only consumers "benefited" is tantamount to reducing the slave trade to economic triviality. This view of import trades has informed historical understanding not only of the factors leading to industrialization in Europe but also of those apparently retarding similar development in the Third World, including Africa and the West Indies (Bairoch 1975: 198–99).

In the present article we suggest that the slave and sugar trade (along with the importation of other "colonial goods") was essential to European industrial development precisely because it stimulated and ultimately reshaped the entire pattern of Western consumer demand. We will review the role assigned to "luxury" consumption in the literature on industrialization, suggest some ways in which this factor can be better understood, and conclude with comments about sugar-based and related consumerism in later stages of modern economic history.

The simplest measure of the relationship between sugar and industrialization, employed both by Thomas and Bean and by Eric Williams (1944), is the profitability of the Atlantic triangle, which is then linked to protoindustrial capital accumulation. A more sophisticated argument, advanced by several contributors at a recent conference dedicated to the "Williams thesis," is to reevaluate the share of the Atlantic triangle(s) in overall British trade during the seventeenth and eighteenth centuries (Inikori 1987; Richardson 1987). Even more complex is the argument that efforts to maintain large-scale long-distance trade in exotic goods, no matter what its immediate economic value was, created new institutional capacities for lowering transaction costs, which were then adaptable to the more productive undertakings of an industrial economy (Austen 1987: 110; North 1991). At a more basic level, Immanuel Wallerstein (1974) has contended that the caloric content of imported sugar was critical to the labor capacity of early-modern Europe.

In all of these arguments, the attraction of sugar as a nonessential consumer item in Europe is either explicitly or implicitly treated as negative. For Thomas (1968) and Coelho (1974), the Atlantic triangle was a positive misallocation of resources inspired by the mistaken notions of mercantilist economics. Wallerstein and others go to great lengths to emphasize that the importance of sugar lay in its linkages with the production of other commodities, in part because they do not regard consumption as significant in itself.[1] Thomas and Bean's allusion to the physical harm resulting from sugar consumption is consistent with Sidney Mintz's (1985) view of sugar as a drug disguising real deteriorations in British popular diet. However, Mintz (ibid.: 180ff.), in the most challenging account we have of consumerism in the development of European capitalism, insists that it was precisely through their negative nutritional qualities that "sugar and other drug foods" contributed to industrialization; "by provisioning, sating—and, indeed, drugging—farm and factory workers, [these items] sharply reduced the overall cost of creating and reproducing the metropolitan proletariat."

The literature dealing more generally with European economic history on the eve of the industrial revolution (Mokyr 1977, 1984) has given greater attention to consumption issues—even when they systematically deny that demand factors are autonomously relevant to such change—than most historians of overseas trade have.[2] However, the explanations for evidently very dramatic rises of domestic European consumption standards from the late seventeenth century are usually framed outside the process of consumption itself and linked instead to changes in agricultural productivity and demography.[3] Imports of sugar and related goods become, in these arguments, mainly indicators of increased European effective demand rather than causal factors in new patterns of consumption.

Without denying either that the Atlantic sugar triangle had some role in the development of European productive capacity or that independent changes in that capacity were necessary conditions for consuming new imports, we are convinced that the significance of sugar in the protoindustrial economy can be better understood if we take more seriously its function in the transformation of European consumerism. Our assumption here is that consumption of a commodity like sugar is not a given of human nature, merely waiting for incomes and prices to reach the proper equilibrium, but that consumption systems are social and cultural constructs, linked to broader historical factors no less vitally than production systems are. The importation of large quantities of sugar and the closely related beverage commodities, cocoa, coffee, and tea, in the early-modern era had a decisive role in changing not only the patterns but also the organization and meaning of consumption in Europe. These changes can be seen in the levels and distribution of sugar consumption, in the economic and social institutions linked to this increased consumption capacity, and in the concep-

tions of economy and society provoked by the contemplation of
entirely unprecedented experiences of consumption.

MEASUREMENT: SUGAR AS A
MASS-CONSUMPTION COMMODITY

Measurement is the aspect of sugar consumption which has been
most carefully studied by previous historians. There is a consensus in the literature that per capita consumption rose markedly
from the latter 1600s. What we need to know more fully and precisely, however, is the rate at which such consumption rose before
industrialization set in. To what degree did it extend beyond the
elite and reach what could be called a "mass market"? Existing
studies are ambivalent or even negative upon this point, mainly
because the industrial revolution made possible an acceleration of
mass consumption on a scale far greater than anything that had
appeared before.[4] However, it is our argument that the qualitative break from elite to mass consumption took place before the
industrial revolution and thus was as much its cause as its effect.
Quantitative evidence does not suffice to identify the new form
of consumerism we seek to define, but it is nonetheless important
to examine carefully the relevant numbers and anecdotal evidence
indicating how much was consumed in the protoindustrial era and
by whom.

Table 1 is drawn mainly from a historian, Sheridan (1973),
who has already argued strongly for the role of sugar (and its
accompanying beverage, tea) as a major element of expanding
consumption in Britain before the industrial revolution. From the
rising rate of per capita consumption implied by the retained import statistics, we see that this increased use of sugar must have
extended well beyond the elite (however defined) into the middle and even lower strata of society. Sheridan, Mintz, and others
have provided ample anecdotal evidence to support such a view.
It would be useful also to know something about the urban versus
the rural distribution of sugar consumption. If, as naive logic (and
the French case, discussed below) would lead us to suspect, a
disproportionate part of this consumption did take place in urban
areas, then the probability of "mass," that is, wide lower-class,
consumption would rise, since the per capita figures within the
urban population would be considerably higher. This last issue is
even more important in the French situation (Table 2).

Table 1   British sugar consumption, 1698–1775

	Net import (1,000s cwt.)	Growth (%)	Population (1,000s)	Pounds consumed per capita	Growth (%)
1698–1700	280.7	—	6,122	4.6	—
1701–5	262.4	−6.5	—	—	—
1706–10	300.5	14.5	6,352	4.7	3.1
1711–15	342.5	13.9			
1716–20	473.1	38.1	6,253	7.6	59.9
1721–25	571.9	20.8			
1726–30	686.2	19.9	6,183	11.1	46.7
1731–35	741.7	8.0			
1736–40	720.1	−2.9	6,153	11.7	5.5
1741–45	678.4	−5.7			
1746–50	761.5	12.2	6,336	12.0	2.7
1751–55	892.9	17.2			
1756–60	1,102.1	23.4	8,000	13.8	14.6
1761–65	1,063.6	−3.4			
1766–70	1,379.2	29.6	8,500	16.2	17.8
1771–75	1,542.9	11.8			
Net growth		449.7	—	—	253.9

Sources: Net imports, Sheridan 1973: 22; population, Mitchell 1962: 5. We have taken the highest of the England and Wales population series given here and added approximations from the one figure given for eighteenth-century Scotland.

A comparison of Tables 1 and 2 reveals that during the eighteenth century French sugar imports generally equaled, and sometimes exceeded, those of Britain. However, a far lower proportion of French sugar was retained for domestic consumption: France was obviously more committed to mercantilist policies of export balances than to internal consumer demand. Given the much larger French population, this means that per capita consumption was far lower than in Britain and, even within its absolute limits, subject to a much less sustained pattern of growth.

These data appear to support the observations of Sheridan (1973: 24–25) and others, based on literary evidence and more limited statistics, that France did not experience the same sugar

Table 2   French sugar consumption, 1730–90

	Total import (1,000s cwt.)	Retained import (1,000s cwt.)	Retained growth (%)	Population (1,000s)	Pounds consumed per capita
1730–34	590	240	—	23,000	1.0
1735–39	860	260	8.3	23,800	1.1
1740–42	900	380	46.2	24,200	1.6
1743–45	1,000	400	5.3	24,500	1.6
1750–52	900	400	.0	24,600	1.6
1753–55	1,200	450	12.5	25,000	1.8
1767–70	1,200	500	11.1	26,500	1.9
1770	1,640	800	—	27,066	3.0[a]
1771–73	1,400	650	30.0	27,200	2.4
1774–78	1,200	400	−38.5	27,700	1.4
1784–87	1,600	550	37.5	28,300	1.9
1788–90	1,850	600	9.1	28,560	2.1
Net growth			213.6		1.1 = 110%

Sources: Stein 1980: 5–6; Dupâquier et al. 1988: 64–68.
[a] This is the only single year for which Stein (1988b: 163–64) gives fairly precise import retention statistics. We have corresponded with him, but he is no longer able to supply us with the tabular import data which went into his 1980 published graphs.

and beverage consumer explosion as Britain. Indeed, French sugar consumption at its eighteenth-century high point (1770–73) did not match the level of Britain in 1698–1700.[5] Moreover, we know that even in the consumption of more basic domestic staples, France had not achieved Britain's security by the 1780s, a decade in which bread shortages remained a major factor in the French national economy (Rogers 1980).

In short, high levels of imported luxury food consumption appear to be linked to other indicators of economic growth pointing toward industrialization, in which France has always been assumed to have lagged considerably behind Britain. However, just as comparisons of French and British economic growth have lately undergone considerable revision, so the role of sugar consumption in these two societies may not be contrasted as simply as national statistical comparisons suggest.[6]

Much less research has been done on sugar consumption in eighteenth-century France than in Britain. However, Robert Stein (pers. com., 1988a; 1988b: 164) has discovered evidence of the distribution of sugar within France which suggests that per capita consumption in Paris during the 1780s may have been as high as 50 pounds and in Marseilles in 1755, nearly 10 pounds. Moreover, sugar shortages were the immediate cause of the popular Paris riots, which led in 1792 to the final overthrow of the French monarchy.[7] Thus, by the late eighteenth century sugar was sufficiently accessible to populations in the best-supplied centers of France as to be an established article of mass consumption.

Obviously, we need to know a good deal more about the role of sugar in eighteenth-century French commerce and industry as well as about consumption patterns before we can draw any definitive conclusions about its prominence in comparison to the more evident British case. What the French quantitative evidence does suggest is that the emergence of mass sugar consumption is not primarily created by the labor needs of an emerging industrial economy.[8] But does such a shift in consumption represent anything more than a "natural" response to cheaper commodities entering an invisible-handed market?

CONSTRUCTING A COLONIAL-GOODS MARKET

The measurement of European consumption of sugar and other colonial products allows us to establish the existence of greatly extended markets for such goods by the eighteenth century, but in itself such an exercise does not explain the structures of the markets, the extent to which their formation was related to major institutional and cultural changes, or the connection (if any) between enhanced colonial-goods consumption and the expansion of industrial production in the eighteenth century. An overview of the issues involved in these matters is possible if one thinks in terms of active construction of a broader European market for overseas goods in the seventeenth and eighteenth centuries, construction in the sense both of establishing institutions which promoted certain consumer behavior patterns and of assigning new meanings to colonial commodities in European conceptions of the economy.

The structural outlines of the seventeenth-century European market for overseas products are well known. It consisted of a network of interconnected urban markets arranged in a roughly concentric pattern, with Amsterdam (and, by the eighteenth century, London) at the center. The European marketing system was linked to its suppliers in a variety of ways, but most notably, for a wide range of Asian products, through large, bureaucratic, and more or less monopolistic companies. Smith (1982) has argued that an entirely new approach to marketing evolved from the peculiar circumstances of the Dutch East India Company. The company imported large quantities of new or previously rare goods for buyers who themselves sold on a continental scale. The bureaucracy in Asia which supplied these commodities (often in the form of "surprize" cargoes) represented a huge overhead cost, was only partly controllable from Holland, and, at best, required an unprecedentedly long lead time for orders. To deal with this ·situation, the Dutch East India Company (and its English rival) instituted a series of innovations in planning, research, and advertising that were later adapted to selling the output of industrial factories.

To what extent was sugar a part of all this? Sugar was, of course, distributed within Europe through the same general marketing structure as the other overseas products, but it was not really a new commodity, and it was never controlled by semimonopolistic organizations such as the East India companies. And, although it was a subject of considerable public discussion on the grounds of its possible effects on personal and national well-being, there seems to have been relatively little advertising or large-scale promotion of its use.[9] The expansion of sugar consumption was thus in some sense "invisible," quite literally so when sugar was incorporated into the preparation of other food and drink, such as pastries, puddings, and punches.

And yet, indirectly, sugar also participated in the institutional restructuring of consumer-goods markets, because its consumption came to be tied to that of tea, coffee, and cocoa, the first two of which were introduced in large quantities by the East India companies. The process by which it became a necessary complement to these items changed the nature of demand for sugar at the end of the seventeenth and the beginning of the eighteenth centuries. As Mintz (1985: 78, 108–50) explains, sugar became a "sweetener" more than a medicine, spice, decorative material, or preservative.[10] The markets for sugar in the latter forms, although dynamic in the seventeenth century, were limited compared to the tea-coffee-cocoa-sugar complex, which grew explosively in the eighteenth. So it was not by itself but as part of a broader and more complex consumption pattern, one actively expanded by new commercial institutions, that sugar came to have the immense impact that it did.

But how did sugar come to play so central a role? In the areas from which the "bitter" beverages were imported, they were seldom taken with sugar, nor were they originally so consumed in Europe. There is little evidence for a deliberate institutional promotion of the sweetening habit until it had already appeared.[11] In any case, the extent to which early-modern institutional marketing could actually create new consumption patterns, as opposed to exploiting opportunities presented by current fashions, was quite limited. It is obviously necessary to take into account the interaction between the set of items of which sugar was a part and sociocultural changes in Western Europe within which the consumption of those items had meaning. We can only point to a few features of this interaction here.

The actual process by which sugar became attached to tea and coffee consumption is not wholly known, but it may have started in the last quarter of the seventeenth century, not in order to sweeten those beverages but rather to encourage the use of tea as a medium for consuming sugar, whose negative effects on teeth and the body were becoming apparent, in a healthy way.[12] However it happened, sometime around 1700 tea and sugar, like coffee and sugar, became part of the daily routine that increasing numbers of Europeans, especially in Britain, practiced in their homes. Previously, the consumption of exotic beverages, usually without sugar, had taken place in aristocratic gatherings or in coffeehouses and teahouses. Much of the increase in coffee consumption in England between 1660 and 1700 had been due to the central role which coffeehouses had come to play in urban social, commercial, and political life. By 1700, the taking of tea and sugar with other foods in the morning and late afternoon had become a central domestic ritual in Britain and some other parts of Western Europe.[13] It was the generalization of this ritual that sustained the growing demand for tea and sugar throughout the eighteenth century. It also created the institutional and cultural framework within which the tea-and-sugar custom became a source of true mass consumption by the end of the eighteenth century, as tea prices continued to fall and people at lower levels of income adopted the custom.

The significance and impetus of these rituals have been debated. Chandra Mukerji (1983) suggests that they were related to similar developments in dress, which in turn arose from an increasing "materialism" in European social perceptions in the early-modern era. This materialism emerged out of the interaction between new printing technologies and the changing dynamics of European society. The new consumption patterns created a demand for printed Asian textiles which, by engendering competition between importers and domestic textile producers in Britain, helped stimulate technical innovation among the latter and therefore the industrial revolution. One could, in fact, demonstrate a similar linkage between the widespread adoption of the sugar-and-tea ritual and innovations in the pottery industry, but clearly textiles were far more important to early industrialization than "china." [14] More significant is Mukerji's linking of demand to social perceptions through rituals of consumption. But where did the rituals come from?

Many scholars have emphasized the effects of "bourgeois" imitation of elite dress and behavior in the seventeenth and eighteenth centuries. It is argued that, like most fashions, the taking of sugar by itself and with exotic beverages started as an elite custom and then "trickled down" to a "rising" bourgeoisie anxious to ape its betters (Freudenberger 1963). [15] When the trickle became a flood in the course of the eighteenth century, as yet poorer classes imitated *their* immediate superiors, mass consumption arose. Reductions in price, due to economies of scale in production and (in the late eighteenth century) lower duties on tea, sugar, and the like, obviously played a role as well. The "emulation" theory presupposes an ongoing change in class structure, with luxury consumption a sign of the rising importance of the middle class and accelerating individual social mobility, not an autonomous factor contributing actively to social restructuring.

There are several weaknesses in this sort of explanation. The reason that the emulation process continued for a century and a half—long after sugar and its associated beverages had ceased to be distinctively elite luxuries—is difficult to explain. Mintz (1985: 180–83) is undoubtedly on the right track in indicating that each social group that adopted the sugar-coffee-tea ritual in fact interpreted the meaning of the ritual in its own way, which limits the trickle-down explanation to the initial introduction of a commodity to a new group of potential users. Second, the explanation tends to ignore the fact that the mode of taking sugar, tea, and so on and the links to other social behavior actually changed markedly several times over the space of a few generations, and not always because of innovations introduced at the apex of society. The movement of coffee and tea use (at different times) from aristocratic parlors to public establishments to domestic houses shows this, as does the convergence of sugar taking with these forms of consumption. Each form had, for example, different political associations: with inner-elite politicking, with the primary system for clearing political and commercial information (in the coffeehouses), and, finally, with a domestic context in which public affairs were relatively insignificant.

In our opinion, the relationship between the sugar-tea-coffee-cocoa consumption complex and the broader culture of the immediate preindustrial period centered primarily on the phenomenon of respectability.[16] Respectability was not simply a matter of emulating elite fashions, although that was of course part of it. It was a distinctive cultural pattern, incorporating rather strict guidelines for individual and group behavior and an elaborate system of moral legitimation, that evolved in several European countries in the seventeenth and eighteenth centuries. Its emergence appears to have been connected to an array of economic changes, probably including a degree of income redistribution to the "middling" classes in an expanding commercial economy, but the connection was not an automatic or in every respect a direct one. Such a redistribution does not necessarily produce a particular, clearly defined cultural pattern; a rise in income among a group of people does not automatically mean that they will decide to spend a substantial part of it on sugar and tea. Economic factors fit themselves into broader patterns of thought and action that have immediate meaning to the participants, while deep coherence (such as the connection of respectability to the growth of a commercial middle class) is often the result of later rationalization. Material objects are also fitted into the same sort of pattern, to be manipulated, often in ritual fashion, to produce meaning. From this standpoint, the use of commodities such as sugar, coffee, and tea is not simply a sign of more "real" or "basic" socioeconomic changes but an active process of cultural construction in itself. As signs of deeper social phenomena, tea, sugar, printed cottons, and the like could easily have been interchanged with other products without much effect; indeed, if their consumption had simply been a matter of fashion, they almost certainly would have been.[17] But they persisted, apparently because the nature and the interpretation of these particular commodities came to play a significant role in shaping the rituals of respectability and thus of respectability itself.

In very-late-seventeenth- and early-eighteenth-century England, the consumption of sugar with tea and, to a lesser extent, with coffee became one of a number of significant elements of a cultural pattern that had meaning because it both signified and constituted the respectability of the people who participated in it. In a functional sense, one could say that respectability centered on a demand on the part of certain people for respect from people above them, below them, and at the same level in their society —respect that was to be manifested in different ways, depending on the social position from which the respect was to come. In this sense, taking tea and sugar in certain ways, with the proper implements, at the proper times of day, was connected to a wider array of cultural practices such as wearing fashionable clothes, following the now-generalized rules of "polite" behavior, and so forth. All of these things constituted a demand for respect. Most were tied to modes of moral justification for the respect demanded. Tea was especially significant in this regard, because it was consciously presented as a substitute for alcoholic drink and therefore not only symbolized but also was an aspect of respectable sobriety and concern for health (Short 1750: 28–33). Taking sugar in tea, as opposed to other forms of using it, such as in sugared decorations for foods, displayed and constituted similar qualities. Sugared food decorations symbolized exactly the aspects of aristocratic fashion that respectable people (regardless of their official or conventional social standing, which could in fact encompass nobility) rejected: immoderation and wastefulness, not to mention excessive ornateness. Consuming sugar in tea symbolized contrasting virtues, but it also was an alternate form of behavior that could be seen to have beneficial social consequences (by stimulating commerce without waste and, as part of the tea ritual, sociability without inebriation).[18]

That the tea-and-sugar pattern was fitted into the larger cultural pattern of respectability was of course of immense importance to Britain's overseas trade, especially as respectability became an increasingly significant element of British life after 1700. The lesser importance of the domestic market for sugar and tea in France may have been due in part to the evolution of alternate patterns and rituals of respectability (which featured unsweetened wine rather than tea, one suspects)—although the behavior of the revolutionary mob noted above may indicate that some of the same pattern appeared at the petit-bourgeois level even of French society.

The relationship between the sugar trade and eighteenth-century industrialization, seen from the demand side, is thus an extremely complex one. The rituals of respectable consumption of sugar and its related products did directly stimulate some industrial demand, especially in the pottery industry. But more important was the effect that the availability of commodities like sugar, tea, calicos, chinaware, and the like had on the formation of the rituals themselves and on the way those rituals were related to the social perceptions, political aspirations, and moral expectations that came to be seen as respectable. Respectability was one of the main sources of demand for the products of the early industrial revolution (cottons, tableware, etc.). Respectability is not a general condition of human social life but a very specific cultural pattern that developed in the period immediately preceding industrialization. Much more work on this subject needs to be done, but we can say that to the extent that sugar played a role in the construction of respectability, it contributed to the conditions that made industrialization historically possible.

TOWARDS A WORLD OF (EVER-EXPANDING) COMMODITIES AND CONSUMERS

It is widely recognized that eighteenth-century economic thinkers such as Adam Smith failed entirely to recognize the incipient industrialization whose posthumous ideologues they were to become (Caton 1985). What did capture the attention of economic discourse in the seventeenth and eighteenth centuries, however, was the spread of luxury consumption beyond the limited boundaries of elite society.

In the specific cases of sugar and tea, this discussion encompassed concern for the medicinal value frequently claimed by sellers of these commodities. In the late seventeenth century, evidence of the damage to physical, including dental, health that sugar could inflict was increasingly cited in opposition to the proponents of sugar. As we have seen, the habit of taking sugar in tea may have arisen out of an attempt to reconcile these perceptions.[19] However, the more significant issue was not the effect of hitherto rare or unknown foodstuffs on individual bodies but the social consequence of making such goods available cheaply enough that large numbers of people could consume them.

It is not necessary to explain at length the contradiction between these new conditions and traditional "sumptuary laws" (class-specific restrictions on various forms of consumption) as well as theories about backward-bending labor supply curves (assertions that cheaper consumer goods would decrease incentives to work). The intellectual confrontation between continuing belief in such restrictions and the expanding early-modern consumer market took place very publicly during the period itself and has been widely noted by economic historians (De Vries 1976).

The most serious form of this confrontation came in the debates over doctrines and policies generally referred to as mercantilism. Whether or not a self-defined ideology ever existed under this name, European states did systematically seek to maximize balances of trade and bullion accumulation by encouraging reexport rather than domestic consumption of colonial goods such as sugar. Mercantilist writers were driven not only by their belief in the correctness of these policy goals but also by the interplay of government revenue needs and the wishes of economic interest groups. Sugar importers and plantation owners, like the importers of Asian products, took an active part in the politics of mercantilism in Britain and France, inconsistently over time and frequently in conflict with other, similar interests. On the whole, however, the importing interest tended to argue against the idea that widespread consumerism endangered society and the economy. This position ultimately contributed to the nonzero-sum view of consumerism as public economic virtue advanced in Smith's *Wealth of Nations*, which thus, even without its author's foreseeing industrialism, became the canon of liberal economics. [20]

Among the forms of individual self-interest thus vindicated, sugar consumption is quite prominent, if for no other reason than that it grew so rapidly and conspicuously despite the prevalence of anticonsumerist doctrine in the first half of the eighteenth century. To see the economic role of sugar in these terms is to stand a major portion of the Williams thesis upon its head. Williams argued that the sugar-slave triangle and mercantilism were bonded together as an aspect of "primitive" capital accumulation, to be dispensed with once industrialism and free trade had triumphed. If instead we associate sugar with free trade and consumerism, we can appreciate its importance to industrialization independently of capital accumulation. This change in the evaluation of the products of West Indian slavery parallels our new understanding of slave labor itself, not as an inefficient anachronism of the ancien régime but as a precursor of industrial capitalist production. Even in the late eighteenth century, despite Adam Smith's denunciation of the inefficiency of bonded workers, other free-trade economists, such as Turgot, recognized the rationality of slave plantations under southern New World conditions (Davis 1975: 132–33).

Viewed from a cultural perspective, the very overvaluation of colonial trade by mercantilist theorists can be understood to have had a positive impact on the development of capitalist culture, whatever it may have done for or against the attainment of maximal monetary returns on available eighteenth-century capital. As students of political culture in eighteenth-century France and of contemporary U.S. election campaigns have noted, the outcome of any public debate may depend less on which side wins specific points than on which set of terms becomes the basis for subsequent discourse. Colonial commodities and their consumers, because of their visibility, gave rise to a debate about economics which, though temporarily won by the mercantilists, assured the eventual triumph of a position fully based upon a world of commodities and consumers. Mukerji (1983), with her emphasis upon media of communication and intraclass demonstration effects, addresses aspects of early-modern culture necessary for full communication of market information and propaganda. But more critical to the substance of modernism in this era is contemplation of the market itself as the central object and model of discourse for both economics and broader social issues.

CONSUMERISM, UNDERDEVELOPMENT, AND A ZERO-SUM UNIVERSE

Not the least appealing element of the Williams thesis was the connection it made between the anguish of slavery and what is regarded in both Marxist and liberal terms as the core of capitalist development. Slaves and proletarians may be victims of capitalism, but if industrialization is essentially based upon the material fruits of their labor, they remain part of its consciousness and may ultimately, as Marx promises, become its heirs. The present consumerist argument implies an alienation for third world primary producers far more cruel than what Marx ascribes to industrial workers. If the capitalism "constructed" from their efforts is essentially a cultural entity, its reality exists only for those who participate in the central arena. It is only the commodities and those who consume and exchange them, not the primary producers (despite the new construction of blacks in Africa and the New World by the abolitionist movement), who are visible and can visualize.

Within the mercantilist version of protoindustrial capitalism, Africans and West Indian slaves were valued as consumers of goods manufactured in Europe. However, as Eric Williams painfully noted, the triumph of liberalism brought a decline in concern for markets which lacked the dynamism of the Europeans' own world. Nonetheless, in absolute terms, Africa and the West Indies received far larger quantities of consumer goods from Europe and North America in the nineteenth century and afterwards than they had during their era of mercantilist prominence. Initially, these goods were mainly textiles, but eventually sugar/beverage consumption ("coca-colanization") played its role in this process.

The result of this kind of consumerism has not, however, been the replication of European industrialization processes in the tropics. Instead, economists have pointed to a negative demonstration effect in which a few import-substitution industries fail to close the gap between heightened consumption expectations and limited local productivity (Felix 1974).[21] Moreover, the experience of integration into the world market has not only failed to transplant "modernization" into third world culture but (at least in Africa) directly encouraged an economy of patron-client practices and witchcraft beliefs, based upon zero-sum visions of the material and social world (Berry 1985; Austen 1986).

The orthodox response to this problem among development economists is to recommend that third world countries place more emphasis on production and in particular adjust food pricing and other policies so as to stop favoring urban consumers over rural producers (World Bank 1981). However, it has been argued recently, on the basis of successful industrialization in Asia, that the formula for economic development in the Third World should include the encouragement, or at least endorsement, of mass consumerism, with all its emphasis on urbanization, nonessential commodities, and advertisement (McGee 1985).[22] The relevance of earlier European experience for contemporary issues thus remains ambiguous.

Clearly, a study of consumerism in the pre-nineteenth-century connections between Africa, Europe, and the slave plantations of the New World cannot claim to resolve twentieth-century debates over worldwide development and underdevelopment. However, in revising our models for the international dimensions of the first industrial revolution, we can at least expand the intellectual, moral, and practical vision with which we contemplate the dilemmas of the present.

NOTES

1   The theoretical basis for this evaluation among dependency theorists such as Wallerstein is Sraffa 1960; however, similar arguments can be found in liberal economic literature following the less pretentious "linkage" arguments of Hirschmann (1958). In more empirical terms, this kind of argument does establish important links between *Asian* "luxury" trade and industrialization, since European tastes for both Chinese pottery and, more importantly, Indian cottons eventually led to the development of innovative import-substitution industries. However, this is not true for sugar, which inspired (at least within protoindustrial Europe) only the proliferation of small-scale food-processing enterprises. The affinity between the New World sugar plantation and the European industrial factory has often been remarked upon, but without any demonstration of an influence of the former upon the emergence of the latter; the influence suggested here came through the marketing and cultural assimilation of mass-produced consumption goods.
2   The major exceptions to this statement are Mintz (primarily an anthropologist rather than a historian) and the excellent, although essentially descriptive, chapter on British sugar and tea consumption in Sheridan 1973: 18–35.
3   This is the central argument of the very valuable chapter on consumption in De Vries 1976: 176–209; see also Eversley 1967. A more autonomous role for consumption is postulated by Jones (1973).

4   See Ewen 1976, Fraser 1981, and Zaretsky 1976; for a useful discussion of recent historiography on preindustrial consumerism, see McCracken 1988: 1–30.

5   This point holds even if we accept the maximum consumption figure of four pounds per capita given in Stein 1988b: 164.

6   For a review of studies closing the "development gap" between Britain and France see Cameron and Freedeman 1983.

7   For an indication of the kind of public discourse on sugar consumption which arose from these events and might form the basis of a fuller investigation of the French case, see Mathiez 1927: 29ff.

8   Mintz (1985: 188ff.) is thus unjustified in his self-righteous lipsmacking over the relative absence of sugar in the superior cuisine of France and China, as opposed to that of the drugged victims of industrialism and imperialism in Britain and the Third World.

9   Sugar, though retailed through the same channels as other colonial goods, appears to have been either omitted from marketing campaigns or incorporated into them as a "loss leader" (McKendrick et al. 1982: 93–94); however, there is one example of a folded and illustrated German handbill advertising sugar during the first half of the eighteenth century (see Baxa and Bruhns 1967: 48–49). Normally, however, sugar appears in British handbills as an element of trade policy under debate, as in the 1698 publication "On the State of the Sugar Plantations in America" (Goldsmith's Library 1698).

10 Ongoing research by Smith indicates that the British domestic fashion of drinking tea with sugar probably took hold widely between 1695 and 1700.

11 Unlike sugar, tea and coffee were regularly advertised in Britain in the late seventeenth and early eighteenth centuries (McKendrick et al. 1982: 146ff.; Cranfield 1962: 211: "The ordinary necessities of life were rarely advertized in these newspapers. . . . The only goods advertized with any frequency were luxury goods such as millinery from London, tea, coffee and chocolate, and wines and spirits"). See also the career of John Houghton, "Father of Publication Advertising" and seller of "coffee, tea, chocolate and other commodities" in late-seventeenth-century England (Presbrey 1929: 56ff.).

12 This possibility and the dating of the process to the end of the seventeenth century are based upon Smith's ongoing research in contemporary British literature and family account books.

13 On coffeehouses and teahouses see Ukkers 1935, 1: 38–43. The importance of domestic consumption of tea with sugar is emphasized in Short 1750: 32, 40.

14 See McKendrick et al. 1982: 99–145 on Josiah Wedgwood.

15 McCracken (1988: 11–16, 93–103) pushes the fashion changes back to Elizabethan England and refines the "trickle-down" theory of fashion changes.

16 For an indication of the complex relationships which might have existed between social identity and consumption in early-modern Europe, see Schama 1987: 130–220.

17 This apparently happened in France during the late seventeenth century,

when the coffee and tea fashion was simply displaced (Dufour 1685: 27–40).

18 "Then consider the many sober Companies it [tea drinking] assembles both in Coffee-houses (which in London are only about six hundred) and private Houses. Observe we further the Business, Conversation and Intelligence it promotes, the Expence and Debauchery it prevents. Nor is its consumption of Sugar, which is a great Encouragement to our American Colonies to be forgot" (Short 1750: 32).

19 Baxa and Bruhns (1967: 44–46) cite treatises from as early as 1693 indicating potential damage to the teeth from sugar; the earliest such statement known to us is Blankaart 1683: 39–43.

20 The above argument has been developed most strongly by Appleby (1978); for a critique of Appleby's entire opus (which does not, in our opinion, diminish its value for the present argument), see Winch 1985.

21 For a Marxist version of this view, with special attention paid to the negative effects of mass-marketing culture, see Langdon 1981.

22 McGee not only counters the austerity doctrines of development economists but also suggests a productive role for "informal sectors," as opposed to the views of Berry (1985).

REFERENCES

Appleby, J. O. (1978) Economic Thought and Ideology in Seventeenth-Century England. Princeton: Princeton University Press.

Austen, R. A. (1986) "The criminal and the African cultural imagination: Normative and deviant heroism in precolonial and modern narratives." Africa 56: 385–98.

——— (1987) African Economic History: Internal Development and External Dependency. London: James Currey.

Bairoch, P. (1975) The Economic Development of the Third World since 1900. Berkeley and Los Angeles: University of California Press.

Baxa, J., and G. Bruhns (1967) Zucker im Leben der Völker: Ein Kultur- und Wirtschaftsgeschichte. Berlin: A. Bartens.

Berry, S. (1985) Fathers Work for Their Sons: Accumulation, Mobility, and Class Formation in an Extended Yoruba Community. Berkeley and Los Angeles: University of California Press.

Blankaart, S. (1683) Die Bogerlyke Tafel: Om lang gesond sonder ziekten te leven. Amsterdam.

Cameron, R., and C. E. Freedeman (1983) "French economic growth: A radical revision." Social Science History 7: 3–30.

Caton, H. (1985) "The pre-industrial economics of Adam Smith." Journal of Economic History 45: 833–53.

Coelho, P. R. P. (1974) "The profitability of imperialism: The British experience in the West Indies, 1768–1772." Explorations in Economic History 10: 253–80.

Cranfield, G. A. (1962) The Development of the Provincial Newspaper, 1700–1790. Oxford: Clarendon.

Davis, D. B. (1975) The Problem of Slavery in the Age of Revolution. Ithaca: Cornell University Press.

De Vries, J. (1976) The Economy of Europe in an Age of Crisis, 1600–1750. Cambridge: Cambridge University Press.

Dufour, P. S. (1685) Traitez nouveaux et curieux du café, du thé, et du chocolat. The Hague.

Dupâquier, J., et al. (1988) Histoire de la population française. Vol. 2, De la Renaissance à 1789. Paris: Presses universitaires de la France.

Eversley, D. E. C. (1967) "The home market and economic growth in England," in E. L. Jones and G. E. Mingay (eds.) Land, Labour, and Population in the Industrial Revolution. London: Arnold: 206–59.

Ewen, S. (1976) Captains of Consciousness: Advertising and the Social Roots of the Consumer Culture. New York: McGraw-Hill.

Felix, D. (1974) "Technological dualism in late industrializers: On theory, history, and policy." Journal of Economic History 34: 194–238.

Fraser, W. H. (1981) The Coming of the Mass Market, 1850–1914. Hamden, CT: Archon.

Freudenberger, H. (1963) "Fashion, sumptuary laws, and business." Business History Review 37: 37–48.

Goldsmith's Library (1698) "On the state of the sugar plantations in America." Broadsheet Collection, vol. 1, no. 87. London: Goldsmith's Library.

Hirschmann, A. O. (1958) The Strategy of Economic Development. New Haven: Yale University Press.

Inikori, J. E. (1987) "Slavery and the development of industrial capitalism in England." Journal of Interdisciplinary History 17: 739–93.

Jones, E. L. (1973) "The fashion manipulators: Consumer tastes and British industries, 1660–1800," in L. P. Cain and P. J. Uselding (eds.) Business Enterprise and Economic Change. Kent, OH: Kent State University Press: 198–226.

Langdon, S. W. (1981) Multinational Corporations in the Economy of Kenya. New York: St. Martin's.

McCracken, G. (1988) Culture and Consumption. Bloomington: Indiana University Press.

McGee, T. G. (1985) "Mass markets, little markets: Some preliminary thoughts on the growth of consumption and its relationship to urbanization: A case study of Malaysia," in S. Plattner (ed.) Markets and Marketing. Monographs on Economic Anthropology, No. 4. Lanham, MD: University Press of America: 205–33.

McKendrick, N., J. Brewer, and J. H. Plumb (1982) The Birth of a Consumer Society: The Commercialization of Eighteenth-Century England. London: Europa.

Mathiez, A. (1927) La vie chère et le mouvement social sous la Terreur. Paris: Payot.

Mintz, S. W. (1985) Sweetness and Power: The Place of Sugar in Modern History. New York: Viking.

Mitchell, B. R. (1962) Abstract of British Historical Statistics. Cambridge: Cambridge University Press.

Mokyr, J. (1977) "Demand versus supply in the industrial revolution." Journal of Economic History 37: 981–1008.

——— (1984) "Demand versus supply in the industrial revolution: A reply." Journal of Economic History 44: 806–9.

Mukerji, C. (1983) From Graven Images: Patterns of Modern Materialism. New York: Columbia University Press.

North, D. C. (1991) "Institutions, transaction costs, and the rise of merchant empires," in J. D. Tracy (ed.) The Political Economy of Merchant Empires, vol. 2. Cambridge: Cambridge University Press: 22–40.

Presbrey, F. (1929) The History and Development of Advertising. Garden City, NY: Doubleday, Doran.

Richardson, D. (1987) "The slave trade, sugar, and British economic growth, 1748–1776." Journal of Interdisciplinary History 17: 739–93.

Rogers, J. W., Jr. (1980) "Subsistence crises and political economy in France at the end of the ancien régime." Research in Economic History 5: 249–301.

Schama, S. (1987) The Embarrassment of Riches: An Interpretation of Dutch Culture in the Golden Age. New York: Knopf.

Sheridan, R. B. (1973) Sugar and Slavery. Baltimore: Johns Hopkins University Press.

Short, T. (1750) Discourses on Tea, Sugar, Milk, Made-Wines, Spirits, Punch, Tobacco, Etc. London.

Smith, Woodruff (1982) "The European-Asian trade of the seventeenth century and the modernization of commercial capitalism." Itinerario 6: 68–90.

Sraffa, P. (1960) The Production of Commodities by Means of Commodities. Cambridge: Cambridge University Press.

Stein, Robert (1980) "The French sugar business in the eighteenth century: A quantitative study." Business History 22: 3–17.

——— (1988a) Personal communication, November.

——— (1988b) The French Sugar Business in the Eighteenth Century. Baton Rouge: Louisiana State University Press.

Thomas, R. P. (1968) "The sugar colonies of the old empire: Profit or loss for Great Britain?" Economic History Review 21: 30–45.

———, and R. N. Bean (1974) "The fishers of men: The profits of the slave trade." Journal of Economic History 34: 885–914.

Ukkers, W. H. (1935) All about Tea. 2 vols., New York: Tea and Coffee Trade Journal Co.

Wallerstein, I. (1974) The Modern World System, vol. 1. New York: Academic.

Williams, E. (1944) Capitalism and Slavery. Chapel Hill: University of North Carolina Press.

Winch, Donald (1985) "Economic liberalism as ideology: The Appleby version." Economic History Review 38: 287–97.

World Bank (1981) Accelerated Development in Tropical Africa. Washington: World Bank.

Zaretsky, E. (1976) Capitalism, the Family, and Personal Life. New York: Harper and Row.

8

The Slave(ry) Trade and the Development of Capitalism in the United States: The Textile Industry in New England

RONALD BAILEY

THE SIGNIFICANCE of the slave trade and slavery-related commerce—what I will call the slave(ry) trade—in contributing to the development of colonial America and the United States has been a persistent theme in the work of Afro-American scholars. Two scholars in particular should be cited in this regard. W. E. B. DuBois (1896: 27) pointed out that slave labor was not widely utilized because the climate and geography of New England precluded the extensive development of agriculture: "The significance of New England in the African slave-trade does not therefore lie in the fact that she early discountenanced the system of slavery and stopped importation; but rather in the fact that her citizens, being the traders of the New World, early took part in the carrying slave trade and furnished slaves to the other colonies." DuBois's account of the role of Massachusetts and of Rhode Island, which later became "the clearing house for the slave trade of other colonies," was similar to what was popularized as the "triangular trade" thesis. Geometric analogies were used in an attempt to convey the complex economic and geographical scope of the trade, especially its impact in facilitating the expansion of commerce.

> This trade formed a perfect circle. Owners of slavers carried slaves to South Carolina, and brought home naval stores for their ship-building; or to the West Indies, and brought home molasses; or to other colonies, and brought home hogsheads. The molasses was made into the highly prized New England rum, and shipped in those hogsheads to Africa for more slaves. Thus, the rum-distilling industry indicates to some extent the activity of New England in the slave-trade. [Ibid.: 28–29][1]

The general development of commerce and industry in the United States has similarly been viewed as closely intertwined with the slave trade and slavery. Lorenzo Greene's (1942: 68–69) classic but largely unheralded study, *The Negro in Colonial New England*, boldly asserted that

> the effects of this slave trade were manifold. On the eve of the American Revolution it formed the very basis of the economic life of New England; about it revolved, and on it depended, most of her industries. The vast sugar, molasses and rum trade, shipbuilding, the distilleries, a great many of the fisheries, the employment of artisans and seamen, even agriculture—all were dependent on the slave traffic.[2]

Professor Greene's list could be extended, I will argue, to include commerce beyond the colonial period and the all-important textile industry, generally acknowledged as the pivotal enterprise in the industrial revolution in the United States (as it had been in England).[3]

The logical extension of the work of DuBois, Greene, and others provides the thesis of this article: that the commercial and industrial activity related to the slave(ry) trade were essential ingredients in the process of industrialization in the United States, particularly in textiles. Moreover, beyond the era of the slave trade, slave-produced cotton played a pivotal role in the expansion of interregional trade. This division of labor among regions laid the basis for a national economy that emerged between 1815 and 1865.

Three factors need to be considered as background to the slave(ry) trade's role in the rise of industrial capitalism in the U.S.: the fact that Africa supplied the majority of the population and the bulk of the workers during the European expansion into the Americas; the involvement of New England merchants in the slave trade; and the critical dependence of New England on trade revolving around the slavery-based economies of the West Indies.

The main subject of this article is the growth and development of the cotton textile industry in New England between 1790 and 1860. It is argued that the industry's development during the period was strongly connected, through various routes, to the slave trade and the slave-based Atlantic economic system. This is demonstrated in stages. First, we show the dependence of the Atlantic economic system on African slave labor from the seventeenth to the nineteenth centuries. Second, the significance of the direct involvement of New England's merchants in the slave trade is established. Third, evidence is produced to show the dependence of New England's maritime trade and shipping in general on the slave-based economies of the Atlantic. Fourth, it is shown that the early industries in New England—shipbuilding, rum manufacturing, and the production of spermaceti candles (as three examples)—were all derived from maritime activities dependent on the slave-based Atlantic economic system. Fifth, we show how slave-grown southern cotton stimulated a tripartite regional specialization which created a large domestic market for New England's cotton textile industry. To illustrate all these linkages and show that the initial capital for the cotton textile industry in New England came from sources directly and indirectly connected to the slave trade and the slave-based Atlantic economic system, we present detailed case studies of two entrepreneurial groups in the cotton textile industry. The evidence provided by these case studies enables us to draw a firm conclusion on the subject.[4]

THE AFRICANIZATION OF THE AMERICAS

While much debate has centered on the numbers of slaves imported to the New World, this has obscured a more central issue.[5] Far more important than the number of Africans taken from their homeland and sold into slavery are the labor of African peoples

Table 1   Cumulative net migration into and populations of selected American regions, c. 1820

	Net migration		Population	
	African	European	Black and free colored	White
United States	550,000	651,000	1,771,656	7,866,797
British West Indies	1,600,000	210,000	839,000	57,000
French, Danish, and Dutch West Indies	2,235,000	254,000	814,600	73,600
Brazil	2,942,000	500,000	2,660,000	920,000
Spanish America, excluding Peru	1,072,000	750,000	5,150,000	3,429,000
Totals	8,399,000	2,365,000	11,235,256	12,346,397

Source: Eltis 1983: 278.
Note: The totals were not included in the original table. See additional explanatory notes in Eltis 1983.

and the profitability of their products in the various sites where they were enslaved and exploited.

More African peoples than Europeans entered the Americas during the period under discussion (Table 1). Up to 1820, among those people who were transported across the Atlantic, Africans outnumbered Europeans by a ratio of over three to one: almost 8.4 million Africans and 2.4 million Europeans. Between 1820 and 1840, the number of Africans imported as slaves totaled 1,165,900, while the number of free migrants totaled only 824,500 (Eltis 1983), continuing the pattern of African numerical dominance for another 40 years. Eltis (ibid.: 255) is quite clear on the point, linking the phenomenon of African population dominance in the New World to industrialization in Europe:

Indeed, in every year from about the mid-sixteenth century to 1831, more Africans than Europeans quite likely came to the

Americas, and not until the second wave of mass migration began in the 1880s did the sum of net European immigration start to match and then exceed the cumulative influx from Africa. . . . In terms of immigration alone, then, America was an extension of Africa rather than Europe until late in the nineteenth century.[6]

The centrality of the African population to the population dynamics of the Americas is thus established. The islands of the British West Indies, for example, were about 90% African! When we discuss such matters as the dynamics of the Atlantic economy, the role of the slave trade or slavery, the significance of slavery-based economies such as that of the West Indies, the impact of slave-produced commodities like sugar and its derivatives, and cotton, we are likewise discussing the central role and contributions of "those valuable people, the Africans" and their descendants in the Americas.[7]

NEW ENGLAND MERCHANTS
AND THE SLAVE TRADE

The enslavement of Africans in New England occurred first in what was to become the state of Massachusetts, sometime between 1624 and 1638. "Combined with Negro slavery in New England were the several kinds of unfree labor current in that day; white, Negro and Indian indentured servitude, Indian slavery and, in occasional instances, the slavery of white people" (Greene 1942: 18–19). Although relatively small in numbers, African slaves were connected to almost every aspect of the New England economy, working as house servants, in agricultural production, and in industry. In short, slavery was as viable and as often utilized in relieving the general shortage of labor in New England as it was in other British American colonies and the rest of the New World. Lorenzo Greene (ibid.: 123) is right in concluding that, "despite frequent assertions to the contrary, the Negroes were a valuable and essential part of New England's labor supply and . . . unquestionably played a role in the commercial and industrial development of that section." Greene's Appendix 2 contains a list of 162 leading slave-holding families of colonial New England.

In addition to the direct employment of African slave labor,

New England's merchants were very much involved in the transatlantic slave trade, which supplied African slaves to New England itself but more heavily to the West Indies and the southern colonies. In fact, Massachusetts was the first British North American colony to enter the slave trade, in 1638. Rhode Island subsequently came to dominate the trade.

Coughtry's (1981) exhaustive work on Rhode Island reveals much about New England's involvement in the slave trade. A total of 523 Rhode Island slaving ships (from a total of 934) were identified by destination or slave market. These ships carried slaves to more than 40 New World ports, but nearly two-thirds of the slaves were sold in the West Indies and 31% in various mainland North American markets. Coughtry's work enables us to put one matter to rest and contributes to the resolution of another. Regarding the triangular trade, labeled by some a myth, Coughtry (ibid.: 6–7) is definitive:[8]

> Most Rhode Island slaving voyages originated at one of two principal ports [Newport and Bristol] and conformed to the triangular pattern long associated with both the English and the American slave trade. . . . The trade assumed its classic three-point configuration almost from the outset. . . . A second leg or "middle passage" was probably added to the itinerary in the 1730s, if not sooner. Most of these so-called "middle passages" terminated in the Caribbean, where the slaves were exchanged for specie, bills, and return cargoes of sugar or molasses. The standard textbook diagram featuring a triangular trade in rum, slaves, and molasses is therefore substantially correct.

Coughtry's data also contribute to a clarification of the factors which shaped New England's involvement in the slave trade. A part of my earlier research (Bailey 1979) was an effort to understand the pattern of U.S. involvement and to explore the view that the high moral standards found in the colonies mitigated against extensive participation in that "notorious traffic." Drawing on the Naval Office lists available through the British Public Record Office, I analyzed 4,747 ships which entered Boston and South Carolina between 1718 and 1764, including 122 slave carriers.[9] I found that the British carried 58% of 630 slaves in 30% of all slave ships entering these ports in 1718, 82% of the 799 slaves in

58% of the ships in 1724, and 80% of 4,417 slaves in 41% of the ships in 1764.

Using these data and data in Donnan 1930–35 and Coughtry 1981, I analyzed ports in South Carolina, Massachusetts, Virginia, and Georgia and voyages for Rhode Island merchants. Another complementary pattern was discovered. Into Savannah, for example, North American merchants played a leading role as slave traders, importing 38.9% of the slaves in 45.8% of the ships between 1755 and 1767 (British merchants imported only 29.1% of the slaves). North American merchants had a much smaller carrying capacity: 15.1 slaves per ship as compared to the 116.0 slaves per ship of British merchants. British merchants averaged 173.9 slaves per ship on the 46 ships which brought 8,001 slaves from Africa to South Carolina during the period, almost twice the 90.9-slave capacity of all ships which imported slaves into that state.

In short, using total shipping tonnage and average ship size (tons) as measures, the data reveal that the pattern of New England involvement—its subordinate role when compared to Britain—was a result of colonial domination rather than of morality. British merchants dominated the more lucrative routes direct from Africa to large ports like those in South Carolina. Colonial merchants, especially New England merchants, were the leading traders on less lucrative long-distance routes, like those between Africa and Savannah and the shuttle traffic between the West Indies and the southern colonies. Thus, the distinguished president of the American Antiquarian Society, Charles Deane (1886), was not entirely correct when he asserted "that the work of transporting Negroes from Africa to the mainland and islands of this continent was almost exclusively done by Englishmen and in English ships." To accept this view should not lead one to conclude, however, that direct participation in the slave trade did not form an important part of New England's overseas trade.

Apart from the overall quantitative importance of the slave trade in New England's maritime commerce, its concentration among a few merchant capitalists made it an important source of capital for industrial investment in subsequent decades.

In these [New England] towns there grew up a privileged class of slave-trading merchants whose wealth was drawn largely from the Negro traffic. They enjoyed the highest social position and held public offices of the greatest trust and responsibility. The Belchers, Waldos, Fanueils, and Cabots of Boston; the Royalls of Charlestown; the Pepperells of Kittery; and the Crowninshields of Salem, Massachusetts, were but a few of the leading slave merchants of the Bay Colony. Equally representative were the Malbones, Gardners, Ellerys, and Champlins of Newport; the Browns of Providence, the DeWolfs of Bristol, and the Robinsons of Narragansett, Rhode Island. [Greene 1942: 28–31]

These same families provided the foundation for social and political leadership as well.

THE WEST INDIAN CONNECTION

"I don't know why we should blush to confess that molasses was an essential ingredient in American independence," said John Quincy Adams. The significance of this statement lies in the role played by New England in the Atlantic-wide division of labor imposed through colonial domination by the countries of western Europe. Economically, this division of labor rested on African slave labor. What distinguished New England from most of the New World colonies is that its lack of easily exploited natural resources both allowed and compelled it to squeeze (de facto and de jure) from British mercantilism some part of the functions usually limited to the colonial mother country—maritime commerce and shipping. Ultimately, this worked to the mutual benefit of New England and Britain, as it enabled the former to obtain the income with which to pay for imported British manufactures. Thus, New England, as it struggled to offset the debt it incurred by importing British goods, was able to supply valuable goods and services to the West Indies and to other colonies. This made the entire British "realm" more productive, which was the main goal of mercantilism.[10]

Molasses and rum became "the customary currency" (Hedges 1952: 24) by which the colonists could obtain a variety of goods both domestic and foreign to ship to the West Indies or other colonies. Between 1768 and 1772, Massachusetts alone imported some 8.3 million gallons of molasses—8.2 million gallons from non-British colonies in the West Indies. Adding to this the 2.3 million gallons imported by Rhode Island during this period, these

Table 2   Destinations and average annual value (£) of commodity exports from New England, 1768–72

Commodity	Great Britain	Ireland	Southern Europe	West Indies	Africa	Total
Fish	206	—	57,195	94,754	—	152,155
Livestock, beef, pork	374	—	461	89,118	—	89,953
Wood products	5,983	167	1,352	57,769	—	65,271
Whale products	40,443	—	804	20,416	440	62,103
Potash	22,390	9	—	—	—	22,399
Grains, grain products	117	23	3,998	15,764	—	19,902
Rum	471	44	1,497	—	16,754	18,766
Other	6,991	1,018	296	247	—	8,552
Total	76,975	1,261	65,603	278,068	17,194	439,101

Source: McCusker and Menard 1985: 108.

two colonies alone accounted for almost three-fifths of the 18 million gallons imported into the mainland colonies (Ostrander 1948: 78). "It is this quantity of molasses which serves as an engine in the hands of the Merchant to effect the great purpose of paying for British manufactures" (Hedges 1952: 22).[11]

There were other key commodities which reflected the close relationship between New England and the West Indies (Price 1984: 27). Nine commodities made up more than 75% of the value of all British North American goods exported in 1770, shown here with the percentage of the colonial total exported to the West Indies and Africa in parentheses: tobacco (0.2); bread and flour (51.3); fish (35.0); rice (27.1); wheat, oats, and maize (31.4); pine, oak, and cedar boards (84.0); staves and headings (54.1); horses and livestock (100); and beef and pork (98.5). Most of these represented exports to the West Indies from the New England colonies (see Table 2).

The West Indies also imported substantial quantities of other New England goods; these quantities, though lower in value, nevertheless represented a significant percentage of the total quantities of these goods produced and exported by particular colonies. This included over 85% of the quantities of the following commodities: spermaceti and tallow candles, peas and beans, meal, potatoes, butter, cheese, soap, shoes, onions, framed houses, hoops, shook hogsheads, poultry, tallow, and lard. Clearly, New England's economic prosperity was intertwined and dependent on the West India connection. Between 1768 and 1772, 63% of New England's exports were destined for the West Indies (Table 2).

The preponderance of foodstuffs in this list is noteworthy. The West Indies were so deeply engaged in producing and exporting sugar to serve the British that they relied heavily on the mainland colonies to supply their food, even fish—astounding for islands so richly endowed with seafood. This can be explained only through colonial domination and the distorted patterns of economic relationships founded on exploitation of the people of the colonies. For colonies struggling for independence from Britain, the contribution of slave labor and the slave(ry) trade became all the more important.

Finally, the evidence shows that the West Indies were not just an important source of imports into the U.S. and an important market for New England goods. New England shipping houses were also greatly involved in carrying goods between the mainland colonies and the West Indies. Colonial shipping, which New England dominated, accounted for the bulk of the shipping between the British (and foreign) West Indies and various regions of the U.S. between 1768 and 1772. In studying tonnage flows, Walton (1968: 365) concludes: "By far the most important route to shippers and traders in New England was the route to the West Indies. This route accounted for slightly less than half the New England clears and enters." For ownership proportions, except for imports into the lower South, colonial shipping houses clearly dominated shipping with the West Indies (shipbuilding also benefited).

As early as 1679, Boston could be labeled "the mart town of the West Indies."

In the 6 months from March 25 to September 29, 1688, out of 141 ships clearing from Boston, 84 were in the

West Indies traffic. Nearly all these were Boston-owned and Massachusetts-built. Of the more than 140 arrivals during the same 6 months, 89 came with cargoes from the West Indies, 37 others from other American colonies and 21 from England. One of the impulses for the establishment of the famous New England mint in 1652 was the need for coining and recording the bullion and currency which poured in from the southern islands. [Writers Project 1941]

This pattern continued until the American Revolution, as indicated by the 2,443 ships in the sample I studied. While the West Indies remained an important partner, the major change was the expansion of the domestic market. In 1752, 1762, and 1764, for example, 444, or 21.8%, of all the ships came from the West Indies, 335 ships came from North Carolina, 254 from Philadelphia, and 176 from Maryland. Only 100 came from London. This growth of domestic trade—of the home market—was the foundation upon which industrial capitalism in the U.S. could effectively fasten.

Thus, overseas shipping was an important source of profits and capital for New England. Shepherd and Walton estimate that New England's merchants earned an average of £427,000 per year from the sale of freight and commercial services between 1768 and 1772. Lord Sheffield estimated that mainland merchants collected freight charges of £245,000 from the West Indian markets in 1770. For a region with chronic deficits, such sums were of some considerable importance (McCusker and Menard 1985: 110, 157).

In discussing the significance of the West Indies, Jacob Price (1984: 36) has raised several counterfactual questions:[12]

If there had been no West Indies, how much trade would New England and the Middle Colonies have had? How many people then would have been content to emigrate to or reside in those areas? If there had been no slavery, would there have been any West Indies trade? What about Virginia, Maryland and the Carolinas? I detect a certain impatience with counterfactual propositions in much recent critical literature. These nevertheless are not unreasonable questions, even though we may never obtain answers to them that will give general satisfaction.

Price suggests that slavery was not necessary for tobacco production in the Chesapeake and North Carolina but is less sure
whether nonslave economies were conceivable in South Carolina,
Georgia, and the West Indies. He concludes: "These are some
of the questions we must at least consider before we attempt to
pass on the absolute indispensability of slavery. However, since
such questions are uncongenial to most professional historians,
most analysis will prefer to start with slavery and the slave trade
as givens" (ibid.: 36).

It is not so much "impatience with counterfactual propositions"
as distaste for hypothetical history, especially when the historical record is so abundantly clear about what actually happened.
And the claim for indispensability is not one I am making yet.
The fact is that the economy of New England and colonial commerce were bound to a West Indies economy dependent on slavery
and the slave trade. Had there been no slavery, the West Indies
trade would not have been as substantial. And had there been
no substantial West Indies trade, there would have been much
less trade for New England and the mainland colonies. The result
would have been a much narrower field and a markedly slowed
pace for the economic movement of the colonies toward political
independence and industrial capitalism in a developing United
States.[13]

EARLY INDUSTRIES BASED ON MARITIME COMMERCE

Shipbuilding

In constructing an index of industrial output for New England
in the early nineteenth century, Zevin (1975: 1–3) suggests that
seven sectors (cotton textiles, woolen textiles, cotton textile machinery, pig iron, cast iron, rolled and slit iron and products, and
shipbuilding) probably accounted for roughly one-half to three-
quarters of the manufacturing value-added and "between 30% and
40% of employment in the sector." "Before 1816 shipbuilding is
predominant among the index industries. In 1810 it accounts for
78% of the total index. . . . Shipbuilding declines to 29% of the
total in 1820 and 6% in 1831."

In my sample of 4,747 ships, 49% of the slaves imported into
Virginia and 67% of the tonnage consisted of ships "made in

America." Klein (1978: 133–34) has confirmed this, concluding that "most of the ships involved in the trade were built in
America," and makes an additional point of importance.

American-built ships not only dominated the West Indian and
Coastwise trades, where they accounted respectively for 96
percent and 93 percent of the ships, but were even important
in the shipping coming directly from Africa. On this route,
they accounted for 44 percent of the ships, with English-built
ships making up the rest. . . .

In a comparison of construction with ownership, the dominance of American-built shipping is again impressive. Fully
100 percent of the ships owned by Southern and West
Indian merchants, and 93 percent of the Northern and Middle Atlantic colonial-owned ships, were colonial-built. Of
the shipping owned by English merchants, 40 percent were
American-made.

Price (1976: 722) estimates that between 1763 and 1775, "shipbuilding in the Thirteen Colonies totalled about 40,000 measured
tons annually and was worth about £300,000 sterling, of which
at least 18,600 tons worth £140,000 were sold abroad." He concludes that "American colonial shipbuilding, a neglected industry,
does appear to have made a significant contribution to late colonial
export earnings."

Rum Manufacturing

One of the factors which encouraged the commercial relationship
between New England and the West Indies was the trade in West
Indian molasses needed in New England for the production of rum
for export. For his profits the sugar planter depended upon getting
rid of the rum and molasses left over from sugar production; sugar
alone was not profitable (Pitman 1917: 415). New England merchants were quite willing to import molasses and rum. That rum
making was a natural consequence of such large importations of
molasses could be anticipated.

Rum was distilled and exported from New England as early
as 1708. In 1770, over 6.5 million gallons of molasses were
imported. Some 140 distilleries, 30 in Rhode Island and 63 in
Massachusetts, turned out 5 million gallons of rum. In fact, "the

best known of this type of colonial manufacture was the North American distillation of West Indian molasses" (McCusker and Menard 1985: 290).

Spermaceti Candles

Spermaceti candles were made from the head matter of whales, that is, from a good grade of oil that burned cleanly. The oil was also used to burn in streetlights and in home lanterns. New England exports of spermaceti candles to the West Indies between 1768 and 1772 averaged 271,168 pounds, at an annual value of £18,255, over 6% of the total of all goods shipped from New England to the West Indies (Shepherd 1970: 38–40). This was not an insignificant trade. "Spermaceti candles were a part of the cargo of virtually every ship the Browns [a prominent Rhode Island family of merchants] sent to the Caribbean area during the score of years preceding the outbreak of the War for Independence" (Hedges 1952: 90). In addition, many slave ships took consignments of these candles to Africa. For example, the Browns supplied such well-known slave traders as the Wantons and Malbones of Newport and Simeon Potter and the DeWolfs of Bristol (Greene 1942). The editors of a volume of papers illustrating the commerce of Rhode Island made a special mention in the introduction: "Two branches deserve mention, the purchase and manufacture of spermaceti, which were controlled by agreement among the large manufacturers in New England as closely as by any trust agreement of later times; and the African slave trade, of the greatest importance to Newport" (Massachusetts Historical Society 1914–15, 1: 69, vi).[14]

These early industries provided the foundation and part of the initial capital for the industrialization of New England. They were all closely tied to the slave(ry) trade. In the section that follows, an attempt is made to demonstrate the role of slave-grown southern cotton in the emergence of a national economy in the United States between 1790 and 1860. It becomes evident that the size of the market for the products of New England's cotton textile industry during the period was a function of interregional specialization, which was due largely to the growth of the slave-based cotton economy of the southern states. The growth of the market, in turn, made the production of cotton textile machinery economical.

SLAVE-PRODUCED COTTON AND THE EMERGENCE
OF A NATIONAL ECONOMY

One of the great travesties in the study of U.S. history is the suggestion that only the South benefited directly and substantially from slavery. The benefits from what we are calling the slave(ry) trade to the North and to the U.S. as a whole were far from indirect.[15] It is quite easy to argue that the growth of the U.S. national economy directly depended on the fruits of the labor of slaves.

For many years, the staple crop produced and sold widely was sugar. But in the nineteenth century, it was cotton, "the fabric of civilization," which could be "sold in the markets of the world." And it was the common perception that "cotton and slavery were so complementary as to seem to be made for each other" (Nettels 1962: 188). Nettels argues that slavery and cotton were the key to the South's development. Douglass North (1961: 166–67) explains why:

By all odds, the most important influence [on American manufacturing development before the Civil War] was the growth in the size of the domestic market. . . . The growing localization of industry, specialization of function, and increasing size of firm were all basically related to the growth in the market, which stemmed from the regional specialization and growth of interregional trade beginning after 1815, but was *really* accelerated with the surge of expansion in the 1830's. The markets for textiles, clothing, boots and shoes, and other consumer goods were national in scope, reflecting the decline of self-sufficiency and the growth of specialization and division of labor. Derived demand for machinery and products of iron expanded in response to the consumer goods industries. The cotton trade was the immediate impetus for this regional specialization, and the growth of cotton income in the 1830's was the most important proximate influence upon the spurt of manufacturing growth of that decade.

North (ibid.: 181) later pinpoints the expanding cotton economy as the main impetus for the development of the West, since "the extension of cotton cultivation into the new South meant a growing market for flour, cornmeal, livestock products, and whiskey."

In 1790, the U.S. produced approximately 1.5 million pounds of cotton. By 1800, owing to the success of the cotton gin, which had been invented in 1791, and the new life it breathed into the institution of slavery, this amount had risen to 35 million pounds, a remarkable increase of over 2,200%. By 1820, 160 million pounds were produced by the U.S., and by 1860 this amount had grown to 2.3 billion pounds (Hammond 1897). This places the U.S. share of total world production at 9% in 1801, almost 29% in 1821, and 66% in 1860 (Bruchey 1967: 7).

Cotton became central to the U.S. economy. On the export side, cotton constituted the largest share of exports from the U.S. to Great Britain. In 1816, unmanufactured cotton accounted for almost 40% of the U.S. exports, increasing to 54% in 1856. Raw tobacco, wheat, and flour declined relatively over this same period as the importance of domestic manufactures increased. Cotton also made up the bulk of the value of all U.S. exports from 1815 on, reaching 57.5% in 1860. This gave the U.S. substantial foreign exchange to purchase overseas goods and services.

In 1800, the proportion of the total U.S. cotton crop exported to Great Britain was already over 45%; it still averaged more than 50% in the two decades preceding the Civil War. Similarly, from providing 29% of Britain's cotton imports in 1800, the U.S. became its leading supplier, furnishing over 50% of its imports from 1820 to 1860, 88.5% in 1860 (ibid.: 9–17).

As the South increasingly concentrated its resources on the production of raw cotton for export to Britain, it had to purchase services from New England and foodstuffs from the West. These interregional purchases expanded as income from raw cotton exports to Europe grew. New England's shipping houses transported southern cotton to Europe and brought European manufactures for southern consumers. New England's merchants and financiers also found expanding markets for their business in the South. In turn, the growing commercial cities of New England became major food markets for western farmers, who in turn purchased services from New England and, later, manufactured goods. This interregional specialization, based initially on southern slave-grown cotton and facilitated by improvements in internal water transportation, provided a large domestic market for the products of New England's cotton textile industry, a market securely protected by the nation's tariff laws.

NEW ENGLAND MERCHANTS AND THE U.S. INDUSTRIAL REVOLUTION IN TEXTILES

Industrial activity prior to the development of the textile industry in the early nineteenth century was very low. The census of 1810 indicates that agriculture was the dominant form of economic activity. Of the 2.3 million people estimated to be in the labor force, almost 2 million worked in agriculture (Sobel and Sicilia 1986: 92). Few people wanted to risk financial loss from investment in an untested arena like manufacturing. The Navigation Acts, which prohibited the export of some manufactured goods or confined it to British needs, were another fetter on colonial development (Harper 1939).

The textile industry was central to the industrial revolution in the U.S. In 1816, large-scale manufacturing enterprises in New England employed about 5,000 people, or slightly more than 1% of the regional labor force. By 1840, this number had grown to about 100,000 people, about one-seventh of the New England labor force, with 20 to 30 factories employing up to 1,500 employees each. As Zevin (1971: 123) puts it:

> This remarkable explosion of industrial activity was dominated in every sense by the expansion of the cotton textile component of manufacturing. The cotton industry was the only major New England industry to expand steadily in the very earliest years of the period from 1816 to the early 1820's. In the late 1830's cotton textiles accounted for two-thirds of the value added in all large scale New England manufacturing.

Cotton textiles had accounted for only 10% of manufacturing in 1810, and its growth influenced other important industries (e.g., iron). By 1860, cotton manufacturing became the leading industry in the U.S. as measured by the amount of capital and labor it employed and the net value of the product. Industrial use of raw cotton increased from 5 million pounds in 1790 to 433 million in 1860, over eight times as rapidly as the U.S. population. The production of cotton machinery provided an additional boost to the U.S. economy.[16]

In the following section, I shall point to some evidence linking the slave(ry) trade and two specific entrepreneurial families considered critical to the development of textile manufacturing: the Brown family–Slater group of Rhode Island and Francis Cabot Lowell and the Boston Associates.[17] These two groups correspond to the two stages of the industrialization of textiles: the emergence of water-powered spinning of yarn in Rhode Island and that of the power loom and large mill in Massachusetts.

Moses Brown, Samuel Slater,
and Machine Spinning

Moses Brown was a member of one of the leading families of merchants in the United States. Its commercial, manufacturing, agricultural, and financial dealings included shipping and maritime trade to the East Indies, South America, Europe, Africa, and the West Indies; importing molasses and distilling rum; a virtual monopoly in the manufacture of spermaceti candles; cod fishing; and, later, profitable undertakings in banking and insurance; turnpike, bridge, and canal building; and land speculation in the western territories.

Members of the Brown family were also slave-trading merchants. While Newport slavers were active early in the trade in 1700, the patriarch of the Brown family, Captain James Brown, was the first Providence merchant "to enter this hazardous traffic" in 1736. Upon his early death, a brother, Obadiah, and four sons, "John, Josey, Nickey, and Mosey," were left to carry on the slave trade and the rest of the family's business dealings. The details of their activity show, first, that they got involved without hesitation in "that unrighteous traffic," as Moses Brown called it, but more importantly, that the slave trade was a vehicle through which the Browns sought to realize other aims—selling at a profit the goods which they produced themselves or acquired in their far-flung commercial undertakings, all to finance new ventures. James Brown fitted out the sloop *Mary*, the first "Guinea man" to sail from Providence Plantations; his son Obadiah served as supercargo. Hedges (1952: 71–72) reports that "the first Guinea voyage of the Brown family was not a failure; on the other hand, it was not a conspicuous success."

The voyage of their brig *Sally*, under the guidance of Captain Esek Hopkins, is illustrative. The cargo consisted of "159 hogsheads and 6 tierces of rum, amounting to 17,274 gallons, 25 casks of rice, 30 boxes of spermaceti candles, 10 hogsheads of tobacco, 6 barrels of tar, 40 barrels of flour, a quantity of loaf sugar, 2 tierces of brown sugar, 96 pounds of coffee, and 1800 bunches of onions." Also on board was "a small arsenal," including guns and pistols, 40 "hand Cufs" and 40 "Shakels," 3 "Chanes," 13 "Cutleshes," and a dozen "padlocks" (ibid.: 75–76). The products of the Browns' rum-making business and the goods obtained from trading with various colonies thus were being disposed of. In addition, the venture provided an outlet for the products of an iron-making business; witness the arsenal, handcuffs, shackles, and other items.

But it was also the *Sally* which probably helped to discourage at least three of the Brown brothers from engaging more extensively in the slave trade. First, an inordinate amount of time, rum, and other resources was expended in gathering a cargo of slaves because of stiff competition from other slave-trading vessels in the "Road," as the coast of Africa was called. After nine months, Hopkins secured 196 slaves. Second, 21 slaves died between 21 April and 21 August. But the worst was yet to come. On 28 August, Hopkins wrote that when the "Slaves Rose on us was obliged to fire on them and Destroyed 8 and Several more wounded badly 1 Thye & ones Ribs broke." Over the next few weeks, slaves died almost daily, and when Hopkins reached Antigua, he reported that the brutal suppression of the revolts left many Africans "so disperited" that "some drowned themselves, some starved and other sickened and died." Almost 90 slaves were dead, and those who were left were "very sickly and disordered [in] manner" (ibid.: 79–80). Twenty-four were sold for £417:4:3. A total of 109 slaves died, and 38 remained unaccounted for. Hedges (ibid.: 80) remarks that "*Sally* had traded her cargo of rum for tragedy, disease and death." The loss on the voyage was estimated at $12,000.

While this voyage shows that not every slaving venture ended in profits, the general expectations of the business community indicate that profits were far more frequent than losses. In fact, the expectations of the Browns reveal how large Africa and the West Indies loomed in launching industrial enterprises in the U.S. Prior to 1765, Hedges (ibid.) reports, the Browns sent ships to the Caribbean to make money to expand their candle-making business. But the main objective in 1765 was to make money with which to enter the iron-making business.

> Three of their vessels were to rendezvous at Surinam. One of them was later to go to Barbados to meet Captain Esek Hopkins, fresh from his slave-trading voyage to the Guinea coast in *Sally*. Another carried an especially valuable cargo, including "the best parcel [of horses] shipped out of this place, several of which were too superior to be used in the sugar mills and were, therefore, to be sold as riding horses. From the sale of this and the other two cargoes at Surinam, plus the anticipated profits from the sale of Esek Hopkins' slaves in the British Islands, Nicholas Brown and Company hoped to realize handsomely." The profits were to pay part of the initial costs of their new experiment in iron. [Ibid.: 123]

Many such voyages and plans were undertaken, with similar results in mind. We have no direct evidence of the returns from these slaving ventures. One can only infer from the general view of contemporaries that they met the expectations of their owners. It was with good reason that these contemporary observers regarded the slave trade and the West Indian trade as yielding a "golden harvest" (Peterson 1853: 104). In the words of Duignan and Clendenen (1963: 5): "It was probably no exaggeration to say that the slave trade was the lubricating oil that kept the colonial economy moving smoothly. For this reason, the trade was as vital to New England as to the South."

John Brown remained in the slave trade to the very end. As a U.S. congressman, he fought in the early 1800s to reopen the slave trade. "That John Brown was one of the foremost champions of the African slave trade in his day there can be no doubt" (Hedges 1952: 84). Moses Brown, on the other hand, was active in the slave trade only for a short period and later became an ardent abolitionist, a "paradox" that continues to perplex historians. No doubt it has something to do with the fact that Moses was converted and became a Quaker in the 1770s.[18] But the roots of the paradox are to be found in the broader economic context. The few slave-trading ventures in which Moses Brown participated had not been as profitable as those of other merchants. He found greater success in other lines, notably iron works and candle making, which in part depended on the slave trade, and textile manufacturing.

The postrevolutionary crisis after the late 1770s had disrupted overseas commerce, and Brown "was greatly concerned over the deteriorating economic situation of the state, particularly as it affected the Quakers." According to his biographer, the moral code of the Quakers prevented their participation in certain industries, and many Quakers were worried over the debt that increasing English imports were piling up. He became convinced that "Americans must develop their own manufacturing as a means of lessening their economic dependence on England. To Moses, it seemed that cotton manufacturing would, at one and the same time, improve the lot of the Friends and contribute to the greater economic independence of his country" (Hedges 1968: 160–61).

Certainly inspired by the industrial successes in Europe and facing a mounting economic crisis at home, Moses Brown himself conducted detailed investigations of the existing state of cotton manufacturing in the United States and engaged in a brief period of scientific experimentation.[19] He purchased all of the technology then available in Rhode Island but failed because of "inadequate machines and unskilled mechanics" (ibid.). Soon, however, he received unexpected help. In 1789, Samuel Slater, a management trainee in the textile mill of Jedidiah Strutt, a partner of the famous Richard Arkwright,[20] violated the British laws forbidding the emigration of skilled textile mechanics and came to America, disguised as a farm laborer. Within a few months, Slater was in touch with Brown, who agreed to finance him in "perfecting the first water-mill in America" (ibid.: 163). Slater was taken on as a full partner and, as Hedges (ibid.: 164–65) states, "on December 20, 1790 . . . set in motion the power-driven machinery he had made. . . . Thus was born cotton manufacturing in America, which marked the entrance of the young country into the first stage of the Industrial Revolution."

Francis Cabot Lowell, the Boston Associates, the Power Loom, and Large-Scale Factory Production

It is at another stage of the commercial crisis after the 1808 embargo and the War of 1812 that we find Francis Cabot Lowell and the Boston Associates and explore another prime example of the relationship between the slave(ry) trade and the rise of industrial capitalism in the U.S.

The Slater mill financed by the Brown family in the 1790s marked a tremendous advance over hand methods of spinning raw cotton into yarn and thread. But it still relied on the putting-out method of manufacturing finished products like cloth; that is, the yarn was turned over to individuals for home production. In 1810, "only 2 per cent of the cloth made in America was produced in factories" (Wright 1941: 275). The Embargo Act and the War of 1812 between the United States and Great Britain disrupted the New England economy, and many small firms, like that of the Browns and Slater, were unable to sustain themselves through the hard times (Ware 1931: 39–59).

Both the embargo and the war must be viewed as a further installment in the continuing political struggle that had already led to the American Revolution. The newly independent bourgeoisie in the United States was still struggling to consolidate its control over its new economy and political state. Great Britain and France actively attempted to restrict American commerce, seized United States ships, and allegedly encouraged warfare between Native Americans and the United States on the U.S.-Canadian border (there was ample reason for warfare without British encouragement). The U.S. declaration of war against Great Britain in 1812 was a response to this. Cotton manufacture in the U.S. expanded during the war, mainly because British goods were kept out of the U.S. market. But the war's end resulted in the dumping of even more British commodities, including cheaper cotton cloth, on the American market.

It was during this period that Francis Cabot Lowell introduced the first power loom and a new form of business into the American textile industry. "It was . . . the prototype of the big modern corporation, organized for mass production and integrating all processes from the raw materials through the finished product under one management and, as far as possible, in one plant" (ibid.: 60). This development signaled a new stage of capitalism in the United States: a shift from small-scale manufacturing and home production to that of large-scale machine industry. The importance of this development can be seen from the estimate that the compound annual growth rate of cotton cloth production between 1815 and 1833 was 29%. Adjusting for the shift of production from home to factory, the growth rate of output was still 15.4%, while the introduction of the power loom accounted for about 5% of this growth rate. Thus these two components account for about two-thirds of the overall growth in cloth output (Zevin 1971: 146).

Francis Cabot Lowell was a wealthy merchant and brilliant mathematician. After graduating from Harvard, he entered commerce with an uncle, William Cabot, and made a fortune. He eventually joined in the construction of India Wharf, the second largest commercial wharf in Boston. While in Scotland and England, ostensibly recuperating from an illness, he used his considerable connections to secure visits to textile mills.

If Lowell really was ill, it was possibly because of the financial losses and general crises Boston merchants suffered from the disruption of commerce by the embargo and the War of 1812. But his industrial espionage almost certainly was planned. His illness was propitious, and some ruse would have been necessary, because England had forbidden any detailed study of textile technology by foreigners.[21] Moreover, Lowell had intimate knowledge of the current state of textile experimentation in the U.S., since his uncle and others had launched the unsuccessful Beverly Mill in 1786 (this effort was one of the earliest experiments in the U.S. textile industry). His letters to his partner Patrick Tracy Jackson chronicle his interest in the industry, and Nathan Appleton, another partner, actually visited Lowell in Scotland, where they "had frequent conversation on the matter of Cotton Manufacture" and discussed Lowell's plan "before his return to America, to visit Manchester, for the purpose of obtaining all possible information on the subject, with a view to the introduction of the improved manufacture in the United States" (Appleton 1858: 7).

On his visits to numerous mills, Lowell memorized all the details regarding the use of power looms in the British cotton textile industry. Returning to the U.S., he joined with Appleton, Jackson, Paul Moody, a mechanic, and others to charter a company and to build a factory and machines to make cotton fabrics. According to Chamberlain (1963: 56), "This was the beginning of the famous Boston Associates, a group that came to include most of the Lowell clan and their connections (Amorys, Cabots, Higginsons, Jacksons, Russels, Lees, and others of the old trading aristocracy), as well as the new merchant tribe of the Lawrences, who were eventually to intermarry with the Lowells."

The importance of this observation is that it correctly identifies the group of capitalists that put up the initial $100,000 to finance "the Waltham mill," as the Boston Manufacturing Company came to be called. Soon after its initial success, this same group "started buying shares with a madness all their own," enabling several other larger mills to be started. The initial success lay in providing the United States, after the embargo and the War of 1812 had stopped the importation of English textiles, with "some thirty miles of cotton cloth in a day and paying 10 to 20 per cent in dividends." Further, the impact of the shift from small-scale manufacture to the power loom and large-scale factory production can be clearly seen in the drastic reduction in the price of the cloth first manufactured by Lowell and his associates (Appleton 1858: 16): from 30 cents per yard in 1816 to 13 cents in 1826 to 6.5 cents in 1843.

In short, the power loom lowered the price of cotton cloth and increased the quantity produced. Combined with other factors— the growth of the population, lower transportation costs, rising per capita income, and changing consumer tastes—it "produced growth that was not merely rapid, but truly spectacular" (Davis et al. 1972: 419–27).

New England and the Slave(ry) Trade: A Summary

To summarize and reiterate some general points which demonstrate links between the textile revolution and slavery and the slave(ry) trade, the textile industry was financed by a relatively small group of wealthy merchants with capital derived especially from trade connected to the slave trade and slavery. This is clearly illustrated by the activities of the entrepreneurial groups we have been discussing.

In assessing the particular importance of the slave trade and slavery during this period, it is essential to keep in mind the general economic context. Rhode Island, for example, was a leading slave-trading center until 1808; merchants there had been among the most active slave traders since 1720. The expansion of the slave trade and that of general trade, which followed in its wake, ushered in the expansion of other activities from which entrepreneurial groups profited greatly. The Brown family, for example, who mainly supplied rum, candles, and other commodities, were closely connected to others more active as slave traders. A similar argument can be made for Massachusetts and its merchants. Thus, it is necessary to stress both the accumulation of capital derived from direct participation as slave traders and the accumulation of capital and expansion of commerce and manufacturing in economic sectors directly dependent on the slave(ry) trade.

The Brown family became a prime example of the important transformation of the U.S. economy from one based on merchant capital during the colonial period to one based on industrial capital during the post–Revolutionary War period. As Hedges (1952: xiii–xiv) summarizes:

> As colonial merchants the Browns were first concerned with sea-borne trade and, in a small way, with that important adjunct to the maritime commerce of the period, the distilling of rum. Gradually, in line with the pre-Revolutionary trend, they began to transfer their capital from sea to land. They became important manufacturers of spermaceti candles and of pig iron; by 1775 their mercantile and maritime interests had become ancillary to those of manufacture.
>
> The Browns . . . went into banking and insurance; they promoted the building of turnpikes and, later, of canals; and, most important, they introduced the cotton manufacture into this country. This last venture was financed originally by the transfer of funds acquired in maritime pursuits.

In this context, the importance of trade with the slave-based economies of the West Indies must be emphasized. "To the Browns, trade with the Caribbean region was of major importance. So closely were other features of their business integrated with this commerce that stoppage of it for any length of time would have thrown their whole way of life out of gear. Not content merely to traffic with British possessions, they constantly sent their ships to the foreign colonies in the area" (ibid.: 46). Clearly the slave(ry) trade was the soil that nourished the activities of the Brown family. The family was reported to own two distilleries, and several of the Browns were considered master distillers. There is clear evidence that they used considerable amounts of molasses and rum (ibid.: 42).

The families of several of the Boston Associates were also involved directly in the slave(ry) trade. In addition, their general mercantile activities were closely intertwined with the slave(ry) trade. Porter (1937: 79–80) makes this observation about four of the families:

> The highly speculative African trade was a different matter and the triangular trade in molasses from the West Indies, rum from the West Coast, and slaves to the West Indies, etc., came nearer than any other to producing a group of pre-Revolutionary specialized merchants, but it was a Rhode Island rather than a Massachusetts specialty. Neither Jonathan Jackson, nor the Tracys, nor Joseph Lee, Sr., nor the Cabots, ever participated personally in the slave trade. They confined themselves to selling rum to those who did so participate, as in the early nineteenth century their descendants similarly supplied slavers with gaudy India cottons while expressing pious and probably sincere hopes for the slave trade's abolition.

But there is evidence which contradicts Porter's claim about non-involvement in the slave trade. Francis Cabot Lowell is said to have "marched with the Independent Cadets under Major T. H. Perkins" while a student at Harvard. But his relationship to Perkins goes much farther than this. Samuel Cabot married Eliza Perkins, daughter of Thomas Handasyd Perkins, in 1812. "T. H. Perkins, like other merchants of his day, engaged in the slave trade, for there was not a merchant of any prominence who was not then directly or indirectly engaged in this trade" (Briggs 1927: 386). Perkins wrote in 1791 to a Haitian contact: "When the disturbances of Y'r Colony have passed, you will probably be in want of Cargoes for the Coast of Africa. Rum, Tobacco, and Coarse Cloths are always to be had here [at] low [prices], such as suits the Guinea Market." On 17 November 1792, Perkins wrote about slaves to the captain of *The Willing Quaker*: "He is to take care that they are *young & healthy without any defects* in their Limbs,

Teeth & Eyes, & as few females as possible." On 1 December 1792, he informed his contacts that "this money you will appropriate to the purchase of the Slaves & other articles specifi'd. . . . If you cannot readily buy the slaves in the road [off the coast], we hope you will find some new negroes from on shore, who know nothing of the language" (ibid.).

In describing extracts of letters from various firms in which Perkins was a member, Briggs (ibid.: 469) had this to say:

> John and Andrew Cabot of Beverly and Samuel Cabot, Sr. were interested in many of the ventures of these firms. Until the uprising in St. Domingo, the Perkins and Cabot ships seem to have been engaged in the slave trade. Rum and molasses were also an important part of many of the cargoes. The "Guinea ships" spoken of in these letters were ships in the slave trade with the western coast of Africa.

Various letters from Perkins and his associates confirm the purchases and sales of a "Negro Wench" or a "Negro Man." Special orders were also placed: "If it should be in your power to purchase a few serviceable stout negroes, some Tradesmen (as Carpenters, Blacksmiths, & a Cooper) & others acquainted with the Culture of Tobacco, we sh'd be glad you would do it on our acct. & ship them here, one or two at a time, as opportunity offers." Reporting a few months later that "the Ports of St. Domingo, Caracas & Havanna are opend [*sic*] for the reception of Negroes in foreign bottoms, for the space of two years, free of duty," Perkins was enthusiastic about the prospects for profits: "There is a fine field opened for Guinea Speculations" (ibid.: 475, 476).

The quote from Porter also indicates another close connection to the slave trade: distilling and supplying rum. And it appears that this was a primary interest of Frances Cabot Lowell and his family: "As to the rum trade. There are literally hundreds of receipts in Salem and Beverly records of excised goods and almost invariably New England Rum is the principal item of export. As invariably, molasses is recorded among West Indian imports— evidently to make more rum! The following indicate only some of the activities of the Cabots in this line" (ibid.: 150f.).

Writing to a merchant in 1804, Perkins stated: "Mr. F C Lowell applied to know if we w'd guarantee you in the sale of some Rum he proposes to ship to yr. address. . . . As this gentleman is very extensively concerned in a Distillery it will be quite an object to secure his good will" (ibid.: 514).[22] In fact, rum making occupied the attention of the ancestors and associates of close relatives of Francis Cabot Lowell and Patrick Tracy Jackson of the Boston Associates and laid the basis for some of their fortune. Jonathan Jackson was the father of Patrick Tracy Jackson, and Francis Cabot Lowell first entered into the import-export business with William Cabot, the brother of John, Andrew, and George Cabot. "Joseph Lee and Co. distillers" was half owned by Joseph Lee, and William Bartlett, John and Andrew Cabot, and George Cabot each owned one-sixth. "For a time the manufacturer seemed to take precedence over the merchant. . . . Rum, naturally, became predominant among the goods in which he dealt" (Porter 1937: 393). Porter (ibid.: 20) also reports that "Jonathan Jackson and the Tracys, Joseph Lee and the Cabots, readily turned from the importation of British manufactures and molasses, the shipping of salt fish and flaxseed, and the distilling of rum, to the fitting out of privateers" in the era of the American Revolution.

Finally, the comment on "gaudy India cottons" suggests that the East India trade of the Browns and that of the Boston Associates must be investigated as another of the slave trade–related sources of industrial investment capital. The East India trade is generally portrayed as a replacement for the slave trade, but this quote suggests that the East India trade supported rather than replaced the slave trade.[23] In any case, it is another example of colonial labor contributing to the expansion of capital accumulation in Europe and in the United States.[24]

T. H. Perkins became the prime mover behind the development of the Lowell Manufacturing Company in 1823. Among the investors were members of the same investment group that had backed Francis Cabot Lowell: Patrick Tracy Jackson and his brothers, the Thorndikes, and others (Gibb 1950; Dalzell 1987). Perkins also served as vice president of the Massachusetts Hospital Life Insurance Company, a key vehicle for raising and controlling investment and personal funds for the Boston Associates. Many officers of the company were also members of the associates (ibid.).[25]

A study of capital mobility and American growth during this period further demonstrates the role of merchants in financing the early textile industry in Massachusetts:

That the textile firms tended not to finance expansion through sale of equity is obvious. . . . The [stock] issues themselves were very narrowly held. A study of eleven of the largest mills showed that the original holders of equity totalled only slightly over 500 people, and even as late as 1859 three-quarters of the stock was still held by less than 750 persons . . . , almost all . . . concentrated in Massachusetts. Less than one half of one percent of the original stockholders lived outside the state and even in 1859 this percentage had risen to only slightly above three. Occupationally the owners were concentrated in mercantile enterprises. . . . In short, although it may appear that capital was mobilized through the sale of securities, the relevant area of mobilization was very small indeed, limited as it was to a relatively small group of Massachusetts merchants. [Davis 1971: 294–95]

CONCLUSION

The slave trade and the economic activities which depended upon it are an embarrassing chapter in U.S. history. Many of the most prominent families on the East Coast and especially in New England were involved. Such embarrassments, however, must not become the reason for important parts of the history of the U.S. and the world to be rendered invisible. W. E. B. DuBois (1935: 722) was absolutely correct when he said: "Somebody in each era must make clear the facts with utter disregard to his own wish and desire and belief. What we have got to know, so far as possible, are the things that actually happened in the world."

The significance of the contribution of the slave(ry) trade, I have argued, does not hinge mainly on proving that New England's merchants were active as slave traders, nor does it rest on showing that individual merchants made substantial profits in this business. Both are unquestionably true. As I have argued in the case of British capitalism, such a narrowing of the slave(ry) trade's contribution is a convenient strawman which can be easily knocked down.

I have argued in this article, as others have done, that New England's maritime trade and shipping laid the foundation for, raised the infrastructure of, and funded early industrial development. This was particularly the case for the cotton textile industry between 1815 and 1860. Maritime trade and shipping depended largely on the slave trade and on the slave-based Atlantic economic system of the seventeenth, eighteenth, and nineteenth centuries. The early industries, such as shipbuilding and rum distilling, were directly tied to the slave trade and to maritime activities in general. These helped pave the way for the establishment of the cotton textile industry, which, together with the production of cotton textile machinery, became the leading sector of U.S. industrialization in the nineteenth century. The linkage between the cotton textile industry, the slave trade, other maritime activities, and the early industries in New England has been demonstrated with evidence taken from detailed case studies of some entrepreneurial groups in this important industry.

Cotton textile production in New England was not directly dependent on maritime activities as such, although its initial capital was. It was an import substitution industry and the markets for its products were internal (Inikori 1992). However, these internal markets were created by the slave-based cotton economy of the southern states and the maritime activities of New England. The tripartite division of labor which developed among the southern states, New England, and the West was based on the staple economy of the South. Expanding incomes from the production of raw cotton for export to Europe, using African slave labor, fueled the whole process. New England graduated from shipping southern cotton to Europe and importing European manufactures (including cotton textiles) for distribution in the United States to manufacturing these goods for the domestic markets in the South and West. No firm figures for regional sales are available; however, one recent estimate shows that southern purchases of cotton goods from U.S. producers amounted to $27 million for the year ending 20 June 1860 (Huertas 1979: 91). This was about one-third of the total output of New England's cotton textile industry for the period and over one-quarter of the combined output for New England and the Middle Atlantic (U.S. Bureau of the Census 1862: 180–81). The rapid settlement of the West after 1816, which depended on the expanding markets for food in the South and New England, provided an additional, and fast-growing, market for the cotton textile industry in New England. The combination of these several factors—increasing incomes from raw cotton exports to Europe, expansion of commercial and manufacturing activities in

New England (with the attendant growth of urban populations), and rapid migration to and settlement of the West—gave rise to sustained growth in the domestic market for the products of New England's cotton textile industry for many decades. This prevented the usual stagnation encountered by import substitution industries after the initial stage of rapid growth. Thus, New England's cotton textile output grew continuously after the adoption of tariff protection (Zevin 1971: 123–25). With this sustained growth, New England became the most rapidly expanding market for southern cotton producers. In this way, southern dependency moved from Britain to New England, to the great advantage of the latter's commerce and industry, especially the cotton textile industry. The contribution of the slave trade and New World slavery to the entire process is hard to exaggerate.

NOTES

1   The term *triangular trade* has a long history as an accurate description of the deep involvement of European merchants in the slave trade. For example, Bean (1971: 65) points out that of the 218 ships entering the British West Indies from Africa in 1685–1778, 212, or 97%, originated in England (i.e., had English port registry) and would presumably return there. This is the triangular trade—a voyage from England to Africa, on to the West Indies, and then back to England. Unfortunately, as I discuss in note 8 below, many scholars have sought to deny the participation of European and U.S. merchants in the slave trade simply by showing the absence of triangular patterns. The concept includes the carrying of produce from the West Indies by slave ships, general trade in slave-produced commodities, and other activities dependent on such trade.

2   Professor Greene, who died in 1987, was most helpful in my efforts to develop this research. I will be forever indebted to him for our long walks and talks during the conventions of the Association for the Study of Negro Life and History, and to his visit to Cornell in 1976 to discuss the research which led to *The Negro in Colonial New England*. The story of his work with Carter G. Woodson, the association, and the *Journal of Negro History* is particularly inspiring. This article is dedicated to his memory.

3   The long-standing conventional wisdom that the slave trade and slavery made a significant contribution to industrial capitalism was clearly stated by contemporary mercantilist theorists, of whom Malachi Postlethwayt (1745) is very representative. This view has been widely echoed over the centuries. Wilson E. Williams's *Africa and the Rise of Capitalism* (1936: 39f.) is one of the best statements in the twentieth century: "The African trade was a very important factor in the growth of the capitalist economy in England. . . . Without the Negro slave it is likely that neither the African trade nor

the West Indian economy could have played an important part in the development of English capitalism; and hence it is unlikely that without the slave trade, English capitalism could have shown the phenomenal growth it did."

Eric Williams, in *Capitalism and Slavery*, popularized this view of the development of capitalism in England. "By 1750 there was hardly a trading or a manufacturing town in England which was not in some way connected with the triangular or direct colonial trade. The profits obtained provided one of the main streams of that accumulation of capital in England which financed the Industrial Revolution" (Williams 1944: 51–52). That the slave trade made important contributions to industrial development in England has been not only seriously challenged but, if we accept the words of the challengers, definitively repudiated. Focusing on *Capitalism and Slavery*, Stanley Engerman (1972: 441) provided the initial repudiation: "The aggregate contribution of slave trade profits to the financing of British capital formation in the eighteenth century could not be so large as to bear weight as *the*, or *a*, major contributing factor. Its role was . . . of a relatively minor magnitude." Scholars who have embraced this denial of the positive contribution of the slave trade, many of whom trace their objections to Engerman's initial critique, include Anstey (1975), Rawley (1981), Hughes (1983), Davis (1984), McCusker and Menard (1985), and Reynolds (1985). Patterson (1979, 1982) and Davis (1975, 1984) substantially revised earlier views to conform with Engerman.

Inikori, Darity, Solow, Bailey, and others have reiterated the conventional argument that the slave trade was significant. Solow and Engerman 1987 is a useful discussion of "the legacy of Eric Williams."

4   I have only summarized the discussion of capitalism and slavery in Europe, since that subject is more thoroughly covered by Joseph Inikori, and I have expanded the focus on New England. Professor Inikori has been particularly helpful in sharing his important work and inspiring and cajoling me to complete my manuscript. It was Stanley Engerman (1972) whom I credited with initiating the effort to overthrow the conventional wisdom that the slave trade was important to European industrialization (Bailey 1979, 1986). Since I have been rather harsh in my criticism of what I see as serious errors in his work, Professor Engerman's critiques and encouragement of my efforts sustain his widespread reputation for assisting other scholars. William Darity of the University of North Carolina at Chapel Hill and Patrick Manning of Northeastern University have also been particularly encouraging. A fuller picture of the 15-year history of research on this topic is covered in Bailey 1986, with other acknowledgments.

5   The controversy over how many Africans were taken as slaves has been intense. Curtin (1969, 1975) makes the initial statement which spurred additional research and commentary. Inikori (1976a, 1976b, 1982) makes important corrections to Curtin's estimates, and Lovejoy (1982) attempts a synthesis. The debate on the number of slaves is most important for the study of the historical demography of Africa. For the slave trade's contribution to the U.S., most commentaries have not emphasized that it is the quality and quantity of the African input into the New World labor pool

and not mainly the quantity of Africans taken as slaves in Africa that is the critical issue.

6   Given the magnitude of the African input into the American population, the argument of Bernard Bailyn's *Peopling of British North America* (1986) is questionable. He elaborates four propositions that "do not involve to any significant extent the movements of either of the two non-Caucasian peoples —the Native Americans and the Africans—whose histories are so vital a part of the story," arguing that "relatively little" is known about the histories of "both of these groups" (ibid.: 20). Ralph Davis (1973: 125–42), in presenting these matters in his chapter on the peopling of the Americas, notes, "Some six and a half million people migrated to the New World in the three centuries between its discovery by Columbus and the American Revolution of 1776; a million of them white, the remainder Africans, who came unwillingly to slavery."

7   *Those Valuable People, the Africans: An Afrocentric Interpretation of the Slave(ry) Trade and the Rise of Industrial Capitalism in Europe and the United States* is the working title of a book which I hope to complete soon. It is taken from a quote by one of the leading mercantilist theorists of the era, Malachi Postlethwayt (1745: 6): "But is it not notorious to the whole World, that the Business of Planting [plantations] in our British Colonies, as well as the French, is carried on by the labour of Negroes, imported thither from Africa? Are we not indebted to *those valuable People, the Africans,* for our Sugars, Tobaccoes, Rice, Rum and all other Plantation Produce? And the greater the number of Negroes imported into our Colonies, from Africa, will not the Exportation of British Manufactures among the Africans be in Proportion; they being paid for in such Commodities only?"

I have used the term *Afrocentric* with considerable hesitation. The term should denote an interpretation in which the vantage point of people of African descent—the main force of the slave trade—is utilized. But the concept of "Afrocentricity" is laden with the ideological baggage associated with the position known as "cultural nationalism," and some view Afrocentricity as they preach it as the most correct or only perspective to be had. The debate over a paradigm for Afro-American studies is a long and involved one, not to be recounted here. Suffice it to say that my use of the phrase *an Afrocentric interpretation* is to remind us that perspectives in the field are quite diverse. See, for example, Asante 1987 for an elaboration of "the Afrocentric idea." This paper is an application of an alternative paradigm for understanding the Afro-American experience which is elaborated in Alkalimat and Associates 1986.

8   Ostrander (1973: 641) has gone farther than any other scholar in branding the triangular trade a myth: "The history of world commerce affords innumerable examples of triangular patterns of trade, but every schoolboy knows that *the* triangular trade was the one in rum, slaves, and molasses between colonial New England, Africa, and the West Indies. Popularly believed to have been one of the mainstays of American colonial commerce, this famous triangular trade is, in fact, a myth, for no such pattern of trade

existed as a major factor in colonial commerce. It is also a myth in the
sense of possessing mythic appeal, evidently requiring little in the way of
evidence to establish itself as historical 'fact.' " McCusker (1970: 1–24)
has a useful overview of the history of the concept, but his conclusion is
equally flawed. He mentions that "after years of work in New England
shipping records, Clifford Shipton [1963] could not recall having found a
single example of a ship engaged in such a triangular trade" (McCusker
1970: 21).

   Shepperson (1975: 102) makes a comment on the concept with which
I fully agree: "I am, however, wondering just how useful this triangular
trade concept is. This geometrical metaphor has, I think, been overworked
by historians for far too long. The slave trade was, if we must employ
geometrical images, often part of a quadrilateral trade across the Atlantic."
Unfortunately, geometrical understanding has often been pursued at the
expense of historical understanding; see note 1 above.

9   The Naval Office lists, designated Colonial Office (C.O.) 5 by the British
   Public Record Office, were prepared by colonial agents to facilitate the
   collection of tax revenue for the British government. The records cover the
   period from 1680 to 1784, though a complete series is not available for any
   port. The records I used initially were filmed—actually photographed—at
   the British Public Record Office in the 1930s by assistants working under
   the direction of Lawrence Harper of the University of California, Berkeley.
   Compilations from these data became the basis for the section on colonial
   statistics in the U.S. Bureau of the Census (1960). I am deeply grateful to
   Professor Harper for making his office and resources available to me during
   a 1976–77 dissertation fellowship at the University of California, Santa
   Barbara, and to the Center for Black Studies there for a productive year's
   stay and for financial support to travel to Berkeley.

10   The writings of the mercantilists such as Mun, Davenant, Gee, and Cary
   all elaborate a view of colonies as sources of raw materials, as outlets or
   "vents" for goods produced in the mother country, and as sources of supplies to other colonies within the realm. For discussion of this point and of
   mercantilism more generally, see the standard work Heckscher 1935. Dobb
   1947 is also useful.

11   Blaut (1989: 285) has provided some additional insight into the world
   context for gauging the importance of sugar. In Brazil, sugar production
   produced a profit which doubled its productive capacity every two years.
   By 1600, sugar exports were valued at £2 million—"twice the annual
   value of England's *total* exports to *all* the world." This underscores the
   observations of the mercantilists comparing the relative value of British
   and colonial workers. Blaut's conclusion is thus as appropriate for the U.S.
   as it is for Europe: "These and other statistics tending in the same direction suggest that in 1600 and thereafter the sugar plantation system, with
   its attendant economic and geographic characteristics, including the slave
   trade, shipping, refining, etc., was the single most important protocapitalist
   industry of the period." Blaut's other main contribution is his reiteration
   that, fundamentally, "colonial enterprise was from the outset a matter of
   capital accumulation" (ibid.: 280), and that "colonialism involved massive

production, massive exchange, and massive capital accumulation" (ibid.: 282). There are several ways in which this capital was generated: gold and silver mining (and plunder); plantation agriculture, especially Brazil; trade, colonial production, and commerce; slaving; and piracy. Blaut stresses the role of labor in capital accumulation and compares the contributions of the labor provided in the colonized sectors with the labor contributed within the colonizing nation.

12 I have already presented my views on the distortions of the slave trade's role which appear to result from biases in the neoclassical paradigm as it is utilized by several of the "cliometricians" or new economic historians (Bailey 1986: 34–40). For other insights see Coats 1980, McClelland 1978, Redlich 1971, Union for Radical Political Economics 1971, and Sutch 1982. Nevertheless, Darity (1982a, 1982b) and Solow (1985) both use the tools of neoclassical economics to argue for a positive role for the slave trade.

13 In January 1987 Gavin Wright of Stanford University wrote me a long and encouraging letter responding to the paper I had delivered at the annual meeting of the American Economics Association/National Economics Association in New Orleans. "The important point, however, is that showing widespread involvement with the slave trade is entirely different from showing that the trade was pivotally important. . . . To show that slavery was 'pivotal' requires a more precise economic argument. . . . I think such an economic argument can be made, but I also think one has to be tentative about claiming either ultimate indispensability (whatever that might mean) or a gargantuan magnitude of a contribution."

14 In one of the most intriguing episodes of the candle business, the Brown family joined with other manufacturers to form one of the earliest-known monopolies in U.S. history. The United Company of Spermaceti Candlers, later called the Spermaceti Trust, was formed on 5 November 1761, with the leading producers from Newport, Boston, and Providence involved. The group effectively monopolized the technology, governed the price of raw materials and finished products, and generally colluded to make their enterprises more profitable (Hedges 1952: 86–122).

15 See, e.g., O'Connor 1968: 47: "After 1830 the industrial North had become wedded, not only to the South's production of cotton, but to the institution of slave labor which made such valuable production possible"; cf. Genovese 1971: 157: "Capitalism in the North did not depend for its growth and development on the forced labor of Blacks, although it indirectly profited from the slave trade and from Southern slave labor."

16 George S. Gibb (1950: 179) stressed, in addition to the importance of the manufacture of cotton textile products, the significant impact of industrial activity related to the cotton textile industry, particularly the manufacture of textile machinery: "From the textile mills and the textile-machine shops came the men who supplied most of the tools for the American Industrial Revolution. From these mills and shops sprang directly the machine tool and locomotive industries, together with a host of less basic metal-fabricating trades. The part played by the textile machinery industry in fostering American metal-working skills in the early nineteenth century was a crucial one."

17 Vera Shlakman, in *Economic History of a Factory Town* (1935), is reported by Dalzell (1987: 253n) to be the first historian to use the term *Boston Associates*. I assume that the usage stems from the "Articles of Agreement between the Associates of the Boston Manufacturing Company," signed on 4 September 1813 and later incorporated into the company's bylaws (ibid.: 27).

18 The slave ship *The Willing Quaker* is a clue as to the attitudes of Quakers to involvement in the slave trade. See Briggs 1927: 386.

19 The textile industry in Britain expanded rapidly in the first decades of the nineteenth century. "Cotton was the leading industry in the British industrial revolution"; "*circa* 1770, [cotton] contributed only about half a million pounds a year to British national income. By 1801–3, with a net value added of about £11 m., it accounted for nearly 5 per cent of total national income and was second only to the woolen industry. By 1811–13, it had outstripped wool and contributed about 7½ per cent of national income. Retained imports of raw cotton, a conservative indicator of the volume of output for the industry in this period, had increased by a factor of 19 in [the] space of about fifty years" (Deane and Cole 1967: 182, 163).

20 Arkwright had perfected the spinning frame and further revolutionized cotton manufacture, following such earlier inventions as the "spinning jenny" and the "mule," all making for greater efficiency in spinning cotton into yarn (Rivard 1974). It is no mere coincidence that some early textile technology in Britain was financed by profits from the slave(ry) trade. Eric Williams (1944: 70) described Samuel Touchet as a member of the Company of Merchants Trading to Africa and a member of a great textile-manufacturing house in Manchester who represented Liverpool on the governing body of the company: "He was concerned in the equipping of the expedition which captured Senegal in 1758 and tried hard to get the contract for victualling the troops. A patron of Paul's unsuccessful spinning machine intended to revolutionize the cotton industry, and accused openly of trying to monopolize the import of raw cotton, Touchet added to his many interests a partnership, with his brothers, in above twenty ships in the West Indian trade." Similar connections between slave traders, West Indian merchants, and cotton manufacturers can undoubtedly be found.

  Though Williams says that Paul's invention was unsuccessful, other scholars see his efforts as "the first of the series of inventions which revolutionized cotton textile production in England" (Inikori 1992: 163; cf. Wadsworth and Mann 1931: 425, 427, 444–45).

21 I was delighted to read in late 1989 that Dalzell (1987: 10), author of the most detailed study of the Boston Associates, makes the same observation that I first made in 1975: "The evidence is that his [Lowell's] weakened health—the announced reason for his trip abroad—was the result of anxiety over business. More to the point, the same anxiety almost certainly explained Lowell's interest in textile manufacturing." The book opens: "As the story is usually told, the Waltham-Lowell system had its beginnings in a stunning act of industrial piracy. And so in a sense it did, though the individual responsible probably did not look like a man on such a mission" (ibid.: 5).

22   Greenslet (1946: 154) confirms the involvement with rum making: "While John Lowell was hurling hot verbal shot at Jefferson and his Embargo, the realistic mind of Francis had been casting about for opportune enterprises to take up the slack of the slump in commerce and distilling."

23   There are ample data on the export of India cottons to Africa as a commodity to trade for Africans destined for the slave trade. In 1751, 54,958 pieces of East India cotton goods were sent from England to West Africa; in 1792, this trade reached a high of 413,652 pieces. In fact, only in seven years between 1787 and 1807 did the value of English cotton pieces sent from England to West Africa exceed the value of East India cotton sent (Inikori 1989: Appendix 2). There is considerable evidence on the importance of East India cottons in the correspondence of the New England slave traders. See, for example, Porter's (1937) two-volume compilation of the correspondence of the Jacksons and the Lees. In fact, Francis Cabot Lowell's successful effort to have a duty levied on Indian cotton goods flooding the U.S. market in 1815 is a good illustration of the importance of these goods (O'Connor 1968: 19–27). Asia is vitally important in the history of cotton textiles. In 1791, India produced 130 million pounds of cotton and the rest of Asia 190 million pounds—almost 70% of the world's total. In 1821, though displaced from the leading position by slave-grown cotton from the U.S. South, Asia's combined production was still almost 50% of the total. The region was a victim of "the development of underdevelopment." "The East Indies had been . . . the traditional exporter of cotton goods, encouraged by the East India Company. But as the industrialist vested interest prevailed in Britain, the East India mercantile interests (not to mention the Indian ones) were pressed back. India was systematically deindustrialized and became in turn a market for Lancashire cottons: in 1820 the subcontinent took only 11 million yards; but by 1840 it already took 145 million yards" (Hobsbawm 1968: 53).

The connection of New England merchants to the opium trade, also extensively referenced in the correspondence, and its role in financing industrial investment, will be fully explored in a later essay.

24   There has been considerable debate over the relative importance of trade with the "metropolis"—the European nations—and trade with the "periphery"—the underdeveloped nations—in the economic development of Europe and the U.S. The issue is sometimes phrased as the significance of the role of the "home market" or of export-led development. See, for example, Goldin and Lewis 1980 and Crouzet 1980. Lenin 1899 is one of the best explications of the Marxist view on home markets and the development of capitalism. Blaut 1989 is a strong argument for the pivotal role of colonial labor. North 1961 remains one of the best discussions on this topic for the U.S.

25   Similarly, 7 of the first 11 directors of the Suffolk Bank were members of the Boston Associates. The Suffolk Bank, founded in 1818, was not the first, but it became the most important because of the aggressive role it played as a central bank (Dalzell 1987: 95f.). Lamoreaux (1986), focusing on the Brown and Ives group of Rhode Island and the Boston Associates, details how early banks in New England operated more like the financial

arms of extended kinship networks. These networks provided additional capital for industrial investment, stabilized the financial system for the smoother operation of New England industry, and are another link to the slave(ry) trade.

REFERENCES

Alkalimat, A., and Associates (1986) Introduction to Afro-American Studies: A People College Primer. Chicago: Twenty-first Century Books and Publications.

Anstey, R. (1975) The Atlantic Slave Trade and British Abolition, 1760–1810. London: Macmillan.

Appleton, N. (1858) Introduction of the Power Loom and Origin of Lowell. Lowell, MA: Proprietors of Locks and Canals.

Asante, M. K. (1987) The Afrocentric Idea. Philadelphia: Temple University Press.

Bailey, R. (1979) "The slave trade and the development of capitalism in the United States: A critical reappraisal of theory and method in black studies." Ph.D. diss., Stanford University.

——— (1986) "Africa, the slave trade, and the rise of industrial capitalism in Europe and the United States." American History: A Bibliographic Review 2: 1–91.

Bailyn, B. (1986) The Peopling of British North America: An Introduction. New York: Knopf.

Bean, R. N. (1971) "The British trans-Atlantic slave trade, 1650–1775." Ph.D. diss., University of Washington.

Blaut, J. M. (1989) "Colonialism and the rise of capitalism." Science and Society 53: 260–96.

Briggs, L. V. (1927) History and Genealogy of the Cabot Family, 1475–1927. Boston: Charles E. Goodspeed and Co.

Bruchey, S. (1967) Cotton and the Growth of the American Economy, 1790–1860. New York: Harcourt, Brace, and World.

Chamberlain, J. (1963) The Enterprising Americans: A Business History of the United States. New York: Harper and Row.

Coats, A. W. (1980) "The historical context of the new economic history." Journal of European Economic History 9: 185–208.

Coughtry, J. (1981) The Notorious Triangle. Philadelphia: Temple University Press.

Crouzet, F. (1980) "Toward an export economy: British exports during the industrial revolution." Explorations in Economic History 17: 48–93.

Curtin, P. D. (1969) The Atlantic Slave Trade: A Census. Madison: University of Wisconsin Press.

——— (1975) "Measuring the Atlantic slave trade," in S. L. Engerman and E. D. Genovese (eds.) Race and Slavery in the Western Hemisphere: Quantitative Studies. Princeton, NJ: Princeton University Press: 107–28.

Dalzell, R., Jr. (1987) Enterprising Elite: The Boston Associates and the World They Made. Cambridge, MA: Harvard University Press.

Darity, William, Jr. (1975) "The numbers game and the profitability of the

British trade in slaves." Journal of Economic History 45: 693–703.

———— (1982a) "Mercantilism, slavery, and the industrial revolution." Research in Political Economy 5: 1–21.

———— (1982b) "A general equilibrium model of the eighteenth-century Atlantic slave trade: A least-likely test." Research in Economic History 7: 290–321.

Davis, D. B. (1975) The Problem of Slavery in the Age of Revolution, 1770–1823. Ithaca, NY: Cornell University Press.

———— (1984) Slavery and Human Progress. New York: Oxford University Press.

Davis, L. E. (1971) "Capital mobility and American growth," in R. W. Fogel and S. L. Engerman (eds.) The Reinterpretation of American Economic History. New York: Harper and Row: 285–301.

Davis, L. E., et al. (1972) American Economic Growth: An Economist's History of the United States. New York: Harper and Row.

Davis, R. (1973) The Rise of the Atlantic Economies. Ithaca, NY: Cornell University Press.

Deane, C. S. (1886) "Report of the council: The connection of Massachusetts with slavery and the slave trade." American Antiquarian Society Proceedings, 2d ser., 4: 177–222.

Deane, P., and W. A. Cole (1967) British Economic Growth, 1688–1959: Trends and Structure. Cambridge, U.K.: Cambridge University Press.

Dobb, M. (1947) Studies in the Development of Capitalism. New York: International Publishers.

Donnan, E. (1930–35) Documents Illustrative of the History of the Slave Trade to America. 4 vols., Washington, DC: Carnegie Institution.

DuBois, W. E. B. (1896) The Suppression of the African Slave Trade to the United States, 1638–1870. London: Longmans, Green and Company.

———— (1935) Black Reconstruction in America, 1860–1880. New York: Harcourt, Brace, and World.

Duignan, P., and C. Clendenen (1963) The United States and the African Slave Trade, 1619–1862. Stanford, CA: Stanford University Press.

Eltis, D. (1983) "Free and coerced transatlantic migrations: Some comparisons." American Historical Review 88: 251–80.

Engerman, S. L. (1972) "The slave trade and British capital formation in the eighteenth century: A comment on the Williams thesis." Business History Review 46: 430–43.

Genovese, E. D. (1971) In Red and Black: Marxian Explorations in Southern and Afro-American History. New York: Pantheon.

Gibb, G. S. (1950) The Saco-Lowell Shops: Textile Machinery Building in New England, 1813–1849. Cambridge, MA: Harvard University Press.

Goldin, C. D., and F. D. Lewis (1980) "The role of exports in American economic growth during the Napoleonic Wars, 1793 to 1807." Explorations in Economic History 17: 26–47.

Greene, L. J. (1942) The Negro in Colonial New England, 1620–1776. New York: Columbia University Press.

Greenslet, F. (1946) The Lowells and Their Seven Worlds. Boston: Houghton Mifflin.

Hammond, M. B. (1897) The Cotton Industry: An Essay in American Economic History. New York: American Economic Association.

Harper, L. A. (1939) The English Navigation Laws. New York: Columbia University Press.

Heckscher, E. F. (1935) Mercantilism. London: Allen and Unwin.

Hedges, J. B. (1952) The Browns of Providence Plantations: Colonial Years. Cambridge, MA: Harvard University Press.

—————— (1968) The Browns of Providence Plantations: The Nineteenth Century. Providence, RI: Brown University Press.

Hobsbawm, E. (1968) Industry and Empire: The Making of Modern English Society. New York: Pantheon Books.

Huertas, T. F. (1979) "Damnifying growth in the antebellum South." Journal of Economic History 39: 87–100.

Hughes, J. R. T. (1983) American Economic History. Glenview, IL: Scott, Foresman.

Inikori, J. E. (1976a) "Measuring the Atlantic slave trade: An assessment of Curtin and Anstey." Journal of African History 17: 197–223.

—————— (1976b) "Measuring the Atlantic slave trade: A rejoinder." Journal of African History 17: 607–27.

—————— (1982) Forced Migration. New York: Africana Publishing.

—————— (1992) "Slavery and the revolution in cotton textile production in England," in Joseph E. Inikori and Stanley L. Engerman (eds.) The Atlantic Slave Trade. Durham, NC: Duke University Press: 145–81.

Klein, H. S. (1978) The Middle Passage: Comparative Studies in the Atlantic Slave Trade. Princeton: Princeton University Press.

Lamoreaux, N. R. (1986) "Banks, kinship, and economic development: The New England case." Journal of Economic History 46: 647–67.

Lenin, V. I. (1899) The Development of Capitalism in Russia. Moscow: Progress Publishers.

Lovejoy, P. E. (1982) "The volume of the Atlantic slave trade: A synthesis." Journal of African History 23: 473–501.

McClelland, P. D. (1978) "Cliometrics versus institutional history." Research in Economic History 3: 369–78.

McCusker, J. J. (1970) "The rum trade and the balance of payments of the thirteen Continental colonies, 1650–1775." Ph.D. diss., University of Pittsburgh.

——————, and R. R. Menard (1985) The Economy of British America, 1607–1789. Chapel Hill: University of North Carolina Press.

Massachusetts Historical Society (1914–15) Commerce of Rhode Island, 1726–1800. Massachusetts Historical Society Collections, 7th ser. 2 vols.

Nettels, C. P. (1962) The Emergence of a National Economy, 1775–1815. New York: Holt, Rinehart and Winston.

North, D. C. (1961) The Economic Growth of the United States, 1790–1860. Englewood Cliffs, NJ: Prentice-Hall.

O'Connor, T. H. (1968) Lords of the Loom: The Cotton Whigs and the Coming of the Civil War. New York: Charles Scribner's Sons.

Ostrander, G. M. (1948) "The molasses trade of the thirteen colonies." M.A. thesis, University of California, Berkeley.

—————— (1973) "The making of the triangular trade myth." William and Mary Quarterly, 3d ser., 30: 635–44.

Patterson, H. O. (1979) "The black community: Is there a future?" In S. M. Lipset (ed.) The Third Century. Stanford, CA: Hoover Institution Press: 244–84.

—— (1982) Slavery and Social Death: A Comparative Study. Cambridge, MA: Harvard University Press.

Peterson, E. (1853) History of Rhode Island. New York: J. S. Taylor.

Pitman, F. W. (1917) The Development of the British West Indies, 1700–1763. New Haven, CT: Yale University Press.

Porter, K. W. (1937) The Jacksons and the Lees: Two Generations of Massachusetts Merchants, 1765–1844. Cambridge, MA: Harvard University Press.

Postlethwayt, M. (1745) The African Trade: The Great Piller and Support of the British Plantation in America, by a British Merchant. London: J. Robinson.

Price, J. M. (1976) "A note on the value of colonial exports of shipping." Journal of Economic History 22: 704–22.

—— (1984) "The transatlantic economy," in J. P. Greene and J. R. Pole (eds.) Colonial British America: Essays in the New History of the Early Modern Period. Baltimore, MD: Johns Hopkins University Press: 18–42.

Rawley, J. A. (1981) The Transatlantic Slave Trade: A History. New York: W. W. Norton.

Redlich, F. (1971) "New and traditional approaches to economic history and their interdependence," in Steeped in Two Cultures: A Selection of Essays, by F. Redlich. New York: Harper Torchbooks: 339–55.

Reynolds, E. (1985) Stand the Storm: A History of the Atlantic Slave Trade. London: Allison and Busby.

Rivard, P. (1974) Samuel Slater: Father of American Manufacturers. Pawtucket, RI: Slater Mill Historic Site.

Shepherd, J. F. (1970) "Commodity exports from the British North American colonies to overseas areas, 1768–1772." Explorations in Economic History 7: 5–76.

Shepperson, G. (1975) "Comment," in S. L. Engerman and E. D. Genovese (eds.) Race and Slavery in the Western Hemisphere: Quantitative Studies. Princeton, NJ: Princeton University Press: 99–106.

Shipton, C. K. (1963) "Documents and the historian." New England Social Studies Bulletin 21.

Shlakman, V. (1935) Economic History of a Factory Town: A Study of Chicopee, Massachusetts. Northampton, MA: Smith College.

Sobel, R., and D. Sicilia (1986) The Entrepreneurs: An American Adventure. Boston: Houghton Mifflin.

Solow, B. L. (1985) "Caribbean slavery and British growth: The Eric Williams hypothesis." Journal of Development Economics 17: 99–115.

——, and S. L. Engerman, eds. (1987) British Capitalism and Caribbean Slavery: The Legacy of Eric Williams. Cambridge, U.K.: Cambridge University Press.

Sutch, R. (1982) "Douglass North and the new economic history," in R. Ransom, R. Sutch, and G. Walton (eds.) Explorations in the New Economic History. New York: Academic: 15–40.

U.S. Bureau of the Census (1862) Preliminary Report on the Eighth Census, 1860. 37th Cong., 2d sess. H. Exec. Doc. 116.
———(1960) Historical Statistics of the United States, Colonial Times to 1957. Washington, DC: U.S. Government Printing Office.
Union for Radical Political Economics (1971) "On radical paradigms in economics" (special issue). Review of Radical Political Economics 3(2).
Wadsworth, A. P., and J. Mann (1931) The Cotton Trade and Industrial Lancashire. Manchester, U.K.: Manchester University Press.
Walton, G. M. (1968) "New evidence on colonial commerce." Journal of Economic History 27: 363–89.
Ware, C. F. (1931) The Early New England Cotton Manufacture: A Study in Industrial Beginnings. Boston: Houghton Mifflin.
Williams, E. (1944) Capitalism and Slavery. Chapel Hill: University of North Carolina Press.
Williams, W. (1936) "Africa and the rise of capitalism." M.A. thesis, Howard University.
Wright, Chester (1941) Economic History of the United States. New York: McGraw-Hill.
Writers Project, Works Project Administration (1941) Boston Looks Seaward: The Story of the Port, 1630–1940. Boston: Bruce Humphries.
Zevin, R. B. (1971) "The growth of cotton textile production after 1815," in R. W. Fogel and S. L. Engerman (eds.) The Reinterpretation of American Economic History. New York: Harper and Row: 122–47.
———(1975) The Growth of Manufacturing in Early-Nineteenth-Century New England. New York: Arno.

9
British Industry and
the West Indies Plantations
WILLIAM DARITY, JR.

Is it not notorious to the whole World, that the Business of *Planting* in our *British Colonies*, as well as in the *French*, is carried on by the Labour of *Negroes*, imported thither from *Africa*? Are we not indebted to those valuable People, the *Africans* for our *Sugars*, *Tobaccoes*, *Rice*, *Rum*, and all other *Plantation Produce*? And the greater the Number of *Negroes* imported into our Colonies, from *Africa*, will not the Exportation of *British* Manufactures among the *Africans* be in Proportion, they being paid for in such Commodities only? The more likewise our Plantations abound in *Negroes*, will not more Land become cultivated, and both *better* and greater *Variety* of *Plantation Commodities* be produced? As those Trades are subservient to the Well Being and Prosperity of each other; so the more either flourishes or declines, the other must be necessarily affected; and the general Trade and Navigation of their *Mother Country*, will be proportionably benefited or injured. May we not therefore say, with equal Truth, as the *French* do in their before cited *Memorial,* that the general Navigation of *Great Britain* owes all its *Encrease* and *Splendor* to the Commerce of its *American* and *African Colonies;* and that it cannot be maintained and enlarged otherwise than from the constant Prosperity of both those branches, *whose Interests are mutual and inseparable?* [Postlethwayt 1968c: 6]

THE ATLANTIC slave trade remains oddly invisible in the commentaries of historians who have specialized in the sources and causes of British industrialization in the late eighteenth century. This curiosity contrasts sharply with the perspective of eighteenth-century strategists who, on the eve of the industrial revolution, placed great stock in both the trade and the colonial plantations as vital instruments for British economic progress. Specifically, Joshua Gee and Malachy Postlethwayt, once described by the imperial historian Charles Ryle Fay (1934: 2–3) as Britain's major "spokesmen" for the eighteenth century, both placed the importation of African slaves into the Americas at the core of their visions of the requirements for national expansion. Fay (ibid.: 3) also described both of them as "mercantilists hardening into a manufacturers' imperialism." For such a "manufacturers' imperialism" to be a success, both Gee and Postlethwayt saw the need for extensive British participation in the trade in Africans and in the maintenance and development of the West Indies.

However, for historians of the industrial revolution, British involvement in the Atlantic slave trade brings forth, at most, a proper and perfunctory moral abhorrence.[1] It plays no part in the stories they weave about the origins of the industrial revolution. Not a single essay in the Floud and McCloskey (1981) volume on British economic history since 1700 discusses the possibility of an important connection between Caribbean and/or North American slavery and the industrialization of England. Neither Nicholas Crafts (1987) nor Jeffrey Williamson (1987) nor Joel Mokyr (1987) gives even passing notice, in the special issue of *Explorations in Economic History* devoted to Britain's industrial revolution, to the potential relevance of Eric Williams's (1966 [1944]) hypothesis that the development of British industrial capitalism bore intimate links to the Atlantic slave system. And in a slightly earlier collection of notable articles by the "new" economic historians on the industrial revolution, only Mokyr (1985), the editor, offers a single sentence that refers to the Williams hypothesis.

In a discussion of the venerable puzzle of the initial sources of finance for British industry that later could have triggered a cumulative process of reinvestment of profits, Mokyr (ibid.: 35) observes dismissively,

> While some curious mechanisms have been proposed to solve this problem such as the Williams . . . thesis, which attributed the "original accumulation" to profits generated in the slave trade, the difficulty seems a bit overstated, since in the early stages of the industrial revolution the fixed-cost requirements to set up a minimum-sized firm were modest and could be financed from profits accumulated at the artisan level.

Thus, the Williams hypothesis is reduced to the status of a "curious mechanism" advanced to handle an "overstated" problem.

The intellectual invisibility of the economic significance for British industry of the British trade in slaves is reinforced by the peculiar attitude of some economic historians over what constitutes true items of commerce. Apparently only nonhuman commodities merit consideration. We find the following strange passage in W. Arthur Lewis's (1978: 4–5) Janeway lectures:

> At the end of the eighteenth century, trade between what are now the industrial countries and what is now the Third World was based on geography rather than on structure; indeed India was the leading exporter of fine cotton fabrics. The trade was also trivially small in volume. It consisted of sugar, a few spices, precious metals and luxury goods. It was then cloaked in much romance, and had caused much bloodshed, but it simply did not amount to much.

Similar sentiments were advanced by T. S. Ashton (1964: 34) in his analysis of British industrialization over the period 1760–1830: "The overwhelming bulk of [British] import and export trade was with the Continent and, in particular, with the countries nearest to Britain. Compared with this the traffic with India, the West Indies, and North America was small, and that with Africa insignificant." So much for the more than 1.5 million African slaves transported from the African coast to the Americas by British slavers between 1761 and 1807 alone (see Darity 1985: 697–701).[2]

What accounts for the muteness of the economic historians of the industrial revolution on the slave trade and slavery in their analyses of British industrialization? Has there been a conspiracy of silence, or have they had a sound intellectual foundation for ignoring the Williams hypothesis? Or has it simply been a more innocent oversight among a group of scholars so passionately engaged in supporting or debunking one another's pet explanations for the rise of British industry that they have failed to consider explanations put forward by others outside their loop?

The polite explanation is, of course, that the historians of the industrial revolution have a valid reason for not mentioning arguments that assign a leading role in British industrial expansion to the foreign sector and, more specifically, to the slave trade and plantation slavery. The modern economic historians, ostensibly, have considered the case for the Williams hypothesis in careful, deliberate fashion and have simply found it wanting. For them, commerce with the colonial plantations and with the African coastal regions was no more than a handmaiden to the British process of industrialization, and a minor handmaiden at that—so minor that it can be ignored. The position taken by Mokyr (1985: 22–23) is blunt and by no means unrepresentative:

> Foreign trade expanded considerably faster than output throughout the Industrial Revolution. Between 1700 and 1800 the volume of foreign trade grew sixfold. Although the expansion was studded with leaps and bounds followed by sharp retreats, it was on the whole much faster than output and population growth. Perhaps this has led many historians to conclude that foreign markets were indispensable to British industrial growth. They were not.

SMALL RATIOS?

The most prevalent justification for the foregoing attitude consistently appears to be Stanley Engerman's (1972) well-known "small ratios" argument. Engerman constructed what he viewed as overstated estimates of the profits earned from the slave trade by British capitalists. He then sought to demonstrate that slave trade profits, as a percentage of national income, investment, and commercial and industrial investment for Britain in several years during the eighteenth century, were too small to matter in an explanation of British industrialization. Note, first, that Engerman's intentionally overstated estimates are limited to profits from the British slave trade alone; they do not encompass the entire returns from the trade as well as the colonial plantation system in the British West Indies (see Darity 1982; Solow 1985).[3] Second, in light of the more recent range of estimates of the profits from the slave trade, it is not clear that Engerman's numbers constitute a gross overstatement (see, e.g., Darity's [1985] profit estimates, which use Inikori's [1976] importation estimates).[4]

Third, it is not apparent that Engerman's percentages actually are small in a historical or relative sense, despite their apparent absolute smallness. In a critique of Engerman's argument, Barbara Solow (1985: 105–6) makes exactly such a point:

> Focusing on 1770 . . . we find that [Engerman's] overstated slave trade profits form one half of 1 percent of national income, nearly 8 percent of total investment, and 39 percent of commercial and industrial investment.
>
> These ratios are not small; they are enormous. The ratio of *total* corporate profits of domestic industries to GNP in the United States today (1980) amounts to 6 percent. The ratio of total corporate domestic profits to gross private domestic investment for that year amounts to over 40 percent. And the ratio of total corporate domestic profits to 1980 investment in domestic plant and equipment (non-residential fixed investment) runs at more than 55 percent. . . .
>
> How can we be sure the ratio of slave trade profits to national income in 1770 is "small" at half a percent, when the ratio of total corporate profits to GNP today is only 6 percent? If slave trade profits were 8 percent of investment in Britain in 1770, is that "small" when today total corporate profits amount to 40 percent? No industry manages as much as 8 percent. Is the potential contribution of an industry whose profits can "only" amount to 39 percent of commercial and industrial investment to be ruled out because it is "small"?

Naturally it is not my intention to make a serious comparison between 1770 and 1980, nor to claim that these figures
make a case for Williams. Engerman never claims that they
measure anything but an upper limit on what the slave trade
could have contributed to British growth. On the evidence of
his figures, the contribution *could have been* enormous.

The best-developed application of Engerman's small ratios
argument to the period of the industrial revolution is Patrick
O'Brien's (1982) attempt to dismiss the importance of trade with
the entire periphery (Asia, Africa, and the Americas) for European economic development. O'Brien marshalls estimates of the
shares of foreign trade in overall economic activity for all of
eighteenth-century Europe to show that the numbers are too small
to give credence to the importance of trade of any sort as a critical
engine of economic expansion. Presumably, European economic
development was predominantly an internal affair that would have
proceeded if the rest of the world had not existed from the eighteenth century onward.

O'Brien (ibid.: 4) points out that by the 1790s "the flows of
commodities transshipped between Western Europe and regions
at the periphery of the 'modern world system' might amount to
20 per cent of exports and 25 per cent of imports." The bulk
of trade by European states was between themselves. He goes
on to observe that the volume of all exports of European nations
during the period 1780–90 amounted to about 4% of Europe's
GNP, with "perhaps less than 1 per cent . . . sold to Africa, Asia,
Latin America, the Caribbean, and the southern plantations of the
young United States" (ibid.: 14). The proportionate volume of
imports was a bit larger but still small, according to O'Brien.

Again, smallness in an absolute sense tells us nothing about
the contextual or causal significance of Europe's trade with
the periphery. In 1837, the German nationalist Friedrich List
(1983: 174–75) expressed concern about the misleading impression Huskisson, the British ambassador to the United States, had
given while using a similar small ratios argument in the early
nineteenth century:

> Huskisson declared that the exports of the United States to
> England amounted to half her total exports but that England's
> exports to the United States amounted to only one sixth of

her total exports. From this he concluded that the Americans were more in England's power than England was at the mercy of the United States. This superficial argument may sound plausible but every American farmer knows perfectly well the true nature of Anglo-American trade. He knows that the exports of the United States to England are all raw materials that England cannot do without and that the value of these products is increased tenfold in the manufacturing process. On the other hand he also knows that all England's exports to the United States are manufactured goods which the United States can very well do without since she can either make such goods herself or she can buy them from France or Germany. Consequently England is in the power of the United States in two ways.

Without consideration of the composition of trade, the interindustry linkages, and differential multiplier effects, O'Brien's small ratios are empty.

Furthermore, ratios for Britain, the major economic success story of the latter half of the eighteenth century, were much greater than for Europe as a whole. Consider the following passage from O'Brien (1982: 4–5) himself:

> For particular countries [external] trade would be more important; especially for smaller maritime powers such as Portugal, Holland, and Britain, where ratios of domestic exports to gross national product probably approach 10 per cent by the second half of the eighteenth century; but less than half of these sales overseas consisted of merchandize sold to residents of the periphery. Imports for maritime economies perhaps fell within a similar range of 10 per cent to 15 per cent of gross national product, again with smaller proportions purchased from the periphery.

Plus, the British shares were moving in the proper direction to establish the significance of external trade—progressively upward. Total net imports, for example, rose from 10% of GNP in the 1780s to 25% by 1850 (Mokyr 1985: 21). Furthermore, one can ask whether or not ratios of exports or imports to GDP or GNP of 10% and a ratio of 3–5% with a subset of trading partners—the periphery—are small.

Table 1   Export and import shares, 1986

	GDP[a]	Exports[a]	Imports[a]	Exports/GDP	Imports/GDP
U.S.	4,185.5	217.31	387.08	.052	.092
U.K.	468.29	106.93	126.33	.228	.270
Brazil	206.7	23.4	15.56	.113	.075
Hong Kong	32.25	35.44	35.37	1.10	1.10
South Korea	98.15	34.72	31.58	.35	.32
Singapore	17.35	22.50	25.51	1.29	1.47
Philippines	30.54	4.7	5.4	.15	.18
Argentina	69.82	6.85	4.72	.098	.068
Venezuela	49.98	10.03	9.57	.20	.19
Mexico	127.14	16.24	11.99	.13	.09
Thailand	41.78	8.79	9.18	.21	.22
Peru	25.37	2.51	2.83	.10	.11

Source: World Bank 1988.
[a] In billions of dollars.

Following Solow's comparative technique, consider some contemporary estimates of overall export and import shares in GDP (see Table 1). Aside from the spectacularly high ratios for Hong Kong and Singapore, the statistical share of overall trade for Britain's economy in the late 1700s compares quite favorably with that of major modern industrial centers, the U.S. and the U.K. today, as well as such newly industrializing countries (NICs) as Brazil, Venezuela, Mexico, Peru, Argentina, and the Philippines. Ratios for the modern U.K., in the aftermath of the imperial period, are about double what they were in the 1790s and similar to the ratios for the 1850s. Only South Korea, among the NICs listed here, has ratios well above Britain's in the late eighteenth century. Moreover, it is not evident that foreign trade is less important to modern Brazil or Venezuela than to the U.K. today, because their export and import ratios to GDP are smaller, particularly given their having to service large external debts.

Admittedly, O'Brien (1982: 5) acknowledges that the trade ratio data are not sufficient to make his case for the marginal importance of trade in general and trade with the periphery specifically. The more fundamental questions, he admits, are, "How important was capital formation for the economic growth of Western Europe, and did profits from trade with the periphery supply a significant percentage of the funds utilized to finance the invest-

Table 2   Profit ratios in the British slave trade and American automobile industry

Great Britain (£ million)		United States ($ billion)	
Gross investment expenditures at home and abroad by British investors[a]	10.30(a)	Gross private domestic investment[c]	671.0(e)
Total flows of profits to British capitalists engaged in trade with the periphery[a]	5.66(b)	Corporate profits[c]	284.4(f)
Profits from commodities made or grown for export to the periphery[a]	1.20(c)	Manufacturing profits[c]	69.4(g)
Profits from the slave trade[b]	.318(d)	Profits of motor vehicles sector[c]	5.9(h)
Ratio of (b) over (a)	.55	Ratio of (f) over (e)	.42
Ratio of (c) over (a)	.12	Ratio of (g) over (e)	.10
Ratio of (d) over (a)	.03	Ratio of (h) over (e)	.009

[a] See O'Brien 1982: Table 1.
[b] See Anstey 1975: 3–31.
[c] See U.S. Department of Commerce 1987.

ment required for economic growth after 1750?" Not surprisingly, O'Brien's answers to both questions are negative.

But again, comparatively, O'Brien's ratios look anything but small. In Table 2, entries (a)–(c) are O'Brien's (ibid.: 6) own estimates. Entry (d) is a conservative estimate, based upon Anstey's (1975) calculations (also see Darity 1985), of profits from the slave trade over the three-year span 1784–86. Note that the ratio of the total flows of profits accruing to British capitalists trading with the periphery alone to gross investment expenditures during that interval exceeds the ratio of total corporate profits to gross private domestic investment in the United States in 1986. The ratio of profits from Britain's export trade to the periphery over gross investment expenditures during 1784–86 exceeds the ratio of manufacturing profits to gross private domestic investment in the U.S. in 1986. Most striking, the ratio of Anstey's conservative estimate of slave trade profits—again, separate from the profits of the West Indies slave plantations—to gross investment spending in Britain from 1784 to 1786 is three times as large as the ratio of profits from the U.S. motor vehicle industry—the largest manufacturing sector in 1986—to gross private domestic investment. If it is legitimate to ascribe a substantive analytical interpretation to these ratios, independent of a well-specified theory of the role of trade and industrial expansion, one would be hard pressed to dismiss the importance of either the "periphery" or the slave trade for Britain once these ratios were assessed from a historical-comparative perspective. Inikori (1988) indicates that the emergent credit system in England that financed urban industrial development in Birmingham and Manchester, in particular, was stimulated by the credit needs of the African trade but also was promoted by the flow of profits from the African trade.

SUPERNORMAL PROFITS?

The small ratios argument is the crux of the empirical basis for dismissing the proposition that the slave trade and the colonial plantation system were instrumental in British economic development. It is a weak basis. Another a priori argument that emerges with less frequency (see Anderson and Richardson 1983; O'Brien 1982: 8–9) is that the slave trade was a highly competitive industry where only "normal" profits could be earned. The inference then drawn is that in the absence of supernormal profits, the slave trade could not have played a key role in Britain's accumulation of wealth prior to or during the industrial revolution. But this is an insubstantial argument. As I have pointed out elsewhere (Darity 1985: 694; 1989), conclusions about the degree of competition in the slave trade industry provide no information about the volume of slave trade profits, slave trade profitability, or the specific channels into which slave trade profits subsequently flowed.

Ironically, O'Brien (1982: 9) suggests that in the early stages of the slave trade, what he terms "superexploitative" profits were earned until additional entrants drove the profit rate in the slave trade into line with other sectors. This suggests that the slave trade, at least for a while, offered an investment outlet that propped up the general rate of profit. In fact, depending upon one's theory of the determination of the general profit rate, it is possible to argue that the slave trade led to a higher rate of profit than otherwise would have prevailed, thereby contributing a powerful stimulus to British industry. The important issue is the determination of the general profit rate and the mechanisms that led to equalization of profit rates across all activities. The monopoly versus nonmonopoly nature of slave trade profits is a false issue.

THEORIES OF GROWTH, TRADE, AND SLAVERY

O'Brien (ibid.: 7) does recognize correctly that a comprehensive assessment of the role of commerce with the periphery (or the role of the slave trade, for that matter) requires "historians [to] construct financial flow tables which reveal the sources of funds *actually* used to pay for the net and gross investment expenditures which occurred in Britain for a century after 1760." He then asserts that, unfortunately, construction of such flow tables "is not even a remote possibility" because of inadequate data.

But there are some clues to how such a flow table might look; they give a critical role to the slave trade. For example, two major British banks, Barclay's and Lloyds, developed rapidly from slave trade profits acquired during the mid-eighteenth century. Both later became important sources of credit for British industry (see Rodney 1972: 96; Williams 1966 [1944]: 101, 204; Inikori 1988). Wilson Williams (1938: 11–27) documented the extent to which the development of the port cities of Bristol and Liverpool was linked directly to the trade in Africans but, more provocatively, the extent to which the development of the manufacturing center of Manchester derived from that of Liverpool via credit relations and export activities. Manchester's businessmen, recognizing that the slave trade offered a major market for their products, erected a vast network of warehouses in Liverpool to store their goods for transport to Africa. Of special note was the Hibbert family, whose business activities included a 3,000-acre sugar plantation in Jamaica and a sugar commission enterprise in London as well as a cotton cloth manufactory in Manchester—an intrafamily triangle trade (see Sheridan 1958: 255).

Eric Williams (1966 [1944]: 98–107) itemized various routes taken by the capital accumulated by West Indian sugar planters and Liverpool slave traders to promote British industry: (1) A large number of eighteenth-century banks that developed in Liverpool and Manchester were established with funds generated by the triangle trade. These included the Heywood Bank, founded in Liverpool in 1773 and absorbed a century later by the Bank of Liverpool.[5] Thomas Leyland's involvement in banking in the early nineteenth century followed his acquisition in the late eighteenth century of a fortune in the trade in Africans. The same was true of banking in Bristol, Glasgow, and London, the latter dominated by the aforementioned example of Barclay's. (2) Heavy industry received its stimulus as well. Williams (ibid.: 102–3) highlights the examples of "capital accumulated from the West Indian trade [financing] James Watt and the steam engine" and ironmongers Antony Bacon and William Beckford, whose capital originated in the Africa trade and the West Indies. (3) The insurance industry also was nurtured by the triangle trade. In addition to Lloyds, the Phoenix and the Liverpool Underwriters' Association both possessed important West Indian planter connections. If a flow-of-finance matrix could be designed for Britain in the 1780s and 1790s, the point of origin of the flows often would have been the African trade.[6]

This is indicative of an overarching scheme of expansion, of which the slave trade and plantations were a critical linchpin and a valuable direct source of funds. Ronald Bailey (1986: 32) finds the answer to Mokyr's puzzle precisely at this point, suggesting that Eric Williams's solution is far from "peculiar": "Thus, for a source of capital sufficient to finance industrialization, and to support the expensive habits of the British ruling elites, we need look no further than the profits from the overseas trade to the Caribbean, of which the slave trade and related commerce was an indispensable prop." But what might be the precise nature of a scheme of British expansion that locates slave trading and plantation slavery at its core? A surprisingly wide variety of answers are available in various economic theories. The point in the discussion that follows is not to establish a single correct approach but to indicate a range of reasonable arguments compatible with a vital role for the slave trade and slavery in the analysis of British industrialization.

These potential answers must hinge on the inability of British growth strategists—or perhaps, more generally, European growth strategists—to develop an adequate labor force in the Americas and the Caribbean without resorting to enslavement of Africans. The native population was decimated by the European wars of conquest and exposure to new diseases. The natives also could flee inland. The "free" white laborers in a new and seemingly unsettled territory would be predisposed to acquire their own land, a point often made by the Marxists (see Marx 1977: 931–40; Wolfe 1935–36: 37), rather than work at another's behest for wages. To work instead as a wage laborer, the free laborer would have to have been paid relatively more, and the differential may have been prohibitive from the standpoint of profitability. Similarly, the expenses required to lure large numbers of free laborers to the Americas might have reduced perceived profitability relative to the use of slave labor.

Extensive proletarianization in the New World required slavery. British economic expansion required colonies. Therefore, British economic expansion required slavery in the colonies.

Even Adam Smith's (1976 [1776], 1) emphasis on extension of the market as the animus of growth via its positive effects on the division of labor constitutes a case for the importance of a colonial system. Despite Smith's (ibid., 2: 103–58) aversion to the monopolistic aspects of British commerce with the American colonies, despite his moral abhorrence of slavery, and despite his pragmatic belief that slave labor is inherently costlier than wage labor (ibid., 1: 90), Smith viewed the American colonies as a major economic benefit to Britain—so much so that the benefits more than outweighed the dead-weight loss from what Smith saw as excessive regulation of the colonial trade:

> We must carefully distinguish between the effects of the colony trade and those of the monopoly of that trade. The former are always and necessarily beneficial; the latter always and necessarily hurtful. But the former are so beneficial, that the colony trade, though subject to a monopoly and notwithstanding the hurtful effects of that monopoly, is still upon the whole beneficial, and greatly beneficial; though a great deal less so than it otherwise would be. [Ibid., 2: 122]

There can be little doubt that Fay's (1934: 3) description of Smith as "an imperialist, passing to internationalism through affection for colonial America" is as apposite as his characterization of Gee and Postlethwayt. Apparently, Smith had no objection to the opening up of the colonies. Nor could he genuinely sustain an objection to the use of slave labor if free labor was not available in adequate amounts to man colonial production, although he did seek to make the psychological case that proprietors resorted to allegedly costlier slave labor in the most profitable fields of colonial enterprise, sugar and tobacco, out of an intrinsic "love to domineer" (Smith 1976 [1776], 1: 412). Nor is it obvious that Smith's assessment of the relative cost of free versus slave labor in the colonies was correct, given (a) the opportunity free laborers would have to stake out their own claims to tracts of land, and (b) the migratory premiums that would have to have been paid to pull sufficient numbers of British subjects into an adequately staffed colonial work force. Perhaps Smith's assertion is more fruitful for explaining the lack of any record of endeavors to utilize African slaves directly in British industry.

Smith's liberalism is not evident in his general colonialist sentiments. It is evident in his claim that after the colonies had been opened up, trade with them would best be conducted on a laissez-faire, rather than a monopoly, basis. Of course, this was, Smith argued, in the best interest of the colonizer as well as the colony. Indeed, even in Smith's intensely antimercantilist vision of proper political economy, the slave plantation system definitely could function as a vital engine of economic growth, although preferably with unrestricted trade in products.

From the standpoint of Smith's theory, the importance of colonial commerce is not to be assessed by calculating trade shares, export or import ratios, or the like. It is the positive contribution, on the margin, of colonial markets to the growth in effectual demand that sustains the dynamic of economic "progress." In Smith's economics, the key to technical progress and growth is the producer's expectation that a growing market will exist for his wares.

Much attention has been given to the idea that the industrial revolution was primarily characterized not by an increase in the available factors of production in Britain but by increased productivity of the available factors. While Nicholas Crafts (1987: 248–56) stands somewhat apart as a skeptic of the magnitude of productivity increases in the industrial revolution, most contemporary economic historians give pride of place to the role of technical change in British industry in the late eighteenth century (see, e.g., Mokyr 1985: 25–29; McCloskey 1985; Williamson 1987; Findlay 1982). In McCloskey's (1985: 65) words, the pace of technical change was such that "Britain from 1780 to 1860 ate a massive free lunch." This comes close to the "wave of gadgets" characterization of the industrial revolution.

But what prompted such a rapid rate of technical change? For Smith, it was the widening of markets that stimulated more efficient organization of labor and the development of new machinery. The colonies in the Americas could play a prominent role in sustaining "the extension of the market." Phyllis Deane (1965: 51–68) has offered an intensely Smith-like reading of the industrial revolution premised on exactly this chain of reasoning.[7] Since there were serious limitations in the prospects for growth in continental demand for British products, the development of the West Indian islands and North America was crucial.

Deane (ibid.: 55) stressed, in particular, the immense growth in British reexports of colonial produce to the rest of Europe: "By the 1790's Europe was absorbing between 80 and 90 per cent of Britain's re-exports, and the West Indies and the Far East were supplying about half of Britain's imports" to meet the rapidly expanding "European demand for the commodities which could not be produced in temperate climates." O'Brien (1982: 14) contends that the most important trading partner for Western Europe as a whole was the Baltic region (Russia, Poland, Prussia, Estonia, and Scandinavia), a source of "grain, timber, and other intermediate goods for shipbuilding." Deane (1965: 53) said that trade with that region could not have been as extensive for Britain in particular without reexports of tropical produce.[8]

McCloskey (1985: 69) also has given serious consideration to the possibility that the technical progress of the industrial revolution was "initiated by increases in demand." But he commits a Say's law type of fallacy by questioning the significance of such an effect on the grounds that "increase in one demand . . . must be achieved at the expense or decrease in another." This could be true only if real domestic income were at its full employment threshold, and McCloskey is contemplating a closed economy. There is no reason to think that eighteenth-century Britain exhibited either of these features. For Adam Smith and Phyllis Deane, the foreign sector is where the action really begins. Keynesian multiplier effects *cum* linkage effects could follow close behind, particularly in an economy with surplus labor (Lewis 1954).

Ricardian economics leads to similar conclusions about the potential importance of the colonies, albeit from a different route. For Ricardo, the more advanced a nation, the closer it must be to the day of perpetual zero economic growth, or the so-called stationary state. For Ricardo, the approach to the stationary state is induced by the secular fall in the rate of profit, attributable in turn to the squeeze on profits caused by rising rents and rising labor costs as growth proceeds. The rise in rents and rise in wages, in their turn, are consequences of diminishing returns in agriculture associated with differential fertility of land.

Foreign trade can function as a source of "corn" to supplement home production. If corn can be obtained from abroad more cheaply than at home, home wages can fall in terms of gold without a corresponding reduction in labor's standard of living, insofar as corn is a major component of the laborer's consumption basket. A fall in home wages implies a rise in the home profit rate and therefore a stimulus to renewed accumulation (see Ricardo 1951 [1817]: 131–33). Importation of food or other "necessaries and conveniences" of the laborer can delay the onset of the stationary state (Kregel 1977: 4). But what happens to the country whose comparative advantage leads it to export food? It experiences a rise in home wages as its tendency to specialize in food leads it to produce food on progressively less fertile tracts of land. This means, in turn, that its profit rate must fall. Accumulation necessarily decelerates in the country exporting food (Findlay 1975: 323–24).

Given the logic of Ricardo's analysis, the unsalutary effects of exporting food should give any nation pause whose comparative advantage lies in agriculture rather than manufacturing. Accepting the dictates of comparative advantage means accepting a more rapid approach to the steady state than otherwise. Such countries may have political leaders who seek to diversify and develop a domestic manufacturing capability. These leaders may consciously seek to alter their nations' comparative advantage over time. But if the food exporter is a colony, the food importer can better exercise control over the pattern of specialization. The metropole can actively block colonial efforts to develop manufacturing. Metropolitan dominance can be maneuvered into a metropolitan growth advantage.

In a related context, Ricardo (1951 [1817]: 338–40) actually disputed Smith's position that invariably both trading partners would gain from free trade, arguing that while the colony always is the loser under a regime of trade restriction, the "mother country" could benefit. Ricardo was, after all, de facto the most mercantilist of the classical economists.

The relevance of this aspect of Ricardo's trade theory to Britain's experience in the late eighteenth century is open to conjecture. For the argument can carry through only if colonial products were among "the food and necessaries and conveniences" of the laborers. Should sugar or tobacco be considered to have become staple elements of the British working class diet by then? Presumably, raw cotton as a primary input for the textile industry had those characteristics. Therefore, another aspect of Ricardo's theory may have greater relevance: his view that natural wage and profit rates differ internationally (Kregel 1977). Coupled with Ricardo's (1951 [1817]: 136–37) belief in the incomplete mobility of capital internationally in response to profit rate differentials, at any point in time there will be regions coexisting with low and high rates of profit. Capitalists in low-return countries will seek outlets for some (not all) of their capital in high-return countries.

In the context of Britain's colonial system, suppose that the profit rate at home was persistently lower than in the West Indian islands. Then the existence of the British West Indies prevented British growth from slowing to a rate commensurate with its own lower domestic rate of profit, if British capitalists repatriated and reinvested at home a significant portion of the profits they earned in the West Indies. This seems to be the essence of Barbara Solow's (1985: 109–13) interpretation of Eric Williams's *Capitalism and Slavery*, although the textual basis for her interpretation of Williams as a neo-Ricardian seems somewhat obscure.

It is in the pages of Marx's *Capital* that the straightforward suggestion is made that the colonial system functioned as an offset to the fall in the rate of profit in Britain. For Marx, once capitalism is in its mature phase, machinery is introduced to save on socially necessary labor and thereby to extract surplus value in relative form. Machine production entails a buildup of constant capital, and the explosive growth in constant capital is the proximate cause of the fall in the rate of profit. But Marx (1981: 346) identified six counteracting factors that would "delay . . . and in part even paralyse . . . the fall in the general rate of profit," noting that "these [countereffects] do not annul the law, but they weaken its effect." These six factors included (1) lengthening the working day and intensifying the pace of work, that is, resorting back to extracting surplus value in absolute form; (2) reducing wage payments below the value of labor power; (3) reducing the cost of production of constant capital; (4) developing new lines of production that have relatively low organic compositions of capital while utilizing members of the relative surplus population as their work force; (5) foreign trade; and (6) the absence of share (or "dividend") capital from the process of equalizing the general rate of profit.

In a colonial setting, especially with slave labor in place, all of these countereffects except the sixth can be operative. The lash and the whip can lengthen the workday and intensify the pace of work. Support for slave labor in the form of means of subsistence can be driven intermittently below the value of the labor power of the slaves, particularly before the closing of the formal British trade in slaves in the early nineteenth century. To the extent that raw materials are a component of constant capital, colonies that produce raw materials, such as raw cotton and raw sugar, can lower the cost of constant capital. Colonies also are open to the extension of production in venues where the ratio of constant to variable capital is low.

It is under the heading of foreign trade that the most important function of a colonial system as a prop to the metropolitan profit rate is most evident in Marx's (ibid.: 344–46) discussion of the fifth counteracting factor:

> In so far as foreign trade cheapens on the one hand the elements of constant capital and on the other the necessary means of subsistence into which variable capital is converted, it acts to raise the rate of profit by raising the rate of surplus-value and reducing the value of constant capital.
>
> . . . As far as capital invested in the colonies, etc. is concerned . . . the reason why this can yield higher rates of profit is that the profit rate is generally higher there on account of the lower degree of development, and so too is the exploitation of labour, through the use of slaves and coolies, etc. Now there is no reason why the higher rates of profit that capital invested in certain branches yields in this way and brings home to its country of origin, should not enter into

the equalization of the general rate of profit and hence raise this in due proportion, unless monopolies stand in the way. There is in particular no reason why this should be so when the branches of capital investment in question are subject to the laws of free competition.

The net effect in Marx's (1977: 918) estimation was that "the colonial system ripened trade and navigation as in a hothouse." Furthermore,

> the colonies provided a market for the budding manufactures, and a vast increase in accumulation which was guaranteed by the mother country's monopoly of the market. The treasures captured outside Europe by undisguised looting, enslavement and murder flowed back to the mother-country and were turned into capital there. . . .
>
> Today [c. 1860], industry supremacy brings with it commercial supremacy. In the period of manufacture [c. 1760] it is the reverse: commercial supremacy produces industrial predominance. Hence the preponderant role played by the colonial system at the time. [Ibid.]

Finally, even if the terrain of analysis is confined to the neoclassical supply-and-demand apparatus, the existence of a colonial system in its general equilibrium form can promote the growth of the colonizer. Darity (1982) showed that a three-cornered neoclassical model of international trade, under perfect competition and under plausible parameterizations for the eighteenth century, could be used to demonstrate that Europe episodically would experience a (low) positive rate of growth, while Africa and the colonies would experience (low) negative rates of growth. Cumulatively, this laid the groundwork for the origins of uneven international development. Findlay (1989) has developed a dynamic general equilibrium model of the Atlantic slave trade that illustrates a potential connection between the occurrence of the agricultural revolution and the industrial revolution in Europe and the slave plantation system in the Caribbean.

In sum, there are several theories of growth and trade that give a prominent role to the African slave trade and slave plantations in British industrialization. Each is potentially rich and complex, and none can be dismissed or disproven by the small ratios argument. But what was the nature of the vision that served as the basis for actual British commercial policy in the eighteenth century? For one set of useful answers, we turn at last to Fay's two spokesmen for Britain in the eighteenth century, mercantilist writers Joshua Gee and Malachy Postlethwayt. What is especially notable is how many of their concerns about the importance of the slave trade and the West Indies plantations overlap with the various arguments advanced in this section of the essay.

GEE AND POSTLETHWAYT ON
BRITISH TRADE AND NAVIGATION

The substance of Gee's views can be found in two documents that date from the 1720s: the monograph *The Trade and Navigation of Great Britain Considered* and an open letter addressed to a member of Parliament on pending legislation concerning naval stores. In the former work, first published in 1729, Gee (1750: 52) explicitly described the African trade as "very profitable to the nation in general" because

> it carries no money out, and not only supplies our plantations with servants, but brings in a great deal of bullion for those that are sold to the Spanish West-Indies, besides gold dust, and other commodities, as redwood, teeth, Guinea grain, etc. some of which are re-exported. The supplying our Plantations with negroes is of that extraordinary advantage to us, that the planting sugar and tobacco, and carrying on trade could not be supported without them; which Plantations . . . are the great causes of the increase of the riches of the kingdom.

The nexus of economic progress for Gee (ibid.: xi) was the triumvirate of "manufactures, commerce and Plantations." Gee (ibid.) recognized, with respect to the latter, that the only source of riches for Spain and Portugal, aside from the wines and fruits they produced domestically for export, were their colonies. Their example demonstrated to Gee (ibid.: ix–x) the importance of the plantation system as an outlet for manufactured exports:

> Tho' they [Spain and Portugal] buy the manufactures of all nations in Europe to transport thither (having none of their own) we see what a mighty treasure is brought into these kingdoms, and how rich and powerful they are made thereby.

If they draw such riches from their mines and merchandize so disposed of, what a boundless wealth might be brought into this kingdom, by supplying our Plantations with everything they want, and all manufactured within ourselves.

Success for Gee (ibid.: vii) was contingent on "prudent regulation of our trade and our foreign settlements." This would necessitate in part a strengthening of the Navigation Act to require all vessels that arrived in Portugal to come to Britain before returning to the colonies (ibid.: 82–88).

Gee devoted a substantial portion of *The Trade and Navigation* to a catalog of Britain's trade balance with a variety of partners. It soon becomes evident that France was Britain's chief rival in international trade. Trade with a particular country was deemed "very useful," as in the case of Turkey, if Britain exported manufactures while importing raw materials (ibid.: 32–33). Trade with Italy had had those characteristics as well—Britain's exports were manufactures, fish, and reexports of East Indian products; its imports were raw commodities—until France began to supply Italy with woolen manufactures, tending to shift the trade balance with Italy against Britain (ibid.: 33). Similarly, there had been a lucrative trade with Spain. British trade surpluses generated a substantial bullion inflow, but now, Gee (ibid.: 35) complained, the trade surpluses had diminished since, after the accession of the House of Bourbon, "French stuffs and fashions" had made their way into Spain. The Portuguese trade was similarly advantageous to Britain, aside from French intrusions. Gee (ibid.: 36) also noted pregnantly that Portuguese industry had declined since the discovery of gold and silver in Brazil.

Gee (ibid.: 37–38) worried most about Britain's direct deficit with France and the associated drain of specie, an especially unfortunate state of affairs since imports of French wine and brandy could be replaced by rum from the plantations if "importation [were] sufficiently encouraged." In fact, Gee (ibid.: 38) condemned the Anglo-French trade as absolutely the worst for Britain: "France above all other nations, is the worst for England to trade with: it produces most things necessary for life, and wants very little either for luxury or convenience, some few materials excepted to help carry out on their manufactures, the chief of which are wool, and some dying stuffs."

Flanders, Germany, Norway, Denmark, and Sweden all were

countries that Gee (ibid.: 39–45) estimated, however crudely, to be running trade surpluses against Britain. Russia's balance was ambiguous. This simply meant that the sugar and tobacco plantations took on increased importance because "they are entirely dependent on us." Here was the ideal trade. Britain sent out wrought goods and in return received raw goods, consumer goods, and bullion.[9] Substantial portions of the raw goods and consumer goods were destined for the valuable reexport trade.

Gee (ibid.: 75–81) expressed concern that increased home consumption of sugar left too little for reexport, and that if a similar increase had occurred with other luxuries "the nation would be reduced to a miserable condition." He advocated a system of bounties to encourage greater production of sugar and a policy, modeled on the French, of sending the industrious poor to the plantations with funds to enable them to purchase African slaves. Gee (ibid.: 66) was anxious to transform "idle vagrant persons" into industrious types as well; there was much work for them to perform on the plantations. The streets of London needed to be cleansed of its beggars, including those with deformities, who showed "their nauseous sights to terrify people"—although he was reluctant to send the severely maimed abroad, since their productivity would be too low (ibid.: 74).

The doctrine of the utility of poverty also surfaces briefly in *The Trade and Navigation*, leading Gee (ibid.: 68) to argue implicitly that there was an optimal price for "corn." When corn was too cheap, it was difficult for manufacturers to get enough hands. This would be the case when two or three days' wages could buy food sufficient for a week. However, Gee (ibid.) noted, "when corn has been dear they [laborers] have been forced to stick all the week at it." Such reasoning is not necessarily contra-Ricardian, for in Ricardo's analysis, when corn was cheap the manufacturers could correspondingly lower their money (gold) wage outlays, preserving the same standard for the laborers and raising their own profit rate. But Gee's concern was that access to a higher standard would take the form of increased leisure for the working class. He did not make this point, but presumably a large (voluntary) export of British subjects to the New World as wage laborers would have had the undesired effect of raising the wage standard at home.

Concerns about the behavior of labor are absent from Gee's (1972 [1720]) open letter on the naval store bill, but commercial policy is very much a part of his discussion. Here the central protagonist was Sweden, rather than France, in a rivalry-centered vision of international trade. Gee (ibid.: 18) perceived that "our Trade and Riches came in but very slowly till our Plantations began to be settled; and as they throve, our Trade and Riches encreased, our Lands rose in value, and our Manufacturies encreased also." According to Gee (ibid.: 18–20), the sugar and tobacco plantations served several economically energizing functions: (1) They led to the hire of 300 ships providing employment for 6,000 sailors and, correspondingly, support for their families. There also were backward linkages to a host of individuals in occupations allied to the building and maintenance of ships, whose incomes, therefore, depended indirectly on the plantations. (2) British West Indian produce had come to substitute for more expensive produce from the Spanish and Portuguese colonies. Moreover, the colonies also "send us above the Value of 500,000 £. yearly for Re-exportation." (3) An estimated four jobs in England were generated for "every white Man in the Sugar Plantations . . . and his Negroes" providing them "with Wearables, Household-Goods, and all other Necessaries for carrying on the Work of the Plantations." [10]

Some reforms were advocated by Gee to extend further the benefits of the colonial trade for Britain. Gee (ibid.: 35) recommended restraining extensive development of manufactures in the colonies to prevent competition with Britain's own produce, but he was especially adamant that cheaper African labor should be kept out of manufacturing altogether: "No body will think it reasonable that a Nation has spared her people to settle a colony, that their Arts, Mysteries, and Skill in Manufactures, should be transmitted to the Slaves of those Planters." After all, the Africans were "only intended for Planting, and doing the Drudgery of the Plantations" (ibid.). Penalties, including loss of ownership by the planter, were to be assessed if a slave was found working in manufacturing on the plantations. Such restraints, of course, are more readily imposed on colonies than on rival sovereignties.

Here again, Gee (ibid.: 38) insisted "that all ships belonging to Plantations, who take in a Loading of Fish or Lumber for the *Straits,* shall be obliged before they return to the Plantations, to come to *Great Britain,* and bring the produce of their Cargoes with them, and then clear out for the Plantations." The intent was to get ships stopping in Portugal and Spain to go to Britain before returning to the Americas, presumably so that they would be likely to load more British manufactures to be imported into the New World. Gee was an ardent believer in trade-led growth for Britain, with Britain performing a classic function as a workshop to the eighteenth-century world.

It is in Malachy Postlethwayt's ponderous writings that the most comprehensive statement of British mercantilist statecraft can be found. Economic growth and national power intertwined as the objectives Postlethwayt sought from British policy, with foreign trade at the fulcrum. For Postlethwayt (1967 [1757]: 234), "the Balance of Trade . . . is in Fact the Balance of Power."

Postlethwayt, writing largely in the mid-eighteenth century, advanced a perspective similar to but not identical with Joshua Gee's. For example, he was much less a bullionist than Gee or Adam Smith's (1976 [1776]) stereotyped practitioners of the mercantile system. Postlethwayt (1967 [1757]: 204–10), while desiring specie acquisition, appears to have ascribed a near neutrality to augmentation of the quantity of money and the quantity of credit. Although matters became more complex and precarious in the face of public sector indebtedness, Postlethwayt generally argued that an increase in the quantity of money merely augmented all prices proportionally. Whereas Gee (1750: 52–53) believed that the slave trade was best conducted by "private adventurers," rather than by the Royal African Company as its exclusive preserve, Postlethwayt (1968a [1757], 2: 150–56; 1968b: 1–44) was a fervent advocate of privileged trade for the company. He claimed that restricting trade to its own national company accounted in large measure for France's successes. There is, of course, some speculation that Postlethwayt was a paid propagandist for the Royal African Company, and hence that his advocacy of the company's superiority in the provision of slaves to the colonies was not purely objective. Postlethwayt's (1968b: 10–13) stated reason was to mimic the French practice of selling slaves more cheaply to their plantations. France was to be a still more bitter rival for Britain in Postlethwayt's writings than in Gee's.

Nonetheless, on remaining matters of substance, Postlethwayt appears to be Joshua Gee in far more grandiose and expansive dress, with a crudely pragmatic bent. For instance, in the entry entitled "Africa" in his version of Savary de Brulon's *Universal Dictionary of Trade and Commerce*, Postlethwayt (1971 [1755]) expresses some dismay over African slavery but concludes, "We must, however, at present take the state of the trade as it stands and men as they now are." After all, "this trade, in its present state, is of as great advantage as any we carry on."

The slave trade had numerous benefits in Postlethwayt's eyes. In a 1746 pamphlet, he argued that the provision of black labor for the colonies had distinct advantages over that of white labor. Specifically, the use of African slaves on the plantations would not depopulate Britain; colonies dependent on African slave labor for planting were unlikely to become independent; and such colonies would not become rival manufacturers (Postlethwayt 1968c: 3–4). Furthermore, in the true spirit of humanitarianism, he suggested that such an arrangement was better for the Africans, who were better off being sold into slavery by warring African princes than being made into human sacrifices (ibid.: 4–5). The planters, Postlethwayt (ibid.: 4) argued, would have an economic self-interest in treating their slaves "with great Levity and Humanity."

But it was the perceived contribution of black labor to British expansion, particularly of industry, that gave the African trade its decisive significance for Postlethwayt (ibid.: 1–8):

> The Trade to Africa is the Branch which renders our *American Colonies* and *Plantations* so advantagious to *Great-Britain*, that Traffic only affording our *Planters* a constant supply of *Negroe-Servants* for the Culture of their Lands in the Produce of *Sugars, Tobacco, Rice, Rum, Cotton, Fustick, Pimento,* and all other our Plantation-Produce: so that the extensive Employment of our Shipping in, to and from *America,* the great Broad of Seamen consequent thereupon, and the daily Bread of the most considerable Part of our *British Manufacturers,* are owing primarily to the Labour of *Negroes.* . . .
>
> The *Negroe-Trade* . . . may be justly esteemed an inexhaustible Fund of Wealth and Naval Power to the Nation. And by the Overplus of *Negroes* above what have served our own Plantations, we have drawn likewise no inconsiderable Quantities of Treasure from the *Spaniards.* . . .
>
> . . . near Nine-tenths of those *Negroes* are paid for in *Africa* with *British Produce* and *Manufactures* only; and the Remaining with *East-India* Commodities. We send no Specie or Bullion to pay for the Products of *Africa,* but, 'tis certain,

we bring from thence very large Quantities of *Gold;* and not only that but *Wax* and *Ivory.* . . .
. . . the Trade to *Africa* may very truly be said to be as it were, all Profit to the Nation.

To run the desired trade surpluses with other European states would require continued development of the plantations. That, in turn, would require a prosperous African trade, since the colonies could not progress without a stable supply of slaves. Otherwise, Postlethwayt (ibid.: 7) contended, the British colonies would sink into "Distress and Poverty."

For Postlethwayt, it was always what he perceived as Britain's national advantage that was at stake, not any individual's or group's private advantage (aside from, perhaps, that of the Royal African Company). Postlethwayt (1746) mused about the terms of a future treaty of navigation and commerce with Spain, hoping for renewal of the Assiento that would sustain Britain's contract to supply slaves to the Spanish colonies. He noted that blacks transported from the African coast to New Spain by British vessels were bought with British manufactures (ibid.: 21). This would create employment in the shipping sector as well as employment for seamen. The Assiento, then, would make manufacturing exports to Africa larger than otherwise, giving Britain an edge in the competition with omnipresent France (ibid.: 12–13).

Postlethwayt's (1750: 3) estimate of the annual British gain from slaves landed at Jamaica was £60,000. But even more striking was his estimate of an annual gain of £1,648,600 from British participation in the slave trade as a whole (ibid.: 10–12). Finally, consider the correspondence from Postlethwayt to the Duke of Newcastle, serving as secretary of state, which brings the mercantilist themes of trade and power together with great force. Reacting to the hostilities that took place in the 1750s and 1760s between England and France, Postlethwayt sought to maximize Britain's gains from the peace treaty. The treaty would have to alter interstate relations because the existing "System of Europe can never produce anything of a lasting Peace for Great Britain" (Postlethwayt 1768: 323).

Containment of France was an urgent objective for Postlethwayt. He proposed the formation of a Protestant commercial confederacy with the Dutch, to be opposed to what he saw as an implicit Catholic confederacy headed by France (ibid.). The Protestant confederacy was conceived of as part military alliance and part customs union. Ultimately, what was at stake, once again, was control of coastal Africa and colonial America. Postlethwayt (ibid.: 324–26) hoped to impose a global Pax Protestantus that would, presumably, best serve Britain's economic and political interests. He even advocated a partition of the Americas, like the late-nineteenth-century partition of Africa, among the members of his hoped-for Protestant confederacy (ibid.: 326), with Britain receiving the most valuable territories. Not one to broach even an incipient cosmopolitanism, Postlethwayt (ibid.: 329–30) concluded his letter to Newcastle with an encouragement to hurry in forming the alliance to preempt similar actions by France and her allies: "And the same perhaps might be done by the Roman Catholic Potentates, if they determined to form and support a Commercial Alliance, in the nature of this proposed for the Protestant States. But it is to be hoped that they will never think of any thing of this kind, till they see the same first executed by the Protestant allies; and then it will be too late."

No such formal alliance of Protestant Europe was ever made, but British mercantilism was sufficiently thorough and effective to make Britain the world's industrial leader by the start of the nineteenth century. Britain was the first to win in pursuit of the grand mercantilist scheme of commercial conquest, naval power, colonialism, slavery, and metropolitan industrialization. Nevertheless, historians of British industrialization have suppressed this story of the industrial revolution, consciously, subconsciously, or unconsciously. A blanket of scholarly silence, a cloak of historical invisibility, has been laid by these disputants over the causes of British industrialization and over the significance of the slave trade and the slave plantations. But it is not a golden silence, for it has served only to obscure the richer and brutal story of how the modern world took shape, "small" import and export ratios and nonmonopoly profits notwithstanding.

NOTES

The author expresses his gratitude to Ronald Bailey, Ronald Findlay, Henry Gemery, and Joseph Inikori for several helpful criticisms and suggestions, and to the National Endowment for the Humanities and the Kenan Fund at the University of North Carolina at Chapel Hill for support during a fellowship year at the National Humanities Center while he completed this article.

1   For example, T. S. Ashton (1964: 34), while downplaying the significance of all foreign trade outside continental Europe for British development between 1760 and 1830, does comment that "cloth, firearms, hardware, and trinkets were sent to Africa and exchanged for slaves, who were shipped to the West Indies to pay for the luxuries and raw material which constituted the final cargo in this disreputable, triangular trade." For Ashton, the trade in Africans was not only disreputable but peripheral to the critical streams of British commerce. Economic historians who specialize in the slave trade, of course, have considered the Williams hypothesis seriously. See Gemery and Hogendorn 1979; Minchinton 1979; Inikori 1981, 1988; and the essays in Solow and Engerman 1987, especially Richardson 1987.

2   This estimate refers to the slaves actually landed in the Caribbean; it does not include the numberless others who died on the drive from the interior of Africa to the coastal entrepôts in the West and who died on the middle passage.

3   Ronald Bailey (1986: 32) has recomputed Engerman's ratios by replacing profits from sales of slaves with overseas trade profits from the British West Indies, estimated at £2.58 million (relative to a GNP estimate of £62.5 million), and reports that "the Caribbean trade profits comprise a peak contribution to British national income of 4.2 percent in 1770 as compared to a peak of .54 percent for slave trade profits during the same period. Using Engerman's assumption, we find that over eighty-two percent of the total capital formation in Britain in 1770 could have been provided out of the profits British merchants collected on their overseas trade to the Caribbean, a substantial increase from the 10.8 percent calculated for the profits from the slave trade alone."

4   The share of slaves directly imported into British North America also was small in percentage terms, perhaps less than 5% of the total. Nor should this "small" number be taken as an indication that the continental slave trade was unimportant. As Darold Wax (1973: 373) has observed, "English merchants operating out of London, Bristol and Liverpool, as well as colonial traders in such port towns as Philadelphia, New York, Boston and Newport, found the African slave trade a worthwhile, i.e., profitable form of economic activity. Furthermore, planters in the Chesapeake area, rice and indigo growers in the Carolinas and Georgia, and, though to a lesser extent, farmers and tradesmen from Pennsylvania northward took a serious interest in the slave traffic. The very livelihood and well-being of their communities could depend upon the flow of slaves from outside areas, including, but not limited to, Africa."

5   A detailed study of the Heywood's experience and its role in the general development of banking in Lancashire is provided in Inikori 1988. Inikori also demonstrates that industrial development in Birmingham was linked to credit generated by the slave trade.

6   O'Brien (1982: 10) also acknowledges that "some 'dynamic' benefits certainly emanated from exports to the periphery." He lists the following potential gains: "From the beginning Europeans exchanged manufactured goods for primary produce and precious metals. The governments regulated

trade to promote this tendency by restricting manufacturing in their imperial possessions. Europeans also specialized in the sale of shipping, banking, and insurance services to other continents (partly because they pioneered technical breakthroughs in these spheres of business) but basically to obtain means (other than gold and silver) to pay for the persistently adverse balance of commodity trade with India and China. The efficiency of Chinese and Indian industry pushed the maritime nations towards specialization in commercial services. European ships captured an increasing share of the waterborne trade on the Indian Ocean and the China seas from the fleets of the Orient, and by the seventeenth century a sizeable share of European imports from Asia may have been financed from the sale of transport and mercantile services. Such patterns of specialization stimulated shipbuilding. And the development of banks, insurance, and shipping companies to service oceanic trade are all part of the commercial and institutional development which promoted industry and urban development. The direction of such effects is not in doubt" (ibid.: 10–11). But after introducing this array of "dynamic benefits," which seem to undermine his case for the insignificance of the periphery in Europe's economic development, O'Brien (ibid.: 11) immediately downplays their importance by invoking his small ratios argument: "Nevertheless, the feedbacks to industry and shipbuilding as well as the obvious spinoffs to commercial development are not understated by the small ratios of exports sold to and imports purchased from other continents."

7   Deane (1965: 51), echoing Smith, wrote: "One of the ways—the commonest way perhaps—by which an economy can develop from a pre-industrial to an industrial state is to exploit the opportunities open to it from international trade. By selling abroad goods which are in surplus at home in return for goods which are scarce at home, it is possible both to widen the range of goods and services coming on to the home-market and to increase the value of domestic output, and so to improve the national standard of living both qualitatively and quantitatively. In widening the potential market for domestic producers, foreign trade encourages them to specialize, to develop special skills and techniques of economic organization, and to reap the economics of large-scale production. This broadening of their economic horizons constitutes an incentive to greater productive activity and helps to break up the economic inertia which so often inhibits material progress."

8   Deane (1965: 53–54) observed: "The immense importance of the tropical commodities lay in the fact that they increased British purchasing power on the continent of Europe. Britain needed her European imports for vital productive purposes and not merely to meet the upper-class demand for wine and brandy. She needed foreign timber, pitch and hemp for her ships and buildings, high-grade bar iron for her metal trade, raw and thrown silk for her textile trades. Her industrial expansion along traditional lines was severely restricted by the fact that the demand for woollen products was inelastic and already near [the] saturation point in traditional markets. Had it not been for the tropical products with their elastic demand and growing markets in temperate regions it would have been difficult to expand British trade with Europe.

"The tropical products also had to be paid for, of course, and it was not easy to buy them with woollen manufactures. The tropical demand for woollen goods was naturally limited by climatic considerations, and there were no other British goods with a special advantage in most markets. In Africa, for example, the demand for British manufactures was further restricted by low incomes, in China by the fact that local manufactures were often as good and always a great deal cheaper. In the end the solution to the numerous problems of matching demand and supply in the international market was found by developing a complex world-wide network of trading transactions centred on London. In this network the West Indian islands, administered by a British plantation *elite* on the basis of a slave society, constituted the most valuable and intimate link. Weapons, hardware, spirits from Britain and calicoes from India were shipped to West Africa and exchanged for slaves, ivory and gold. The slaves were sold in the West Indies for sugar, dyestuffs, mahogany, logwood, tobacco and raw cotton. The gold and ivory was shipped to the East and Near East for teas, silks, calicoes, coffee and spices. The tropical goods were sold in Europe for Baltic timber, hemp, pitch and tar (all essential naval stores), Swedish and Russian iron; and, in the fourth quarter of the century, they paid for the foreign grain which was vital when the harvest failed and which was regularly required in most years even when the harvest had not failed."

9   O'Brien (1982: 12–16) also seeks to downgrade the importance to European development of precious metals obtained from the Americas and Africa. His discussion, oddly enough, does not consider the specie inflow as an addition to the monetary bases of the colonial powers and hence, through the credit-bank multiplier, fundamental to the expansion of finance. O'Brien (ibid.: 14) also indicates that there was a net drain of bullion from Europe to settle trade deficits with the Far East and the Baltic states. However, one would be hard-pressed to establish that there was a net drain over time for Britain given the Anglo-Portuguese trade. Early in the eighteenth century, the Portuguese trade alone brought an estimated £50,000 worth of bullion from Brazil's mines into London each week (Birnie 1935: 175, 180).

10 Gee's claim about the employment multiplier effect in Britain of the slave plantation system came from the work of the seventeenth-century mercantilist writer Josiah Child (n.d.: 205), who also viewed slave trading and slavery as critical to British economic expansion.

REFERENCES

Anderson, B. L., and David Richardson (1983) "Market structure and profits of the British African trade in the late eighteenth century: A comment." Journal of Economic History 4: 713–21.

Anstey, Roger (1975) "The volume and profitability of the British slave trade, 1761–1807," in S. Engerman and E. D. Genovese (eds.) Race and Slavery in the Western Hemisphere: Quantitative Studies. Princeton: Princeton University Press: 3–36.

Ashton, T. S. (1964) The Industrial Revolution, 1760–1830. New York: Oxford University Press.

Bailey, Ronald W. (1986) "Africa, the slave trade, and the rise of industrial capitalism in Europe and the United States: A historiographic review." American History: A Bibliographic Review 2: 1–91.

Birnie, A. (1935) An Economic History of the British Isles. London: Methuen.

Child, Josiah (n.d.) A New Discourse of Trade. 4th ed., London: J. Hodges on London-Bridge.

Crafts, N. F. R. (1987) "British economic growth, 1700–1850: Some difficulties of interpretation." Explorations in Economic History 24: 245–68.

Darity, William, Jr. (1982) "A general equilibrium model of the eighteenth-century Atlantic slave trade: A least-likely test for the Caribbean school." Research in Economic History 7: 287–326.

——— (1985) "The numbers game and the profitability of the British trade in slaves." Journal of Economic History 45: 693–703.

——— (1989) "The profitability of the British trade in slaves once again." Explorations in Economic History 26: 380–84.

Deane, Phyllis (1965) The First Industrial Revolution. Cambridge: Cambridge University Press.

Engerman, Stanley L. (1972) "The slave trade and British capital formation in the eighteenth century: A comment on the Williams thesis." Business History Review 46: 430–43.

Fay, C. R. (1934) Imperial Economy and Its Place in the Formation of Economic Doctrine, 1600–1932. Oxford: Clarendon.

Findlay, Ronald L. (1975) "Implications of growth theory for trade and development." American Economic Review 65: 323–28.

——— (1982) "Trade and growth in the industrial revolution," in C. Kindleberger and G. Tella (eds.) Economics in the Long View: Essays in Honour of W. W. Rostow, vol. 1. New York: New York University Press.

——— (1989) "The 'triangular trade' and the Atlantic economy of the eighteenth century: A simple general equilibrium model." Graham Lecture, Columbia University.

Floud, R. C, and D. N. McCloskey (eds.) (1981) The Economic History of Britain since 1700, vol. 1. Cambridge: Cambridge University Press.

Gee, Joshua (1750) The Trade and Navigation of Great Britain Considered. 5th ed., Glasgow: Robert Urie.

——— (1972 [1720]) "A letter to a member of Parliament concerning the naval store-bill," in British Imperialism: Three Documents. New York: Arno: 3–43.

Gemery, Henry A., and Jan S. Hogendorn (1979) "Introduction," in H. A. Gemery and J. S. Hogendorn (eds.) The Uncommon Market: Essays in the Economic History of the Atlantic Slave Trade. New York: Academic: 1–19.

Inikori, Joseph E. (1976) "Measuring the Atlantic slave trade: An assessment of Curtin and Anstey." Journal of African History 17: 197–223.

——— (1981) "Market structure and the profits of the British African trade in the late eighteenth century." Journal of Economic History 41: 745–76.

——— (1988) "The credit needs of the African trade and the development of the credit economy in England." Unpublished manuscript.

Kregel, Jan (1977) "Ricardo, trade, and factor mobility." Economia Internazionale 30: 3–13.

Lewis, W. A. (1954) "Economic development with unlimited supplies of labour." Manchester School of Economic and Social Studies 22: 139–91.
───── (1978) The Evolution of the International Economic Order. Princeton: Princeton University Press.
List, Friedrich (1983) The Natural System of Political Economy, 1837. London: Frank Cass.
Marx, Karl (1977) Capital, vol. 1. New York: Vintage Books.
───── (1981) Capital, vol. 3. New York: Vintage Books.
McCloskey, Donald (1985) "The industrial revolution, 1760–1860: A survey," in Joel Mokyr (ed.) The Economics of the Industrial Revolution. London: George Allen and Unwin: 53–74.
Minchinton, W. E. (1979) "The triangular trade revisited," in H. A. Gemery and J. S. Hogendorn (eds.) The Uncommon Market: Essays in the Economic History of the Atlantic Slave Trade. New York: Academic: 331–52.
Mokyr, Joel (1985) "The industrial revolution and the new economic history," in Joel Mokyr (ed.) The Economics of the Industrial Revolution. London: George Allen and Unwin: 1–51.
───── (1987) "Has the industrial revolution been crowded out? Some reflections on Crafts and Williamson." Explorations in Economic History 24: 293–319.
O'Brien, Patrick (1982) "European economic development: The contribution of the periphery." Economic History Review 35: 1–18.
Postlethwayt, Malachy (1746) "Considerations on a future treaty of navigation and commerce with Spain (November 25, 1746)." MS. 493 (1), Palaeography Room (Sterling Library). Senate House, University of London Library.
───── (1750) "The advantages to the nation in general of the Royal Assiento, and to the South Sea Company in particular asserted and maintained (1750)." MS. 493 (2), Palaeography Room (Sterling Library). Senate House, University of London Library.
───── (1768) "The sequel to considerations upon the measures necessary to be taken by the Court of Great Britain to obtain a very good and a very durable peace (1768)." Additional MS. 33053, folio 323–330, Newcastle Papers, vol. 343. British Library.
───── (1967 [1757]) Great Britain's True System. New York: Augustus M. Kelley.
───── (1968a [1757]) Britain's Commercial Interest Explained and Improved. 2 vols., New York: Augustus M. Kelley.
───── (1968b) Selected Works. Vol. 1, 1745–1751. London: Gregg International.
───── (1968c) Selected Works. Vol. 2, 1746–1759. London: Gregg International.
───── (1971 [1755]) The Universal Dictionary of Trade and Commerce. New York: Augustus M. Kelley.
Ricardo, David (1951 [1817]) On the Principles of Political Economy and Taxation. Cambridge: Cambridge University Press.
Richardson, David (1987) "The slave trade, sugar, and British economic growth, 1748–1776," in B. Solow and S. Engerman (eds.) British Capitalism and

Caribbean Slavery: The Legacy of Eric Williams. Cambridge: Cambridge University Press: 1–30.

Rodney, Walter (1972) How Europe Underdeveloped Africa. London: Bogle L'Ouverture.

Sheridan, Richard B. (1958) "The commercial and financial organization of the British slave trade, 1750–1807." Economic History Review 11: 249–63.

Smith, Adam (1976 [1776]) An Inquiry into the Nature and Causes of the Wealth of Nations. 2 vols., Chicago: University of Chicago Press.

Solow, Barbara (1985) "Caribbean slavery and British growth: The Eric Williams hypothesis." Journal of Development Economics 17: 99–115.

————, and Stanley Engerman, eds. (1987) British Capitalism and Caribbean Slavery: The Legacy of Eric Williams. Cambridge: Cambridge University Press.

U.S. Department of Commerce (1987) Survey of Current Business 67: 2–4.

Wax, Darold D. (1973) "Preferences for slaves in colonial America." Journal of Negro History 58: 371–401.

Williams, Eric (1966 [1944]) Capitalism and Slavery. New York: Capricorn Books.

Williams, Wilson E. (1938) "Africa and the rise of capitalism." M.A. thesis, Howard University.

Williamson, Jeffrey (1987) "Debating the British industrial revolution." Explorations in Economic History 24: 269–92.

Wolfe, Bertram (1935–36) "Marxism and the Negro." Race 1: 37–40.

World Bank (1988) World Development Report 1988. New York: Oxford University Press.

Part III

Atlantic Slavery, the World of
the Slaves, and
Their Enduring Legacies

10

The Dispersal of
African Slaves in the West
by Dutch Slave Traders,
1630–1803

JOHANNES POSTMA

MISCONCEPTIONS ABOUT the American destinations of African slaves can easily arise when current population statistics are used to project the number of arrivals. People in the United States, for example, are invariably astonished when they hear that the 25 million Americans who claim African descent are the progeny of only about 6% of the Atlantic slave trade, or some 600,000 slaves who were landed here (Fogel and Engerman 1974: 14). A country like Surinam, by contrast, imported approximately 200,000 slaves from Africa, but only about half of its current 400,000 population can claim African descent. Before such intriguing demographic problems can be solved, however, we need to know more precisely when and where the African slaves were disembarked and settled in the Americas. This chapter addresses that basic question, although its scope is limited to the Dutch share in the Atlantic slave trade.

Subjects of the Dutch republic were engaged in the Atlantic slave trade during most of the seventeenth and eighteenth centuries. The Dutch began to show serious interest in the traffic after 1630, when they acquired a plantation colony in northern Brazil.

By the end of that decade they had chased the Portuguese from most of their West African strongholds in order to control the sources of the slave traffic. During the 1660s, the Dutch gained a share of the so-called *asiento* trade, which regulated the importation of slaves to the Spanish colonies. Toward the end of the seventeenth century, when the Dutch lost the asiento trade, they began to expand their plantation colonies on the Guiana coast of South America. These settlements, particularly that of Surinam, became the most significant slave markets for the Dutch during the eighteenth century.

During this period of nearly two hundred years, Dutch slavers exported approximately 543,000 slaves from Africa, as is illustrated in Table 1. During the transatlantic crossing about 15% of these slaves lost their lives and a few consignments were captured by enemies, which brought the total number landed in the West to approximately 457,000.[1] This chapter attempts to delineate the destination of slaves transported by the Dutch across the Atlantic. The framework in which this study is cast is determined in part by the internal developments of the operation of the traffic, although the activities have been broken down into convenient time spans (mostly decades) that will facilitate correlation with comparable studies.

During the early decades of the seventeenth century, the Dutch involvement in the Atlantic slave trade was limited to an occasional capture of a foreign slave ship. Uncertain about the value of the captured cargo, Dutch captains apparently disposed of the slaves in a haphazard manner. In 1619, for example, a Dutch warship landed 20 slaves at the young English settlement at Jamestown in return for needed food supplies (Arber and Bradley 1910: 541). The commercial potential of the Atlantic slave trade was not understood by the Dutch until they established their own plantation settlement in the Americas. Thus, the catalyst for the Dutch slave trade was the acquisition of northern Brazil in 1630. This action prompted the Dutch to get more deeply involved in African affairs in order to secure the slaves needed for their plantation colony. In 1637 they captured the Portuguese headquarters at Elmina, in present-day Ghana, and after that they were able to acquire a steady supply of slaves.

The Dutch slave trade to Brazil was brief but intense. In little more than a decade more than 26,000 slaves were landed in "New

Table 1 Slave exports from Africa by the Dutch

Years	WIC trade Documented	WIC trade Adjustment[a]	Free trade Documented	Free trade Adjustment	Total	Annual averages
1600–45	30,182	3,000			33,182	721
1646–64	11,039	2,500			13,539	713
1665–74	43,412	500			43,912	4,391
1675–99	66,692	5,500			72,192	2,888
1700–09	28,596	3,500			32,096	3,210
1710–19	20,575	4,500			25,075	2,508
1720–29	38,580	3,000			41,580	4,158
1730–39	24,911		19,169		44,080	4,408
1740–49			47,574		47,574	4,757
1750–59			49,362	1,416	50,778	5,078
1760–69			59,501	2,912	62,413	6,241
1770–79			51,095	1,706	52,801	5,280
1780–95			22,544		22,544	1,409
1802–3			1,206		1,206	603
1600–1803	263,987	22,500[a]	250,451	6,034	542,972	2,659
1665–1795					495,730	3,784

Source: Postma 1990: 110, 118, and 285 (Tables 5.1, 5.6, and 12.1).
[a] Includes 14,000 from the interloper trade.

Table 2 The Dutch slave trade to Brazil, 1630–1651

Year	From Guinea	From Angola	Other	Imported total	Deaths[a]	Left Africa
1630		280		280	49	329
1636		1,046		1,040	183	1,229
1637	1,211	346		1,557	109	1,666
1638	1,267	66	419	1,752	210	1,962
1639	1,393	326	77	1,796	359	2,155
1640	1,316			1,316	184	1,500
1641	1,062	297		1,359	258	1,617
1642	1,616	762		2,378	579	2,957
1643	1,553	2,461		4,014	682	4,696
1644	1,111	4,354		5,465	1,420	6,885
1645	594	3,179		3,773	943	4,716
1646	24	251		275	48	323
1649	290	200		490	86	576
1651		785		785	137	922
Total	11,437	14,353	496	26,286	5,247	31,533

Source: Van den Boogaart and Emmer 1979: 367–69.
[a] Mortality on the middle passage.

Holland," as the Dutch called their Brazilian colony (see Table 2). The traffic reached a peak in 1644 when more than 5,000 slaves were disembarked. Although these figures are not high compared to later years, this was perhaps the only time that the Dutch were the dominant European slave-trading nation.[2]

When the Portuguese reconquered northern Brazil during the late 1640s, the Dutch lost their one and only slave market, and their participation in the traffic declined accordingly. But having acquired experience and a taste for profits from the traffic, they soon found other outlets for their human merchandise. Since the Spanish had no African bases, and the Portuguese, their traditional suppliers, had lost control over the high seas, the Spanish colonies were a logical target for the Dutch. Since the Spanish officials were unwilling to trade with these Protestant "heretics" and recent adversaries in war, the Dutch initially engaged in illicit trade with the Spanish American colonies. The Dutch also delivered some slaves to other foreign markets in the Caribbean; for example, 460 slaves were shipped to Trinidad in 1606 (Harlow

Table 3   The Curaçao/asiento trade, 1658–1729

Period	Spanish Main	Curaçao	Unspecified	Totals
1658–62		1,089	940	2,029
1662–74		23,466	10,273	33,739
1675–88	1,770	17,748	7,245	26,763
1689–99	645	8,231	2,660	11,536
1700–1716	2,921	16,017	1,590	20,528
1717–29		2,537		2,537
Total	5,336	69,588	22,708	98,277

Source: Postma 1990: 35, 45, and 48 (Tables 2.2, 2.3, and 2.4).

1925: 125). The French Caribbean islands are also mentioned occasionally in connection with the early Dutch slave trade. The documentation for the early years and the traffic to foreign markets is meager, which forces us to rely on a good deal of estimation, if not speculation, in determining volume and destinations of that part of the Dutch trade.

The intensity of the Dutch slave trade increased in 1662, when they negotiated their first asiento contract with the Spanish authorities. Now they could legally take slaves to the Spanish colonies, resulting in a significant increase in their slave traffic. The documentation is still sparse and difficult to obtain for the early years of the Dutch asiento trade, but it is better for the period after 1675.[3] The Spanish mainland colonies were at this time by far the most significant, if not the only slave market for the Dutch. The vast majority of slaves were shipped via the island of Curaçao, and then trans-shipped to the mainland ports of Cartagena, Portobelo, and Vera Cruz Llave. Occasionally, a few slave consignments were shipped directly to these ports. A significant number of slaves were illicitly sold at the Caracas coast, particularly when there were conflicts over the asiento agreements.

In 1668, the Dutch gained a monopoly over the asiento trade, which they maintained for the next two decades. During the 1680s, the Spanish authorities even appointed the Dutch financier Balthazar Coymans to direct the whole asiento operation. This brought the Dutch slave trade to another peak, with approximately 8,000 slave disembarkations during the years 1687–88. Table 3 lists the volume of the Dutch asiento and Curaçao trade in its entirety.

The asiento trade did not always operate smoothly. On the contrary, there were frequent conflicts over payments and renewal of agreements. Coymans's control of the asiento was greatly resented by many influential Spaniards, who preferred to see the traffic returned to the Portuguese. And with Coymans's death in 1688, the Dutch lost control over the asiento, although occasionally they still participated through subcontracts. They also continued to participate in the slave trade to the Spanish colonies through illicit trade via the island of Curaçao and through Dutch slave ships sailing directly to the Caracas coast (see Wright 1924: 24ff.)

In addition, international tensions periodically disrupted the slave trade. The Third Anglo–Dutch War (1672–74), for example, contributed to the financial collapse of the West India Company (WIC) in 1674. The WIC enjoyed a monopoly over the Dutch slave trade until the 1730s, and its bankruptcy and reorganization in 1674 brought a temporary decline in the traffic.

At the same time that the Dutch were losing their Spanish colonial slave markets, they were expanding their plantation settlements on the Guiana coast. This was an incentive for them to continue their slaving operations. The oldest surviving Dutch settlements in today's Guyana were started on the Essequibo and Berbice rivers, in 1618 and 1627 respectively. Much later, in 1746, another plantation colony was started on the Demerara River in Guyana. None of these settlements became significant slave markets, however, at least not until the middle of the eighteenth century. The Guyana settlements were captured and retained by the English in 1795.[4]

The bulk of the Dutch slave trade, after the asiento trade was lost, was directed to the colony of Surinam, to the east of the Guyana settlements. This colony was founded by the English in 1651, but the Dutch captured it in 1667. For several years, the Dutch were unable to make the settlement prosper in the same way as their predecessors had. But after a stable government was established under the so-called Society of Surinam in 1682, the settlement began to expand. This is clearly noticeable in the growing numbers of slaves that were disembarked in the colony. Conflicts among the European settlers and with the indigenous American population, however, still hindered the expansion of Surinam. In addition, an invasion by a French fleet in 1712 gave the colony another serious setback. By 1720, its total population was approximately 15,000, of which about 14,000 were slaves

Table 4   The Dutch slave trade to Surinam, 1668–1803

| Years | Documented | | Estimates | | | Annual |
	Ships	Slaves	Mixed[a]	Adjustments[b]	Totals	averages
1668–74	11	3,404			3,404	486
1675–79	3	1,160		400	1,560	312
1680–84	6	2,418	100	260	2,778	556
1685–89	17	7,072			7,072	1,414
1690–94	4	2,076	150		2,226	445
1695–99	10	5,079	40		5,119	1,023
1700–1704	7	3,433			3,433	687
1705–9	9	4,250	90		4,340	868
1710–14	4	2,065		280	2,345	469
1715–19	11	5,212	60		5,272	1,054
1720–24	7	2,191		400	2,591	518
1725–29	15	7,432	115	400	7,947	1,589
1730–34	21	9,423		400	9,823	1,965
1735–39	17	7,980		400	8,380	1,676
1740–44	31	7,872		400	8,272	1,654
1745–49	44	14,062		400	14,462	2,892
1750–54	41	10,169		500	10,669	2,134
1755–59	50	15,079	164	500	15,743	3,149
1760–64	47	13,919	455	500	14,874	2,974
1765–69	76	19,309	250		19,559	3,912
1770–74	69	17,535	412	500	18,697	3,639
1775–79	24	6,320	439	250	7,259	1,402
1780–84	6	1,856	161	250	2,267	453
1785–89	13	2,423			2,423	485
1790–95	19	3,605	88	250	3,943	789
1802–3	6	1,087		250	1,337	669
Total	568	176,429	2,524	5,680	185,443	

Sources: Binder (see note 3); Postma 1990: 186, 212, and 225 (Tables 8.2, 9.2, 9.8, and 9.9).
[a] Partial slave consignments shared with other settlements.
[b] Estimated arrivals from slave ships for which no destination has been verified.

of African descent (suggestive of a high rate of mortality and defection). Then, during the following decade, the colony began to grow extensively as its tropical production grew and became more diverse.[5]

Yet, as Table 4 shows, the slave trade to Surinam never became a big operation during the seventeenth century. Only slightly more than 22,000 slaves were landed in the colony during the first 33 years under Dutch control, and this trend increased only haltingly during the first decades of the eighteenth century. Before 1725, annual slave imports (averaged for five-year periods) rarely exceeded 1,000. After that year, however, they were generally above 2,000, and sometimes even above 3,000 per year. Importation reached a peak in the period 1765–73, when the annual average was close to 4,000 slaves. After a financial crisis struck in 1773, depriving the planters of credit to purchase slaves and other necessities, the colony's importation of slaves declined drastically. The slave traffic never recuperated from this crisis. Instead, international tensions drove the Dutch completely out of the Atlantic slave trade during the next few decades. During the years of the French and Napoleonic wars, 1795–1815, very few slave ships were outfitted by the Dutch, and none at all during the period 1796–1801. The temporary peace that followed enabled the Dutch to ship their last human cargoes: nearly 1,100 slaves have been documented as having been disembarked at Surinam during the years 1802–3.[6]

The small Dutch plantation settlements in Guyana were far less significant than those of Surinam. Yet, collectively, Essequibo, Berbice, and Demerara represented an important slave market in the eighteenth-century Dutch slave trade. Unfortunately, the documentation on slave imports for this region is less complete than that for Surinam and Curaçao, which has made it necessary to make several estimates.

The volume of the slave trade to Essequibo was modest in the extreme during the seventeenth century. There is documented evidence of only ten slave ships that disembarked their full human cargoes at the settlement during the years 1618–99. A few additional slaves were brought in by small boats from Surinam and/ or Curaçao, and a few Dutch slavers landed portions of their cargoes at Essequibo. Slave importation increased during the turn of the century, and again in the 1730s, but this was followed by a long period of stagnation. During the years 1760–75, the colony experienced its most rapid growth, with an average of about 400 slaves imported annually. In total, Dutch slave traders shipped approximately 15,300 slaves to Essequibo, as is illustrated in Table 5, the vast majority of these during the eighteenth century.

Table 5   Slave imports at Essequibo, 1618–1795

Years	Documented		Estimates			Annual averages
	Ships	Slaves	Mixed[a]	Adjustments[b]	Totals	
1618–69	1	100		400	500	10
1670–79	3	225		25	250	25
1680–89	1	170	110	50	320	32
1690–99	5	987	227	50	1,264	126
1700–1709	4	1,079	90	50	1,219	122
1710–19	3	709	60	50	819	82
1720–29	2	395	200	50	645	65
1731–39	1	306		750	1,056	101
1740–49				1,000	1,000	100
1750–59				1,000	1,000	100
1760–69	1	269	1,478	1,000	2,752	276
1770–79	8	2,207	663	750	3,620	362
1780–89	1	437	100		537	54
1790–95			102	250	352	59
Total	30	6,884	3,030	5,425	15,334	

Source: Binder (see note 3); Postma 1990: 191, 220, and 225 (Tables 8.3, 9.4, and 9.9).
[a] Partial slave consignments shared with other settlements.
[b] Estimated arrivals from slave ships for which no destination has been verified.

The settlement on the Berbice River equaled that of Essequibo in many ways, including the volume of slave importation. The colony had a very slow start during its 73 years in the seventeenth century, when judged by its slave imports. Only one complete slave cargo has been found recorded for those years; most of its few slaves were shipped in on small boats from nearby Surinam. The colony expanded slightly more during the 1720s and 1730s and then stagnated again for many years. The peak of slave importation to Berbice came in the years 1765–75, when an average of 400 to 500 slaves were imported annually. The total Dutch traffic to Berbice numbered slightly more than 14,000, as is shown in Table 6.

The Dutch settlement on the Demerara River, started in 1746, was essentially an extension of the neighboring Essequibo settlement. Because of this close proximity, and often joint leadership, many slave ships divided their human cargoes between the two

Table 6   Slave imports at Berbice, 1627–1795

| | Documented | | Estimates | | | Annual |
Years	Ships	Slaves	Mixed[a]	Adjustments[b]	Totals	averages
1627–99	1	90	327	600	1,017	14
1700–1709	1	50	90	100	240	24
1710–19	2	422	60	300	782	78
1720–29	2	770	200	100	1,070	107
1730–39	6	1,847		750	2,597	260
1740–49				1,000	1,000	100
1750–59	1	730		1,000	1,730	173
1760–69	6	1,753	100	500	2,353	235
1770–97	7	1,516	214	750	2,480	248
1780–89						
1790–95	2	530	104	250	884	147
Total	30	7,708	1,095	5,350	14,153	

Sources: Binder (see note 3); Postma 1990: 195, 218, and 225 (Tables 8.4, 9.3, 9.8, and 9.9).
[a] Partial slave consignments shared with other settlements.
[b] Estimated arrivals from slave ships for which no destination has been verified.

colonies. After a relatively slow start, Demerara expanded rapidly during the 1760s. Its peak of development, measured in slave imports, came during the years 1780–95, when the other Guyana settlements were importing very few slaves. Nearly 11,000 slaves were disembarked at Demerara during its half-century under Dutch control, as is shown in Table 7.

The Dutch-controlled Caribbean islands of Curaçao and St. Eustatius functioned for many years as transit slave markets, as has been shown already in connection with Curaçao and the asiento trade. Both islands did have several small plantations, but the local demand for slaves was not significant. After the loss of the asiento trade (see Table 2), Curaçao decreased in importance as a slave transit market. From 1718 to the early 1740s, there was indeed very little evidence of slave-trading activity at Curaçao. During the next twenty years, however, the traffic increased to 500 to 600 slaves annually. But after 1775, the Curaçao slave trade appears to have been limited to local demands. Table 8 lists the volume of the Curaçao slave importations for the period 1730–95. A combined total of about 36,000 slaves

Table 7   Slave imports at Demerara, 1746–95

| Years | Documented | | Estimates | | | Annual |
	Ships	Slaves	Mixed[a]	Adjustments[b]	Totals	averages
1746–49				500	500	125
1750–59				1,250	1,250	125
1760–69			1,260	1,000	2,260	226
1770–79	1	270	456	750	1,476	148
1780–89	12	3,633	102		3,735	374
1790–95	4	1,177	100	250	1,527	255
Total	17	5,080	1,918	3,750	10,748	

Source: Postma 1990: 221 and 225 (Tables 9.5, 9.8, and 9.9).
[a] Partial slave consignments shared with other settlements.
[b] Estimated arrivals from slave ships for which no destination has been verified.

Table 8   The Dutch slave trade to Curaçao, 1731–95

| Years | Documented | | Estimates | | | Annual |
	Ships	Slaves	Mixed[a]	Adjustments[b]	Totals	averages
1731–39	2	418		2,500	2,918	324
1740–49	7	2,450		2,000	4,450	445
1750–59	4	1,438	400	1,000	2,838	284
1760–69	7	2,124	100	1,000	3,224	322
1770–79	2	508	158	1,000	1,666	167
1780–89			91	250	341	34
1790–95				250	250	42
Total	22	6,938	749	8,000	15,687	

Source: Postma 1990: 223 and 225 (Tables 9.6, 9.8, and 9.9).
[a] Partial slave consignments shared with other Dutch settlements.
[b] Estimated arrivals from slave ships for which no destination has been verified.

was disembarked at Curaçao during all of the eighteenth century (see Table 2). Continuing previously developed practices of illicit trade with the Spanish colonies, the vast majority of these slaves were smuggled to the Spanish mainland, primarily to the coast of Venezuela.

The small island of St. Eustatius, one of the upper Leeward Islands, was of little significance in the Dutch slave trade before the eighteenth century, although it had been a Dutch possession since 1635. Its limited local needs were initially supplied by small shipments of slaves from Curaçao. During the turn of the century, St. Eustatius was periodically used as a base for the Dutch interloper slave ships, trading primarily with the French islands in that region. Not long after Curaçao's role in the asiento trade was terminated, St. Eustatius became for a short time an important transit station in the Dutch slave trade.

During the period 1722–27, 22 Dutch ships disembarked approximately 10,000 slaves at St. Eustatius. It seemed as if the island had replaced Curaçao as a Dutch slave trade depot. Some of the slaves landed at St. Eustatius were sold to asiento agents, but the majority were trans-shipped to surrounding islands. St. Eustatius's role as a significant slave trade center was short-lived, however. The island continued to function as Caribbean "general store," but its slaving activities remained modest for the remainder of the eighteenth century. However, there was a significant but brief rise in the island's slave trade during the late 1770s, when it became involved in supplying the rebellious North American colonies.[7] Nearly 6,000 slaves were traded and trans-shipped via St. Eustatius during the 1770s, as is shown in Table 9. Some of these slaves may have ended up in the United States, but the majority were undoubtedly taken to the nearby French islands, since France was unable to supply its colonies because of its involvement in the war. After a brief English occupation of the island (1782–84), St. Eustatius did not play a significant role in the slave trade again.

Not included in the above destination tables are slaves shipped across the Atlantic by Dutch interloper ships. Interlopers were unauthorized intruders into Atlantic regions where the WIC enjoyed a monopoly. The company lost a significant portion of its monopoly in 1730, and this ended the interloper traffic. Actually, the interloper factor was never significant in the Dutch slave trade, since most of this activity was focused on the direct Afro-European trade. For the period 1688–1725, the most active years for the Dutch interloper traffic, records of 28 interloper slave ships have been identified.[8] On the basis of these findings, it can be estimated that 14,000 slaves were shipped to the West by Dutch interlopers (included in the "adjustment column" in Table 1), and 12,000 of these have been counted among the arrivals in the West. While the documentation on such unauthorized activities is sketchy, I surmise that the most active period for interlopers was

Table 9   The Dutch slave trade to St. Eustatius, 1689–1795

Years	Documented		Estimates			Annual averages
	Ships	Slaves	Mixed[b]	Adjustments[c]	Totals	
1689	1[a]	175[a]			175	
1701	1[a]	400[a]			400	
1719	2[a]	700[a]			700	
1720	1[a]	340[a]			340	
1721	1	450			450	
1722	3	1,579			1,579	
1723	5	2,744			2,744	
1724	3	1,067	221		1,288	
1725	3	1,324			1,324	
1726	5	2,238	104		2,342	
1727	1	570			570	
1729	1		75		75	
1731–39				2,500	2,500	250
1740–49				2,500	2,500	250
1750–59	3	1,129		1,500	2,627	263
1760–69	3	902	336	1,000	2,238	324
1770–79	14	3,849	830	1,000	5,679	568
1780–89	1	443		500	943	94
1790–95				250	250	42
Total	48	17,910	1,566	9,250	28,726	

Source: Postma 1990: 225 and 320–48 (Tables 9.8 and 9.9 and Appendix 2).
[a] These were interloper ships; their cargo sizes are estimates.
[b] Partial slave consignments shared with other settlements.
[c] Estimated arrivals from the slave ships for which no destination has been verified.

during the first quarter of the eighteenth century, and that the vast majority of the slaves transported by interlopers were destined for markets outside of Dutch jurisdiction.

Another problematic factor in this study is how to account for the Dutch slave ships for which the American port of destination has not been verified. For the WIC monopoly period before 1730, the number of unverified destinations is limited, involving an estimated 23,000 slaves for the period 1658–1729. Since the Surinam trade has been thoroughly researched, there is little doubt that the vast majority of the slaves unaccounted for were part of the asiento trade or the illicit trade to the Spanish mainland

Table 10 Estimates for unknown slave destinations

Years	Total	Surinam	Berbice	Essequibo	Demerara	Curaçao	St. Eustatius	Foreign markets
1730–34	7,020	400	350	350		1,000	1,000	3,920
1735–39	8,207	400	400	400		1,500	1,500	4,007
1740–44	8,080	400	500	500		1,000	1,500	4,180
1745–49	8,117	400	500	500	500	1,000	1,000	4,217
1750–54	6,735	500	500	500	500	500	1,000	3,235
1755–59	5,424	500	500	500	750	500	500	2,174
1760–64	6,862	500	500	750	750	750	750	2,862
1765–69	2,450			250	250	250	250	1,450
1770–74	5,940	500	500	500	500	750	750	2,440
1775–79	2,452	250	250	250	250	250	250	952
1780–84	1,375	250					250	875
1785–89	685						250	435
1790–95	2,197	250	250	250	250	250	250	697

Source: Postma 1990: 225 and 320–48 (Table 9.8 and Appendix 2).

Table 11   Aggregate Dutch slave destinations

	Brazil	Surinam	Guyana	Dutch Antilles	Spanish America	Other foreign markets
17th c.	26,500	27,000	3,500	7,000	64,000	11,000
18th c.		162,000	38,500	10,000	77,500	29,000
19th c.		1,000				
Total	26,500	190,000	42,000	17,000	141,500	40,000
Percentage	5.8	41.6	9.2	3.7	30.9	8.7
Grand total	457,000					

Source: Tables 2–10 and Postma Data Collection.
Note: The last three columns involve considerable speculation; they are rounded off to the nearest 500.

colonies (see Table 2). For the years after 1730, the so-called free trade period, the problem becomes more complex. There was a greater variety of markets, and the number of unverified destinations is much larger, involving an estimated 65,500 slaves during the period 1730–95. On the basis of familiarity with the records and the historical situation, I estimate that these unaccounted-for slaves were distributed in the manner shown in Table 10. These figures have been included as adjustments in the destination tables given above.

Table 11 presents a summary of slave destinations in the Dutch slave trade, including estimates for unverified slave voyages and projected interloper slavers. The figures have been rounded off to the nearest 500, and the sources have been listed below the relevant statistics. The grand total of 457,000 disembarkations is within 1% of the projected export figures from Africa given in Table 1, assuming a mortality rate of 15%. The discrepancy might partially be explained by the capture of a few slave consignments that were counted among the African departures but not among the arrivals.

In summary, the destinations in the Dutch slave trade started with Brazil during the first half of the seventeenth century; during the second half trade shifted to the Spanish American colonies; and during the eighteenth century its focus shifted primarily to the Guiana plantation colonies. Surinam was clearly the largest market, accounting for nearly 42% of the Dutch slave trade. This was followed by the Spanish colonies with about 31%, while the settlements in Guyana absorbed a generous 9% of the slaves carried by the Dutch. The volume of the slave trade to the foreign markets and to the Dutch Antilles is highly conjectural, due to the nature of the trade at both Curaçao and St. Eustatius. I estimate the slave retention in the Dutch Antilles at 3.7%, and the shipments to markets not under Dutch jurisdiction at 8.7%, of the total number of slaves landed by Dutch slavers (see Table 11).

The following conclusions may be drawn from this assessment in regard to the use of these statistics as a base for future demographic analysis. It is clearly evident that the Dutch slave trade to Brazil is an insignificant fraction of the total importation of slaves to that country, which imported more than 3.5 million African slaves over a period of three centuries (Curtin 1969: 268). Slave destination figures for the Spanish colonial markets are useful only for general purposes; additional examination of secondary disembarkments at Spanish colonial ports would be necessary for such figures to be useful in population analysis for specific regions. Most reliable and useful are the slave landings in Surinam, particularly when supplemented with English importation figures for the late eighteenth and early nineteenth centuries. The findings for Guyana are more conjectural. In the first place, the statistics are based on frequent use of estimates, and there is also a strong possibility that there were additional illicit slave imports by foreign carriers. For the Dutch Antilles, slave imports may forever remain a mystery because of the transit roles of Curaçao and St. Eustatius. Since traffic to and from these islands was generally carried out by a variety of small boats, mostly owned by private vendors, for which no accurate records were kept, the peopling of these islands and their smaller neighbors may be an insolvable riddle.

NOTES

1   I provide a detailed survey in Postma 1990.
2   Statistics for the Brazil slave trade have been derived from van den Boogaart and Emmer 1979: 360–64.
3   Franz Binder has done extensive research on the Dutch slave trade for the period 1650–74, but he has never published any of his findings on this sub-

ject. Fortunately, he was very generous in sharing his notes. My assessment for this period is based on his findings.

4   See Netscher 1888 for a survey of the early history of Guyana.
5   For a detailed assessment of Surinam's development, see Postma 1990: 174–226.
6   See Postma 1990: 284–303, concerning the end of the Dutch slave trade.
7   Jameson 1903 provides an assessment of the role played by St. Eustatius during the American revolutionary period.
8   Kors 1987 provides valuable insights into the Dutch interloper trade.

REFERENCES

Arber, Edward and A. G. Bradley (eds.) (1910) The Travels and Works of Captain John Smith. Edinburgh: Burt Franklin.
Curtin, Philip D. (1969) The Atlantic Slave Trade: A Census. Madison: University of Wisconsin Press.
Fogel, Robert William and Stanley L. Engerman (1974) Time on the Cross: The Economics of American Negro Slavery. Boston: Little, Brown and Company.
Harlow, Vincent (ed.) (1925) Colonizing Expeditions to the West Indies and Guiana, 1623–1667. Series 2, vol. 56. London: Hakluyt Society.
Jameson, J. F. (1903) "St. Eustatius and the American Revolution." American Historical Review 8: 683–708.
Kors, M. J. G. (1987) "Lorrendraaien in het vaarwater van de Westindische Compagnie: De Nederlandse smokkelhandel op de Westkust van Afrika in de periode 1700–1734." M.A. thesis, Leiden University.
Netscher, P. M. (1888) Geschiedenis van de Colonieën Essequibo, Demerary en Berbice. The Hague: Nijhoff.
Postma, Johannes (1990) The Dutch in the Atlantic Slave Trade, 1600–1815. Cambridge: Cambridge University Press.
Van den Boogaart, E. and P. C. Emmer (1979) "The Dutch participation in the Atlantic slave trade, 1596–1650," in Henry A. Gemery and Jan S. Hogendorn (eds.) The Uncommon Market. New York: Academic Press: 353–75.
Wright, I. A. (1924) "The Coymans asiento, 1685–1689." Bijdragen voor vaderlandse geschiedenis en oudheidkunde 6: 23–62.

11
Slave Importation, Runaways, and Compensation in Antigua, 1720–1729

DAVID BARRY GASPAR

THE ATLANTIC SLAVE TRADE left its mark on all the societies that it touched, directly or indirectly, in Africa, Europe, and the Americas. While both slave traders and slaveowners were in business to make a profit, they did not always gain, or often not as much as they expected, because of the risky nature of slave trading and of plantation agriculture with slave labor. One general consequence of the slave trade that contributed to the anxiety and unease of the plantocracy in various parts of the Americas was the possibility of slave revolt, which the troublesome day-to-day resistance of the slaves might nurture under suitable conditions. "Such is the danger, which . . . menaces the planter, who is surrounded with slaves," wrote Clement Caines, a former slaveowner in the British Leeward Islands, in 1801 (Caines 1801: 284). Slave resistance saddled slaveowners and society with certain costs which were inherent in the maintenance of slavery.

In making a case for the abolition of the slave trade before the General Council of the Leeward Islands in 1798, Caines drew attention to the "horrors which have desolated" the French colony of St. Domingue. He argued that "it is the same trade which menaces us with the same horrors. For it is this trade, with its dangerous facility of procuring slaves and the treacherous submission of their demeanour, that has multiplied the lurking assassins, till they swarm wherever the planter turns his eyes" (ibid.: 285–87). Much earlier, in 1736, the Virginia planter and slaveowner William Byrd had expressed similar reservations about the rapid increase of the slave population in that colony, and in a letter to the Earl of Egmont, trustee of the Georgia colony, he hoped that slavery would not be introduced there. But Georgia adopted slavery later and thenceforth faced the same dangers of slave rebellion as other slave societies in the Americas (Land 1969: 69–71). Slavery and slave rebellion, or the possibility or threat of rebellion, were inseparable, and in slave societies such as those of the British Leeward Islands in the Caribbean, which relied heavily upon the slave trade for supplies of African labor, planters were acutely aware of the potential dangers of an increasing black majority. Rather than abandon the potentially lucrative production of sugar with slave labor, however, they resigned themselves to facing the inherent risks of slave resistance. While there are numerous important ways in which the slave trade or the African migration influenced the development of slave society in the Leeward Islands, this study attempts to uncover whether there are any traceable connections with slave resistance during the 1720s, particularly as they relate to Antigua, the leading island among the four major colonies of the group.

During the last three decades of the seventeenth century, the four main island colonies of the British Leeward Islands—Antigua, St. Christopher, Nevis, Montserrat—followed Barbados and plunged into sugar production with slave labor. The sugar revolution that followed transformed the society and economy of the Leewards in fundamental ways. Because the islands relied on the slave trade for supplies of labor, the demographic changes were striking, and certainly by the 1720s, if not earlier, the slave population in each island outnumbered whites by significant margins. The slave-white ratios presented in Table 1 reflect the demographic, agricultural, and other changes of the drive toward sugar monoculture. The early planters obtained their slaves from Dutch traders, from independent British traders, and from the Royal African Company. By the early 1700s, after the company had lost its monopoly, the islanders continued to rely upon British

Table 1   Slave-white ratios of the Leeward Islands, 1708–29

	Year	White	Slaves	Total	Slave-white ratio
Antigua	1708	2,892	12,960	15,852	4.48
	1720	2,954	19,186	22,140	6.49
	1724	5,200	19,800	25,000	3.80
	1729	4,088	22,611	26,999	5.53
St. Christopher	1708	1,670	3,294	4,964	1.97
	1720	2,740	7,321	10,061	2.67
	1724	4,000	11,500	15,500	2.88
	1729	3,976	14,663	18,360	3.97
Nevis	1708	1,600	3,676	5,276	2.30
	1720	1,275	5,689	6,964	4.46
	1724	1,100	6,000	7,100	5.45
	1729	1,296	5,648	6,944	4.36
Montserrat	1708	1,545	3,570	5,115	2.31
	1720	1,593	3,772	5,365	2.37
	1724	1,000	4,400	5,400	4.40
	1729	1,053	5,855	6,908	5.56

Source: Watts 1987: 313; Gaspar 1985: 83.

supplies, which were usually not sufficient to satisfy their needs. Barbados and Jamaica, strong competitors in the demand for slave cargoes, attracted the bulk of the trade. The planters of the undersupplied Leeward Islands therefore exploited other ways to obtain slaves. They participated in a clandestine traffic with Dutch traders at the neighboring island of St. Eustatius, and some of them who had the necessary resources also sent ships from the islands direct to the West African coast, thus cutting out the European slave trader as middleman (Dunn 1972: 118–26; Sheridan 1973: 184–207; Gaspar 1985: 65–92; Watts 1987: 313; Pitman 1917: 61–90; Galenson 1986; Journal of the Commissioners for Trade and Plantations 1928: 255).

Reports from the Leeward Islands before the 1720s convey the impression that these colonies were often in need of more slaves than they got. In 1719 Governor Hamilton complained that slave imports had lately declined and that slave prices had been rising, both trends proving to be "a great Hindrance to the Improvement of the Sugar Plantations." Referring later to Antigua in 1722, the governor reported that the island was "of a fruitfull Soil, but to be wrought with a good deal of labour" (Gaspar 1985: 84–85; Pitman 1917: 74; CO 152/14, R43). During the 1720s slave ships called regularly at the Leeward Islands, and Antigua planters bought up large numbers of adult slaves. The details of the Antigua deliveries are recorded in the Naval Office and customs papers showing the names and types of vessels, their dates of arrival, the names of the captains as well as owners of vessels and consignees of the cargoes, where the ships had loaded the slaves, and the number of slaves transported (CO 152/15, R190; 152/16, S65; 152/18, T78). Table 2 presents some of this data for Antigua, which imported 4,633 slaves in 32 shipments for the period 20 December 1721 to 25 December 1726, at an average rate of 1,148.25 a year. For the period 25 March–20 November 1727, the number of slaves delivered was 1,658. Combining the two estimates, Antigua received 6,291 slaves from December 1721 to November 1727, for an annual average of 1,048.5 (Table 3). For the longer period of 25 December 1720 to 25 December 1729, one report places the importation figure at 11,278, or 1,253.11 a year. The planter Josiah Martin reported from Antigua in 1729 that prices for imported slaves had been falling, "for we have had a great many & there is now 4 Ships of Negroes in St. Johns," the main port (Martin Papers 1729). The overall impression from both the quantitative and qualitative evidence is that Antigua was well supplied with slaves in the 1720s after some relatively lean years in the previous decade. Some of the slave ships came directly to the Leeward Islands from the African coast, while others, like the Snow *Judith* in 1728, belonging to the prominent London trader Humphrey Morrice, were under orders to touch first at Barbados (Donnan 1931: 368–69). Of the 41 vessels entering Antigua with slaves in 1721–27, 38 arrived from the African coast and 3 from Nevis, Boston, and Barbados.

While the estimated number of a little over eleven thousand slaves imported into Antigua for 1720–29 may not by itself seem that large, it must be remembered that the compact little island was only 280 square kilometers in area, with perhaps close to 150 sugar plantations of varying size. By the late seventeenth century, slaveowners were already fully aware of the dangers of a black majority and had begun to take measures not to curtail the volume of slave imports but to prevent the slaves' awareness of their

Table 2   Slaves imported into Antigua
20 December 1721–20 November 1727

Date of entry	Vessel	Point of departure	Slaves
9 Mar. 1722	Ship *Lady Rachel*	Africa	244
12 Jun. 1722	Ship *Margaret*	Coast of Africa	205
14 Mar. 1723	Sloop *Great Caesar*	Coast of Africa	143
7 Sept. 1723	Sloop *John & Elizabeth*	Coast of Africa	242
12 Sept. 1723	Snow *Lady's Adventure*	Coast of Africa	97
13 Sept. 1723	Snow *Unity*	Africa	102
28 Jan. 1724	Snow *Mary*	Coast of Africa	30
7 Apr. 1724	Brigantine *Ruby*	Coast of Africa	79
21 Apr. 1724	Sloop *Success*	Coast of Africa	47
12 May 1724	Brigantine *Negroes Nest*	Coast of Africa	154
27 May 1724	Ship *Gaboone*	Coast of Africa	120
18 Jan. 1725	Ship *John & Elizabeth*	Coast of Africa	272
28 Jan. 1725	Sloop *Charles*	Nevis	32
22 Feb. 1725	Sloop *Newport*	Coast of Africa	78
23 Apr. 1725	Ship *Sarah Galley*	Africa	355
15 May 1725	Brigantine *Negroes Nest*	Coast of Africa	167
11 Jun. 1725	Ship *Gaboone*	Coast of Africa	182
16 Jun. 1725	Snow *Hester & June*	Coast of Africa	147
17 Jul. 1725	Brigantine *Sarah & Rebecca*	Boston	1
28 Aug. 1725	Ship *Byam Gally*	Coast of Africa	70
8 Oct. 1725	Brigantine *Ruby*	Coast of Africa	45
13 Dec. 1725	Ship *Sea Nymph*	Africa	166
4 Jan. 1726	Ship *Betty Gally*	Coast of Africa	226
5 Feb. 1726	Snow *Kingfisher*	Coast of Africa	197
30 Mar. 1726	Snow *Gold Coast Gally*	Coast of Africa	180
18 Apr. 1726	Ship *John & Elizabeth*	Coast of Africa	150
18 Apr. 1726	Brigantine *Negroes Nest*	Coast of Africa	140
2 Jun. 1726	Brigantine *Catherine & Elizabeth*	Coast of Africa	176
22 Jun. 1726	Sloop *Three Friends*	Coast of Africa	155
6 Sept. 1726	Ship *Stannage*	Coast of Africa	180
13 Sept. 1726	Snow *London Spy*	Coast of Africa	141
7 Nov. 1726	Snow *Flying Horse*	Coast of Africa	200
8 Apr. 1727	Snow *Judith*	Africa	220
11 Apr. 1727	Snow *Gold Coast Gally*	Africa	160
1 May 1727	Ship *Byam Gally*	Africa	180
31 July 1727	Ship *Stannage*	Africa	152
21 Aug. 1727	Sloop *Catherine*	Africa	77

Table 2   Continued

Date of entry	Vessel	Point of departure	Slaves
14 Oct. 1727	Sloop *George*	Barbados	80
4 Nov. 1727	Ship *Catherine Gally*	Africa	550
20 Nov. 1727	Snow *Codrington*	Africa	139
20 Nov. 1727	Snow *Tryall*	Africa	100

Source: Great Britain, Colonial Office (CO) 152/15, R190; 152/16, S65.

Table 3   Annual slave imports to
Antigua 1722–27

Year	Slaves	Shipments
1722	449	2
1723	548	4
1724	430	5
1725	1,525	11
1726	1,645	10
1727	1,658	9

Source: Great Britain, Colonial Office
(CO) 152/15, R190.

numerical advantage from leading to attempts to seize the island. This is not to say that Antigua slaveowners developed a full-blown siege mentality. Slave resistance was rarely on the scale of island-wide revolt. The threat of massive resistance had surfaced in the 1680s; although in the ensuing decades there was frequent cause for alarm over the restlessness of the slaves, particularly the activities of runaways, a real threat did not emerge again until the 1730s (Gaspar 1985). The slave-white ratio, which was 3.80 in 1724, rose to 5.53 in 1729, but the slave population only increased by a little over three thousand for 1720–29, although about four times that many had been imported. Antigua did not have a significant reexport trade in slaves, so the failure of the slave population to show a greater increase must be attributed to a much higher death rate than birth rate. While the slave population climbed during the 1720s, the white population peaked in 1724 and then fell absolutely and relatively thereafter (CO 152/15, R190; 152/16, S65; 152/18, T78; Gaspar 1985: 82–83; Watts 1987: 313).

In tracing whether there was any relation between slave importation and slave resistance in Antigua in the 1720s, the concern is not so much with the significance of a crude black demographic majority which historians have sometimes unquestioningly cited as contributing to the potential for slave unrest in some societies. To a greater extent, the concern is with the significance of the rate of importation and its interaction with other less variable dimensions of slavery in the colony, including the process of adjustment of recently arrived Africans to their new environment, which was often complicated by drought which periodically struck Antigua. The possible relation between slave resistance and importation cannot be traced through a simple correlation. On the side of importation there are many other considerations beside the mere arrival of Africans that should be taken into account to determine their influence in both the general and the more specific contexts of resistance. Although their precise role is not yet clear, sometimes because of the lack of data, such elements of the slave trade might include the time of the arrival of cargoes, slave prices, the ethnic composition of cargoes, the size and composition of purchases, and also the distribution of purchases to different owners.

When Antigua slaves were executed for crimes, or when they were hunted down and killed as fugitives, their owners were entitled to compensation from public funds after they had filed claims or petitions to the legislature. These claims, which are located in the minutes of the legislature, do not give as much detail about the slave offender and the crime committed as do the newspaper notices for fugitives that historians continue to mine for information about slave resistance and culture in societies of the Americas. Antigua compensation claims frequently recorded only the names of slaves, their estimated value, their owner's name, and the offense committed. However useful such claims might be for examining slave crime and resistance, they represent only those cases that actually came before the magistrates and the legislature; they therefore underrepresent the frequency of such activity. Claims for the period 1722–29 show 38 for fugitives who were executed, 5 for fugitives killed "in pursuit," 6 for theft, 1 for highway robbery, 1 for assault on a white person, 4 for murder of another slave, 8 for unspecified felonies, 1 for rape, 3 for murders not specified, and 26 for other undisclosed offenses (most of these probably for running away). Altogether there were 93 claims, or nearly 12 a year for the eight-year period (Gaspar 1985: 191–94; CO 9/5–12).

As running away was the most prevalent form of slave resistance, even after the island had been deforested (Gaspar 1985: 151–62, 171–84; 1979: 3–13; 1984: 45–59), we may focus on this activity in the 1720s. From 2 claims in 1723 for fugitives either executed or hunted down and killed, the number increased to 3 in 1724 and swelled to 21 in 1725 following passage of a comprehensive slave act late in 1723 (Laws of Antigua 1805: vol. 1). There were 3 such claims in 1726, 8 in 1727, 1 in 1728, and 5 in 1729. The number of claims underrepresents, of course, the actual number of fugitives at large, and, except for 1725, it does not reflect the true proportions of the fugitive problem, which is better captured in the legislation of the period. Of the 43 claims for fugitives executed or killed while out, 9 were for women. Three slave women were also executed for other serious offenses. It is striking that even though there was no real possibility for an alternative existence outside the sugar plantations (in the hills and forests, as in Jamaica before 1739–40), the slaves of tiny deforested Antigua still took flight, provoking the legislature and individual slaveowners to take punitive and preventive action.

In 1715, the Antigua assembly admitted that despite previous action taken against fugitives, "great Quantitys of Runaway Negroes (and some of them Notorious Offenders) do still Continue so as to Indanger peoples lives and goods travelling lawfully." By 1723, the fugitive problem was much more serious, and the legislature passed "An Act for attainting several Slaves now run away from their Master's Service, and for the better Government of Slaves." Devoted almost exclusively to fugitives, the act was the second such comprehensive legislation of the eighteenth century. It refined parts of earlier Antigua acts of 1697 and 1702, and followed or may have been modeled on a similar act of neighboring St. Christopher of 1722 (CO 9/3; Laws of Antigua 1805: vol. 1; CO 8/3; Acts of St. Christopher, 1739: 69–74). As Governor Hart noted in a report to the Board of Trade (CSP 1936: 58), the title and preamble of the act fully expressed its intent. According to the preamble,

it has been found by Experience that the Laws now in Force for the better Government of Negroes and Slaves, and for punishing such as do withdraw from the Service of their Masters, have proved too mild and gentle to curb and restrain them and that they have so abused the Lenity of the Laws, that great Numbers of them have deserted the Service of their Masters, and fled to the Mountains and Rocky Parts of this Island, and have armed and assembled themselves in Bands to oppose their Masters, and any that come in pursuit of them; and in the Night-time, when they cannot be easily discovered or taken, do frequently commit divers Thefts and Robberies in the Plantations . . . to the insupportable Wrong and Damage of many of His Majesty's good Subjects: And . . . they are daily inticing other Negroes to resort to and join with them, and it is much to be apprehended their Numbers will greatly increase, without the Aid of some Law to give extraordinary Encouragement for the taking their Chiefs and Ringleaders, and inflicting condign Punishment upon such as shall be taken.

Apart from the numerous clauses that covered the problem of fugitive slaves in general, the act made special mention of the notorious ringleaders Frank, Papa Will, Africa, and Sharper, who "have for a long Time past headed several armed Fugitive Slaves, and do all that in them lies to intice other Negroes to desert their Master's Service, and join them, and have themselves committed, and been the Occasion of committing many flagrant Thefts and Felonies." The act does not say whether these ringleaders were African-born or island-born Creoles, and their ethnic origin cannot be established from other existing evidence. But whether they were Africans or Creoles, could these fugitive ringleaders have capitalized on the restlessness and discontent of Antigua slaves whose lives were worsened by the hard times of drought; on the lax enforcement of the slave laws by both individual masters and authorized officials; and on the restlessness of recently arrived Africans struggling to adjust to their new environment?

Recurrent drought was a striking feature of life in Antigua and the rest of the Leeward Islands during the 1720s, affecting masters and slaves and the economic prospects of the colonies. The drought frequently struck during the dry season months from about January to June, which coincided with crop time, when the labor of the slaves was intensely applied to reaping the cane crop and manufacturing sugar and rum; but sometimes the drought could hang on much longer. Writing in 1732, the Nevis pastor and slaveowner, Robert Robertson, observed that drought was the "surest and severest" of the disasters wrought by nature or by man to which the sugar colonies were prone, especially the Leeward Islands. Robertson said that the drought was "generally followed by an Army of Worms, Flies, and other Insects, which eat up what little green things are left on the Earth." Next came "a scarcity of Indian Provisions, and a proportional Dearth of these from England, Ireland, and the North Continent," which was accompanied by "a most dreadful Mortality among the Negroes and Livestock, Crops next to nothing, and Ships returning with dead Freight." Robertson referred to the impact of such effects for the years 1717, 1718, 1721, 1724, and 1726, when all of the islands suffered. In 1718 and 1721 many plantations fell into debt. Throughout the 1720s in Antigua, the governor often ordered the inhabitants to fast and pray for rain. Governor Hart reported in May 1726 that eight months of dry weather had resulted in the loss of the Antigua cane crop for 1726 and 1727. Their ponds dry and cisterns empty, the planters of the riverless colony had been forced to import water from neighboring Guadeloupe and Montserrat. Many cattle and slaves had died. Hart predicted that many of the "midling and poorer Planters will be utterly undone" because of the loss of crops for two years and the added burden of buying provisions on credit from the merchants (Robertson 1732: 49–50; Gaspar 1985: 141–42; Dirks 1978: 137–53, 163–64; Dirks 1975: 86–87; CSP 1933: 49–50; CO 152/14, R38; CSP 1934: 238; CSP 1936: 74, 220; Martin Papers 1729). In 1725 Antigua produced an estimated 7,471 tons of sugar; production in 1726 was down to 3,882, nearly a 50% drop. These figures are based on the calculations of Noel Deerr, who does not record any figures for 1727 (Deerr 1949: 195).

The hardships brought on by drought and famine could precipitate restlessness and aggressive behavior among Antigua slaves. During the severe drought of 1726, fugitives "plagu'd everybody" in Nevis, which was as dry as Antigua. Reporting on the death of several slaves belonging to the Nevis plantation of Sir William Stapleton, the manager explained that they had "kill'd themselves by running away in the hard times." One Pompey, a slave driven to theft, "was cut to pieces stealing of corn." In Antigua in 1727 nearly half (8) of the slaves for whom compensation was claimed (18) were fugitives (Gay 1928: 157–58; CO 9/6), but there were many more at large. While the pressure of drought could have driven many of these slaves to aggressive action and also many others who were not represented in the usual sources that bear on slave crime, relief from such stress or deprivation could also cause similar patterns of behavior through the process of "relief-induced agonism."

Scholars who have studied the behavioral responses to relief in different societies have observed that the typical response to "the early refeeding of famished groups is the sudden appearance of symptoms of irritability, the aggressive voicing of complaints, and the other general, often intense, displays of hostility." Robert Dirks has argued that this phenomenon may help to explain the clustering of slave revolts and conspiracies in the British Caribbean during the month of December, and the annual practice of the Black Saturnalia at Christmas time, when the slaves channeled their explosive energies toward ritualized festivities. From December to June, which were the dry months of crop time, yields of local provisions were low. This recurrent food scarcity became worse by the wet season of July–November, when ships that brought supplies avoided the Caribbean and its hurricanes. The effects of this cycle were most pronounced in colonies such as the Leeward Islands which relied heavily upon imported provisions. At planting time in the wet season, the field slaves "endured a prolonged period of backbreaking labor while subsisting on stingy rations, storable grains and starchy tubers." The strain upon the slaves began to be relieved by late November, when imported supplies started arriving after the hurricane season, and work also slackened before the onset of crop time in late December or early January. According to Dirks, this relief coincided with an upsurge of aggressive slave behavior (Dirks 1978: 122–80; Dirks 1987a: 167–84; Dirks 1987b: 167–94). In the Leeward Islands during the 1720s, periodic drought could have accentuated slave resistance in several ways besides flight which did not result in the appearance of offenders before the magistrates.

What effect did the rate of importation of Africans into Antigua in the 1720s have on the flight of slaves (Geggus 1986: 121)? It is not easy to say because the sources do not address the question in any direct way. For example, fugitives were not designated as either Africans or Creoles, just simply slaves. There is therefore no basis for a quantitative assessment. On the other hand, the question can perhaps be approached indirectly, building upon the information about the effect of drought, by looking at the difficulty that African newcomers experienced in adjusting to their new environment as slaves, and how such responses would have resulted in various forms of resistance, including running away.

Planters realized that the entry of the Africans into the strange environment of plantation slavery was traumatic, and to protect their investment, they tried to keep the newcomers alive and contented by allowing them a seasoning period of from one year to perhaps as many as three, during which they learned the ropes of their new life. On the basis of his own experience of life in the Leeward Islands, Robertson noted that "notwithstanding self-Interest obliges the Purchasers to take all imaginable Care of the Salt-Water" slaves or newcomers, at least two-fifths were likely to die during the seasoning period. Recognizing that survivors might still need to be gradually transformed into valuable workers, the absentee slaveowner William Codrington instructed the manager of one of his Antigua plantations in 1715 to "be sure you take care of the new ngrs. and see that they are well fed and have there feet kept clean from Chegoes." Codrington also told the manager to give the slaves time off every Friday so that they could work on their provision grounds, "especially the New Negrs. and let them have ground by ym selves and not with the old Negrs." To minimize the risks of breaking in or seasoning newly imported Africans, some planters purchased them in small groups. Others preferred to buy young slaves. As David Stalker, a white employee on a Nevis plantation, explained in 1730, it was best to buy slaves between twelve and fifteen years old. "They are fully seasoned by 18 and is full as handy as them that is born in the country; but them full grown fellers think it hard to work never being brought up to it. They take it to heart and dye or is never good for any things" (Robertson 1730: 11; Robertson 1732: 44; Codrington Papers 1715; Gay 1928: 164).

Stalker's comments throw some light on slave resistance during the seasoning period and make it conceivable that many of the Antigua runaways of the 1720s were recent arrivals, although it is impossible to say what number. It is also possible that these newcomers set an example for others to follow who had their own problems coping with the hard times of drought. In other words, the arrival of large numbers of what one might call unassimilated slaves may have had a destablizing effect on general patterns of slave behavior at a time when the resident slaves were restless and discontented for other reasons (Gaspar 1985: 152–60, 199–201).

Evidence from the Antigua slave laws shows that slaveowners were quite aware that recent arrivals had a propensity to run away. The slave act of 1702, referring to a clause in an earlier act of 1681, declared that the clause "by Experience is sometimes found too severe, by reason of new ignorant Slaves." The act therefore repealed the clause that had imposed the death penalty for fugitives who were absent for three or more months, and instead prescribed that punishment—"Death, Loss of Limb, or Member, or publick Whipping"—should be at the discretion of two justices of the peace before whom the offenders must appear. By 1723, when the legislature had every reason to fear the escalation of slave flight and related forms of resistance, the new slave act reimposed the death penalty for fugitives who had been in the island for a year and had fled for at least three months, or had fled several times amounting to six months over a two-year period. But it must be noted that to encourage such fugitives to return to their owners the legislature promised them a pardon if they returned within three months of the publication of the act (Laws of Antigua 1805: vol. 1). Both slave acts of 1702 and 1723 illustrate the thorough approach that the Antigua legislators took to the problem of slave flight, but in giving their attention to the special difficulties of recently arrived Africans, they were arguably more concerned with the interests of slaveowners than with the well-being of the Africans. While it is not possible to estimate the number of recently imported African slaves among fugitives in Antigua during the 1720s, qualitative evidence about related considerations suggests that they were likely to run away, though not necessarily more so than other slaves who had resided longer in the island or who had been born there.

If the direct impact of the rate of slave imports upon slave flight and other forms of resistance in Antigua in the 1720s cannot be easily traced, it can be shown that it did have some bearing on other facets of the problem of slave flight in connection with compensation to slaveowners. The Antigua authorities recognized, and wrote into the 1723 slave act, that running away could be an individual or collective response. In the case of slaves who ran away in gangs of ten or more from the same plantation, often, according to the act, "upon slight or no occasions," it was lawful for only one of them, "the greatest Offender," presumably the ringleader, to be executed as a felon. There would seem to be more to this way of dealing with collective flight (which has been described as a striking pattern among recently imported Africans in South Carolina and Virginia) than simply decapitating these efforts so that the rest of the fugitives might return, or that flight might be discouraged. While it is possible that here too the legislature may have taken into account that in some ways the policing of runaways was unfair to recently imported Africans, and therefore to their owners, a more compelling explanation of the legislation may be that the lawmakers were concerned about the drain on public funds because there were so many fugitives at large, and because the ninth clause of the act awarded compensation for them at full appraised value (Laws of Antigua 1805: vol. 1; Mullin 1972: 42–43; Wood 1974: 249–53).

The earliest law that awarded full compensation covered all felonies, including running away. Passed in 1669 in response to increased resistance among the slaves, whose number had "increased to great Multitudes," the law ruled that appraisement should be done by two "indifferent" free white men. It was repealed in 1682 because it was "found by Experience to be very prejudicial to the Interest of all the Inhabitants of this Island," most likely, perhaps, because of the drain on the treasury. If this was the case, a similar concern surfaced again in 1688 (CO 154/2; CO 154/3; CSP 1899: 496). By 1723 the Antigua legislature had a history of wrestling with the problem of how best to encourage masters to prosecute their rebellious slaves. A law of the comprehensive slave act of 1702 had limited compensation for fugitives to £18 island currency (Gaspar 1984: 45–59; Laws of Antigua 1805: vol. 1). Perhaps repeated complaints that this payment was not sufficient, combined with the concern with fugitives, influenced the slaveowning legislators to change the law in 1723 and allow compensation at full appraised value. Newly imported African slaves sold in Antigua for as much as £33 island currency each in January 1702, and for about £38 in November 1703 (Records of the Royal African Company, T70/13). After 1702, the money that owners might lose when their fugitives were appraised, and the difficulty of finding replacements at low enough prices, ultimately discouraged them from initiating prosecution, and this was one reason why so many fugitives were at large and apparently brazenly committing other crimes during the first two decades of the eighteenth century. Not surprisingly, the slaveowning justices of the peace also did not regularly enforce the law as they should have. For the new system of compensation of 1723 to work, slaveowners would at least have had to have easy enough access to new supplies of slaves to replace those executed or killed as fugitives.

The revived state of the slave trade to Antigua in 1723 (584), in 1724 (430), and 1725 (1,525) resulted in a sizable increase in the number of runaways prosecuted and for whom compensation was claimed. The 21 claims reported for 1725 dwarf the 5 claims for 1723 and 1724 together. By November 1724, once the 1723 act had begun to take effect, the lieutenant governor and council voiced their concern to the assembly that part of the act was "too Severe" because the justices were authorized to impose only the death penalty, although the seriousness of the fugitives' crimes varied. "We therefore believe it reasonable," these men suggested, "that the Magistrates have power to take of a Limb or inflict any other punishment they shall judge proper according to the nature of the offence by which means the Publick will be eased of a great charge." The assembly, however, quickly disagreed "because the good effects of that Severity have been plainly seen & we have great reason to imagine there will be dayly fewer Objects to exercise it on." The assembly also reminded the complainers that the amendment they proposed had turned out to be "a very great defect"—clause 12—in the 1702 slave act. By April 1725 the lieutenant governor and council were back again to insist that the drain on the treasury for that year in compensation for fugitives would be "very great" and "will perhaps continue to be so." They saw no reason why, for the next few years, slaveowners would not continue to vigorously prosecute fugitives. Their remedy was to limit compensation to £30, "especially since . . . a Negro that deserves death for running away cannot be worth more than that sum," and also to match the punishment with the seriousness of the fugitives' offenses. The assembly later agreed to limit compensation to £35 for male fugitives and £30 for females. However, these limits did not apply to fugitives who were executed for fleeing in gangs. An act to that effect was passed in 1725. It acknowledged that compensation for fugitives at full appraised value had "amounted to great Sums, and thereby encouraged too vigorous Prosecutions" (CO 9/5; CO 155/6; Laws of Antigua 1805: vol. 1; CO 152/15, R166).

The legislature seems to have realized that there would be problems when compensation payments were either too low, as after 1702, or too high, as after 1723. One solution was to set aside more public funds for payments, but this the legislature would not do. The solution finally arrived at in 1725 was closer to that of 1702 than that of 1723, though compensation was now adjusted upward, presumably to approximate slave prices. In 1728 Humphrey Morrice hoped that the slave cargo of his Snow *Judith* would fetch £24 to £25 sterling a head, or about £36 to £38 Antigua currency. In 1727 the quoted average price for such slaves was £20 sterling or £30 Antigua currency (Donnan 1931: 369; CO 152/16, s65; McCusker 1978: 256–60). The limits on compensation claims therefore did not perhaps discourage masters from prosecuting fugitives whose value was less than or close to these rates. Indeed, there were complaints in 1727 that some masters were abusing the new laws by prosecuting old and worn-out fugitives whom they would have largely ignored earlier. The tendency may have been for unscrupulous masters to overvalue such slaves in seeking compensation. Although only eight fugitives were definitely paid for in 1727, the legislature was still concerned about cost, and admitted that in this regard the laws against fugitives had not produced the desired results, and that perhaps now magistrates should sentence offenders to be "hamstringed in one legg" because "one living instance Constantly before their Eyes would have a better Effect on the Slaves than many Executed who are no more thought on" (CO 9/6). In any case, limited compensation after 1725 would have discouraged masters from prosecuting fugitives who were valued higher, in spite of the regular arrival of slave cargoes. This might explain the fall in the number of claims for compensation from 21 in 1725 to 17 for 1726–29.

In 1728–29 the Antigua authorities unearthed an alleged slave conspiracy for a general revolt, but the sources are frustratingly silent about its origins. The affair generated 14 compensation claims; 4 slaves were executed and 10 were banished (Gaspar 1985: 209–10; CO 9/6; CO 152/17, T25; CO 8/6; CO 152/43). Though the precise connection with the arrival of hundreds of

Africans in the preceding years of the 1720s may not be clear, if the plot was genuine, is it possible that the leaders hoped to capitalize on the dislocations and restlessness among the slaves (recently arrived Africans, acculturated Africans, Creoles) caused by the presence of unassimilated Africans, and by drought and hardship? Better information than is now available would certainly be needed to find an answer.

After many lean years in the early 1700s, Antigua received regular supplies of slaves from the west coast of Africa during the 1720s. For the same period, the Antigua authorities remained markedly concerned about the resistance of the growing slave population, many of whom commonly became fugitives. The striking coincidence between these two trends raises the question about whether they might be connected in some way. Using compensation claims or petitions that slaveowners brought before the legislation when their fugitive slaves were either executed or hunted down and killed, it is possible to count at least how many such slaves were actually dealt with officially, but these would probably represent only a fraction of the total number of fugitives at large for any period. Because these claims do not supply details about whether fugitives were Africans or Creoles, we cannot estimate the proportion of recently imported Africans among them. Other qualitative evidence, however, points to the likelihood that newcomers would run away or simply stray because of the difficulty of adjusting to their new environment during years of intermittent drought, though not necessarily more so than acculturated Africans or Creoles. One interpretation of this evidence might be that the arrival of large numbers of unassimilated adult slaves may have had a destabilizing effect on general patterns of slave behavior at a critical period of recurrent drought and subsistence crises and other related problems when resident slaves already had sufficient reason for restlessness and discontent. The argument about the relation between slave importation and resistance therefore relies upon circumstantial evidence, but the evidence of compensation claims, and of the deep concern of the Antigua authorities about the mounting public cost for executing or paying for fugitives killed, strongly indicates that masters more vigorously prosecuted their fugitive slaves because they could rely on the Antigua market for newly imported slaves to find replacements.

REFERENCES
Acts of Assembly Passed in the Island of St. Christopher, From 1711, to 1735, inclusive. (1739). London.
Caines, Clement (1801) Letters on the Cultivation of the Otaheite Cane. London: Robinson.
Codrington Papers D1610/C2, Gloucestershire County Record Office, Gloucester, England.
Colonial Office (CO), Public Record Office, Kew, Surrey, England:
Minutes of (Antigua) Council in Assembly, 7 May 1715, CO 9/3.
Minutes of Assembly, 29 Jan., 20 Feb. 1722, CO 9/5.
Minutes of Council in Assembly, 27 Nov. 1724; 2 April 1725, CO 9/5; 17 April 1725, CO 155/6.
Minutes of Legislature, CO 9/5–12 (compensation claims).
Minutes of Council in Assembly, 17 March 1727; 24, 28 Jan., 28 Feb. 1729, CO 9/6.
Minutes of Council, 8, 25, 31 March, 29 April, 12 Nov. 1729, CO 9/6. "An Act for publique recompense to the Masters of Slaves putt to death by Law," 28 Oct. 1669, CO 154/2.
"An Act for repealing an Act, intituled, An Act for Publick Recompence to Masters of Slaves putt to death by Law," 24 May 1682, CO 154/3.
"An Act for the better Government of Slaves," 16 Dec. 1697, CO 8/3.
"An Act for the Banishment of Several Negroe Slaves Concerned in the Late Conspiracy," 8 March 1729, CO 8/6.
Governor John Hart to Board of Trade (BT), 2 May 1722, CO 152/14, R38; 11 July 1722, CO 152/14, R43; 20 May 1726, CO 152/15, R166; 15 Feb. 1727, CO 152/15, R190; 1 Dec. 1727, CO 152/16, s65; CO 152/18, T78.
Gov. Londonderry to BT, 5 April 1729, CO 152/17, T25.
Provost Marshal Accounts, Jan.–April 1729, Minutes of Council, 20 July 1730, CO 152/43.
Calendar of State Papers (CSP), Colonial Series, America and West Indies. Sainsbury, William Noel et al. (eds.) (1862–). London: Her Majesty's Stationery Office.
(1899) CSP (1685–1688), no. 1630: 496.
(1933) CSP (March 1720–Dec. 1721), no. 107: 49–50.
(1936) CSP (1724–1725), no. 82: 58.
(1936) CSP (1726–1727), no. 151: 74, no. 441: 220.
Deerr, Noel (1949) The History of Sugar. Vol. 1. London: Chapman and Hall.
Dirks, Robert (1975) Slaves' holiday. Natural History 84: 86–87.
——— (1978) "Resource fluctuations and competitive transformations in West Indian slave societies," in Charles D. Laughlin and Ivan A. Brady (eds.) Extinction and Survival in Human Populations. New York: Columbia University Press: 122–80.
——— (1987a) The Black Saturnalia: Conflict and Its Ritual Expression on British West Indian Slave Plantations. Gainesville: University of Florida Press.
——— (1987b) "The Black Saturnalia and relief induced agonism," in Kenneth F. Kiple (ed.) The African Exchange: Toward a Biological History of Black People. Durham, NC: Duke University Press: 167–94.

Donnan, Elizabeth (ed.) (1931) Documents Illustrative of the History of the Slave Trade to America. Vol. 2. Washington, DC: Carnegie Institution of Washington: 366–71: Instructions from Humphrey Morrice to Capt. Anthony Overstall of the Snow *Judith*. London, 8 July 1728.

Dunn, Richard S. (1972) Sugar and Slaves: The Rise of the Planter Class in the English West Indies, 1624–1713. Chapel Hill: University of North Carolina Press.

Galenson, David W. (1986) Traders, Planters, and Slaves: Market Behavior in Early English America. Cambridge: Cambridge University Press.

Gaspar, David Barry (1979) "Runaways in seventeenth century Antigua, West Indies," Boletin de Estudios Latinoamericanos y del Caribe: 3–13.

——— (1984) " 'To bring their offending slaves to justice': Compensation and slave resistance in Antigua 1669–1763." Caribbean Quarterly 30: 45–59.

——— (1985) Bondmen and Rebels: A Study of Master-Slave Relations in Antigua. Baltimore: Johns Hopkins University Press.

Gay, Edwin F. (1928) "Letters from a sugar plantation in Nevis, 1723–1732." Journal of Economic and Business History 1: 149–73.

Geggus, David (1986) "On the eve of the Haitian revolution: Slave runaways in Saint Domingue in the year 1790," in Gad Heuman (ed.) Out of the House of Bondage: Runaways, Resistance and Marronage in Africa and the New World. London: Frank Cass: 112–28.

Journal of Commissioners for Trade and Plantations (Jan. 1723–Dec. 1728) (1928). London: Her Britannic Majesty's Stationery Office.

Land, Aubrey C. (ed.) (1969) Bases of the Plantation Society. Columbia: University of South Carolina Press: 69–71.

The Laws of the Island of Antigua consisting of the Acts of the Leeward Islands, 1690–1798, and Acts of Antigua 1668–1845. Vol. 1 (1805). London.

"An Act for the better Government of Slaves, and Free Negroes," 28 June 1702, act no. 130: 158–64.

"An Act for attainting several Slaves now run away from their Master's Service, and for the better Government of Slaves," 9 Dec. 1723, act no. 176: 214–31.

"An Act for explaining a certain Act of this Island, past the ninth Day of December, one thousand seven hundred twenty and three, intituled, An Act for attainting several Slaves, now run away from their Master's Service; and for the better Government of Slaves," 9 Aug. 1725, act no. 183.

Martin Papers, 7, part 1, Add. ms. 41352 (1): Josiah Martin correspondence.

McCusker, John (1978) Money and Exchange in Europe and America, 1600–1775: A Handbook. Chapel Hill: University of North Carolina Press.

Mullin, Gerald W. (1972) Flight and Rebellion: Slave Resistance in Eighteenth-Century Virginia. New York: Oxford University Press.

Pitman, Frank Wesley (1917) The Development of the British West Indies, 1700–1763. New Haven: Yale University Press.

Records of the Royal African Company, Abstracts for the Committee of Correspondence, 13 Feb. 1702–9 May 1704, T70/13 (Treasury Records, Public Record Office, Kew, Surrey, England).

Robertson, Robert (1730) A Letter to the Right Reverend the Lord Bishop of London. London: J. Wilford.

———— (1732) A Detection of the State and Situation of the Present Sugar Planters of Barbadoes and the Leeward Islands. London: J. Wilford.

Sheridan, Richard B. (1973) Sugar and Slavery: An Economic History of the British West Indies, 1623–1775. Baltimore: Johns Hopkins University Press.

Watts, David (1987) The West Indies: Patterns of Development, Culture, and Environmental Change since 1492. Cambridge: Cambridge University Press.

Wood, Peter H. (1974) Black Majority: Negroes in Colonial South Carolina. New York: Alfred A. Knopf.

12
Mortality Caused by Dehydration during the Middle Passage

KENNETH F. KIPLE AND

BRIAN T. HIGGINS

ACCOUNTS ABOUND of slaves suffering from lack of water during the middle passage, many of them collected during testimony before the British Parliament and by British abolitionists. A Captain Hayes spoke of a cargo "labouring under the most famishing thirst . . . being in very few instances allowed more than a pint of water a day" (Buxton, 1844: 154–155). Thomas Clarkson (1969 [1789]: 573) claimed that he had seen slaves "almost dying from want of water," and Thomas Buxton (1844: 151–152) alleged that "there is nothing which slaves during the middle passage suffer from so much as want of water." [1]

Similar testimony was offered for the Brazilian trade. Dr. Luis Antônio de Oliveira Mendes (1812: 18–34) stated that "the slaves are affected with a very short ration of water," while a male slave who had made the journey from Africa to Brazil (Moore, 1983 [1854]: 27) testified that "we suffered very much for want of water but was [sic] denied all we needed. A pint a day was all that was allowed and many slaves died upon the passage." Dr. Joseph Cliffe, a physician in the Brazilian trade (House of Commons, 1983 [1848]: 34), claimed that when he was on shipboard, "the want of water" was so great among the slaves that they were not brought on deck because "if they were to see water alongside," thirst would drive "a great number of them to jump overboard without considering that it was salt water." When questioned about the amount of water given the slaves, Cliffe stated that in one case water only in the amount of a "teacup-full" was given every three days.

The last bit of testimony notwithstanding, the daily ration of a single pint of water, mentioned twice in the testimony quoted, was pronounced standard during the middle passage by Dr. Alexander Falconbridge (1788: 22) and has come to be accepted as such by many modern students of the slave trade. Now it is true that the slaves supposedly received another quart of water or so in their souplike meals of boiled vegetables doled out twice a day. Yet the same sources also speak of a shortage of food on the voyages—as if the slaves were begrudged even their soup—and in the process have left a physiological puzzle behind. For even had slaves been provided a pint of water and a quart of soup daily, they would certainly have suffered the thirst alleged by the abolitionists, and in fact it seems inconceivable that anyone could have endured the thirty-five–to–seventy–day passage to the Americas without dying of dehydration.[2]

It has been determined that a young man of about 145 pounds, in good health, leading a sedentary life, and consuming two thousand calories daily, will take in a bit over a quart of water in beverage form and close to a quart and a half in his foods. In all, then, his normal fluid requirements amount to about two and a half quarts of water daily. His output, again assuming good health, will be approximately the same, with urine and evaporative water accounting for almost all of the loss and fecal water for a very little (Davidson and Passmore, 1975: 94–95). The body of our hypothetical 145-pound man contains about forty quarts of water. If his water intake is diminished or his water output is increased, then that forty quarts in his body will begin to diminish. He has only to lose 10 percent or four of those quarts before he will show unmistakable signs of acute dehydration, and at that point his life will be at risk (Wolf, 1958: 9–10; Davidson and Passmore, 1975: 95).

The experience of United States soldiers in the desert during World War II provided E. F. Adolph and his associates with the opportunity to observe and identify the symptoms of severe dehydration caused by the interruption of water intake. The sensation of thirst was noticeable quite early in the process but did not really increase very much as water deficit continued. Muscular fatigue was observed next, along with anorexia, and by the time 5 to 8 percent of the body water had been lost, individuals had become "fatigued and spiritless." The tongue began to swell until swallowing was impossible, the eyes retreated into their orbits, and delirium followed (Adolph, 1947: 226–240). Similar symptoms also appear with dehydration caused by increased water output, such as occurs during illnesses that precipitate sweating, vomiting, or diarrhea or all three together. In the case of dehydration caused by cholera, for example, lethargy and sunken features, especially sunken eyes, have invariably been among the most prominent signals of impending death (Wolf, 1958: 219–221; Davidson and Passmore, 1975: 98). In addition, fever is often present with both conditions. If the dehydration is caused by increased water output due to illness, then the invading organism often produces it. In the case of decreased water intake, fever can develop as dehydration becomes progressively severe (Adolph, 1947: 221–223; Strickland, 1984: 272, 308; McGrew, 1985: 59).

Sodium depletion is usually associated with dehydration because of the body's efforts to maintain water balance. As the body progressively loses sodium, muscle cramps characteristically develop along with mental apathy, and vomiting is common. The risk of shock in dehydration is increased enormously with sodium depletion: as the blood pressure plunges, the loss of sodium pulls potassium out of the cells and it is excreted. This process affects the brain cells in such a way that victims are not aware of thirst and their need for water, and they enter a dreamlike state which ends in sudden death when potassium loss finally produces heart failure (Williams, 1973: 158–161; Davidson and Passmore, 1975: 94–98).

These, then, are the most prominent features of dehydration. Next, let us consider what an incredibly dehydrating experience the middle passage would have been even had the slaves received plenty of liquids. First, they were subject to serious water losses from perspiration alone. In coastal Nigeria, which witnessed the embarkation of more slaves to the Americas than any other region of West Africa, the average annual temperature is a bit over eighty degrees Fahrenheit, and the humidity is always high, at least 77 percent except around midday. The hottest months are November through May, precisely those months in which slaves were most likely to be shipped if they were destined for the Caribbean region or North America, since slaving captains did their best to avoid those waters during the hurricane months of July through September.[3]

Had it been the case that slaves were kept on deck while on the coast, there would have been no special problem with perspiration losses to consider, for presumably they either were accustomed to the heat and humidity or had become accustomed to it during their stay in the barracoons. But as long as slave vessels were prowling the coast in search of a full cargo for sale, the practice was to keep the slaves below deck. This was also the case during the first days in which the ship was sailing clear of the Africans' homeland (Falconbridge, 1788: 6–7, 29; Buxton, 1844: 114, 115, 118–119; Donnan, 1969, 1: 228–232; 2: 353; Ransford, 1971: 84–85; Stein, 1979: 86–87; Chandler, 1981: 11–14; Seção de Manuscritos, 1983 [1612]: 15). In his testimony, one slave trader estimated that the temperature below deck was between 120 and 130 degrees Fahrenheit. While at first blush this seems incredible, if the outside temperature was, say, 80 degrees Fahrenheit, then the temperature below deck had to be considerably higher, especially with the heat generated by numerous tightly packed bodies. Given this, it seems no wonder that one slave ship physician wrote that he had almost fainted in just a few minutes from the heat the slaves were forced to endure. Presumably, vents, gratings, and wind sails circulated enough air to mitigate the heat somewhat while the vessel was underway. Indeed something must have done, for water losses from sweating in intense heat have been recorded as high as two and one-half liters per hour, which would bring death in the span of just a few hours. Losses of one-half liter hourly from perspiration are not uncommon and, if unattended to, can also prove deadly in a relatively short period of time (Falconbridge, 1788: 25; House of Commons, 1983 [1848]: 32; Davidson and Passmore, 1975: 95).[4]

After the slaving vessel was well clear of the African coast, the custom was generally to bring the slaves up on deck whenever possible and for as long as possible to let them cool off and take some fresh air. But this was not done when the seas turned rough and when it rained; during these periods the ship was closed up, and the slaves remained below in intense heat and humidity (Snelgrave, 1734: 163–164; Crow, 1830: 150; Mannix, 1962: 116–117). Thus investigators have found that slave mortality aboard ship was systematically higher on vessels that sailed during the rainy season (Rawley, 1981: 294; Chandler, 1981: 23–36; Steckel and Jensen, 1986: 67; Eltis, 1987: 265–268).

Accompanying water loss from perspiration early in the voyage was further loss through the vomiting caused by seasickness. That seasickness was reported as common among the slaves should hardly have been a surprise. Most were not accustomed to the sea, but even if they had been, the heat and stench of the holds, coupled with a lack of fresh air, would have produced the condition, which should quickly have spread as if contagious. Nonetheless, one physician seemed surprised that seasickness affected the slaves "more violently" than Europeans,[5] and that it frequently terminated in death. A modern-day physician would have understood what our slaving surgeon did not: that in addition to being a cause of dehydration, vomiting brings about the voiding of considerable sodium (Falconbridge, 1788: 24; Moore, 1983 [1854]: 27; Nunnelly Hamilton and Whitney, 1978: 307, 315; Kiple, 1984: 61).

The first few days of a voyage, then, must have been a time of severe dehydration for the slaves from sweating and seasickness. After the vessel settled into a steady routine, and assuming that the weather was good, water loss from these causes would have abated, only to be replaced by another even more serious outlet of electrolytes and water: dysentery, which, as the literature makes clear, was rife on slave ships and has been ranked as the major killer of slaves during the middle passage (Hoeppli, 1969: 63–64; Klein, 1978: 201, 234; Rawley, 1981: 291; Eltis, 1983: 276; Cohn, 1985: 692; Steckel and Jensen, 1985: passim). Slaving captains and physicians divided the dysentery or "fluxes" that assaulted their charges into the "white flux" and the "bloody flux," and presumably that differentiation can be taken as an attempt to separate amebic from bacillary dysentery. Bacillary dysentery (shigellosis) spreads by an oral-fecal route, often via unwashed, infected hands, and prevails where sanitary standards and levels of personal hygiene are low and where people are in close contact with one another. Clearly, the holds of a slave ship provided the disease with an ideal environment. Shigellosis is characterized by cramping abdominal pain, fever, and watery diarrhea; nausea and vomiting are also common. The affliction is self-limiting and of relatively short duration, but while it prevails it causes the loss of considerable body water and electrolytes. Today the disease rarely causes death, but in the past various types of the ailment have resulted in significant levels of mortality (Hoeppli, 1969: 63–64; Howe, 1977: 163–165; Warren and Mahmoud, 1978: 30–32).

Bloody stools are not uncommon with bacillary dysentery, but they are a distinctive characteristic of amebic dysentery, which doubtless earned it the name "bloody flux." West Africa today (and presumably yesterday as well) is one area of the world where the risk of acquiring amebic dysentery is very high. Like the bacillary variety, it spreads through contaminated food and water. But unlike bacillary dysentery, which is short-lived, amebic dysentery can persist for weeks, now in remission, now raging, when the feverish patient may pass twenty or more stools daily (Howe, 1977: 119; Warren and Mahmoud, 1978: 42–43; Strickland, 1984: 478).

Bacillary dysentery would, as a rule, have appeared first during the early part of the middle passage, with the outbreak of amebic dysentery delayed until the midpoint of the voyage or even later. The reason is that bacillary dysentery has an incubation period of seven days or less, whereas amebic dysentery has an incubation period of between twenty and ninety days. Because captains and physicians could easily spy individuals afflicted with the latter, it is doubtful that persons with overt symptoms would normally have been taken aboard. On the other hand, the ship's officers could not have identified individuals with the ailment in its latent form, nor, of course, amebas in the water that was loaded. Thus care in inspecting the slaves could not have prevented the disease but only delayed its shipboard appearance. As we will see, the ongoing process of dehydration by definition also meant malnutrition, and malnutrition tends to activate latent amebiasis. Needless to say, once this occurred, the cramped and filthy conditions of the holds would have encouraged the disease to spread like wildfire. Thus slaves must often have been compelled to suffer through two separate epidemics of dysentery, one early and one late in the middle passage. In fact, the bloody flux continued to plague slaves long after they had been landed in the Americas (Hunter, Frey, and Schwartzwelder, 1966: 294; Hoeppli, 1969: 16–17; Wilcocks and Manson-Bahr, 1972: 162–163, 520–528). Michael Craton (1971: 20, 26), for example, has reported the bloody flux to have been the chief cause of "seasoning" mortality in Jamaica.

Modern treatment of amebic dysentery is based on the understanding that the nutritional status of the patient has much to do with the virulence of the disease, and prescribes a diet that is high in protein, low in carbohydrates, and supplemented by ample sources of vitamins, especially the B complex. Unfortunately for slaves with amebic dysentery, the diet aboard ship, laden with carbohydrates and almost devoid of high-quality protein, was just the opposite (Hunter et al., 1966: 302; Burnet and White, 1972: 46–47). In addition to diet, the medicine of the day was also better suited to kill than to cure patients suffering from dehydration. As symptoms of illness began to appear, standard medical procedure which guided the ship surgeons was to further deplete the patient. In the words of one critic (Aubrey, 1729: 107), "because he [the surgeon] does not know what they [the slaves] are afflicted with, but supposing it to be a Fever, [he] bleeds and purges or vomits them and so casts them into incurable *Diarrhoea* and in a few Days they become a Feast for some hungry Shark." In the Brazilian slave trade "enemas" also joined this list of wrongheaded remedies (Miller, 1988b: ch. 11). Obviously this constituted a terribly ironic method of introducing water into slaves who needed it so badly in any other form (ibid.: 420).

For all of these reasons—heat, seasickness, dysentery, and medical practice—the middle passage could scarcely have been a more dehydrating experience, and such symptoms of the condition as apathy, weakness, muscle cramps, emaciation, sunken eyes, and delirium must have been common. Interestingly, there was a mysterious disease reported aboard the slave ships that embraced many of these symptoms. The British called it "fixed melancholy," the Portuguese termed it *banzo,* and both thought it quite deadly. Indeed, one British surgeon told Parliament in 1790 that fully two-thirds of the slave deaths during the middle passage stemmed from it (Blake, 1860: 134–136; Sattamini Duarte, 1951; Mannix, 1962: 121; Carreira and Quintino, 1964: 49–51; Huggins, 1977: 50–51; Rawley, 1981: 291; Miller, 1988b: 379–442). It was a baffling sort of death. A Brazilian dictionary defined *banzo* as the "mortal melancholy that attacks the blacks from Africa"—mortal because slaves seemed to retreat into themselves and successfully will themselves to die (Sattamini Duarte, 1951: 62; translation ours). George Howe, an American medical student aboard a slaver, subscribed to the opinion, held by many, that somehow Africans, unlike other peoples, could commit suicide by holding their breath (Mannix, 1962: 120). Modern writers, on the other hand, have tended to view the condition as a "state of shock" which led to an "involuntary suicide," and one has wondered if "medical science has ever known of such a phenomenon" (Huggins, 1977: 51).

It seems likely that medical science does know of the condition and today would label it extreme dehydration. Certainly, death did not come from holding one's breath, for even if one could do this to the point of unconsciousness, the lungs would then reinflate automatically. But it could certainly have been shock that the British and Portuguese observed—the shock of water and electrolyte loss and the ensuing fall in blood pressure.[6] Recall the swollen tongues the soldiers developed that made swallowing impossible, the way their eyes receded into their sockets, and their apathy, their "fatigued and spiritless" demeanor. Now compare the descriptions of those who died of fixed melancholy, who were surely apathetic and who were reported to systematically refuse food and have the sunken eyes which gave the impression of slaves withdrawing into themselves. The apparently sudden death which bewildered contemporary observers is characteristic of heart failure triggered by potassium loss, which prior to death would have relieved the victim of his thirst and left him in the dreamlike state mentioned above (Blake, 1860: 127–134; Spears, 1900: 68–81; Sattamini Duarte, 1951: 61n; Mannix, 1962: 121; Huggins, 1977: 51).

The victims of fixed melancholy stood out in the minds of the persons who described them because of the number of strange symptoms that were present, and because the condition resulted in death. But if one searches for instances of slaves suffering from just one or two of the symptoms of dehydration, they become overwhelming. Many slave ship accounts list deaths from a refusal to eat; physicians write of those who died "raving mad," those who died from no apparent cause during the night, those who held their breath until death, and those who died of suffocation. "Cramps," which can signal sodium depletion, were often reported by physicians to be fatal. Descriptions are numerous of slaves who could not stand upright because of these cramps and muscular fatigue, and references can also be found to the "sunken visages" of emaciated slaves and to their eyes, which assumed "a sunken appearance . . . almost like the boiled eye of a fish." Finally, the frequent descriptions of whole cargoes as in a "deplorable state," with a "thin and weake" appearance, also indicate the ravages of dehydration as well as malnutrition, which brings up the question of the relationship between the two within the context of the slave trade (Falconbridge, 1788: 31–32; Mayer, 1854: 103; Spears, 1900: 78–79; Pares, 1938: 187; Pope-Hennessy, 1968: 193–195; Donnan, 1969, 1: 280; Huggins, 1977: 50–51; Rawley, 1981: 300; Conrad, 1983: 28–49; Steckel and Jensen, 1985: 61n).[7]

Sometimes slaves were put into the trade because of famine; there is no question that they were, as a rule, fed badly during the forced march to the sea, and most accounts indicate that they fared little better nutritionally in the barracoons. The frequent reports of scurvy on the slave ships—a disease which generally does not develop before four to six months of vitamin C deprivation—alone says much about the poor and unvaried diet the slaves consumed before they ever embarked. Thus, aboard ship, the boiled horsebeans, rice, corn, yams, or even manioc, in some combination laced with red peppers, palm oil, and a bit of salted meat or fish, represented a nutritional improvement. As already noted, however, dehydration produces anorexia, and extreme dehydration makes swallowing impossible. Moreover, it inhibits the body's ability to metabolize. In experiments using laboratory animals, it has been discovered that when the water is restricted to half of that which they will voluntarily consume, there is a one-third reduction in the efficiency of the metabolism of foods consumed.[8]

For all these reasons, then, there seems little question that dehydration was by far the biggest cause of slave mortality during the middle passage. For dysentery does not kill, nor vomiting, nor sweating, but they can all produce dehydration, which does kill. To be sure, when contagious diseases such as smallpox crept on board, they did fearful damage. But their appearance was the exception rather than the rule, while the process of dehydration must have afflicted practically every slave on practically every voyage.[9]

Understanding that dehydration must have been the major cause of mortality aboard slave ships in turn makes it possible to explain what has seemed to be puzzling and often contradictory mortality patterns during the middle passage. Where deaths occurred very early, while the ship was on or near the coast, perspiration losses alone could have caused them, as well as those losses combined with other losses from vomiting induced by seasickness. Thus the findings of Joseph Miller (1988b: 419–424), that a significant number of deaths took place early in voyages from Angola, may be explicable in terms of the rainy season there, where the rains are most intense from January to April (Queiros, 1954), since voyages that began during these months seem to have sustained considerably higher mortality before arrival in Brazil than those that began at other times.[10]

Bacillary dysentery, although not as dehydrating as amebic dysentery, would have precipitated the next round of mortality, while amebic dysentery would have begun its assault on an already water- and electrolyte-depleted group of people from about the midpoint of the voyage onward. Thus other research that has revealed mortality from gastrointestinal causes peaking about thirty-one days into the middle passage may well be indicating dehydration deaths brought about by amebic dysentery (Steckel and Jensen, 1986: 69). In addition, as the voyage grew longer, there was ever greater danger of both a lessening and a fouling of the ship's water supply, assuming that it was not bad to begin with, as it frequently appears to have been, particularly on slave ships sailing from Luanda and Benguela (Miller, 1988a).

Finally, there is the question of the declining middle passage mortality of slaves, from the first decades of the eighteenth century to the first part of the nineteenth century, from close to 25 percent to around 5 to 10 percent. This decline must have been the result, not just of the construction of specialized ships intended for the trade, as has been suggested, but of the construction of specialized ships designed to carry more water than their predecessors and very likely to catch more water from rainfall as well (Klein and Engerman, 1975: 381–398; Stein, 1979: 97; Rawley, 1981: 302; Cohn and Jensen, 1982; Cohn, 1985; Klein, 1986: 142; Miller, 1988b: 418).

To return to the question of the slaves' daily intake of liquids, it will be recalled that a daily ration of one pint of water and a quart of soup would leave a 145-pound individual a quart short of his normal requirements and thus in poor condition to endure the sweating, vomiting, and diarrhea to which the thirty-five–to–seventy–day voyage would subject him. Authorities write that the absolute minimum intake of water to replace normal losses is a quart a day (Lloyd, McDonald, and Crampton, 1978: 27), and yet, as we have seen, the slaves' water losses were far above normal. No doubt the liquid ration of the individual increased as the voyage progressed and the 10 to 20 percent who normally died during the middle passage did so, but this increased ration still does not seem to have been enough to sustain life during the transatlantic crossing.

Moreover, there is the question of sodium replacement, for if the individual is seriously depleted in the mineral, then even an ample supply of water will do no good. Rather, it will create a condition known as water intoxication, whose symptoms are anorexia, weakness, and mental apathy, and later convulsions and coma. Yet the extent to which slaves received salt during the middle passage is difficult to ascertain. Some British physicians advised against feeding the slaves any salted provisions, while at least one Portuguese source, by contrast, mentioned that care should be taken in feeding newly landed slaves who had been so long on a diet of salted foods. Most accounts, however, give the impression that salt, like water, was undersupplied, leaving us with the physiological puzzle referred to earlier (Atkins, 1735: 171; G.A.P.D., 1826: 300; Davidson and Passmore, 1975: 171; Lloyd et al., 1978: 23).

Given what we know about the conditions of the middle passage that would have produced dehydration, and also what we know about dehydration and its effects, the mortality that *did not* occur during the middle passage is a matter of some considerable interest. Joseph Miller (1988b: 419–424) has observed that "it is perhaps remarkable that, overall, 80 to 90% of the slaves taken aboard managed to reach the Americas alive." It is indeed.

NOTES

The authors would like to thank David Eltis, Robert Paquette, and members of the audience for their comments at the conference. They also would like to thank Joseph C. Miller for his splendid suggestions in subsequent correspondence. In addition, Kiple would like to thank the National Endowment for the Humanities for a summer grant in 1988, which provided, among other things, time to research and write his portion of the paper.

1   Testimony presented to Parliament, of course, is considerably tarnished by the conflict between the abolitionists, on the one hand, and the advocates of the trade on the other. Many of the witnesses were closely connected with the slave trade and claimed to have observed few abuses. Clarkson, Buxton, and other abolitionists were likewise determined to present horrific evidence.

2   For other accounts of water rations in the middle passage see Mayer, 1854: 103; Blake, 1860: 127–134; and Reynolds, 1985: 49. By contrast, Herbert Klein (1978: 160n) states that "contemporaries agreed that slaves were given just three pints of water per day." As for sailing times, in the Brazilian trade the voyage from Luanda to Recife averaged thirty-five days, to Bahia forty days, and to Rio de Janeiro fifty to sixty days; see Boxer, 1952: 231, and Russell-Wood, 1982: 27. From Mozambique to Rio de Janeiro the average was seventy days. For this and other information on the slave trade from Mozambique, see Vail and White, 1980. From West African ports to the West Indies, sailing times averaged from five to almost ten weeks, depending on the ports of origin and destination. For a description of such a voyage, see Gurney, 1844, and the testimony of Lieutenant T. A. Craven (U.S. Congress, 1860).

3   Another factor in West Africa was that slavers preferred not to buy slaves during the rainy months of June through August, when diseases were reportedly most prevalent among them; see Galenson, 1986: 47. For information on the climate of West Africa, see Harrison Church, 1963: 52, and Willmott, Mather, and Rowe, 1981; for west-central Africa see Abshire and Saunders, 1969: 3–4. For the major importing season in the Caribbean see Klein, 1978: 239, and Sheridan, 1981: 262.

4   It may be that the water surrounding the ship cooled the slave holds somewhat. Yet, generally, slave decks were well above the waterline and so probably were not subject to any cooling effects the ocean may have had.

5   Emigrants from Europe to North America also frequently suffered temporary malnutrition and dehydration due to seasickness. For this and other information about the North Atlantic passage, see Grubb, 1987.

6   Kiple (1984: 63) advanced this hypothesis, but the "shock" in question is a bit more complicated than the text here indicates. With cholera shock, for example, which comes with extreme dehydration, the volume of urine

decreases as renal failure develops; this in turn further slows the flow of blood, and complete renal shutdown may then end the patient's life. For more detail see Felsenfeld, 1965: 28.

7   Reynolds (1985: 50) cites an insurance manual of the period that states that loss of a slave from "despair" is insurable, suggesting that, as a cause of death, the condition was not unusual. A detailed discussion of the testimony regarding fixed melancholy that many English slave ship surgeons gave before the House of Commons can be found in Chandler, 1981: 34–38. Chandler (ibid.: 30) quotes a Dr. Isaac Wilson, who stated that the "flux" was often a result of melancholy. See also Lima Duarte, 1849: 24, and Donnan, 1969, 1: 206–209.

8   See Eltis, 1989, for a survey which links African rainfall, harvest times, and disease with shipboard mortality. See Miller, 1988b: 413–424, for a summary of much of his fine work on the nutritional state of slaves put into the trade from Angola. For West Africa see Inikori, 1982: 26–27; Winterbottom, 1803, 2: 27; Sheridan, 1985: 105–106; and Kiple, 1984: 59. For scurvy see Postma, 1975: 253; Stein, 1979: 100; and Miller, 1988b: 425. For descriptions of diets aboard ship in the various branches of the slave trade, see Atkins, 1735: 171; Sattamini Duarte, 1951: 24; Saunders, 1982: 13–14; Renny, 1807: 173–174; and Goslinga, 1985: 73. For dehydration and metabolism see Lloyd, McDonald, and Crampton, 1978: 21–35; and Aurand and Woods, 1973: 9.

9   Steckel and Jensen (1985: 7) make the point that smallpox and measles were "virtually absent" as causes of death in the late eighteenth century, at least in the ship logs they consulted.

10   The average passage from Luanda to Rio de Janeiro has been estimated at fifty to sixty days. Thus, slaves embarked in the rainy season of coastal Angola, January through April, would have reached Rio de Janeiro between March and June, which were among the fall and winter months that Klein (1978: 57) and Klein and Engerman (1975: 394) indicate were the months in which slave ships reaching that city sustained the heaviest mortality.

REFERENCES

Abshire, D. M., and M. A. Saunders (1969) Portuguese Africa: A Handbook. London: Pall Mall.

Adolph, E. F. (1947) Physiology of Man in the Desert. New York: Interscience.

Atkins, J. (1735) A Voyage to Guinea, Brazil, and the West Indies. London: C. Ward and R. Chandler.

Aubrey, T. (1729) The Sea Surgeon, or the Guinea Man's *Vade Mecum*. London: Clarke.

Aurand, L. W., and A. E. Woods (1973) Food Chemistry. Westport, CT: Van Nostrand.

Blake, W. O. (1860) The History of Slavery and the Slave Trade. Columbus, OH: J & H Miller.

Boxer, C. R. (1952) Salvador de Sá and the Struggle for Brazil and Angola, 1602–1686. London: University of London Press.

Burnet, M., and D. O. White (1972) Natural History of Infectious Disease. 4th ed., Cambridge: Cambridge University Press.

Buxton, T. F. (1844) The African Slave Trade and Its Remedy. London: John Murray.

Carreira, A., and F. Quintino (1964) Antroponomia da Guiné Portugesa. Lisbon: Memórias da Junta de Investigações do Ultramar.

Chandler, D. L. (1981) Health and Slavery in Colonial Colombia. New York: Arno.

Clarkson, T. (1969 [1789]) "Essay on the efficiency of regulation or abolition," excerpted in E. Donnan (ed.) Documents Illustrative of the Slave Trade to America, vol. 2, The Eighteenth Century. New York: Octagon Books: 571–573.

Cohn, R. L. (1985) "Deaths of slaves in the middle passage." Journal of Economic History 45: 685–692.

———, and R. A. Jensen (1982) "The determinants of slave mortality rates on the middle passage." Explorations in Economic History 19: 269–292.

Conrad, R. E. [ed.] (1983) Children of God's Fire: A Documentary History of Black Slavery in Brazil. Princeton: Princeton University Press.

Craton, M. (1971) "Jamaican slave mortality: Fresh light from Worthy Park, Longville, and the Tharp estates." Journal of Caribbean History 3: 1–27.

Crow, H. (1830) Memoirs of the Late Captain Hugh Crow of Liverpool. London: Frank Cass.

Davidson, S., and R. Passmore (1975) Human Nutrition and Dietetics. 6th ed., Edinburgh: E & S Livingstone.

Donnan, E. [ed.] (1969) Documents Illustrative of the Slave Trade to America. 4 vols., New York: Octagon Books.

Eltis, D. (1983) "Free and coerced transatlantic migrations: Some comparisons." American Historical Review 88: 251–280.

———(1987) Economic Growth and the Ending of the Transatlantic Slave Trade. New York: Oxford University Press.

——— (1989) "Mortality in the nineteenth-century slave trade." Social Science History 13: 315–40.

Falconbridge, A. (1788) Account of the Slave Trade on the Coast of Africa. London: J. Phillips.

Felsenfeld, O. (1965) Synopsis of Clinical Tropical Medicine. St. Louis: C. V. Mosby.

G.A.P.D. (1826) Sketches of Portuguese Life. London: G. B. Whittaker.

Galenson, D. W. (1986) Traders, Planters and Slaves: Market Behavior in Early English America. Cambridge: Cambridge University Press.

Goslinga, C. C. (1985) The Dutch in the Caribbean and in the Guianas, 1680–1791. Assen, Netherlands: Van Gorcum.

Grubb, F. (1987) "Morbidity and mortality on the North Atlantic passage: Eighteenth-century German immigration." Journal of Interdisciplinary History 17: 565–585.

Gurney, W. B. (1844) Trial of Pedro de Zuleta on a Charge of Slave Trading Oct. 1843, at London. London: C. Wood.

Harrison Church, R. J. (1963) West Africa: A Study of the Environment and Man's Use of It. 4th ed., London: Longman Group.

Hoeppli, R. (1969) Parasitic Diseases in Africa and the Western Hemisphere: Early Documentation and Transmission by the Slave Trade. Basel: Verlag für Recht und Gesellschaft.

House of Commons (1983 [1848]) "Second report from the select committee on the slave trade together with the minutes of the evidence and appendix," excerpted in R. E. Conrad (ed.) Children of God's Fire: A Documentary History of Black Slavery in Brazil. Princeton: Princeton University Press: 28–37.

Howe, G. G. M. [ed.] (1977) A World Geography of Human Diseases. New York: Academic.

Huggins, N. I. (1977) Black Odyssey. New York: Pantheon Books.

Hunter, G. W., W. W. Frey, and J. C. Schwartzwelder (1966) A Manual of Tropical Medicine. 4th ed., Philadelphia: Saunders.

Inikori, J. E. [ed.] (1982) Forced Migration: The Impact of the Export Slave Trade on African Societies. New York: Africana.

Kiple, K. F. (1984) The Caribbean Slave: A Biological History. New York: Cambridge University Press.

Klein, H. S. (1978) The Middle Passage: Comparative Studies in the Atlantic Slave Trade. Princeton: Princeton University Press.

————— (1986) African Slavery in Latin America and the Caribbean. New York: Oxford University Press.

—————, and S. L. Engerman (1975) "Shipping patterns and mortality in the African slave trade to Rio de Janeiro, 1825–1830." Cahiers d'études africaines 15: 381–398.

Lima Duarte, J. R. de (1849) "Ensaio sobre a hygiene da escravatura no Brasil." Ph.D. diss., Rio de Janeiro.

Lloyd, L. E., B. E. McDonald, and E. W. Crampton (1978) Fundamentals of Nutrition. 2d ed., San Francisco: W. H. Freeman.

McGrew, R. E. (1985) Encyclopedia of Medical History. New York: McGraw-Hill.

Mannix, D. P. (1962) Black Cargoes: A History of the Atlantic Slave Trade, 1518–1865. New York: Viking.

Mayer, B. (1854) Captain Canot: Or, Twenty Years of an African Slaver. New York: D. Appleton.

Miller, J. C. (1988a) "Overcrowded and undernourished: The techniques and consequences of tight packing in the Portuguese Southern Atlantic slave trade," in S. Daget (ed.) Actes du Colloque International sur la Traite des Noirs (Nantes, 1985), vol. 2, De la traite à l'esclavage. Nantes and Paris: Centre de Recherche sur l'Histoire du Monde Atlantique and Société Française d'Histoire d'Outre-mer: 395–424.

————— (1988b) Way of Death. Madison: University of Wisconsin Press.

Moore, S. (1983 [1854]) "The biography of Mahommah G. Baquaqua, a native of Zoogoo, in the interior of Africa . . . Written and revised from his own words by Samuel Moore," excerpted in R. E. Conrad (ed.) Children of God's Fire: A Documentary History of Black Slavery in Brazil. Princeton: Princeton University Press: 23–28.

Nunnelly Hamilton, E. M., and E. N. Whitney (1978) Nutrition. 2d ed., St. Paul: West.

Oliveira Mendes, Luis Antônio de (1812) Discurso acadêmico ao programa: Determinar com todos os seus sintomas as doenças agudas e crônicas que mais frequentemente acometem os pretos recém-tirados da Africa. Lisbon: Real Academica.

Pares, R. (1938) "Barbados history from the records of the prize courts." Journal of the Barbados Museum and Historical Society 5: 186–189.

Pope-Hennessy, J. (1968) Sins of the Fathers: A Study of the Atlantic Slave Traders, 1441–1807. New York: Knopf.

Postma, J. (1975) "Mortality in the Dutch slave trade, 1675–1795," in H. A. Gemery and J. S. Hogendorn (eds.) The Uncommon Market: Essays in the Economic History of the Atlantic Slave Trade. New York: Academic: 239–260.

Queiros, D. X. (1954) "Os climas das regiões de Luanda, Vila Salazar, Nova Lisboa e Sá da Bandeira." Boletim do Instituto de Angola 3: 57–64.

Ransford, O. (1971) The Slave Trade: The Story of Transatlantic Slavery. London: John Murray.

Rawley, J. A. (1981) The Transatlantic Slave Trade: A History. New York: Norton.

Renny, R. (1807) A History of Jamaica. London: J. Cawthorn.

Reynolds, E. (1985) Stand the Storm: A History of the Atlantic Slave Trade. London: Allison and Busby.

Russell-Wood, A. J. R. (1982) The Black Man in Slavery and Freedom in Colonial Brazil. New York: St. Martin's.

Sattamini Duarte, O. (1951) "Contribução ao estudo clinico-histórico do banzo." Revista Fluminense de Medicina 16: 61–88.

Saunders, A. C. de D. M. (1982) A Social History of Black Slaves and Freedmen in Portugal. Cambridge: Cambridge University Press.

Seção de Manuscritos. Biblioteca Nacional, Rio de Janeiro (1983 [1612]) "Proposta a sua magestade sobre a escravaria [sic] das terras da Conquista de Portugal" (document 7, 3, 1, no. 8), in R. E. Conrad (ed.) Children of God's Fire: A Documentary History of Black Slavery in Brazil. Princeton: Princeton University Press: 11–15.

Sheridan, R. B. (1981) "Slave demography in the British West Indies and the abolition of the slave trade," in D. Eltis and J. Walvin (eds.) The Abolition of the Slave Trade. Madison: University of Wisconsin Press: 259–285.

———(1985) Doctors and Slaves: A Medical and Demographic History of Slavery in the British West Indies, 1680–1834. Cambridge: Cambridge University Press.

Snelgrave, W. (1734) A New Account of Some Parts of Guinea and the Slave Trade. London: J. Wren.

Spears, J. (1900) The American Slave Trade: An Account of Its Origin, Growth and Suppression. New York: Charles Scribner's Sons.

Steckel, R. H., and R. A. Jensen (1985) "Determinants of slave and crew mortality in the Atlantic slave trade" (Working Paper No. 1540). Cambridge, MA: National Bureau of Economic Research.

———(1986) "New evidence on the causes of slave mortality in the Atlantic slave trade." Journal of Economic History 46: 57–77.

Stein, R. L. (1979) The French Slave Trade in the Eighteenth Century: An Old Regime Business. Madison: University of Wisconsin Press.

Strickland, G. T. (1984) Hunter's Tropical Medicine. 6th ed., Philadelphia: Saunders.

U.S. Congress (1860) Message . . . in Reference to the African Slave Trade (House of Representatives Executive Document 7). Washington: Government Printing Office.

Vail, L., and L. White (1980) Capitalism and Colonialism in Mozambique: A Study of the Quelimane District. Minneapolis: University of Minnesota Press.

Warren, K. S., and A. A. F. Mahmoud [eds.] (1978) Geographic Medicine and the Practitioner. Chicago: University of Chicago Press.

Wilcocks, C., and P. E. C. Manson-Bahr (1972) Manson's Tropical Diseases. 17th ed., Baltimore: Williams and Wilkins.

Williams, S. R. (1973) Nutrition and Diet Therapy. St. Louis: C. V. Mosby.

Willmott, C. J., J. R. Mather, and C. M. Rowe (1981) Average Monthly Temperature and Precipitation Data for the World, vol. 1, Eastern Hemisphere. Elmer, NJ: C. W. Thornwaite Assoc.

Winterbottom, T. (1803) An Account of the Native Africans in the Neighbourhood of Sierra Leone. 2 vols., London: C. Whittingham.

Wolf, A. V. (1958) Thirst: Physiology of the Urge to Drink and Problems of Water Lack. Springfield, IL: Thomas.

13

The Possible Relationship between the Transatlantic Slave Trade and Hypertension in Blacks Today

THOMAS W. WILSON AND

CLARENCE E. GRIM

IN 1982, Waldron and coworkers noted higher blood pressure among blacks with a heritage of Western Hemisphere slavery than among those without such a heritage (Waldron et al. 1982). In 1985, Akinkugbe noted that "in both men and women, mean systolic and diastolic arterial pressures were generally lower in Nigerians than in comparable black populations in the United States and the Caribbean" (Akinkugbe 1985). Our recent meta-analysis of numerous epidemiological studies conducted in sub-Saharan Africa, the West Indies, and North America suggests these observations were, indeed, correct: blacks in the Western hemisphere (mostly descendants of slaves) appear to have higher mean blood pressure levels than black populations in Africa (Wilson et al. 1991). However, because of the wide range of sampling techniques in these studies, the lack of standardized measurements, and a host of other problems (Akinkugbe 1985), a confirmation of this finding will require carefully conducted population-based random surveys, similar to the design used in the Intersalt study (Intersalt Cooperative Research Group 1988).

It has been assumed that population differences within the black race are due to environmental factors, such as variations in diet or biobehavioral stress (Akinkugbe et al. 1977; Beiser et al. 1976; Cooper 1984). However, on the basis of historical data from the transatlantic slave trade and modern medical knowledge, we will argue that hypothesized genetic differences in sodium metabolism between these two groups may be partially responsible for the differences in blood pressure levels between Western hemisphere blacks and African blacks that we observe today.

THE EVOLUTION OF SALT CONSERVATION

In 1967, Helmer suggested that in sub-Saharan Africa evolutionary adaptations to the hot, humid environment would emerge to protect against fatal electrolyte depletion from excessive sweating (Helmer 1967). He believed that an enhanced ability to conserve salt would be a major advantage in this ecology, but he also hypothesized that descendants of these populations may be predisposed to hypertension today. Others have supported this general idea that the heat of tropical Africa is partially responsible for the high prevalence of hypertension in blacks today (Schachter and Kuller 1984; Lee 1981; Denton 1982: 616–17). In 1973, Gleibermann (1973) expanded on the evolutionary hypothesis of salt conservation in sub-Saharan Africans by adding that the low intake of dietary salt within Africa would also have acted as a selection pressure.[1] A low salt intake was given a major role in this hypothesis by other investigators as well (Grollmann 1978; Williams and Hopkins 1979; Denton 1982: 616–17). In 1983, this compelling hypothesis was expanded to a non-African setting with the compelling argument that "heat stress and salt and water deprivation during the slave trade" may have acted as further selective pressure (Blackburn and Prineas 1983).[2] All of these writers thought this hypothesis might partially explain the higher blood pressure of blacks when compared to whites.

Many of these authors conceded that their ideas about the evolution of salt conservation were somewhat speculative (Denton 1982: 616–17). In the words of Blackburn and Prineas, "these ideas are too broadly speculative" (Blackburn and Prineas 1983). Grollman (1978) concluded that the hypothesis was not even researchable: "In view of the extensive migrations to which human populations have been subjected and our lack of knowledge of the diets of early man, it is obviously impossible to verify the hypothesis which has been presented here."

We disagree with Grollman. This disagreement stems from our own reviews, and the quantitative analysis by others, of the extensive historical records available on the biohistory of African Americans. For example, in 1986 and 1988 Wilson noted a positive association between the geographical variability of salt in West African history and the geographical variability of blood pressure today in the same region (Wilson 1986; Wilson 1988: 96–108, 144–57). He also concluded that differences in blood pressure among blacks, that is, intraracial differences, are as important as interracial differences between blacks and whites. In addition, he suggested that historical research was a useful adjunct to more traditional methods of hypothesis testing in science. And in 1988, Grim argued that, in addition to heat and a low salt intake, salt-depletive diseases during slavery, such as diarrhea and fevers, may have been an additional force for the natural selection of salt conservation. His formulation of the salt conservation hypothesis can be stated as follows: In the biohistory of African Americans, selective mortality due to heat, salt-depletive diseases, and low salt intake during the slavery period of Western Hemisphere history have acted together to cause the evolution of a Western Hemisphere black population superbly adapted to conserving salt. When this population is exposed to today's high-salt diet it will be more likely to develop increases in blood pressure as a consequence of this better ability to retain salt (Grim 1988).

In this paper we merge historical data with modern physiology in our attempt seriously to address the salt conservation hypothesis as it applies to blacks. We acknowledge that the physiologic testing of this hypothesis will require carefully designed population-based studies. We also acknowledge that such a wide-ranging synthesis of historical evidence on the demography and epidemiology of the slave trade is bound to be in error in specific points, but we believe its overall direction is correct. We encourage more detailed historical research on the demographic, dietary, and disease history of the African diaspora. We also sincerely hope that this overview will encourage others from disciplines besides history and medicine to pursue this compelling biohistorical synthesis of the role of the evolution of salt conservation in the striking variation in the prevalence of hypertension and levels of blood pressure among geographically separated black populations today.

SALT SENSITIVITY AND BLOOD PRESSURE

The concepts of Helmer, Gleibermann, and others about the evolution of salt conservation merge today with the concept of "salt sensitivity" discussed in the hypertension literature for at least 25 years. In 1962, Lewis Dahl and his colleagues were able to use artificial selection to breed (in only three generations) rats that had a blood pressure that was either "salt sensitive" or "salt resistant." The salt-sensitive rats had a sharp rise in blood pressure when fed a diet high in salt, while the salt-resistant rats had little change in blood pressure on the same high-salt diet (Dahl et al. 1962). The Dahl salt-sensitive rats also have a greater propensity to conserve sodium than the salt-resistant rats (Maude and Kao-Lo 1982). In humans, salt sensitivity refers to the effect of current salt intake on blood pressure. Salt-sensitive individuals experience a significant rise in blood pressure following a sodium load. As might be expected, salt-resistant individuals have little change in blood pressure with changes in salt intake (Kawasaki et al. 1978).

In the United States there seem to be clear differences in sodium metabolism between African Americans and whites. The systematic studies by the Indianapolis group have documented that normotensive African Americans are more sensitive to the blood pressure–raising effects of dietary salt than white Americans (Luft et al. 1979b). Hypertensive American blacks are more likely to normalize their blood pressure with sodium-excreting diuretics than other groups (Freis et al. 1988). There are also clear-cut biochemical differences in sodium-regulating systems related to blood pressure between African Americans and whites. Blacks have lower plasma renin activity (Helmer and Judson 1968) and lower urinary kallikrein excretion (Zinner et al. 1976). Although the reasons for these differences are unknown (Luft et al. 1985), it is well known that in both blacks and whites blood pressure is strongly influenced by genetic factors (Grim and Cantor 1986; Grim et al. 1990; Miall et al. 1962). Unfortunately, systematic studies on salt sensitivity have not yet been conducted comparing the American black population to the West African black population.

REGULATION OF SODIUM

Sodium is essential for human life, and numerous mechanisms have evolved to regulate this essential mineral. This exquisitely complex regulatory system is thought to operate around a "set point," conceptually like a thermostat setting (Hollenberg 1980; Simpson 1988). The concept posits that there is a sensor in the body that monitors the level of body sodium and attempts to keep it at an ideal level—the set point—in each individual. Careful metabolic studies on a "normal" sodium intake (in the United States an intake of 150 millimoles (mmols) of sodium or about 9 grams of sodium chloride) can usually account for 95% of ingested sodium. Of this amount, the kidney excretes 96%, while about 2% is lost in the stool and 2% in the sweat (Sanchez-Castillo et al. 1987). Thus, on a daily intake of 150 mmols of dietary sodium, 142 mmols (95%) could be accounted for by 136 mmols of sodium in the urine, 3 mmols in sweat, and 3 mmols in the stool.

The nature of the sensors that detect a change in total body sodium are not clear. When sodium intake is increased, natriuretic systems are activated to bring the sodium balance back to the set point, thus preventing excessive accumulation of sodium (Grim and Scoggins 1986). Conversely, if sodium is reduced below the set point, the body, acting through the kidney, reabsorbs sodium, and loss of the mineral through the renal system is decreased. If sodium intake is further reduced or sodium output from non-renal sources is increased (e.g., from sweating or diarrhea), systems—especially the renin-angiotensin-aldosterone system—are activated which enable the kidneys to attempt to maintain sodium homeostasis by decreasing sodium loss in the urine. If sodium output in the urine is reduced to zero, but sodium loss from nonrenal sources continues, the individual will die of sodium depletion as blood pressure falls and shock develops.

There are important individual and population variations in the time it takes to eliminate an excess of sodium. For example, older people are slower than younger people (Simpson 1988), and African Americans take longer to excrete a sodium load than

American whites (Luft et al. 1979a). Family and twin studies in white subjects have demonstrated that the ability of the kidney to excrete a sodium load with changes in sodium intake are influenced by genetic factors. For example, the amount of sodium retained is increased in first-degree relatives of hypertensives (Grim et al. 1979a), and the rate that a sodium load is excreted is controlled by genetic factors (Grim et al. 1979b). Additional examples of genetic influences on sodium metabolism resulting in excess sodium retention are mineralocorticoid excess due to adrenal steroid biosynthetic disorders (Eberlein and Bongiovanni 1956), Liddle's syndrome (Liddle et al. 1963), and glucocorticoide suppressible hyperaldosteronism (Grim and Weinberger 1980). Thus, there appears to be a genetically controlled variability in the human renal systems which manage sodium regulation.

NONRENAL SODIUM LOSSES

Salt can easily be lost from the body by sweating, diarrhea, and vomiting. The sodium content of sweat in non-heat-adapted individuals can be as high as 90 mmols sodium/liter. Sodium output from the gastrointestinal tract—vomiting or diarrhea—can be dramatic as well. Fecal excretion of sodium under basal conditions is very low, only 2.5–5.0 mmol/day; however, it rises very rapidly with diarrhea (Fordtran and Dietschy 1966). Cholera produces sodium losses in the stool that average 133.0 mmol sodium/liter. Even noncholera diarrheal stools contain about 97 mmol sodium/liter (Rabbani 1986). Finally, vomit can contain up to 60 mmol sodium/liter (Anderson and Linas 1978). Thus, conditions or diseases that cause sweating, diarrhea, or vomiting can result in severe nonrenal sodium loss.

The physiology of the thermoregulatory system plays a key role in salt conservation during increases in environmental temperature or when work is performed. When environmental temperature increases, man must cool by sweating, or he may die from dehydration, shock, and hyperthermia within minutes.

Environmental and genetic factors control variation of the salt content in sweat. Living in a hot environment activates mechanisms that lower the salt content of sweat so that cooling can occur with much less loss of salt in the sweat. This is known as "acclimatization to heat" and occurs as follows: The sodium and water loss from sweating depletes the body of fluid. As this depletion lowers body sodium below the set point, signals are sent to the kidneys which stimulate the enzyme renin. Renin liberates angiotensin I, which is converted to angiotensin II. Angiotensin II causes the kidney to retain salt and also stimulates aldosterone, the major sodium-retaining hormone. This hormone acts on the sweat gland tubule (as well as the renal tubule) to increase salt retention from the sweat and urine. Sweat gland sodium concentration can fall to as low as 1.7 mmols sodium/liter (Conn 1949; Elkington and Danowski 1955: 166–67; Knochel and Reed 1987). Some investigators have commented on possible innate differences between blacks and whites in the ability to work and survive in a hot environment (Ladell 1957; Savitt 1978: 41); however, this has never been systematically demonstrated. More careful studies need to be performed.

There are, however, precedents for genetic influences on sweat sodium control. For example, there are striking individual variations in how quickly sweating begins, how much sweat can be produced, and the distribution of sweat glands (Kuno 1956: 195–211). Perhaps the best-known example of this problem is in patients with cystic fibrosis, the most common genetic disease in whites. These patients have an inherited problem reabsorbing salt from sweat, and their sweat has a very high salt content (Gibson and Cooke 1959).

It is important to note that the standard lifesaving therapy for diarrhea is fluid and electrolyte replacement. Clearly, individuals with an enhanced ability to conserve fluids and electrolytes would have an advantage during episodes of diarrhea. Professor Derek Denton, a leading expert on the physiology of salt, remarked that "it is worth noting that with infectious diseases involving electrolyte loss, the initial defence for survival will be in the area of biochemical and endocrinological regulation since the animal needs to withstand the impact for some days before immunological mechanisms become effective" (Denton 1982: 45). This remark can be attributed to humans as well. Thus, individuals with an enhanced ability to conserve salt, probably mediated by the kidney and sweat glands, would have a survival advantage during any condition, including an infectious disease, that results in sodium loss. Thus, they would be more likely to survive and transmit their salt-conserving, or salt-sensitive, genes to subsequent generations.

THE TRANSATLANTIC SLAVE TRADE

Although slavery existed for centuries within Africa, the expansive transatlantic slave trade of Africans began in the early sixteenth century (Lovejoy 1983). The primary purpose of the Atlantic trade was to supply cheap human labor to the plantation economy of the New World in the Western Hemisphere. After being seized in the interior of Africa, the captives were transported, either on foot or down rivers, to the sea. There they were confined in small shelters (barracoons) along the coast to await transport. After individual captives were loaded, the slave ship often cruised along the coast for more than three months until it had a full load. The ship then began its voyage across the Atlantic (the "middle passage"), often traveling for several months before the captives were unloaded in the Caribbean islands or on the mainland of North, Central, or South America. Slavery was illegal by the late nineteenth century, but during the nearly 400 years of the trade more than 12 million Africans (mostly from West and Central Africa) were imported to the Western Hemisphere; the number exported is unknown. Most of the transported captives were healthy young men and women, although men were typically transported in a greater proportion. During these various stages of the slave trade many of the captive Africans died. A review of the causes of death and the conditions of the slave trade suggests sodium depletion played a major role in these deaths.

The most studied portion of the slave trade has been the "middle passage." This brief discussion is derived from over twenty years of research by historians (Curtin 1969; Dunn 1973; Mannix and Cowley 1976; Klein 1978; Postma 1979; Stein 1979; Rawley 1981; Miller 1981; Eltis 1984; Steckel and Jensen 1986; Galenson 1986; Miller 1988; Eltis 1989). Throughout the 400-year-long trade, the average death rate during the Atlantic passage—from the time of leaving the African coast to arrival in the Western Hemisphere—is estimated by historians at about 12%, although there was considerable between-ship variability in this rate. A similar number (12%) are thought to have died while awaiting transport across the Atlantic. Mortality on the march to the coast has been more difficult to determine because data are lacking, but current estimates are about 10%. Thus, it appears that at least one in three Africans died between the time they were removed from their homeland and the time they were unloaded in the West Indies or the Americas. This high death rate took place in a time span of less than one year and involved the African population of reproductive age. In the unlikely event that those who died were randomly distributed among the captives, the survivors must have been different from those who died. We suggest a major difference between the captives would be in the genetic-based ability to conserve sodium.

Sweating was very common during the slave trade. On the march to the coast, the French traveler Caillie noted the apparent effects of excessive sweating among the captives. He wrote in the early 1800s that "nobody suffered more intensely from thirst than the poor little slaves, who were crying for water. Exhausted by their sufferings and their lamentations, these unhappy creatures fell on the ground, and seemed to have no power to rise" (Buxton 1840: 90).

Those who made it to the coast were confined in barracoons. Body heat produced in these crowded structures would have caused more sweating and salt losses. Individuals able to survive the march and the barracoons were then loaded onto the ships, where they may have remained for many months before beginning passage across the Atlantic.

It is estimated that during the first days of any sea voyage more than a quarter of all unaccustomed passengers suffer from seasickness (Money 1970). Alexander Falconbridge, a slave ship surgeon, confirmed this when he stated that the captives "are far more violently affected by seasickness than the Europeans" (Falconbridge 1788: 24). As vomiting is the major result of seasickness, severe sodium losses could result.

During passage, the Africans usually remained below deck, although at times small groups were allowed on deck for exercise and fresh air. Below deck, the portholes were usually open for ventilation, but the insufficiency of even this "normal" situation was apparent from the words of one African survivor, Olaudah Equiano, of the middle passage: "The closeness of the place, and the heat of the climate, added to the number in the ship, which was so crowded that each had scarcely room to turn himself, almost suffocated us. This produced copious perspirations, so that the air soon became unfit for respiration, from a variety of loathsome smells, and brought on a sickness among the slaves, of which many died" (Curtin 1967: 95).

During storms all portholes were shut tight. Body heat in this confined, unventilated area must have raised the ambient temperature to an unbearable temperature below deck. Passengers on the slave ships were so struck with what they saw below decks during these moments that they wrote about the conditions in some detail (Martin and Spurrell 1962: 110–11). Again from Falconbridge: "But whenever the sea is rough, and the rain heavy, it becomes necessary to shut these and every other conveyance by which air is admitted. The fresh air being thus excluded, the negroes rooms very soon grow intolerably hot. The confined air, rendered noxious by the effluvia exhaled from their bodies, and by being repeatedly breathed, soon produces fevers and fluxes, which generally carry off great numbers of them" (Falconbridge 1788: 24).

A report from a slave ship in the late 1840s noted that during attempts to escape from a British antislaver the portholes were closed and below deck it was an "intensely hot and vitiated atmosphere . . . with the thermometer probably ranging between 90° and 100°" (FO 84/780: 182). Under these hot and humid conditions a better ability to conserve salt would seem to lead to a survival advantage.

It would logically follow that if heat were removed, mortality would decline substantially. As a matter of fact, an experiment was conducted in the eighteenth century to test this hypothesis. Reverend Stephen Hales, a leading physician investigator of the mid-eighteenth century, believed that "noxious putrid Air" accumulated in ships, mines, and other confined areas and caused excessive mortality. This observation led him to develop human-powered ventilators to rid these areas of the bad air. They were mostly installed in mines, but a few were also mounted on slave ships. One ship captain wrote to Hales that the ventilators "kept the inside of the ship cool, sweet, dry, and healthy . . . [and that] . . . the 340 Negroes were very sensible of the benefits of a constant ventilation, and were always displeased when it was omitted" (Hales 1758: 92). Other slave ship captains who used

Hales's ventilator also testified that the death rate on slave ships dropped dramatically. For example, a French captain wrote to Hales "that in the year 1753, Ventilators were put into the Vessels in the Slave-trade . . . the happy Effect of which was, that instead of the loss of one-fourth of those valuable Cargoes in long passages from Africa to the French plantations, the loss seldom exceeded a twentieth" (Hales 1758: 94–95).

We suggest that Hales's device was effective because it lowered the ambient temperature and humidity in the ship holds. Thus, the observation made by the captains and sea surgeons of slave ships of an increased mortality during heating episodes caused by the closure of air passages suggests to us that many deaths were related in some fashion to heatstroke; significantly, fever and diarrhea are also symptoms of the condition (Knochel and Reed 1987). Hales's device would have decreased sweat-induced sodium depletion and thus protected the captives against heatstroke or fatal sodium depletion from diarrhea and vomiting. Unfortunately, it appears his device was not widely employed during the slave trade.

Besides ambient temperature, the disease environment on the ships no doubt played a selective role as well. There is little doubt that diarrhea was the major cause of death on the middle passage. In 1849, a physician wrote that "the great mortality appears to arise from a very intractable and offensive form of dysentery" (FO 84/780: 184). A dramatic example of the disastrous results of diarrhea is revealed by the captain's journal of the slave ship *Le Jeune Louis,* held at the Huntington Library in San Marino, California. On a "clandestine" voyage from Africa to Cuba in 1824–25, this French ship lost over 100 of its 300-plus African cargo to diarrhea. After the Atlantic passage began, about one captive died each day; on one tragic day, the ship lost five Africans from the *dissenterie* (HM 43991). Furthermore, quantitative analysis of records from the 1792–96 "middle passage" confirmed that the greatest mortality was from "fluxes," an ancient term for diarrhea (Steckel and Jensen 1986). Fevers were the second most common cause of death on the ships (Steckel and Jensen 1986). Attempting to cool the body, the thermoregulatory system produces sweat, with its attendant sodium loss.

To dramatize the extraordinary nonrenal sodium losses on slave ships, imagine a worst-case scenario: a relatively non-heat-adapted individual placed for one hour in a confined area, such as a ship hold during a storm, with diarrhea and seasickness. Losses of sodium could be 90 mmols in sweat, 100 mmols in one liter of diarrhea, and 60 mmols in one liter of vomit. Thus, a one-hour loss would exceed 250 mmols of sodium, or about 15 grams of sodium chloride. Continuation of such dramatic sodium losses, not to mention the water losses, would soon be fatal. An enhanced ability to lessen sodium losses by some renal or sweat gland conservation mechanism, a readily available reservoir of exchangeable sodium, or a tremendous intake of sodium would be necessary to survive these threats to sodium homeostasis.

To decrease mortality from salt depletion, the slave traders could have provided captives an abundant supply of dietary sodium. The historian Colin Palmer wrote that he found some eighteenth-century contracts between the Royal African Company and English slave ships that reveal that between two and five bushels of salt were loaded for every 100 slaves (Palmer 1981: 14, 50). In a late-eighteenth-century letter from an African agent of the Royal African Company, the writer advised that "for one-hundred Negroes . . . [load] . . . 4 bushels of salt" (T70/28: 62). Apparently his advice was followed: an examination of over 145 slave ship invoices from the Royal African Company between 1682 and 1704 determined that an average of 3.6 bushels of salt were loaded for every 100 captives. Although the volume of salt per ship varied widely, on the average this would calculate out to an average of about 20 grams of salt (340 mmols sodium) per slave per day on a two-month-long voyage (Wilson 1990). Salt was apparently perceived as an extremely important provision on slave ships by the slave traders.

Of course, this salt was probably not always loaded, or it may have spoiled on the journey. This would explain remarks by contemporaries that the captives received only "a little salt sometimes" (Donnan 1969: 114). If raw salt was not available on the ships, it appears that salted fish provided captives with the important mineral. In 1729, the slave surgeon Thomas Aubrey wrote, "I am very sensible, that it's impossible to maintain the Slaves on Board, after one quits the Coast, without salt Provision, but then Care might be taken to water the Beef and Pork" (Aubrey 1729: 130).

This discovery that slaves (at least those traded by the English) may not have had a low intake of salt is contrary to the theory of salt conservation as formulated by investigators from Gleibermann to Grim. However, after evaluating the physiology of high salt intake, the hypothesis can be refined rather than rejected. We submit that regardless of salt intake, under severe salt-depletive conditions such as apparently existed during the transatlantic slave trade, "sodium conservers" would have a decided advantage over all others. On the one hand, if salt supplies were limited, a "sodium conserver" would minimize the time in salt deficit due to a fast-acting renal, sweat gland, or other system that evolved to conserve the salt, thus conferring protection against salt losses. On the other hand, if salt was readily available, each "dose," as we discussed earlier, would be retained longer in the "sodium conserver" than in others, creating a salt "reservoir" of sorts. This would also offer important protection against salt losses in sweat, stool, or vomit. Thus, in both cases, the "sodium conserver" would have a marked survival advantage over others, minimizing a possible sodium deficit in the former case and maximizing a sodium excess in the latter (Wilson 1990). Of course, one would still expect less mortality on slave ships that carried salt than those that did not, and we are presently developing a research project to test this hypothesis. But it is important to point out that a low salt intake is neither a sufficient nor a necessary component of this theory of the evolution of salt conservation; what is necessary is a high sodium output, which results in differential mortality in the population in question. According to our new formulation of the salt conservation hypothesis, an enhanced genetic-based ability to retain or conserve salt would be increased in populations with high mortality from sodium losses in sweat and the gastrointestinal tract.

Thus, we conclude that those individuals snared into the transatlantic slave trade who possessed an enhanced genetic-based ability to conserve sodium had a significant survival edge over others. This trait, advantageous then, may be medically deleterious in today's world of high sodium consumption because it may lead to hypertension (Freis 1976).

CONCLUSION

We have argued that there is variability in sodium conservation within the human race and that this variability may be due to genetics. Because the transatlantic slave trade was characterized by a death rate that exceeded 30%, and salt-depletion was a major factor in these deaths, natural selection of "salt conservers" was likely. Thus, the nearly 400-year-long transatlantic slave trade may have acted as an evolutionary gate—individuals who survived passage through that gate would possess a different genetic makeup than those who did not. Virtually all sub-Saharan Africans transported to the Western Hemisphere between the sixteenth and nineteenth centuries had to survive these conditions of excessive sodium loss; thus, all passed through the same evolutionary gate. Today's descendants of the captive Africans might possess a different genetic makeup than the descendants of Africans not transported across the Atlantic during the slave trade.

Although other population groups that migrated to the Americas during this period were also transported across the Atlantic, their average death rate was not of this magnitude. In addition, no other population experienced such a death rate for such a long period of history as the African captives. Finally, the conditions of shipment of nonenslaved people were not as well standardized as they were in the slave trade, and the population being transported was not preselected to be the fittest young members of the society (Eltis 1987: 136–37; Hvidt 1975: 73–74).

The slave trade, of course, was only the initial step in New World slavery, and as evolutionary biologists point out, it usually requires several generations of selection pressure for a genetic trait to establish itself in a population. Thus it is important to point out now—a future article will deal with this in more detail—that during the first few years in the Western Hemisphere the Africans went through a period of "seasoning"—the term "seasoned" was attributed to a captive who survived these first crucial years. Like the transatlantic slave trade itself, "seasoning" was characterized by excessive sweating, diarrheas, and fevers. Mortality during the first three years was at least an additional 15% (A Professional Planter [Dr. Collins] 1971 [1811]: 44–74). In addition, in the second, third, and subsequent generations, the mortality rates of slaves remained very high (Kiple 1984: 64–65; Kiple and King 1981: 114, 147–48; Higman 1984: 304–14). Major causes of death in slave societies continued to be diarrheas and fevers (Koplan 1983) even though salt intake was typically high (Wilson 1988). Therefore, it is likely that the natural selection of salt conservers continued throughout the slavery period as well. In fact, in light of these salt-depletive conditions, the salt conservation trait may be found in greater frequency in today's blacks who are descendants of slave populations from the oldest self-sustaining communities, that is, those slave communities with the greatest "natural increase" (by reproduction) of their population (Wilson 1989).

This hypothesis predicts that blood pressure levels and "salt sensitivity" are higher in Western Hemisphere populations than in west and central African populations, the slave-producing regions of sub-Saharan Africa. It would also predict a wide variation in blood pressure within the Western Hemisphere. This latter variation would have emerged because of admixture with a new gene pool (e.g., Amerindian, European, or African) that did not have a high frequency of the salt-sensitive trait. It could also have emerged because of a geographical variation in mortality before reproduction, decreased reproductive capacity, disease ecology, salt intake, or some other natural selective force. Thus, future tests of the hypothesis should include epidemiological studies comparing black populations within west Africa, the Caribbean, and North and South America. These studies should utilize careful, standardized techniques like those used in Intersalt (Intersalt Cooperative Research Group, 1988).[3] Besides blood pressure levels, these studies should examine biochemical factors that influence sodium and water metabolism, such as antidiuretic hormone, angiotensin I, angiotensin II, renin, aldosterone, atrial natriuretic peptide, kallikrein, and sympathetic nervous system activity. Finally, these studies should also examine biobehavioral stress, as several reports reveal that this also influences sodium metabolism (Light et al. 1983; Anderson et al. 1987).

In conclusion, we have reviewed the importance of sodium metabolism in the causes of mortality during the slave trade and estimated sodium losses due to sweating, diarrhea, and vomiting. The magnitude of these potential losses makes it likely that fatal sodium depletion was a major contributor to the high mortality. Thus, we suggest that the slave trade imposed severe demands on sodium homeostasis, and that those who survived were more capable of conserving sodium than those who did not. In today's high dietary sodium environment in the Western Hemisphere, these "sodium-conserving" descendants of African slaves may be more susceptible to "salt-sensitive" hypertension than the populations descended from black Africans without this heritage.

NOTES

Acknowledgments: The historical research in Great Britain was supported in part by a Burroughs-Wellcome Travel Grant, an American Historical Association Schmitt Award, and a National Endowment for the Humanities Travel to Collections Award. We also acknowledge the National Institutes of Health—Research Centers in Minority Institutions award G12RR03026-02, 03, 7 K04HL01885, T32MHL07655-01, RR03026-02 and the American Heart Association—Greater Los Angeles Affiliate award 78-F1 for their ongoing research support in Los Angeles.

We are indebted to the participants of the 1988 Transatlantic Slave Trade: Who Won, Who Lost seminar and the staff/student history seminars at all the University of the West Indies campuses. We also thank Dr. N. A. M. Rodgers at Public Record Office, Chauncery Lane, UK; the archivists at Public Record Office, Kew Gardens, UK; the National Maritime Museum, Greenwich, UK; the Huntington Library, San Marino, California; and, finally, the comments and support of F. J. Meaney, C. M. Grim, D. D. Sun, U. Chettipalli, W. H. Choi, D. M. Wilson, D. C. Allison, and R. Dodds.

1   When "salt" is mentioned in this article we are referring to the sodium portion of the sodium chloride molecule. One gram of salt contains about 17 mmols (millimoles) of sodium.

2   The argument that natural selection in the past has affected the modern distribution of diseases has also been applied to the Polynesians, whose ancestors made the harsh sea passage to Samoa (Baker 1984).

3   We recently conducted a population-based random sample survey, based on the Intersalt design, among rural male Ibos in Eastern Nigeria, the area once known as Biafra. In this population we discovered that in spite of a high salt intake (120 mmols sodium/24 hours) this population had significantly lower blood pressure than those typically seen in black populations in the United States or the West Indies (Wilson et al. 1990). This suggests to us that this population may be a "salt-resistant population," a suggestion which leads to a bit of historical speculation. Historians have noted, but have been unable to explain, the higher death rate on the middle passage from ships leaving from the Bight of Biafra region—about three times greater than from other West Africa regions (Eltis 1989). Could it be that the ancestors of the present-day population were also genetically "salt resistant," and thus had a poorer survival chance during the slave trade? Of course, only detailed metabolic studies using acceptable protocols for salt sensitivity comparing Ibos to other West African tribes will determine if in fact this conjecture about variability of salt sensitivity within West Africa is tenable.

REFERENCES

A Professional Planter (Dr. Collins) (1971 [1811]) Practical Rules for the Management and Medical Treatment of Negro Slaves in the Sugar Colonies. Freeport, NY: Books for Libraries Press.

Akinkugbe, O. O. (1985) "World epidemiology of hypertension in blacks," in W. D. Hall, E. Saunders, and N. B. Shulman (eds.), Hypertension in Blacks, Epidemiology, Pathophysiology, and Treatment. Chicago: Year Book Medical Publishers: 3–16.

Akinkugbe, O. O., F. M. Akinkugbe, O. Ayeni, H. Solomon, K. French, and R. Minear (1977) "Biracial study of arterial pressures in the first and second decades of life." British Medical Journal 1: 1132–34.

Anderson, D. E., J. R. Dietz, and P. Murphy (1987) "Behavioural hypertension in sodium-loaded dogs is accompanied by sustained sodium retention." Journal of Hypertension 5: 99–105.

Anderson, Robert J. and Stuart L. Linas (1978) "Sodium depletion states," in B. M. Brenner and J. H. Stein (eds.) Sodium and Water Homeostasis. New York: Churchill Livingston: 162.

Aubrey, T. (1729) The Sea-Surgeon or the Guinea Man's Vade Mecum. London: John Clark.

Baker, P. T. (1984) "Migration, genetics, and the degenerative disease of South Pacific islanders," in A. Boyce (ed.) Migration and Mobility. London: Taylor and Francis: 209–39.

Beiser, M., H. Collomb, J.-L. Ravel, and C. J. Nafziger (1976) "Systemic blood pressure studies among the Serer of Senegal." Journal of Chronic Diseases 29: 371–80.

Blackburn, Henry and Ronald Prineas (1983) "Diet and hypertension: anthropology, epidemiology, and public health implications." Progress in Biochemical Pharmacology 19: 31–79.

Buxton, Thomas F. (1840) African Slave Trade. New York: American Anti-Slavery Society.

Conn, Jerome W. (1949) "The mechanism of acclimatization to heat." Advances in Internal Medicine 3: 373–93.

Cooper, Richard (1984) "A note on the biologic concept of race and its application in epidemiological research." American Heart Journal 108: 715–23.

Curtin, Philip D. (1967) Africa Remembered: Narratives by West Africans from the Era of the Slave Trade. Madison: University of Wisconsin Press.

——— (1969) The Atlantic Slave Trade: A Census. Madison: University of Wisconsin Press.

Dahl, Lewis K., Martha Heine, and Lorraine Tassinari (1962) "Role of genetic factors in susceptibility to experimental hypertension due to chronic excess salt ingestion." Nature 194: 480–82.

Denton, Derek (1982) The Hunger for Salt: An Anthropological, Physiological and Medical Analysis. Berlin: Springer-Verlag.

Donnan, Elizabeth (1969) Documents Illustrative of the History of the Slave Trade to America. Vol 2. New York: Octagon Books.

Dunn, Richard S. (1973) Sugar and Slaves: The Rise of the Planter Class in the English West Indies, 1624–1713. New York: W.W. Norton.

Eberlein, W. R. and A. M. Bongiovanni (1956) "Plasma and urinary corticosteroids in the hypertensive form of congenital adrenal hyperplasia." Journal of Biological Chemistry 223: 85–90.

Elkington, J. R. and T. S. Danowski (1955) The Body Fluids: Basic Physiology and Practical Therapeutics. Baltimore: Williams and Wilkins.

Eltis, David (1984) "Mortality and voyage length in the middle passage: new evidence from the nineteenth century." Journal of Economic History 44: 301–8.

——— (1987) Economic Growth and the Ending of the Transatlantic Slave Trade. New York: Oxford University Press.

——— (1989) "Fluctuations in mortality in the last half century of the transatlantic slave trade." Social Science History 13: 315–40.

Falconbridge, Alexander (1788) An Account of the Slave Trade on the Coast of Africa. London: J. Phillips.

FO 84/780 Slave Trade: Colonial Office Drafts and Letters. July to December, 1849. Held in Public Record Office, Kew Gardens.

Fordtran, John S. and John M. Dietschy (1966) "Water and electrolyte movement in the intestine." Gastroenterology 50: 263–85.

Freis, E. D. (1976) "Salt, volume, and the prevention of hypertension." Circulation 53: 589–95.

Freis, E. D., D. J. Reda, and B. J. Materson (1988) "Volume (weight) loss and blood pressure response following thiazide diuretics." Hypertension 12: 244–50.

Galenson, David W. (1986) Traders, Planters, and Slaves: Market Behavior in English America. Cambridge: Cambridge University Press.

Gibson, C. E. and R. E. Cooke (1959) "A test for concentration of electrolytes in sweat in cystic fibrosis of the pancreas utilizing pilocarpin by iontophoresis." Pediatrics 23: 545.

Gleibermann, L. (1973) "Blood pressure and dietary salt in human populations." Ecology of Food and Nutrition 2: 143–56.

Grim, C. E. (1988) "On slavery, salt, and the higher blood pressure in black Americans." Clinical Research 36: 426A.

Grim, C. E., F. C. Luft, J. C. Christian, and M. H. Weinberger (1979a) "Effects of volume expansion and contraction in normotensive first degree relatives of essential hypertensives." Journal of Laboratory and Clinical Medicine 94: 764–71.

Grim, C. E., J. Z. Miller, F. C. Luft, J. C. Christian, and M. H. Weinberger (1979b) "Genetic influences on renin, aldosterone, and renal excretion of sodium and potassium following volume expansion and contraction in normal man." Hypertension 1: 583–90.

Grim, C. E. and M. H. Weinberger (1980) "Familial, dexamethasone-suppressible, normokalemic hyperaldosteronism." Pediatrics 65: 597–604.

Grim, C. E. and R. E. Cantor (1986) "Genetic influences on blood pressure in blacks: Twin studies." Clinical Research 34: 98A.

Grim, C. E. and B. Scoggins (1986) "The rapid adjustment of renal sodium excretion to changes in dietary sodium intake in sheep." Life Sciences 39: 215–22.

Grim, C. E., T. W. Wilson, G. D. Nicholson, H. S. Fraser, T. A. Hassell, C. M. Grim, and D. M. Wilson (1990) "Blood pressure in blacks: Twin studies in Barbados." Hypertension 15: 803–9.

Grollmann, A. (1978) "A conjecture about the prevalence of essential hypertension and its high incidence in the black." Texas Reports on Biology and Medicine 36: 25–32.

Hales, Stephan (1758) A Treatise on Ventilators. Wherein An Account is given of the Happy Effects of the several Trials that have been made of them, in different Ways and for Different Purposes: Which has occasioned their being received with general Approbation and Applause, on Account of their Utility for the great benefit of Mankind. Part 2. London: Richard Manby: 82–99.

Helmer, O. M. (1967) "Hormonal and biochemical factors controlling blood pressure," in Roger Heim, Bernard Halpern et al., Les Concepts de Claude Bernard sur le milieu intérieur. Paris: Masson & Cie.: 115–28.

Helmer, O. M., and W. E. Judson (1968) "Metabolic studies on hypertensive patients with suppressed renin activity not due to hyperaldosteronism." Circulation 38: 965–76.

Higman, B. W. (1984) Slave Populations of the British Caribbean: 1807–1834. Baltimore: Johns Hopkins University Press.

HM 43991. French Clandestine Slave Trade Papers. Held in Henry E. Huntington Library. San Marino, California.

Hollenberg, N. K. (1980) "Set point for sodium homeostasis: Surfeit, deficit, and their implications." Kidney International 17: 423–29.

Hvidt, Kristian (1975) Flight to America: The Social Background of 300,000 Danish Emigrants. New York: Academic Press.

Intersalt Cooperative Research Group (1988) "Intersalt: An international study of electrolyte excretion and blood pressure. Results for 24 hour urinary sodium and potassium excretion." British Medical Journal 297: 319–28.

Kawasaki, T., C. S. Delea, F. C. Barter, and H. Smith (1978) "The effect of high sodium intakes on blood pressure and other related variables in human subjects with idiopathic hypertension." American Journal of Medicine 64: 193–98.

Kiple, Kenneth F. (1984) The Caribbean Slave: A Biological History. New York: Cambridge University Press.

Kiple, Kenneth and V. H. King (1981) Another Dimension to the Black Diaspora: Diet, Disease, Racism. New York: Cambridge University Press.

Klein, Herbert (1978) The Middle Passage: Comparative Studies in the Atlantic Slave Trade. Princeton: Princeton University Press.

Knochel, J. P., and G. Reed (1987) "Disorders of heat regulation," in M. H. Maxwell, C. R. Kleeman, and R. G. Narins (eds.) Clinical Disorders of Fluid and Electrolyte Metabolism. New York: McGraw-Hill: 1197–1232.

Koplan, J. P. (1983) "Slave mortality in nineteenth century Grenada." Social Science History 7: 311–20.

Kuno, Y. (1956) Human Perspiration. Springfield, IL: C. C. Thomas.

Ladell, W. S. S. (1957) "Disorders due to heat." Transactions of the Royal Society of Tropical Medicine and Hygiene 51: 189–216.

Lee, M. R. (1981) "The kidney fault in essential hypertension may be a failure to mobilize renal dopamine adequately when dietary sodium chloride is increased." Cardiovascular Reviews and Reports 2: 785–89.

Liddle, G. W., T. Bledsoe, and W. S. Coppage (1963) "A familial renal disorder simulating primary aldosteronism but with negligible aldosterone secretion." Transactions of the Association of American Physicians 76: 199–213.

Light, K. C., J. P. Koepke, P. A. Obrist, and P. W. Willis (1983) "Psychological stress induces sodium and fluid retention in men at high risk for hypertension." Science 220: 429–31.

Lovejoy, Paul E. (1983) Transformations in Slavery: A History of Slavery in Africa. Cambridge: Cambridge University Press.

Luft, F. C., C. E. Grim, N. Fineberg, and M. H. Weinberger (1979a) "Effects of volume expansion and contraction in normotensive whites, blacks and subjects of different ages." Circulation 59: 643–50.

Luft, F. C., L. I. Rankin, R. Bloch, A. E. Weymen, L. R. Willis, R. H. Murray, C. E. Grim, and M. H. Weinberger (1979b). "Cardiovascular and humoral responses to extremes of sodium intake in normal white and black men." Circulation 60: 697–706.

Luft, F. C., C. E. Grim, and M. H. Weinberger (1985) "Electrolyte and volume homeostatis in blacks," in W. D. Hall, E. Saunders, and N. B. Shulman (eds.) Hypertension in Blacks, Epidemiology, Pathophysiology and Treatment. Chicago: Year Book Medical Publishers: 115–31.

Mannix, Daniel, and Malcolm Cowley (1976 [1962]) Black Cargoes: A History of the Atlantic Slave Trade. Harmondsworth, England: Penguin Books.

Martin, Bernard, and Mark Spurrell, eds. (1962) The Journal of a Slave Trader (John Newton), 1750–1754. London: Epworth Press.

Maude, D. L., and G. Kao-Lo (1982) "Salt excretion and vascular resistance of perfused kidneys of Dahl rats." Hypertension 4: 532–37.

Miall, W. E., E. H. Kass, J. Ling, K. L. Stuart, and F. E. Moore (1962) "Arterial pressure and hypertensive disease in a West Indian Negro population: Report of a survey in St. Kitts, West Indies." American Heart Journal 63: 607–28.

Miller, Joseph C. (1981) "Mortality in the Atlantic slave trade: Statistical evidence on causality." Journal of Interdisciplinary History 11: 385–423.

———— (1988) Way of Death: Merchant Capitalism and the Angolan Slave Trade, 1730–1830. Madison: University of Wisconsin Press.

Money, K. E. (1970) "Motion sickness." Physiological Review 50: 1–39.

Palmer, Colin A. (1981) Human Cargoes: The British Slave Trade to Spanish America, 1700–1739. Urbana: University of Illinois Press.

Postma, Johannes (1979) "Mortality in the Dutch slave trade, 1675–1795," in Henry A. Gemery, and Jan S. Hogendorn (eds.) The Uncommon Market: Essays in the Economic History of the Atlantic Slave Trade. New York: Academic Press: 239–60.

Rabbani, G. H. (1986) "Cholera." Clinics in Gastroenterology 15: 507–28.

Rawley, James A. (1981) The Transatlantic Slave Trade: A History. New York: W. W. Norton.

Sanchez-Castillo, C. P., W. J. Branch, and W. P. T. James (1987) "A test of the validity of the lithium marker technique for monitoring dietary sources of salt in man." Clinical Science 72: 87–94.

Savitt, Todd L. (1978). Medicine and Slavery: The Diseases and Health Care of Blacks in Antebellum Virginia. Urbana: University of Illinois Press.

Schachter, J. and L. H. Kuller (1984) "Blood volume expansion among blacks: An hypothesis." Medical Hypotheses 14: 1–19.

Simpson, F. O. (1988) "Sodium intake, body sodium, and sodium excretion." Lancet 1: 25–29.

Steckel, Richard H., and Richard A. Jensen (1986) "New evidence on the causes of slave and crew mortality in the Atlantic slave trade." Journal of Economic History 46: 57–77.

Stein, Robert L. (1979) The French Slave Trade in the Eighteenth Century: An Old Regime Business. Madison: University of Wisconsin Press.

T70/28: 62. Abstract of Letters Received by the Royal African Company. 24 April 1703 to 8 March 1704, folio 62. Held in Public Record Office, Kew Gardens.

Waldron, I., M. Nowotarski, M. Freimer, J. P. Henry, N. Post, and C. Witten (1982) "Cross-cultural variation in blood pressure: A quantitative analysis of the relationships of blood pressure to cultural characteristics, salt consumption, and body weight." Social Science Medicine 16:419–30.

Williams, R., and P. N. Hopkins (1979) "Salt, hypertension, and genetic-environmental interactions." Progress in Clinical and Biological Research 32: 183–94.

Wilson, Thomas W. (1986) "Salt supplies in West Africa and blood pressures today." Lancet 1: 784–86.

——— (1988) "Ancient environments and modern disease: The case of hypertension among Afro-Americans." Ph.D. diss. Bowling Green State University.

——— (1988) "Africa, Afro-Americans, and hypertension: An hypothesis," in Kenneth F. Kiple (ed.) The African Exchange: Toward a Biological History of Black People. Durham, NC: Duke University Press: 257–74.

——— (1989) "Historical evidence for Na+ depleting fatalities among slaves in the West Indies and its relationship to blood pressure today" [meeting abstract]. Journal of Human Hypertension 4: 211.

——— (1990) "Salt consumption on British slave ships, 1682–1704: Historical evidence on the slavery hypothesis of hypertension in blacks" [abstract]. Journal of Human Hypertension 4: 744.

Wilson, T. W., L. H. Hollifield, and C. E. Grim (1991) "Systolic blood pressure levels in blacks in sub-Saharan Africa, the West Indies, and the United States: A metaanalysis." Hypertension 18: I-87–I-91.

Wilson, T. W., C. E. Grim, D. M. Wilson, W. Okoroanyanwu, A. Egbunike, and C. Hames (1990) "Blood pressure does not increase with age in a high sodium intake, rural population in Imo State, Nigeria" [abstract]. Circulation 82: III-553.

Zinner, S. H., H. S. Margolius, B. Rosner, H. R. Keiser, and E. H. Kass (1976) "Familial aggregation of urinary kallikrein concentration in childhood: Relation to blood pressure, race, and urinary electrolytes." American Journal of Epidemiology 104: 124–28.

14
The Ending of
the Slave Trade and
the Evolution of
European Scientific Racism

SEYMOUR DRESCHER

HOW MIGHT a discussion of the ending of the Atlantic slave trade in relation to the development of European racism illuminate the question of who gained and who lost? The question can be approached at three levels. The first concerns the degree to which the racial attitudes of Europeans were affected by the process of termination. The second would be how the people of Europe and of Afro-America were affected by the termination itself. The third and broadest aspect would be the long-term effects of that complex process. It seems to me that the answers become more speculative as the scope of potential impact broadens, as the discussion moves from a concern with attitudes and ideology to social conditions, as the geographical scope broadens, and as the temporal dimension to be considered expands to encompass the twentieth century. The first level, the relation of the processes of abolition to racism, is the primary focus of this paper; a few brief remarks on the second and third issues are reserved for the conclusion.

We must begin by distinguishing between process and outcome. There was a long ending as well as an end to the slave trade. The process extended unevenly over almost a century, and well beyond a century if one includes all overseas and trans-Saharan slaving. Sometimes the ending and the end were virtually simultaneous. The Dutch, for example, lost their trade de facto during the French Revolution and the Napoleonic Wars and then renounced it de jure, under British pressure at the end of that conflict. For the British, the abolition process was drawn out over a century, broadening in clear public stages from a campaign against slaving by British nationals in 1788 into a policy commitment against chattel slavery throughout the world. One could theoretically formulate a complex accounting system for various groups throughout the world who gained or lost from that policy, including nonpecuniary benefits such as status, power, popularity, and organizational experience in almost endless variations.

In opening his recent discussion of Eric Williams's *Capitalism and Slavery* (1944), Gavin Wright (1987: 283) notes that Williams chose to relate "one of the most palpable realities of Western economic history to one of the slipperiest abstractions of the Western intellectual heritage." Some of the same difficulties arise in relating the ending of the slave trade to European racism. The abolition process extended over the same century which witnessed the emergence of European scientific racism. Scholars of the latter, just like scholars of abolitionism, locate both in the Enlightenment and in the religious revivals of the eighteenth century (Mosse 1978; Poliakov 1974; Davis 1966). There is also general agreement that the third quarter of the nineteenth century, which saw the definitive end of the Atlantic slave trade (Eltis 1987), also witnessed the full flowering of scientific racism and its broad diffusion into the popular culture of the West (Lorimer 1978; Biddiss 1970; Bolt 1971).

Both historians of slavery and those of racism have also naturally had a good deal to say about the correlation of one ideology with the other, both in America and in Europe. Although before the rise of political abolitionism[1] those seeking to invoke racial theories sometimes proclaimed antislavery sentiments or lamented the use of their writings in defense of slavery, and slave owners sometimes sneered at racial dehumanization by scientists, there was an increasing crossover in arguments between the two ideologies during the second third of the nineteenth century.

The relationship between abolitionism and racism was, at the very least, more complex than that between racism and the defense of slavery, although many historians have attempted to emphasize the degree of overlap. In the Americas, where large black and white populations lived in close proximity to one another, hostility to the slave trade and slavery was frequently combined with strong hostility to the presence or expansion of the black population. At points in the antislavery debates in the United States, Cuba, and Brazil, aspects of antislavery were linked by some agitators to a program for making their nations safer for Euroamericans. Indeed, there has been a good deal of debate over the degree to which negrophobia played a role in intensifying the debate over the future of slavery in the mid-nineteenth-century United States. The combination of abolitionism and hostility to blacks, however, occurred much more rarely in Europe.

Where the black and white components of the Atlantic empires were largely separated by vast distances, the question of the future status of blacks could be regarded as principally, if not exclusively, a problem of overseas territories. In 1770, on the eve of the age of abolition, black people probably amounted to less than 0.2% of the British metropolitan population and 0.02% of the French. On the American mainland, the black share of the population ranged from 2% in Massachusetts to 60% in South Carolina. And in the French and British sugar islands, the black share of the population was about 90% (a little less in Barbados). In West Africa, the preponderance of the black population was higher still. It was only in the more "mixed" belt of the Americas that antislavery and antislave appeals could overlap.

If nothing else, the temporal conjuncture between racism and abolitionism in Europe should alert us to deep tensions and paradoxes more counterintuitive than those between slavery and racism. Whatever its premises or overtones of cultural imperialism, abolitionism in societies where the slaves and free people were widely separated by oceans, where slavery was "beyond the line," rhetorically assumed a fundamental equality as its core motto. "Am I not a man and a brother?" (and, later, "Am I not a woman and a sister?") was its "inclusive" idiom. Racial thought saw as its goal the division of human beings into group types, usually hierarchically related and often polarized into pairs of opposing characteristics. Its practitioners sought to delineate bio-cultural boundaries, coinciding with innate and heritable mental and moral differences.

Attempts to deal with abolitionism and racism as equally central historical themes reveal some of the difficulties in relating them. The most recent study of race relations and slavery in Britain by a historian who has done much research on both subjects empha-sizes the pervasive long-term hostility by whites toward blacks over the past three centuries. This general current was temporarily interrupted by a massive countercampaign against the slave trade and slavery at the end of the eighteenth and the beginning of the nineteenth centuries. Thereafter there was a wholesale reversion to the more disdainful racial attitudes, intensified by the surge of imperialism in the final third of the nineteenth century (Walvin 1986). Since antislavery was a parenthesis between two eras of racism, the basis of the more benign attitude of the abolitionist era remains somewhat obscure.

I would like to take a slightly different tack in relating the attack on the slave trade to the evolution of racism. The most thorough historians of European responses to blacks during the critical century before 1860 have concentrated upon single countries, chronicling intellectual trends over time (Lorimer 1978; Curtin 1964; Cohen 1980). I would like to look more comparatively at the political environment for racism in the two greatest European imperial powers of the century after 1760, asking whether one can account for divergences in prevailing attitudes toward, or dis-course about, blacks in terms of the political context within each society.[2]

One must first lay out the similarities. Historians have been struck by the durability and continuity of images of African cul-tural inferiority before and after the century of slave trade aboli-tion (Curtin 1964: 479; Cohen 1980: 291–92). French and British reactions were not only analogous in this respect but part of a general Western attitude towards much of the non-Western world. It must be remembered that both before and after the century of the ending of the Atlantic slave trade, Europeans regarded large numbers of people on all continents and of all colors with dis-dain. To wander through the travel books and geographies of the eighteenth century is a voyage through shades of contempt: the "unnatural" Circassians bartered their own of every age and sex; the Georgians sold their children or kidnapped others for the markets of Islam, killing those for whom no market was available; East Asians were linked to wife sacrifice and infanticide; Brazilian Indians were identified with cannibalism, as were the natives of New Zealand (Beauties 1763–64, 10: 140; 11: 132–37; 13: 78; Atlas 1711–17, 5: 271; Carver 1779: 663; Boulle 1986). Thus, if West Africans were categorized as degraded by the selling of their "own," they were neither exclusively condemned for any social or cultural practice nor linked to exclusively negative characteristics. Italians and Russians were as likely to be identified with some "unnatural" (i.e., alien) behavior as the Chinese. The age of abolitionism heightened the intensity and frequency of positive and negative African and black imaging, but those images neither were born nor died with that historical epoch.

Perhaps the most significant point is that such stereotyping was broadly diffused over the peoples of the earth and that there seems to have been little difference of image between the French and British writings of the preabolitionist period. Initial and enduring images of Africans were drawn from a shared international literature deriving from European and Arabic sources as well as from French and British travelers. In addition, both Britain and France established major slave-owning colonies in the Americas and slave-trading enclaves on the African coast (Davis 1984: 51–82; Curtin 1975; Fryer 1984).

Both Britain and France were also confronted by social problems stemming from the importation of slaves from Africa and the Caribbean into Europe. This resulted in black resident populations in the thousands by the second half of the eighteenth century. Both metropolises also faced demands for the termination of their slave trades and slave systems during the last quarter of the eighteenth and the first half of the nineteenth centuries. Finally, race became a major explanation of human variation, behavior, and history only in the period when the Atlantic slave trade was being driven from its last areas of demand in the Latin Americas. Biological and anthropological paradigms were therefore deeply influenced by white and black relationships in slavery, war, revolution, and abolition.

The rise of scientific racism induced not a radical shift in the characteristics ascribed to Africans or to blacks in general but a reworking of those characteristics in different frames of reference. Abolitionists as well as defenders of slavery and the slave trade concurred in many aspects of the image of blacks. Indeed, the most militant abolitionists insisted on a broad range of evils created by the slave trade and the slave environment in Africa, although they often balanced such negative images with an insistence on the greater civility and higher culture of areas not affected by the trade. The issues of typicality or exceptionality, of durability or reversibility, were to play an important role in the debates over the nature of racial relationships. It should be noted that the abolitionist perspective was not confined to whites. Haitian writers also accepted "the idea that civilization was most fully developed in Europe." This was due to "historical and cultural factors, rather than to any racial inferiority of Africans" (Nicholls 1988).

The great difference between abolitionists and anti- (or perhaps non-) abolitionists lay in the emphasis placed upon the potential for rapid change, whatever the supposed deficiencies in African or Afro-American societies in the New World. For agitational purposes the early abolitionists tended to emphasize the distance between slavery and freedom and the dramatic potential metamorphosis entailed in abolition itself. Indeed, it was precisely because the abolitionists linked negative characteristics so causally and so completely to the African slave trade and to colonial slavery that they could assure their contemporaries of a more rapid civilizing of blacks than of any other "backward" people on the globe. For a brief period, at the end of the eighteenth century, more hopes were raised for the transformation of Africa than for any other part of the globe by the elimination of institutions believed to be completely subject to European political legislation. This general frame of reference also made a difference in European assessments of postabolition race relations. Britain and France differed not in the range of racial attitudes but in frequencies, intensity, and timing. It is in this sense that the political context of the abolition of the slave trade seems to have made a critical difference in the intellectual milieu of evolving racial thought and racism.

I have suggested elsewhere that one can empirically distinguish between modes of British and of French abolition (Drescher 1980, 1987: ch. 3). For more than half a century the distinguishing characteristic of the British movement was its breadth and continuity. British citizens brought public pressure to bear on reluctant or hostile economic interests and hesitant politicians decade after decade. Time and again between the 1780s and 1840s they inundated their country with propaganda, newspaper advertisements, lectures, mass meetings, petitions, lawsuits, and boycotts, presenting ever more radical abolition agendas as moral and political imperatives. Organizationally, British abolition tended to be decentralized in structure and rooted in widely dispersed local communities. The movement was increasingly inclusive, welcoming adherents who were otherwise remote from the political process by reason of gender, religion, race, or class. Equally important for our present purpose, abolitionism constituted a continuous social presence, refracting, as we shall see, other forms of cultural production.

French abolition presented a different picture during the six decades between the establishment of the abolitionist Société des Amis des Noirs in 1788 and the second French slave emancipation in 1848. During the Great French Revolution, the first slave emancipation, decreed in 1794, was primarily the result of exogenous pressures, a massive slave uprising in St. Domingue combined with the prospect of British colonial conquest throughout the Caribbean. During almost two-thirds of France's age of abolition (1788–1848), there was simply no identifiable abolitionist movement whatever. What existed during the remaining third was a discontinuous series of small elite groups in the French capital unable, and usually unwilling, to encourage mass appeals. French abolitionists concentrated on formulating plans of abolition, often in their roles as members of the French legislature, including systems of postemancipation labor control and planter compensation. Briefly put, French abolitionism never captured a visible mass following. French slave trade abolition, unlike British abolition, occurred in four uneven surges (1794, 1815, 1831, 1861) with restorations in 1802, 1814, and, depending on definition, 1858–61. British slave trade abolition occurred in a series of increasingly constrictive measures in 1788, 1799, 1806, and 1807, with ever widening moves towards international suppression between 1814 and 1867.

By the second decade of the nineteenth century, the divergent patterns were set. With the passage of British slave trade abolition,

William Wilberforce had become a national hero who symbolized liberty because of his parliamentary leadership in the crusade. His closest counterpart across the Channel, the Abbé Grégoire (one of the few abolitionist who had survived the vagaries of the revolutionary purges, and who lived in internal exile after 1814), was identified as an incendiary of the St. Domingue revolution. Grégoire's very presence inhibited the formation of another French abolitionist organization for almost a generation (Drescher 1980: 59; 1987: 200n.12; Jennings 1988).

France's first and hasty abolition had struck Grégoire and his friends in the Amis des Noirs as a "disastrous measure" (Cohen 1980: 153 and n). Antislavery had not had time to become a settled popular issue in revolutionary France (Drescher 1987: 200n.12; Daget 1980: 67–68). In 1794 the police reported mixed reactions in the streets of Paris. Some people responded favorably, but women in the marketplace were heard to say, "My God, they are giving us black sisters, we shall never be able to live with people like that" (Cohen 1980: 113). Thus, neither organizationally nor socially did abolitionism have the chance to become rooted in France before emancipation as it did in Britain.

Were racial concepts affected by these different political contexts? It is agreed that the first major attack on slavery in England produced a surge in racially justified defenses of the institution. The steady percolation of black slaves into both Britain and France as a result of the slave trade and slavery created legal and social issues about the status of slaves in societies without colonial slave law. A series of attacks on the rights of owners in England culminated in the famous Somerset case of 1772 (Davis 1975: ch. 10; Drescher 1987: ch. 2; Oldham 1988). West Indian racists sought to exploit the image of African cultural inferiority by using it to argue for permanent inferiority and irreversible degeneration (Barker 1978: ch. 3, 77–78).

Soon after the Somerset decision, the Jamaican planter Edward Long (1774) published the most extensive racially grounded argument in defense of slavery written before the age of abolition. *The History of Jamaica*, published in three volumes, contained a vitriolic linkage of Negroes to the animal world. Long assigned blacks to an intermediate species between Europeans and "Orangoutangs." He metaphorically associated blacks with beasts by writing of their "bestial and fetid smell" and categorically affirmed that their children, like animals, matured more rapidly than those of whites; that even their lice were black; and that they were "brutish" people (ibid., 2: 353–71). Long was widely read and accepted as an empirical authority by naturalists and anthropologists for generations.

To what extent did Long's sharp distancing of blacks from whites reflect English as well as planter attitudes? David Davis (1966: 461) warns that we must not presume that Long "was totally unrepresentative of his time." But that statement allows a good deal of leeway between small and substantial agreement with Long's assessment. Peter Fryer (1984: 161) extends Davis's vague caution into the positive statement that Long's "opinions were shared by many and that racism had more than a foothold in England."

Both these statements are too vague for comparative analysis of racism's impact on policy toward slavery in Britain and France. It is important to recall that Long's writings were published in the wake of the most sustained discussion on slavery which had hitherto occurred in England, a discussion which took place in the courts and newspapers as well as in pamphlets and books.

In France the same concern about the presence of blacks induced the French government in 1764 to prohibit their entry into the metropolis. This was modified in 1777 by a decree confining colonial slaves accompanying their masters to special depots to await deportation when their masters returned to the colonies. An equally important explicit racial motive in the decree's preamble stated: "The Negroes are multiplying every day in France. They marry Europeans, the houses of prostitution are infected by them, the colors mix, the blood is changing."

On the other hand, legal restraints were never placed upon black entry into or residence in Britain, despite the fact that the black population there, as a percentage of the general population, was probably more than 10 times greater than in contemporary France (Cohen 1980: 112). Moreover, at the same time that English law was becoming more explicit about the lack of restrictions on incoming blacks, the French government was increasing the level of restraint. This may not mean, as Cohen speculates, that there was less hostility to blacks in Britain than in France. The words of the French decree indicate that part of the problem was precisely the tolerance of many black people by the French as socially acceptable marriage partners. The decree's statement that "they marry Europeans" is an indicator of integration rather than of hostility, and the government appeared to be seeking to stem a popular tendency.

Intermarriage in England was similarly denounced by antiblack writers. The difference between the increasing legal restrictions in France and their absence in Britain probably lay in the countries' different political contexts. The French monarchy was more accessible to highly organized domestic elites, had to consult fewer interests, and allowed for less expression of public opinion in law making (Drescher 1987: 173–74; Boulle 1986: 224). In parliamentary Britain, with its less developed institutions for state policing, the masters utterly failed to win support for legislation affirming their property rights. It seems clear that the political context in which the planters operated had more to do with the different legal response to black people in the metropolis than did a presumed difference in relative racial hostility.

These battles of the 1760s and 1770s were merely preliminary skirmishes. The late 1780s saw the formation of abolitionist organizations in both Britain and France, the former explicitly aiming to achieve the complete and immediate abolition of the slave trade. However, the two movements diverged from the outset. Abolitionism became one of the, if not the, most popular movements of the next 50 years in Britain. Abolitionists sent more petitions to Parliament in 1788 and again in 1792 than the adherents of any other movement in the history of Parliament to that date, or indeed for two decades to come. Meanwhile the short-lived French Amis des Noirs remained confined within their elite membership, unable effectively to counter the proslave mobilization at the beginning of the French Revolution (Drescher 1987: 200; Quinney 1967). They had to look to Britain and the Caribbean to stimulate attention in the French National Assembly.

The difference between the two movements was also reflected in the influence of racial arguments on the debates about legislation for the colonies. When British defenders of the slave trade first became alarmed by the campaign against the trade in 1788, they quickly tested the efficacy of racial arguments in defense of their cause. The most sustained argument for black racial inferiority appeared, significantly, as a series of letters in the same year to the London *Morning Chronicle* over the pseudonym Civis.

Anthony Barker (1978) plausibly argues that Civis's trial balloon actually demonstrated a long-established balance of public opinion in favor of the Negro's human integrity. Civis introduced his own theory of racial hierarchy by announcing that he was entering the argument "on that side of the question, which has scarce found a single defender." By the end of the exchange of letters in the *Morning Chronicle*, the opponents of Civis outnumbered his defenders eight to one (ibid.: 160; Drescher 1987: 180).

Perhaps even more telling in the British discourse was the relative use of racial arguments drawn from Long's *History of Jamaica*. Very few pro–slave trade spokesmen used his racial slurs in their propaganda, and none at all did so in Parliament. On the contrary, it was the abolitionists who quoted Long to illustrate the depth of prejudice among the slave interest (Wilberforce 1807: 54–61). By the end of the campaign to outlaw the British slave trade in 1807, Wilberforce casually referred to the idea "that the Negroes were an inferior race of beings" in the *past* tense, although he acknowledged the persistence of assertions of mental and moral inferiority. He felt free to quote Long at length, with the assurance that his readers would react "with astonishment, as well as with disgust" (ibid.: 57). Neither in the press nor in Parliament was there an indication of preoccupation with theories of racial inferiority, much less an acceptance of them. Abolitionists repeatedly employed the notion of inferiority as an accusation, often vigorously denied, against the slave traders. The opening round of slave trade debates therefore set a pattern which was to last through the debates on British emancipation in the 1830s. The merchants and planters restricted their defense of slavery largely to reasons of law, politics, and, above all, economic expediency (Curtin 1964: 240). Lack of training rather than innate inferiority was the element of black behavior most salient to their argument.

The British abolitionist initiative also led to an upsurge of writings more favorable to the image of Africa, emphasizing the potential for rapid social and cultural change in that continent. Abolitionist literature tended to emphasize African society as desperately requiring change but hitherto imprisoned in the violence of the slave trade. The anti–slave trade campaign thus coincided with a flurry of blueprints for the founding of free settlements in Africa and to the establishment of a "province of freedom" in Sierra Leone. This colonization effort and the one on Bulama

Island marked the high point of expectations for Africa in the decade between the end of the war with the United States in 1783 and the beginning of the war with France in 1793. It also coincided with a peak of "noble savage" literature as applied to Africans, and to writings which emphasized the existence of higher civilizations in the interior, beyond the devastation wrought by the slave trade. The abolitionist initiatives thus led to an upsurge of writings with favorable prognoses for Afro-America, whose regeneration would begin with the ending of the Atlantic slave trade (ibid.: 48–55).

While disappointment with the progress of Sierra Leone was accompanied by a clear diminution of British expectations about the rate of possible change in Africa, that disillusionment was insignificant compared with the impact of the St. Domingue revolution and Napoleon's disastrous failure to subdue the Haitians. In France, the abolitionists found themselves in a much weaker position, and the immediate intrusion of the question of the status of the free colored population in the French islands resulted in the diffusion of caricatures in the brochures distributed by the pro-slave white lobbyists in the National Assembly (Debbasch 1967: 157).[3]

In 1807 it was still possible in Britain to conceive of the formal abolition of the slave trade as part of a progressive providential plan and to hail that event with a poem about Africa, in the noble savage tradition. James Montgomery's (1828, 1: 63–64) poem "The West Indies" could even envision the emergence of a military hero, an African Jenghis Khan, who would unify his continent by conquest. In contemporary France no such evocations were possible. African conquerors rather suggested Dessalines's defeat of Napoleon's army in Haiti. So, while Wilberforce could dismiss hostile racial arguments while being hailed as Britain's symbol of liberation, across the Channel the Abbé Grégoire (1808) was now an isolated voice, reduced to publicizing black literary achievements against a rising tide of antiblack hostility in France.

The French transformation could be observed within the work of a single author. In 1802, just as Napoleon was restoring slavery in the French colonies, Sylvain Golbéry published his *Fragmens d'un voyage en Afrique*, containing his observations in Africa during the late 1780s. Many of the original notes indicated a moment when positive images of Africa were in fashion. Other passages, depicting blacks as savages and slavery as a worthy institution, were "probably added just before publication, in the atmosphere of Negrophobia caused by the St. Domingue uprisings" (Cohen 1980: 69).[4]

Golbéry's book was published only one year before the Englishman Thomas Winterbottom's *Account of the Native Africans in the Neighborhood of Sierra Leone*. While Golbéry ascribed to Africans a natural racial inclination to "sloth," Winterbottom denied all direct influence of race. Golbéry ironically portrayed Africans as happy in their lazy and unconscious ignorance. Winterbottom, an abolitionist doctor in Sierra Leone in the 1790s, found Africa to be plagued by poverty, ignorance, polygyny, and slavery. The dominant frame of reference in both countries had shifted away from expectations of dramatic change, but the revolutions in the French colonies had depressed sympathy for black victims of the slave trade to a far greater extent in France than in Britain. Soon after the renewal of hostilities with France, British cartoons symbolized the imprisonment and death of Toussaint L'Ouverture under Napoleon as one of the crimes of the French despot, despite the fact that L'Ouverture had defeated the British forces in St. Domingue only a few years before.

An analogous trend can be observed in scientific writings as well as in trade accounts and caricatures. As the biologists and anthropologists of the early nineteenth century attempted to disentangle factors of environment and heredity and to relate their findings to the biblical worldview, both British and French scientists generally accepted the premise of African cultural deficiency, a premise they shared with abolitionists and missionaries. They also assumed that blacks belonged to a distinct group, whether characterized as a "race" (subspecies) or a "species." Scientific differences arose concerning the degree to which racial inheritance inhibited the progress of "civilization." This question was frequently related to the "place" of the black in nature and the role of slavery and the slave trade in future relations between Europeans and Africans. As the prestige of scientists increased, developments in their disciplines therefore impinged upon the abolition debates. To the extent that inherited characteristics determined black behavior, the dramatic power of abolition was implicitly diminished.

One of the principal questions facing the scientists was the duration of the racial divisions formulated during the previous century. One position, monogenesis, which derived from biblical texts, was the hypothesis that all humans were descended from a single set of parents. The alternative theory, polygenesis, was at odds with the scriptural account. Polygenesis maximized the biological and permanent distance between races by hypothesizing separate creations for each of them. During the eighteenth century both hypotheses had supporters, although monogenesis was the accepted position of the majority in both countries.

The combined impact of the rise of British abolitionism and the French Revolution seems to have marked a fork in the road for the scientists of Britain and France. The theory of polygenesis was clearly declining in Britain during the early nineteenth century, and English physical anthropologists "were more moderate in their anti-negro strictures" (Curtin 1964: 229). They were less inclined to emphasize the clarity of racial boundaries. Their writings were generally more favorable to Africans than they had been before the 1780s or would become after the 1830s (ibid.: 235).

The dominant figure in British anthropology during this period was James Cowles Prichard, who abandoned the eighteenth century's linkage of racial classification with a traditionally conceived "great chain of being." Prichard, closely associated with the humanitarian movement, emphasized the perfectability of all human beings and insisted upon the overlapping characteristics of human groups. The usual "characters ascribed to the negro" were, for Prichard (1826, 1: 233), "distributed to different nations in all manner of ways, and combined in each instance with more or fewer characters belonging to the European or Asiatic."

Meanwhile, the center of the polygenist school of anthropology of racial hierarchy moved to France, where it was represented by Bory de Saint-Vincent and Geoffroy Saint-Hilaire, aided by the virulently negative descriptions of Jean-Joseph Virey (Poliakov 1974: 181–82, 220). The mental inferiority of blacks became a central thesis of those who insisted upon race as the principal determinant in human behavior and history. The change in French scientific as well as in travel literature may be observed in the writings of Georges de Cuvier, the dominant authority in French comparative anatomy. In 1790 the young Cuvier was among the critics of authors who proclaimed the inherent inferiority of blacks and who likened them to apes. A generation later, although still monogenist, his own *Animal Kingdom* spoke of the similarity of Negro features to those of apes. "The hordes which compose this race," he concluded, "have always been savages" (Cuvier 1817: 94). The English editors of even this French monogenist found it necessary to challenge Cuvier's remarks on African capabilities and to insist upon the importance of education and moral causes in human behavior (Curtin 1964: 235–36).

Philip Curtin attributes British resistance to polygenism largely to the rising current of Evangelicalism and the conservative re-action to the French Revolution. Those variables, if viewed com-paratively, strike me as not fully adequate to explain the diver-gence. It is clear that Evangelicalism was rising in the United States as well as in Britain during the whole first half of the nine-teenth century. Yet this did not prevent Virey's polygenetic and anti-African arguments of 1800 and Long's "facts" from being translated by J. H. Guenebault (1837) of South Carolina in the 1830s, following the first northern mass abolitionist mobilization against southern slavery. Nor did it prevent the rapid emergence of a vigorous polygenist "American school" of anthropology in the following decade (Stanton 1960). Evangelicalism clearly had severe limitations as a brake upon the cultural formation of scientific racial ideology.

Although Curtin may be correct in seeing the evangelical ide-ology as a restraint upon polygenism, environmentalism was in retreat in the United States as early as the second decade of the nineteenth century. Faith in the plasticity of humanity dimin-ished. Curtin himself aptly notes that Britain exported antislavery crusaders to America in the 1830s and received in return the American scientific racism of the 1850s. Finally, in comparative perspectives, attributing the decline of British polygenism to the French Revolution raises the question of why the French scien-tists did not react even more strongly against what was certainly a more traumatic event for them than for their counterparts across the Channel.

A third historical factor might be at least as significant: the presence or absence of an abolitionist political "mentality" dur-ing the early decades of the nineteenth century. The impact of the difference can be illustrated, if not demonstrated, in a num-ber of ways. As early as 1795, when the evangelical movement was certainly less powerful in Britain than it was to become in

the nineteenth century, Charles White challenged the monogenist position with a series of lectures entitled *An Account of the
Regular Graduations in Man*.[5] White, a Manchester doctor, gave
his lectures in the heartland of early popular abolitionism. It is
noteworthy that he felt free to challenge monogenesis but not
slavery. He declared himself in favor not just of ending the British
slave trade (the political target of abolitionists in 1790s) but of
abolishing slavery itself throughout the world. White has often
been cited as evidence that polygenists could be abolitionists, but
it might be truer to say that White concealed himself from an
exposed theological position behind the mantle of a very popular
ideology. Since White was not a prominent member of Manchester abolitionism, even his abolitionism should be treated with
caution (Barker 1978: 167–73). Examples of French polygenist
antislavery writers would make much more convincing evidence
for the polygenist-abolitionist link.

William Lawrence (1819), writing two decades later and at-
tacked on suspicion of unbelief, likewise claimed that his views of
white mental and moral preeminence were no barrier to humanitarianism (Curtin 1964: 232, 239–40). Like White, he included a
vigorous attack on slavery and the slave trade in his scientific lectures. The result is that we have examples of British scientists who
were accused of heterodoxy being stridently antislavery but none,
whether polygenist or monogenist, being proslavery. Lawrence
even softened his stereotype of the "African Character" with a
balancing list of African virtues, so that their "moral inferiority"
would not seem as deep as their "mental."

Against those who infer that the division between polygenists and monogenists was neutral as regards their propensity to
be for or against slavery, Curtin logically concludes that radical polygenesis offered far more rhetorical comfort to proslavery
advocates. Even if abolitionists conceded the inferiority of African culture, the early diminution of biologically racist arguments
in Britain between 1790 and 1840 probably owed much to the
ideological pervasiveness of abolitionism. Historians of British
race thinking may also have underestimated British abolitionism's
cultural impact when they wrote that humanitarians did not claim
full equality for all races but only the admission of common ancestry and the right to freedom out of Christian "charity." There
was far more "rights of man" rhetoric in abolitionist demands and

propaganda than is usually recognized (Walvin 1982; Drescher 1982).[6] But this is a matter for further investigation.

Even within the monogenetic scientific tradition one recalls that the derogatory remarks by the monogenist Cuvier on the capabilities of blacks were not printed in England without editorial challenge. In France, neither leading polygenists nor monogenists apparently felt the need to dissociate themselves publicly from proslavery. Just one year after Napoleon's restoration of slavery in the colonies, Henri de Saint-Simon wrote that the French had erred in emancipating an inferior race: "The revolutionaries applied the principles of equality to the Negroes: had they consulted the physiologists, they would have learned that the Negro, in accordance with his formation, is not susceptible under equal conditions of education, of being raised to the same level of intelligence as [the] European" (Poliakov 1971: 221). The interest in racial science remained strong in the Saint-Simonian tradition. In the 1830s Victor Courtet de l'Isle (1837) identified race as the foundation of political science and the primary cause of human history. At the very moment that colonial slavery was being brought to an end in the British colonies, Courtet de l'Isle justified placing blacks at the bottom of the human scale by referring to their enslavement and to the African slave trade as their most distinguishing characteristic: "They have enslaved no foreign race; they have only enslaved each other" (cited in Poliakov 1974: 228).

In Britain, the strongest resistance to the extreme formulations of racial hierarchy came not just from evangelicals, and certainly not from those most frightened by the French Revolution, but from humanitarians associated with ongoing activities for improving the lot of black slaves. Curtin has uncovered the most telling example of the British pro-African argument in the Reverend Richard Watson's (1834–37, 2: 94) "Religious Instruction of Slaves in the West India Colonies Advocated and Defended," a sermon of 1824. Watson's classic argument, reprinted and paraphrased for decades, linked the planters and the racial scientists as twin spokesmen for racial inequality (Curtin 1964: 242, 285). Humanitarian writers may have entrapped themselves in a theory of inferiority by their own rhetorical distaste for African slavery, customs, and culture, but their commitment to antislavery apparently made some difference in their rhetoric about race. For two full generations, this difference was crucial for the history of slavery and, as we shall speculate, perhaps more than of slavery alone.

Thus far we have investigated the impact of abolitionism on a series of individual thinkers. But it would be useful if we could go beyond the classic terrain of intellectual history to the institutional mentality of the human sciences in Britain and France during the ending of the slave trade. At the beginning of the Victorian era new fields of social inquiry, both humanitarian and scientific, were becoming formalized into separate disciplines and organizations. In Britain, the first anthropological societies came out of a fusion of James Cowles Prichard's biological orientation and the political concerns of humanitarians. A committee formed in 1837 to channel ethnological data to Thomas Fowell Buxton's Parliamentary Committee on the Aborigines became a new humanitarian organization, the Aborigines Protection Society. It functioned partly as a political group and partly as an ethnological society, with Buxton as the nominal chairman and Thomas Hodgkin, a Quaker humanitarian, as its driving force.

Hodgkin wrote to William F. Edwards, an English scientist resident in Paris, and suggested the formation of an analogous French organization. Edwards agreed, but his orientation and that of his interested French colleagues were scientific, not humanitarian. Thus the Parisian Société Ethnologique, formed in 1841, reversed the British priority, making investigation primary and protection secondary. A formal ethnological society was not established in England until 1843, and Hodgkin continued to be its guiding spirit, hosting its meetings at his house. Across the Channel, Edwards had been inspired by the French racial theories of the historians Amédée and Augustin Thierry to develop a racial map of Europe, based upon facial features, head shape, and bodily measurements. Traveling through Europe from France to Hungary, Edwards (1829) designated the boundary lines of transition between one European "race" and another. Consequently, the charter purpose of the Parisian society, to discover "the principal elements that distinguish human races," was a reflection of its founder's priorities (Mémoires 1841–47, 1: 64). Both societies drew up racial/ethnic questionnaires; Hodgkin drew upon Edwards's initial version, but Hodgkin's questionnaire was more concerned with political institutions and Edwards's with material culture and physical measurements.

The difference between the British and French societies did not, of course, reflect only the founders' priorities. The participants in the French society included the Saint-Simonians Courtet de l'Isle and Gustave d'Eichthal, the naturalist Geoffroy Saint-Hilaire, the historian Jules Michelet, the physical anthropologists Armand de Quatrefages and D. M. Morton (of Philadelphia), and, significantly, spokesmen for the French colonial planters (ibid., 1, 3–14).

Ironically, the French society, which had initially distanced itself from directly humanitarian concerns, was the one which became most heavily involved in the question of slavery. Both societies had been formed shortly after the abolition of British colonial apprenticeship (1838) and before the second French emancipation (1848). Seeking to take advantage of the renewed discussion of French slavery in the Chamber of Deputies in 1847, the Société Ethnologique decided to intervene with a parallel scientific discussion. This would demonstrate the national utility of ethnology, "which along with all of the other sciences, must not concern itself solely with gathering facts, but also with establishing doctrines" (ibid., 2: 64). The question which the members thought most relevant was, "What are the distinctive natures of the white race and of the black race and the conditions of association of these two races?" (ibid.). It will be noted that the question was posed in such a way as to maximize racial distinctions explicitly and therefore implicitly to maximize the potential role of those who studied such differences. More important, for the first time in European history the views of ethnologists were to be aired in an open exchange, with the possibility of immediate confrontation.

The meetings on the question extended over several months. The principal speakers included not only leading French anthropologists and ethnologists but representatives of the French slave colonies and Victor Schoelcher, who had recently emerged as France's leading abolitionist writer. As a member of the revolutionary provisional government in 1848, Schoelcher was to preside over the emancipation of French colonial slaves.

The opening speaker was Gustave d'Eichthal, secretary of the society. He made three points which were accepted by the overwhelming majority of those who followed him: (1) that the two groups under discussion divided all of mankind between them in one way or another; (2) that the white race was preeminently the race of intellectual superiority, scientific creativity, and progress; and (3) that the two races were related to each other by differences in social characteristics, psychological constitution, and economic function. D'Eichthal's own analogy was to the relation between the two genders, with whites represented by the male, active, intellectual principle of humanity and blacks by the female, passive, sensual principle. Whatever their future relationship, these essential and opposite characteristics would presumably have to constitute the basis of association between them (ibid.: 64–72).

The past racial relationship of whites and blacks was defined in dyads of domination/subordination and of superiority/inferiority, although the terms of future domination remained unspecified. For those who raised questions about difficulties of racial definition, there were learned references to various anatomical measurements, from skull shapes and cranial cavities to calves. Overlapping characteristics could be explained in terms of the relative mixture between white and black, as elements of a conceptual pyramid running down from fair northern Europeans to south-central Africans.

Significantly, it was not physical measurements which were regarded as the key characteristics, but social relationships of power and, above all, of slavery. When challenged or queried about anomalies in physical measurements, those who were committed to rigorous hierarchical boundaries would ask, rhetorically, which races had given the world slaves and which had produced masters (ibid.: 65–74, 85–92, 186–91). Thus the geographical areas furnishing slaves and fueling the slave trade were offered as prima facie evidence both of group definition and of the empirical relationship between the two major races. The circularity of the argument with regard to the political question which science was supposed to illuminate was not recognized. From beginning to end the bond between the two races was bondage, one group consistently ruling over another. Just one century before, David Hume (1875: 252n) had offered an analogous "bottom line" empirical assertion of a uniform and constant difference of civilization between whites and other "complexions." For the overwhelming majority of the French participants, on the very eve of the second French emancipation, this was still the core distinction in the white/black dichotomy: civilization and domination at one end of humanity, slavery and savagery at the other.

Most speakers seemed indifferent, if not actually hostile, to the process of abolition which had recently been consummated across the Channel. Armand de Quatrefages alluded to the fact that the British planters were attempting to reconstitute new forms of coerced labor, demonstrating the constancy of the traditional relationship between whites and blacks in tropical regions. He echoed the bitter jibes made against "perfidious Albion" in the French Chambers during the early 1840s over an Anglo-French treaty for a mutual right of search. Quatrefages derisively asserted that English ships were hypocritically still being used in the transatlantic slave trade (Mémoires 1841–47, 2: 74–75). This elicited a lively rejoinder from an abolitionist at the society's next meeting. The presiding officer then decided that in light of such a serious charge the minutes should dissociate the society from the opinions of its individual speakers (ibid.: 82).

Another minor fracas arose when one colonial delegate cited a French colonial document which stated that native American Indians were more difficult to civilize than blacks. Two participants quickly rose to defend the mental capacity of the Indians, and a third speaker reiterated the point at the following meeting (ibid.: 93–95). Within the discussion's dichotomous terms of reference, Indians and Asiatics, significantly, were placed closer to whites than to blacks by those major speakers who dealt with the entire racial spectrum. In order to underline the chasm between whites and blacks, Amerasians were placed in the autocivilizing category (ibid.: 64, 185). By all except one major abolitionist participant, blacks were at best allowed compensatory "moral" or emotional capacities in place of their designated lack of "talent" for science, fine art, or monumental architecture. Only certain artistic forms were offered as indicators of such talent.

Given a frame of reference so deeply informed by the master-slave relationship, what were the suggested optimal forms of association for whites and blacks, and how could such associations lead to social change in the direction of "civilization"? Most speakers assumed that the purest characteristics of blacks could be found only on their continent of origin, and even there, only among those Africans least affected by contact with white Arabs to the north and east and by white Europeans to the west, south, and east. This mode of reasoning thus discounted the abundant evidence of economic, political, religious, and artistic development cited by Victor Schoelcher in his vigorous defense of Africans before the society (ibid.: 151–74).

Implicitly taking issue with the abolitionist model, the ethnologists found the "basic" African characteristics to be low technology, little trade, few cities, enslavability, undeveloped cultures, and physical features farthest removed from Europeans. Moreover, these characteristics were documented as the areas of least change in the direction of "civilization." This conformed to an important proslavery argument, that African economic and cultural development had been greatest in those areas of most intense contact with Europeans in the slaving ports of West Africa. The most inferior Africans were the groups generally enslaved by other Africans.

Slavery, not freedom, was thus the primary mechanism of social change at the bottom of the human scale. The French colonial representative at the meetings implied that the slave trade had been the principal mechanism for "improving" the blacks, since improvement for Africans originating in the areas of enslavement occurred only in the slave colonies. Creoles improved both morally and physically in the colonies; the children of Africans lost the "muzzle-like" faces of their parents (ibid.: 85–86, 91–92). The biological orientation of the majority of participants logically led to a discussion of "improvement" by crossbreeding between whites and blacks. There were assertions about the intellectual improvement wrought by such crossbreeding. The colonial delegate, anxious to maximize the positive effects of creolization by racial mixture, declared that mulattoes were virtually identical with whites in intelligence. A metropolitan speaker countered that they must be just average between blacks and whites. A third participant issued the usual scholarly call for more "experimentation" and observation to settle the question; this motion was accepted by the society (ibid.: 93–94, 98).

There was almost no discussion of the implicit premise that, if improvement could occur only in the islands and under conditions of biological crossbreeding, the *ending* of the slave trade was endangering the civilizing process. Nor was any concern expressed about the pattern of extramarital and exploitive behavior implicit in crossbreeding, which had angered abolitionists across the Channel for generations. The Reverend Watson's bitter characterization of planters and racial scientists as conspirators against human equality carried little weight across the Channel. The tone of the discussion was as cool as if one had been discussing the selective breeding of domestic animals. The generally biological metaphors dovetailed well with the first speaker's characterization of the two races as "genders."

There was general accord on the superiority of creoles, although one physical anthropologist wondered whether the change observed in colonial-born children would be permanent (ibid.: 87, 95). Such a concern obviously reflected the central premise of biological determinism which formed the starting point for most anthropometric assertions. Another speaker, obviously with his eye on the impending emancipation of French slaves, wondered if one could breed for a new form of social organization. None of the speakers, of course, anticipated the proximity of French emancipation just a few months later. No African or black Caribbean participants were invited. Blacks were "represented" at the sessions only as objects, through the various African skulls in the society's collection. The one living black brought into the society was a resident of Paris who posed as a model for local artists. He was brought in for visual observation, and no counterpart white model was placed "on stage." The audience presumably needed none.

Only one major dissident voice challenged the cozy consensus of the discussion, its complacent assumptions of clear-cut racial boundaries and immense mental differences, or its offhand use of biological metaphors and analogies. Victor Schoelcher conducted a vigorous but almost solitary counterattack against the empirical premises of the discussants. He began with a ringing affirmation of the absolute equality of all races. To demonstrate that relationships of civilization changed over time, he contrasted the antiquity of Egyptian civilization with the "barbarism" of the Gauls and Germans in antiquity. He cited passage after passage of contemporary travel accounts of Africa to illustrate the existence of fine material cultures, high skills, large towns, legal order, political authority, elite literacy, secure property, market economies, and humane relationships. He conceded that Africa lagged in modern scientific and industrial achievements but insisted that large sectors of the European, and indeed the French, peasantry were at about the same level of social development as their African counterparts.

Above all, Schoelcher emphasized two facets of Afro-American history not considered by the other discussants. The first was that the slave trade itself was responsible for much of the social disorganization and psychological degradation considered by other speakers as inherently African. The second was that the body of evidence which other participants had used in framing their characterizations was limited. Here Schoelcher cited not only examples of African educators, judges, and politicians but accounts of free blacks fulfilling management functions in the newly emancipated British colonies. On evidential grounds Schoelcher was most upset by the society's willingness to accept without question statements about blacks made by a commission of Martinique planters in response to a legislative initiative undertaken by an abolitionist.

For the most part, Schoelcher's approach was heavily empirical. He drew from British and French explorers and from the Abbé Grégoire's catalogue of creative blacks. He patriotically tried to sever the association of abolition with Great Britain by recalling that the first French emancipation had preceded decisive English action. Finally, he insisted that the approach of most speakers offered implicit comfort to the defenders of slavery and even to those who emphasized the beneficent effects of an Atlantic slave trade already condemned by French law (ibid.: 151–74).

Schoelcher's two interventions in the debate were therefore an elaboration on his major premise of the absolute equality of the black and white races. One other member of the society very briefly intervened to plead for discarding the criteria of physical anthropology and ethnology in the name of "spiritual capacities." But that spiritual appeal served only to close the ethnological ranks in the name of scientific objectivity (ibid.: 96–98). Those few participants who felt it necessary to respond to Schoelcher's accusation of abetting the slave owners insisted that they were interested only in the scientific value of the discussion. The possible implications of facts could hardly be allowed to interfere with the advancement of scientific knowledge (ibid.: 173, 191).

Such was the position taken by Victor Courtet de l'Isle. Courtet de l'Isle had already worked out a systematically racial philosophy of history a decade before the Société Ethnologique's discussion of 1847, and before the soon-to-be more famous essays of Robert Knox (1850) in Britain and of Arthur de Gobineau (1853–55) in France.[7] Courtet de l'Isle simply brushed aside Schoelcher's cascade of illustrative facts with one methodological sweep of the hand. The abolitionist had gathered bits and pieces of evidence from all over Africa but had made allowance neither for the exogenous influence of more advanced non-African cultures nor for racial differences within Africa. Thus the original dichotomous notion of a single sub-Saharan African race was now redefined by Courtet de l'Isle to allow for infinite graduations. "True" or "pure" African cultural potential was to be found only in the continent's least developed area (Mémoires 1841–47, 2: 190–96).

Thus, all of Schoelcher's massive counterevidence could be attributed to the presence of Europeans or Arabs, or to the fact that the more gifted Africans were not "true Negroes" but belonged to people with different physical characteristics (indicated by the possession of hair or of anatomical features closer to the European "norm" than in other parts of Africa). All of Schoelcher's evidence could be discounted, concluded Courtet de l'Isle, in the face of a clear, single, worldwide, and color-coded correlation. In the final analysis, he maintained, racial categorizations had an irreducibly aesthetic component. Everywhere in the world, the beautiful, the powerful, and the creative coincided. The closer faces came to resembling the Greek statues of Apollo, the fairer the skin, the bluer the eyes, the greater was their possessor's domination of other racial groups and the greater was the distance between them (ibid.: 184, 187).

Courtet de l'Isle first offered the society a quick world tour through the Americas, the Pacific islands, India, and Europe. Everywhere lighter was brighter, darker was duller; blacker was outcast, savage, or enslaved. Africa merely mirrored the globe. If such "facts" pointed to a constant of superiority/inferiority à la Hume, this was not a defense of abuses of power but a bowing to the power of "sad truths," but truths nevertheless (ibid.: 192).

Thus ended, without resolution, the most extensive discussion of race ever conducted by a scientific body up to that time, in meetings which ran over a period of months during the spring and summer of 1847. A number of its facets are worth summarizing. Most of the discussants adhered to an ideal of rigorous empiricism. In this, they resembled most defenders of the slave trade until the end of the Napoleonic Wars and most supporters of slavery before 1848. The existing racial "map" of the world indicated to them that the relationship between darker- and lighter-skinned peoples, where they overlapped, was one of fair-skinned dominance.

This dominance, significantly, was qualified more as a product of intellectual power and inherent qualities than as a condition imposed by force. The discussants refused to recognize the implications of all examples which did not fit the pattern. Nor did they care to note the trend in Western polities toward the ending of the slave trade and chattel slavery. The ethnological debate of 1847 ended with no resolution to the question it had posed for itself, with no detailed agenda for further research, and without having influenced the political process in the least. By the following summer, French slavery and the Société Ethnologique had both disappeared, fatalities of the Revolution of 1848.

As the Atlantic slave trade lurched to an end during the two decades after 1848, the trends of Anglo-French racial thought again seemed to converge. The British "age of humanitarianism" was drawing to a close and with it the era of Prichard's supremacy in anthropology (Curtin 1964: ch. 15; Stocking 1987: ch. 7). British antislavery, which had been able to mobilize hundreds of thousands in the five decades before 1840, fragmented and ebbed (Temperley 1972). When Courtet de l'Isle published his race-centered analysis of humanity in the 1830s, he had no counterpart in Britain. But within two years of his uncompromising defense of racial science before the Société Ethnologique, Thomas Carlyle (1849) signaled the resurgence of virulent antiblack racism in England with the publication of his "Occasional Discourse on the Nigger Question." By the time Gobineau began to unveil his *Essai sur l'inégalité des races humaines* in 1853, Robert Knox (1850) had already published a book-length work on "the races of man" in Britain (developed out of lectures in 1846). Knox (ibid.: v) declared, "Race is everything: literature, science, art—in a word civilization depends on it." If Knox's ideas about race struggle were still those of a minority, and the British ethnological society still supported potential equality of development, humanitarian abolitionism had clearly ceased to exercise its quasi omnipotence of the previous generation.

A decade later, when the Atlantic trade was drawing to a definitive close, there were already enough Britons who disliked the philanthropic links of the Ethnological Society to break away and form the Anthropological Society of London, under the leadership of a physician, James Hunt. Hunt's papers on the nature and status of the Negro equaled in disdain any assertions of inferiority produced on the other side of the Channel. Hunt by no means went unchallenged; his anti-Negro lecture at the British Association was greeted by "hisses and catcalls" (Lorimer 1978: 138). Hunt consequently believed himself to be breaking new scientific ground against a hostile pro-Negro cultural consensus in England:

> It is not a little remarkable that the subject [the "station" of the Negro in the genus *Homo*] is one which has never been discussed before a scientific audience in this Metropolis. In France, in America and in Germany, the physical and mental characters of the Negro have been frequently discussed, and England alone has neglected to pay that attention to the question which its importance demands. [Hunt 1865]

The Prichardian humanitarian school was his target, as was a supposedly still widespread British opinion of "the equality of the Negro and European" (which Hunt attributed to "little real knowledge" on the part of Europeans; ibid.: 3, 4, 31). Hunt's own theses would probably have satisfied the most rigorous racist of the earlier Parisian meeting, including its slaveholder representatives.[8]

In a faint echo of White and Lawrence before him, Hunt did draw the line against being identified as an outright advocate of the "slave trade" (his quotes). However, a qualification immediately followed. Hunt insisted that the Negro was, after all, much better off as a slave in the Confederate States of America or in the British West Indies before emancipation than as a part of Africa's "savage state" or as a resident, "emancipated (from work?)," of the contemporary West India Islands. Even Hunt's slave trade disclaimer was almost facetious. He advocated that the transporting of those Africans enslaved for crimes be reintroduced (ibid.: 54–56). Indeed, a Confederate agent resident in England who served on the anthropological society's council was sufficiently pleased with its views to donate funds to it through his secret service accounts. He gave special prominence to Hunt's views, which included designation of the Negro as a distinct species, assertion of the proximity of the Negro to the apes, and affirmation of the intellectual inferiority of the black race and its civilizability only under European domination (Lorimer 1978: 138–39). By 1863 the Anthropological Society of London was clearly on the same wavelength as its new French counterpart, the Société d'Anthropologie de Paris, dominated by Hunt's friend, Paul Broca. The Anglo-French patterns of scientific racial thought were far less distinctive by 1860 than they had been during the first four decades of the century.

CONCLUSION

What light can the ending of the slave trade throw upon the concept of winners and losers in relation to the evolution of European racism? If racial attitudes were altered temporarily by the ending of the trade, we must still deal with the contention that the entire abolitionist process altered the path of racism very little. For those who see late-nineteenth-century racism largely as the continuation and intensification of earlier xenophobia and arrogance, toward blacks in particular, abolition was hardly more than a dramatic, quite anomalous interlude in a pattern of general hostility (Walvin 1986: ch. 4, p. 91). On the other hand, for those who see mid-Victorian racism as a novel response to nineteenth-century industrialization and class formation, and one common to all of late-nineteenth-century Europe, the political intensity of the abolitionist process in Britain is equally superfluous (Lorimer 1978: esp. 208). In the latter case, abolition was both too early and too peripheral in orientation to have had an impact on what is conceived to have been a pan-European phenomenon of the last half of the century. In other words, if British and European racism both wound up in roughly the same cultural place by the 1860s, the end of the slave trade, ideologically speaking, was no more than part of the prehistory of late-nineteenth-century scientific and popular racism.

But did European societies end up in quite the same place? First, it must be noted that British policy continued to be more activist against the slave trade and slavery than any of its European counterparts, even during the generation after 1850, the decades usually identified as the period of a more thorough Western shift toward a racialist vision of the world. A much-depleted British antislavery lobby remained in continuous existence and occasionally exercised real influence upon the course of events (Meirs 1975). Thus the new configuration of racist culture was too weak to remove the antislavery component from British policy. That policy continued to subject British diplomacy and colonial rule to greater tensions and outcomes than would probably have emerged without any antislavery pressure. However much the conservative bias of British antislavery may have increased, it continued to provide reasons "for doing something about African savagery," while "racism provided a reason for not doing too much" (Cooper 1980: 32).

The extent to which humanitarian ideology inflected the general trends in European policy toward African slavery can still be best worked out comparatively, rather than in the framework of analysis of a single polity. The postabolition turn toward indentured Asian labor has been designated by one historian as "a new system of slavery" but by another as "the great escape" (Tinker 1974; Emmer 1985). In some ways the new system was clearly uncharacteristic of the previous forced labor transfers from Africa. Once again the abolitionist tradition appears to have exercised a limiting and cost-increasing role in which the old characteristics of the slave trade acted as a negative reference even at the height of late-nineteenth-century European racism.

Another question as to winners and losers concerns the impact of the age of humanitarianism (or the abolitionist interlude, depending on the historian) on the lives of the peoples of Africa. One historian recently concluded that in several important respects the damage to Africa was less severe than has been contended (Eltis 1987: chs. 5, 13). Others may claim that the ending of the slave trade did little to improve the lives of Africans. The analytical point of departure here might have to be counterfactual rather than simply comparative. What would have happened to Africa if the British, like the French under Napoleon and during the early Bourbon restoration, had allowed the slave trade to continue? What if, under the impact of rising racism, governments had used racism as a reason for "not doing too much" and had allowed the unrestricted flow of slaves to Latin America and perhaps elsewhere during the whole of the nineteenth century? David Eltis (ibid.: 64), while denying that the initial impact of British abolition on Africa was significant, concludes that without abolition in the first half of the nineteenth century, the increased demand for slaves under the impact of European economic growth might well have had a major and sustained impact, producing levels of slave exports in excess of the 1780s peak. "Indeed, it is possible that few regions in Africa would have escaped population decline in the face of industrialization in the West" (ibid.: 71). And Eltis takes no stock of the nondemographic consequences or of the whole catalogue of pain and suffering elaborated by the abolitionists.

Thus the question of timing becomes quite important. The earlier (and longer) Britain diverged from the relative Continental passivity toward the slave trade during the early decades of the nineteenth century, the more antislavery ideology provided reasons and pressure for "doing more" against the existing Atlantic slave system, the more these reasons and pressure exceeded those that racism provided for "not doing too much," and the more profound the long-term consequences were for Africa and probably for the Americas as well. David Brion Davis (1983) has imagined a more conservative world as the outcome of a failed American Revolution. One might equally imagine a South African–style outcome for large parts of the British Empire in the absence of the abolitionist movement and its successes. One can easily imagine an analogous outcome in Brazil. The more dependent nineteenth-century capitalism became on slavery, the more difficult, delayed, and perhaps violent the ultimate outcome would have been.

Finally, the long-term impact of the "ending" on European racism must also be considered. Lorimer's (1978: 208–10) study of British racism concludes that, despite differences in the intensity of racial antipathy in late-nineteenth-century Europe, British and Continental racism shared important features: they emerged in the same time period (the 1850s and 1860s), were popularized in the 1870s and 1880s, and persisted, with much-diminished scientific respectability, to the present. Yet in terms of world history the differences of abolitionist intensity may actually have been more important than the racist similarities. Let us allow our imaginations to thrust forward one last time, from the beginning of the last third of the nineteenth century, where we halted our story, to the end of the first third of the twentieth century. In the summer of 1933 the British marked the centennial of their colonial slave emancipation with an international celebration. Despite the self-congratulatory rationalizations for postabolition British imperialism in Africa, the event was primarily hailed as a milestone in the movement of humanity towards common liberty and equality.

However, the same newspapers which reported the flags of 50 nations unfurling together at Wilberforce's birthplace carried vivid accounts of the new Nazi regime driving Jews into the streets to perform forced labor at degrading tasks (Drescher 1985). Given this juxtaposition of events on the pages of British newspapers, one might have expected contemporary editors or historians to note the contrast that the combined centenaries of Wilberforce's death and slave emancipation made with the emerging outlines of the "thousand-year Reich" across the North Sea. After all, in 1807, the triumph of abolition in Britain had been contrasted with the deeds of the warlord of France across the Channel. No one seems to have made the comparison in 1933. Moreover, only a few isolated black voices from the colonies noted that 1933 marked almost 100 years of British metropolitan retreat before the forces of white settler racism abroad and Anglo-Saxon supremacist ideology at home. Perhaps it was too much to ask of a weary and beleaguered empire that it share the memory of its moral zenith with the story of subsequent compromises and accommodations of white supremacy in Africa, the West Indies, Asia, and the South Pacific.

The commemorations of abolition did not, therefore, signal the revival of a new national consciousness against the lengthening shadow of an even more virulent racism to the east. The ultimately antiracist component of the war waged against Hitler was an unanticipated and belated consequence of its horrors and not a primary cause for which the struggle was undertaken by any of the Allies.

Yet the contrast between abolitionism and Nazism was latent, if not evoked, in the centennial of 1933. The British national rituals of black liberation and civic incorporation did contrast sharply with the Nazi rituals of exclusion, racial purification, and dehumanization. The following decade was to show that the logic of racism could ultimately mean the difference between life and death on a new and unimagined scale. At least until the postwar wave of non-European migrations to Europe, the ending of the slave trade, one of the most successful human rights movements in history, may have cast a longer shadow than we recognize.

NOTES

The author would like to thank Stanley Engerman, Henry Gemery, George L. Mosse, and Lionel Rothkrug for their helpful comments.

1   Especially before the rise of abolitionism, West Indians might refuse to align themselves with the emergent scientific racial anatomists of the eighteenth century. The writer of *Observations from a Gentleman in Town to His Friend in the Country Relative to the Sugar Colonies* (1781: 23–24) took issue with a French philosopher "whose scrutinous observations into the interiors of a negro, have pronounced him to be not of the human species." The "observer" rejected the philosopher's findings on the grounds of the Negro's capacity for speech, rationality, and reproduction. On Arthur de Gobineau's discomfort on being linked to proslavery, see Biddiss 1970: 145–47.

2   For analogous attempts to study ideology comparatively, see Kennedy and Nicholls 1981. For an Anglo-French comparison using religious mobilization as a variable, see Drescher 1980.

3   On colonial racial arguments, see, for example, the *Observations sur les hommes de couleur des colonies* (1790), by César de l'Escale de Vérone, quoted in Poliakov 1974: 360n.7. Yet early in the assembly debates most prominent representatives of the slave interest attempted to align themselves with Enlightenment empiricism, arguing for the continuance of the civil restrictions on free blacks and people of color on the grounds of economic necessity and the security of the social order. Like Long's scientific racism, an analogous argument, published in 1790 in St. Domingue, was publicized in France by antislavery writers such as Grégoire, Brissot, and Milscent (see Bénot 1989: 83–85). The turmoil of revolutionary and military change was so swift and erratic in both Franch and the French islands that there was little leisure for the formulation of grand theories of racial inequality. The result was that the prerevolutionary environmental optimism about potential change, which was analogous to British optimism between 1785 and 1795, vanished much more thoroughly from France by the beginning of the nineteenth century with Napoleon's restoration of slavery to the islands and segregationist legislation in the metropolis (see Cohen 1980: 118–20; Debbasch 1967: 234–51). There was a direct relationship between the rate and intensity of revolutionary change and the intensification of racial ideology. On the intensification in France, see Boulle 1986: 227–29.

4   On the literary shift, see Hoffman 1973: 131–36.

5   Published in London in 1799. Robin Blackburn (1988: 154–57), who sees in White part of a racist reaction to the French and St. Domingue revolutions, fails to explain why White took a radical antislavery position while elaborating his doctrines of racial inferiority. Blackburn (ibid.: 156) does not distinguish between postrevolutionary attitudes toward race in Britain, France, or the United States.

6   Where the acquiescence in slavery remained an element of the national ideology, as in the United States (Jordan 1968: 530–38) well into the 1840s, even the hegemony of Christian doctrine, whether in its ritualistic or evangelical variants, did not slow the rapid decline of environmentalism regarding questions of race or of theories of black inferiority.

7   It should be noted that full-blown defenses of slavery which rejected the prin-

Evolution of European Scientific Racism 393

ciple of civic equality could run into more difficulty than books defending racial inequality (see Ride 1843: 57–58).

8   The image of the Negro as a case of arrested human development was being elaborated in the Société d'Anthropologie de Paris at the same time. See Pruner-Bey 1861, especially page 336, comparing blacks to children and likening them to "the most patient, and often the most useful animal." Such was the normal level of discourse in the anthropological societies of London and Paris at the time of the American Civil War.

REFERENCES

Atlas Geographus (1711–17) 5 vols., London: John Nutt.
Barker, Anthony J. (1978) The African Link: British Attitudes to the Negro in the Era of the Atlantic Slave Trade, 1550–1807. London: Frank Cass.
The Beauties of Nature and Art Displayed (1763–64) 13 vols., London: G. Robinson.
Bénot, Yves (1989) La révolution française et la fin des colonies. Paris: Éditions La Découverte.
Biddiss, Michael D. (1970) Father of Racist Ideology: The Social and Political Thought of Count Gobineau. New York: Weybright and Talley.
Blackburn, Robin (1988) The Overthrow of Colonial Slavery, 1776–1848. London: Verso.
Bolt, Christine (1971) Victorian Attitudes to Race. London: Routledge and K. Paul.
Boulle, Pierre H. (1986) "In defense of slavery: Eighteenth-century opposition to abolition and the origins of a racist ideology in France," in Frederick Krantz (ed.) History from Below: Studies in Popular Protest and Popular Ideology in Honor of George Rude. Montreal: Concordia University: 221–41.
Carlyle, Thomas (1849) "Occasional discourse on the nigger question." Fraser's Magazine 40: 670–79.
Carver, Jonathan (1779) The New Universal Traveller. London: G. Robinson.
Cohen, William B. (1980) The French Encounter with Africans: White Response to Blacks, 1530–1880. Bloomington: Indiana University Press.
Cooper, Frederick (1980) From Slaves to Squatters: Plantation Labor and Agriculture in Zanzibar and Coastal Kenya, 1800–1925. New Haven, CT: Yale University Press.
Courtet de l'Isle, Victor (1837) La science politique fondée sur la science de l'homme. Paris: A. Bertrand.
Curtin, Phillip D. (1964) The Image of Africa: British Ideas and Action, 1780–1850. Madison: University of Wisconsin Press.
——— (1975) Economic Change in Pre-Colonial Africa: Senegambia in the Era of the Slave Trade. 2 vols., Madison: University of Wisconsin Press.
Cuvier, Georges de (1817) Le règne animal: Distribué d'après son organisation. Paris: Deterville.
Daget, Serge (1980) "A model of the French abolitionist movement and its variations," in C. Bolt and S. Drescher (eds.) Anti-Slavery, Religion, and Reform. Folkestone, Kent: William Dawson: 64–69.
Davis, David Brion (1966) The Problem of Slavery in Western Culture. Ithaca,

NY: Cornell University Press. Rpt. (1988) New York: Oxford University Press.

———— (1975) The Problem of Slavery in the Age of Revolution, 1770–1823. Ithaca, NY: Cornell University Press.

———— (1983) "American slavery and the American Revolution," in Ira Berlin and Ronald Hoffman (eds.) Slavery and Freedom in the Age of the American Revolution. Charlottesville: University Press of Virginia: 262–80.

———— (1984) Slavery and Human Progress. New York: Oxford University Press.

Debbasch, Yvan (1967) Couleur et liberté: Le jeu du critère éthnique dans un ordre juridique esclavagiste. Paris: Dalloz.

Drescher, Seymour (1980) "Two variants of anti-slavery: Religious organization and social mobilization in Britain and France, 1780–1870," in Christine Bolt and Seymour Drescher (eds.) Anti-slavery, Religion, and Reform: Essays in Memory of Roger Anstey. Folkestone, Kent: William Dawson: 43–63.

———— (1982) "Public opinion and the destruction of British slavery," in J. Walvin (ed.) Slavery and British Society, 1776–1848. London: Macmillan: 22–48.

———— (1985) "The historical context of British abolition," in David Richardson (ed.) Abolition and Its Aftermath: The Historical Context, 1790–1916. London: Frank Cass: 3–24.

———— (1987) Capitalism and Antislavery: British Mobilization in Comparative Perspective. New York: Oxford University Press.

Edwards, William F. (1829) Des caractères physiologiques des races humaines. Paris: Compère Jeune.

Eltis, David (1987) Economic Growth and the Ending of the Transatlantic Slave Trade. New York: Oxford University Press.

Emmer, Pieter C. (1985) "The great escape: The migration of female indentured servants from British India to Surinam," in David Richardson (ed.) Abolition and Its Aftermath: The Historical Context, 1790–1916. London: Frank Cass: 245–66.

Fryer, Peter (1984) Staying Power: Black People in Britain since 1504. Atlantic Highlands, NJ: Humanities.

Gobineau, Arthur de (1853–55) Essai sur l'inégalité des races humaines. 4 vols., Paris: Firmin-Didot.

Grégoire, Abbé (1808) De la littérature des nègres, ou recherches sur leurs facultés intellectuels, leurs qualités morales et leur littérature. Paris: Maradon.

Guenebault, J. H. (1837) The Natural History of the Negro Race. Charleston, SC: D. J. Dowling.

Hoffman, Léon-François (1973) Le nègre romantique: Personnage littéraire et obsession collective. Paris: Payot.

Hume, David (1875) Essays, Moral, Political, and Literary. London: Longmans.

Hunt, James (1865) "On the Negro's place in nature." Memoirs Read Before the Anthropological Society of London 1: 1–60.

Jennings, Lawrence C. (1988) French Reaction to British Slave Emancipation. Baton Rouge: Louisiana State University Press.

Jordan, Winthrop (1968) White over Black: American Attitudes toward the Negro, 1550–1812. Chapel Hill: University of North Carolina Press.

Kennedy, Paul, and Anthony Nicholls (1981) Nationalist and Racialist Movements in Britain and Germany before 1914. London: Macmillan.

Knox, Robert (1850) The Races of Men: A Fragment. London: H. Renshaw.

Lawrence, William (1819) Lectures on Physiology, Zoology, and the Natural History of Man. London: J. Callow.

Long, Edward (1774) The History of Jamaica. 3 vols. London: T. Lowndes.

Lorimer, Douglas A. (1978) Colour, Class, and the Victorians: English Attitudes to the Negro in the Mid-Nineteenth Century. New York: Holmes and Meir.

Meirs, Suzanne (1975) Britain and the Ending of the Slave Trade. New York: Africana Publishing.

Mémoires de la Société Ethnologique de Paris (1841–47) 2 vols., Paris: Dondet-Duprey.

Montgomery, James (1828) Poetical Works. 4 vols., London: Longman, Rees, Orme, etc.

Mosse, George L. (1978) Toward the Final Solution: A History of European Racism. New York: Howard Fertig.

Nicholls, David (1988) "Haiti: Race, slavery, and independence (1804–1825)," in Leonice J. Archer (ed.) Slavery and Other Forms of Unfree Labour. London: Routledge: 225–38.

Observations from a Gentleman in Town to His Friend in the Country Relative to the Sugar Colonies (1781) London: R. Ayre.

Oldham, James (1988) "New light on Mansfield and slavery." Journal of British Studies 27: 45–68.

Poliakov, Leon (1971) Le mythe aryen. Paris: Calmann-Lévy.

——— (1974) The Aryan Myth: A History of Racist and Nationalist Ideas in Europe, trans. Edmund Howard. New York: Basic Books.

Prichard, James C. (1826) Researches into the Physical History of Man, 2d ed. 2 vols., London: John and Arthur Arch.

Pruner-Bey, Franz (1861) "Mémoire sur les Nègres" (lecture of 21 February). Bulletins de la Société d'Anthropologie de Paris 2: 293–336.

Quinney, Valerie (1967) "The Committee on Colonies of the French Constituent Assembly, 1789–91." Ph.D. diss., University of Wisconsin—Madison.

Ride, Alphonse (1843) Esclavage et liberté. Paris: H.-L. Delloye.

Stanton, William (1960) The Leopard's Spots: Scientific Attitudes toward Race in America, 1815–1859. Chicago: University of Chicago Press.

Stocking, George W. (1987) Victorian Anthropology. New York: Free Press.

Temperley, Howard (1972) British Antislavery, 1833–1870. London: Longman.

Tinker, Hugh (1974) A New System of Slavery: The Export of Indian Labour Overseas, 1830–1920. London: Oxford University Press.

Walvin, James (1982) "The propaganda of anti-slavery," in J. Walvin (ed.) Slavery and British Society, 1776–1846. London: Macmillan: 49–68.

——— (1986) England, Slaves, and Freedom, 1776–1838. London: Macmillan.

Watson, Richard (1834–37) Works. 12 vols., London: John Mason.

Wilberforce, William (1807) A Letter on the Abolition of the Slave Trade. London: Luke Hansard and Sons.

Williams, Eric (1944) Capitalism and Slavery. Chapel Hill: University of North Carolina Press.

Wright, Gavin (1987) "Capitalism and slavery on the islands: A lesson from the mainland," in Barbara L. Solow and Stanley L. Engerman (eds.) British Capitalism and Caribbean Slavery: The Legacy of Eric Williams. Cambridge: Cambridge University Press: 283–302.

Index

Contributors

Ralph A. Austen is professor of African history at the University of Chicago.

Ronald Bailey is chair of the Department of African-American Studies and professor of history at Northeastern University.

William Darity, Jr., is professor of economics at the University of North Carolina at Chapel Hill.

Seymour Drescher is University Professor of History at the University of Pittsburgh.

Stanley Engerman is John H. Munro Professor of Economics and professor of history at the University of Rochester.

David Barry Gaspar is professor of history at Duke University.

Clarence E. Grim, M.D., is professor of medicine at Charles R. Drew University of Medicine and Science and UCLA and Director of the Drew/UCLA Hypertension Center.

Brian T. Higgins is visiting assistant professor of history at the University of Toledo.

Jan S. Hogendorn is professor of economics at Colby College.

Joseph E. Inikori is Associate Director of the Frederick Douglass Institute for African and African-American Studies and is professor of history at the University of Rochester.

Kenneth F. Kiple is professor of history at Bowling Green State University.

Martin Klein is professor of history at the University of Toronto.

Paul E. Lovejoy is professor of history and Associate Vice-President (Research), York University, Downsview, Ontario, Canada.

Patrick Manning is professor of history and African-American studies at Northeastern University.

Joseph C. Miller is Commonwealth Professor of History at the University of Virginia.

Johannes M. Postma is professor of history and chair of the History Department at Mankato State University.

Woodruff D. Smith is professor of history at the University of Texas at San Antonio.

Thomas W. Wilson is a research scientist at the Human Population Laboratory and the Western Consortium for Public Health, Berkeley, California.

Library of Congress Cataloging-in-Publication Data

The Atlantic slave trade : effects on economies, societies, and peoples in Africa, the Americas, and Europe / edited by Joseph E. Inkori and Stanley L. Engerman.

p. cm.

Papers presented at a conference "The Atlantic Slave Trade: Who Gained and Who Lost?" held at the University of Rochester.

Includes bibliographical references and index.

ISBN 0-8223-1230-1 : $45.00 (est.). — ISBN 0-8223-1243-3 (pbk.) : $17.95

1. Slave-trade—Congresses.   I. Inikori, J. E.   II. Engerman, Stanley L.

HT855.A85   1992

306.3'62—dc20   92-3258